M000231629

Rule-Following and Realism

Rule-Following and Realism

GARY EBBS

HARVARD UNIVERSITY PRESS
Cambridge, Massachusetts
London, England
1997

Copyright © 1997 by the President and Fellows of Harvard College
All rights reserved
Printed in the United States of America

Library of Congress Cataloging-in-Publication Data
Ebbs, Gary.
    Rule-following and realism / Gary Ebbs.
        p.   cm.
    Includes bibliographical references and index.
    ISBN 0-674-78031-0 (hardcover : alk. paper)
    1. Meaning (Philosophy)—History—20th century.   2. Language and
languages—Philosophy.   3. Realism—Controversial literature.
I. Title.
B840.E23   1997
121'.68—dc21   96–51880

CONTENTS

ACKNOWLEDGMENTS

This book is an attempt to weave together themes and resolve tensions that have gripped me in one form or another ever since I began studying philosophy. I owe thanks to everyone who has instructed, stimulated, or encouraged me along the way.

For giving me my first sense of the attractions and difficulties of philosophy, I thank my principal teachers at Oberlin College—Norman Care, Robert Grimm, Peter McInerney, Daniel Merrill, and Harlan Wilson. I am especially grateful to Robert Grimm for guiding my first attempts to understand the writings of Gottlob Frege and W. V. Quine, and for instilling in me a strong desire to think carefully and systematically.

For setting the framework of my graduate education I am grateful to my principal teachers at the University of Michigan—Paul Boghossian, David Hills, Jaegwon Kim, Peter Railton, Larry Sklar, and Bill Taschek. Paul Boghossian helped me see the force of Saul Kripke's interpretation of Wittgenstein's remarks on rule-following. David Hills exemplified for me the ideal reader of philosophy—tireless, sympathetic, wide-ranging, and wise. Jaegwon Kim set a high standard of philosophical clarity and organization that I will always strive to meet. Larry Sklar's brilliant lectures were filled with delightful and instructive details. I vividly recall when Larry briefly compared W. V. Quine's "analytical hypotheses" with Hans Reichenbach's "coordinative definitions"; at the time I was not sure what to make of this suggestive comparison, but many years later it helped me to develop the interpretation of Rudolf Carnap's view of the relation between semantics and linguistic behavior that I present in Chapter Four.

I am also indebted to my fellow graduate students at Michigan, especially Anne Bezeidenhout, AB Carter, and MR McDonald.

Anne Bezeidenhout and I had many stimulating conversations about the writings of British philosophers of language and mind, including Bertrand Russell, J. L. Austin, P. F. Strawson, and Gareth Evans. AB Carter and I had seemingly endless conversations about Donald Davidson's theory of meaning; we always found something to disagree about, and I learned a great deal from our spirited attempts to resolve our disagreements. MR McDonald was an excellent friend and interlocutor; he sparked my interest in aesthetics and the writings of Ludwig Wittgenstein and Stanley Cavell.

Michael Dummett was my first systematic guide to the philosophy of language. His book *Frege: Philosophy of Language* (2nd ed., Cambridge, Mass.: Harvard University Press, 1981), which I read during my first year at the University of Michigan, convinced me that philosophy of language is a serious subject that I *had* to try to master. At the same time I was captivated by Donald Davidson's elegant essays about how to construct "empirically testable" theories of meaning for natural languages. Although I no longer accept either Dummett's or Davidson's conceptions of the starting point and task of the philosophy of language, I am deeply indebted to their writings.

At an Oberlin College colloquium in 1985, I heard Tyler Burge present his paper "Cartesian Error and the Objectivity of Perception" (later published in Robert Grimm and Daniel Merrill, ed., *Contents of Thought*, Tucson: University of Arizona Press, 1988). In 1986, Burge presented "Individualism and Self-Knowledge" (later published in the *Journal of Philosophy* 85 [1988]: 649-663) as his Nelson lecture at the University of Michigan. Both of these events left a deep impression on me. Like many others, I had been convinced by Hilary Putnam's and Burge's Twin Earth thought experiments, but I could not see how to fit the conclusions of these thought experiments together with the apparent intelligibility of certain skeptical possibilities, and the familiar fact that we can know our own thoughts without special empirical investigation. Anthony Brueckner's article "Brains in a Vat" (*Journal of Philosophy* 83 [1986]: 148-167) deepened my puzzlement about this. In retrospect I can see that Burge's papers and Brueckner's article focused my thinking about a cluster of central issues that gradually led me to some of the views presented in this book.

I am deeply indebted to members of the Harvard Philosophy

Department, especially Warren Goldfarb, Charles Parsons, and Hilary Putnam. During my two years of teaching at Harvard, I gradually glimpsed the possibility of a unified new way of resolving many of the puzzles that gripped me. Each in his own way, Goldfarb, Parsons, and Putnam helped me to see that language use is prior to, and more fundamental than, semantic reflection. As a result, I gained a new appreciation of the classic distinction between use and mention displayed in the disquotational paradigms for reference and truth. This helped me to complete and clarify my earlier methodological shift away from the standard model-theoretic picture of the relationship between language and the world.

At Harvard I also a learned great deal from Frank Arntzenius, John Carriero, Dan Conway, Steve Engstrom, Juliette Floyd, Steven Gross, Fred Neuhouser, Sanford Shieh, and Alan Sidelle. Alan's criticisms of standard metaphysical interpretations of the phenomenon of "necessary a posteriori truth" prompted me to try to develop an interpretation of that phenomenon that does not appeal to analyticity or convention. My debt to Alan is especially evident in the last sections of Chapter Eight. Steven Gross once suggested, to my surprise, that Carnap does not need a criterion of analyticity. I gradually realized that Gross was right; this realization is fundamental to the interpretation of Carnap I present in Chapter Four.

I am indebted to my colleagues at the University of Pennsylvania. Tom Ricketts's systematic and uncompromising interpretations of Frege, early Wittgenstein, Carnap, and Quine, combined with his trenchant criticisms of post-Quinean philosophy of language, led me to rethink my own views from the ground up. From Jay Wallace I received years of friendship, stimulating conversation, constructive criticism, and moral support. I also thank Sally Haslanger for many helpful discussions of my developing views, Charles Kahn for urging me to be bold, and Scott Weinstein for his open-minded yet deflationary reactions to my work.

I am indebted to several others who have taught philosophy at the University of Pennsylvania in the past six years. I enjoyed and learned from my conversations with Wolfgang Mann, who, among other things, recommended that I read R. M. Hare's article "Philosophical Discoveries," which I found stimulating and useful for reasons I present in Chapter Eight. I had many helpful conversations with Alan Richardson about Carnap. I also learned a great deal from Miriam Solomon about Quine and recent work in naturalized epistemology. I am grateful to Miriam for her friendship and her intellectual and professional support of my work.

While writing this book, I participated in a reading group in the philosophy of language. For helping to create and sustain the open and constructive tone of our discussions, I am grateful to Michelle Casino, Peter Dillard, Scott Kimbrough, Tom Meyer, Dan Reynolds, Eric Rosen, and Peter Schwartz. I am also grateful to Katharina Kaiser for guiding us through the labyrinths of Wittgenstein's *Philosophical Investigations*. Our discussions of Wittgenstein's later writings were particularly helpful to me when I was writing Chapters One, Three, and Ten.

For constructive comments on the central strategies and arguments of the manuscript, I am grateful to Lisa Downing, David Hills, Scott Kimbrough, Tom Meyer, and Jay Wallace. I used an early draft of the manuscript as the main text for a graduate seminar at the University of Pennsylvania in the fall term of 1994; I am indebted to the participants in this seminar for helpful questions and criticisms. For comments on particular chapters, I thank Peter Dillard (Chapters One to Four), Warren Goldfarb (Chapter One), Steven Gross (Chapters Four and Five), David Hills (Chapter Nine), Mark Kaplan (Chapters Three and Six), Scott Kimbrough (especially Chapters Three, Six, Eight, and Nine), Tom Ricketts (Chapter Seven), Peter Schwartz (Chapter Seven), and Jay Wallace (especially Chapters One, Three, and Eight). Parts of Chapters Four, Six, and Seven were read at the Graduate Center at CUNY, NYU, and Temple University, respectively; I am grateful for the comments I received on those occasions.

I am indebted to the Philosophy Department and the School of Arts and Sciences of the University of Pennsylvania for two semester-long leaves which allowed me to work full-time on my research and writing. My research for the book was supported in part by a summer research grant from the University of Pennsylvania Research Foundation.

Some of the central themes and arguments of this book are developments of views I first sketched in "Realism and Rational Inquiry" (*Philosophical Topics* 20, no. 1 [1992]: 1-33) and "Skepticism, Objectivity, and Brains in Vats" (*Pacific Philosophical Quarterly* 73, no. 3

[1992]: 239-266). Most of Chapter Nine was previously published under the title "Can We Take Our Words at Face Value?" (*Philosophy and Phenomenological Research 56*, no. 3 [1996]: 499-530); I am grateful to Ernest Sosa for permission to include this material in the book. For comments on various drafts of central parts of Chapter Nine, I am grateful to Gary Hatfield, Charles Kahn, Mark Kaplan, Scott Kimbrough, Wolfgang Mann, Tom Meyer, Alan Richardson, Tom Ricketts, Jamie Tappenden, Jay Wallace, Joan Weiner, and Scott Weinstein.

I am grateful to Saul Kripke, Harvard University Press, and Blackwell Publishers for permission to reprint excerpts from Kripke's book, *Wittgenstein on Rules and Private Language* (Cambridge, Mass.: Harvard University Press, 1982); and to Kluwer Academic Publishers for permission to reprint excerpts from John McDowell's paper "Wittgenstein on Following a Rule" (*Synthese 58* [1984]: 325-363).

I am indebted to Lindsay Waters, Executive Editor for the Humanities at Harvard University Press, for guiding my manuscript through the Press's review process and to Nancy Clemente, Senior Editor, for her careful copyediting and her expert supervision of the final stages in the production of the book.

In a more personal vein, I thank my parents, John and Josette Ebbs, for encouraging me to follow my intellectual and philosophical interests wherever they lead. I am grateful to Deena Adler for helping me to muster the courage and harness the energy to write this book. To my wife, Martha Lhamon, whose unfailing patience, love, and support sustained and refreshed me from the beginning to the end of this project, I owe more than I can say.

Introduction

1. Topics and Aims

My aim in this book is to come to terms with and move beyond currently entrenched ways of looking at central topics in the philosophy of language and mind, including rule-following, meaning, the analytic-synthetic distinction, anti-individualism, realism, skepticism, and self-knowledge. My theme is that to understand these topics, we must investigate them from our perspective as participants in shared linguistic practices. To understand rule-following, for example, we must look carefully at what we count as following a rule or going against it in actual cases. This suggestion remains enigmatic despite countless discussions of Ludwig Wittgenstein's remarks on rule-following. In my view, the effectiveness of these discussions is limited by our lingering loyalties to metaphysical realism—the view that we can make "objective" assertions only if we can "grasp" metaphysically independent "truth conditions"—and scientific naturalism—Quine's view that "it is within science itself . . . that reality is to be identified and described."[1]

To loosen the hold of these views, I expose their roots and develop a different way of looking at our linguistic practices. I explain in detail why the best arguments against the analytic-synthetic distinction are incompatible with both metaphysical realism and scientific naturalism, and I develop a deflationary anti-individualistic picture of our practices of agreeing, disagreeing, evaluating assertions, and resolving disputes. Working from within this deflationary picture, I describe rule-following, meaning, realism, and self-knowledge from our perspective as participants in shared linguistic practices.

2. Structure of the Book and Links between the Topics

The book has three main parts. In the first part (Chapters One to Three) I reconstruct and contrast Saul Kripke's and W. V. Quine's skepticisms about rule-following and meaning, explain my misgivings about John McDowell's transcendental argument for a middle position, and sketch my own strategy for developing a principled alternative to metaphysical realism and scientific naturalism.

Kripke and Quine challenge our commonsense views about meaning. For different reasons they conclude that nothing uniquely determines what our words mean. Their conclusions reflect their respective metaphysical and naturalistic perspectives. I show (in Chapter One) that Kripke's skepticism is the inevitable result of his interpretation of the idea that our use of language commits us to standards relative to which our assertions are true or false. I explain (in Chapter Two) why Quine sees no conflict between our use of sentences to make assertions and his claim that there is no "fact of the matter" about how to "translate" our words. Quine and Kripke present radically different pictures of the relationship between meaning and assertion. For Kripke we *can't* make assertions if nothing determines what our words mean, whereas for Quine we *can* make assertions even if there is no "fact of the matter" about how to "translate" our words. To appreciate this contrast between Quine's and Kripke's views is the first step toward developing an alternative to both.

To articulate an alternative to Quine's and Kripke's views, I propose that we describe meaning and assertion from our perspective as participants in our rule-following practices. Although similar proposals have been made before, the very idea of a participant perspective on meaning and assertion remains elusive. The reason is that previous attempts to view meaning and assertion from our participant perspective fail to come to terms with metaphysical realism and scientific naturalism. In "Wittgenstein on Following a Rule,"[2] for example, John McDowell gives a transcendental argument against metaphysical realism and scientific naturalism, and endorses Wittgenstein's suggestion that "there is a way of grasping a rule which is *not* an *interpretation,* but which is exhibited in what we call 'obeying a rule' and 'going against it' in actual cases."[3] Although it might appear that McDowell has taken a first step toward developing an alternative to metaphysical realism and scientific naturalism, I show (in Chapter Three) that McDowell's transcendental argument rests on enigmatic and questionable claims about what is required for our "intuitive" notions of meaning and assertion to have a "real application." The moral is that it is fruitless to try to argue against metaphysical realism or scientific naturalism until we can articulate a different way of looking at meaning and assertion.

The hegemony of metaphysical realism and scientific naturalism in recent analytic philosophy can be traced back to our collective rejection of the logical positivists' analytic-synthetic distinction. The rhetorical power and wide influence of Quine's arguments against Rudolf Carnap's analytic-synthetic distinction set the context in which scientific naturalism became entrenched. And Hilary Putnam's persuasive arguments against the analytic-synthetic distinction and verificationism led to a resurgence of metaphysical realism. So one way to clarify and evaluate our current attractions to metaphysical realism and scientific naturalism is to reexamine their roots in Quine's and Putnam's arguments for rejecting the logical positivists' analytic-synthetic distinction.

That is why in Part II (Chapters Four to Six) I look in detail at Carnap's analytic-synthetic distinction, and contrast Quine's and Putnam's reasons for rejecting it. I sketch a new interpretation of Carnap's analytic-synthetic distinction (in Chapter Four), highlighting Carnap's pragmatism about the resources investigators may use to codify rules for inquiry and his fundamental distinction between pure and descriptive semantics. I argue (in Chapter Five) that Quine's rejection of Carnap's analytic-synthetic distinction stems from Quine's scientific naturalism, which leads inevitably to his indeterminacy thesis. I show (in Chapter Six) that unlike Quine's reasons for rejecting the distinction, Putnam's are rooted in our perspective as participants in actual practices of agreeing, disagreeing, evaluating assertions, and resolving disputes. My reconstruction of Putnam's reasons for rejecting the analytic-synthetic distinction uncovers the roots of a principled alternative to both scientific naturalism and metaphysical realism.

I develop this alternative in Part III (Chapters Seven to Ten) where I show that Putnam's and Burge's elucidations of anti-individualism can be seen as further consequences of the philosophical project sketched in my reconstruction of Putnam's rejection of the analytic-synthetic distinction. By exploring details and dissolving tempting confusions, I develop a systematic alternative to the standard metaphysical interpretation of anti-individualism. Working from within this alternative picture of anti-individualism, I show why we can't make sense of metaphysical realism, and that related concerns about the compatibility of self-knowledge with anti-individualism are misplaced. I propose that our understanding of rule-following and realism be clarified by careful descriptions of everyday cases in which we see and settle disputes. Finally, I show how my deflationary picture of anti-individualism can help us to overcome the tempting mistakes and confusions that underlie Kripke's and Quine's views of the relationship between meaning and assertion.

3. Method

What will strike most readers as unusual about this book is that it contains detailed reconstructions of arguments with which they already feel familiar. Some may wish I had skipped these details and stated my own position directly. But the reconstructions are integral to my method of working through alternative points of view. My position is inextricably linked to my method.

One central role of my reconstructions is to show in detail that we can suspend commitments to our own starting points and learn to see the same topics from different points of view. Another role of the reconstructions is to propose new interpretations of influential arguments and positions in the philosophy of language. In my view the task of the philosophy of language is to identify and neutralize entrenched ways of thinking that prevent us from describing our linguistic practices from the participant perspective, and to show how to fit familiar aspects of our use of language into a natural and coherent system. I introduce this view of the task of the philosophy of language as part of my reconstruction of Putnam's reasons for rejecting the analytic-synthetic distinction, develop it further in my reconstructions of Putnam's and Burge's arguments for anti-individualism, and use it to clarify such related topics as rule-following, realism, skepticism, and self-knowledge.

Although in my view we must learn to question all the assumptions that have shaped the best work in analytic philosophy, this is not to say that analytic philosophy must come to an end. It can be revitalized by fresh investigations of central issues from rival points of view. As we'll see, these investigations extend our established repertoire of questions and skills to reveal rich dimensions we are just beginning to explore.

I

RULE-FOLLOWING

ONE

Kripke's Skepticism about Meaning

4. Assertion and Meaning

Suppose you and I are dining out with a group of friends seated at two tables. On each table the waiter leaves a check, one for sixty-eight dollars, the other for fifty-seven; I must find the sum and leave a tip. After adding I say, "Sixty-eight plus fifty-seven is one hundred fifteen." "No," you reply, "sixty-eight plus fifty-seven is one hundred twenty-five." Together we add again, and I realize my mistake: I added '8' and '7' to get '15', but forgot to carry the '1'.[1]

Everyday disagreements like this are easy to see and easy to settle. We seldom ask how our disagreements are possible, or how we can be right or wrong. Yet when we raise these questions, we feel compelled to answer them. Our first answers reveal naive and apparently irresistible ideas about assertion and meaning.

We say that we disagreed, that you were right and I was wrong; these evaluations apparently rest on presuppositions about what we meant by our words. We took for granted that I used the sentence 'Sixty-eight plus fifty-seven is one hundred fifteen' to mean sixty-eight plus fifty-seven is one hundred fifteen, and so when I uttered this sentence I thereby *asserted* that sixty-eight plus fifty-seven is one hundred fifteen. Yet we find it natural to say that I might not have used this sentence to mean sixty-eight plus fifty-seven is one hundred fifteen, and so in uttering it I might not have asserted that sixty-eight plus fifty-seven is one hundred fifteen. This possibility highlights our sense that it was *because* I used my sentence to mean sixty-eight plus fifty-seven is one hundred fifteen that when I uttered it I committed myself to standards relative to which I was wrong.

It is tempting to think that we grasp these standards by grasping rules that predetermine the correct answers to all addition problems. When I first added sixty-eight and fifty-seven, I felt I was trying to follow steps that had already been determined by the rule for addition; I later discovered that I failed to match those steps. Since the steps were predetermined by the rule, my assertion was incorrect *before* I discovered my mistake.

If the steps we ought to take are predetermined by the rules we grasp, then to agree or disagree we must both grasp the same rules. Our willingness at the restaurant to evaluate our assertions with a single new calculation showed that we both used 'plus' to mean addition. We added again to decide which of us had properly followed the rule for addition. In this way we resolved our dispute and came to agree that sixty-eight plus fifty-seven is one hundred twenty-five.

5. Kripke's Dialectical Skepticism

These observations evoke the compelling idea that it is *because* we grasp and follow rules that our words are meaningful, that we can make assertions, and that we can agree or disagree at all. In chapter 2 of *Wittgenstein on Rules and Private Language*, Saul Kripke[2] presents his interpretation of this idea, and argues that we *can't* grasp or follow rules. He concludes that our words are meaningless, so we can't make assertions, agree or disagree. My aim in this chapter is to show that Kripke's skeptical conclusion is an inevitable consequence of his tempting interpretation of our naive first thoughts about meaning and assertion.

When presenting his skeptical paradox about meaning, Kripke plays the role of a dialectical skeptic.[3] A dialectical skeptic begins with our firmly entrenched judgments about some topic, and draws a skeptical conclusion from his analysis of those judgments. To succeed he must convince us that prior to encountering his arguments we were already committed to the requirements that lead to his skeptical conclusion.[4] Kripke's skeptical paradox is rooted in his interpretation of our idea that our use of language commits us to standards relative to which our assertions are true or false. To succeed Kripke must convince us that prior to encountering his arguments we were already implicitly committed to his interpretation of this idea.

Previous commentators[5] have ignored or simply missed Kripke's dialectical strategy. They see his skeptical argument as starting from metaphysical principles, not solely from ideas about meaning to which we feel we were already committed before we encountered the skeptic's reasoning. This standard interpretive approach is fundamentally flawed. At best it partly clarifies isolated pieces of Kripke's reasoning. To fit the pieces together we must see them in the context of Kripke's dialectical strategy.

My reconstruction of Kripke's argument features his dialectical strategy. The most important ingredient in Kripke's dialectical strategy is his interpretation of our ordinary understanding of meaning. I begin by reconstructing Kripke's loose formulations of our ordinary understanding of meaning, linking them to our naive first thoughts about meaning and assertion (§§7–11). I then clarify Kripke's strategy and his skeptical challenge (§§12–14), and explain why his skeptical conclusion is an inevitable consequence of his understanding of meaning (§§15–16). In the last two sections of the chapter I adopt a more critical stance: I argue that Kripke's picture of meaning leads us unknowingly to accept an objectifying perspective that obscures our understanding of meaning and assertion (§17), and that this objectifying perspective reflects Kripke's allegiance to metaphysical realism (§18).

6. A First Look at Kripke's Understanding of Meaning

Kripke first characterizes our ordinary understanding of meaning as follows:

> I, like almost all English speakers, use the word 'plus' and the symbol '+' to denote a well-known mathematical function, addition. The function is defined for all pairs of positive integers. By means of my external symbolic representation and my internal mental representation, I 'grasp' the rule for addition. One point is crucial to my 'grasp' of this rule. Although I myself have computed only finitely many sums in the past, the

rule determines my answer for indefinitely many new sums that I have never previously considered. This is the whole point of the notion that in learning to add I grasp a rule: my past intentions regarding addition determine a unique answer for indefinitely many new cases in the future.[6]

To illustrate his point Kripke supposes that he has never before calculated the value of the simple arithmetical formula '68 + 57': "I perform the computation, obtaining, of course, the answer '125'. I am confident, perhaps after checking my work, that '125' is the correct answer. It is correct both in the arithmetical sense that 125 is the sum of 68 and 57, and in the metalinguistic sense that 'plus', as I intended to use that word in the past, denoted a function which, when applied to the numbers I called '68' and '57', yields the value 125."[7] The themes of these earlier passages are repeated with variations throughout Kripke's presentation of the skeptical paradox:

> Ordinarily, I suppose that, in computing '68 + 57' as I do, I do not simply make an unjustified leap in the dark. I follow directions I previously gave myself that uniquely determine that in this new instance I should say '125'.[8]

> Normally, when we consider a mathematical rule such as addition, we think of ourselves as *guided* in our application of it to each new instance. Just this is the difference between someone who computes new values of a function and someone who calls out numbers at random. Given my past intentions regarding the symbol '+', one and only one answer is dictated as the one appropriate to '68 + 57'.[9]

> Even now as I write, I feel confident that there is something in my mind—the meaning I attach to the 'plus' sign—that *instructs* me what I ought to do in all future cases. I do not *predict* what I *will* do . . . but instruct myself what I ought to do to conform to the meaning.[10]

There are four interrelated ideas expressed in these passages, each of which plays a role in Kripke's reasoning: (first) "the rule for addition . . . determines my answer for indefinitely many new sums that I have never previously considered"; (second) "when we consider a mathematical rule such as addition, we think of ourselves as *guided* in our application of it to each new instance," and that "in computing '68 + 57' as I do . . . I follow directions . . . that uniquely determine that in this . . . instance I should say '125' "; (third) when I use 'plus' to mean plus, I "instruct myself what I ought to do to conform to the meaning"; and (fourth) "my past intentions regarding addition determine a unique answer for indefinitely many new cases in the future."

These four ideas are best seen as aspects of our impression that it is *because* we grasp and follow rules that our words are meaningful, we can make assertions, and we can agree or disagree at all. In §§7–11 I'll present this view in detail.

7. Assertion, Meaning, Truth Conditions, and Rules

We saw (§4) that our evaluations of assertions apparently rest on presuppositions about what we mean. Since we presupposed that by 'sixty-eight plus fifty-seven is one hundred fifteen' I meant sixty-eight plus fifty-seven is one hundred fifteen, we took for granted that when I uttered that sentence at the restaurant I asserted that sixty-eight plus fifty-seven is one hundred fifteen. We have the impression that it was *because* I used my sentence to mean sixty-eight plus fifty-seven is one hundred fifteen that when I uttered it I committed myself to standards relative to which I was wrong. Let's try to clarify this impression.

Our impression that it is because we grasp and follow rules that our words are meaningful, that we can make assertions, and that we can agree or disagree at all, goes hand in hand with the view that our assertions are true or false. My sincere utterances of the sentence 'Sixty-eight plus fifty-seven is one hundred fifteen' are true if and only if *sixty-eight plus fifty-seven is one hundred fifteen*. Kripke assumes that to accept such biconditionals I must grasp the rule for addition; to see why, we need a framework within which to place and clarify his sketchy remarks about meaning.

The framework is based in the idea that the meaning of an expression is its contribution to the truth conditions of (our assertions of) sentences in which the expression occurs.[11] This idea lurks in the background of Kripke's discussion; it comes briefly to the foreground when he says that the word 'plus' and the symbol '+' *denote* the addition function.

According to Kripke, if I am to use 'plus' and '+' to denote the addition function, I must grasp a rule for addition. My grasp of the rule for addition simultaneously plays both a linguistic and a non-linguistic role. Its linguistic role is to link the expressions 'plus' and '+' with the addition function. In its nonlinguistic role, my grasp of the rule for addition partly constitutes my grasp of the truth conditions of assertions and judgments I can make by using sentences in which 'plus' and '+' occur. Thanks to the double role of our grasp of the meanings of our words, our grasp of the truth conditions of our assertions *mirrors* the syntactic structures of our sentences.[12]

To evoke our sense of this mirroring, I'll use three new terms. First, an *addition problem* is any expression of the forms '___ plus . . .' and '___ + . . .', where the blanks are filled by English number-words and Arabic numerals respectively. 'Sixty-eight plus fifty-seven' and '68 + 57' are both addition problems in this sense, regardless of how they are interpreted. Second, an *addition sentence* is any sentence of the forms '. . . plus ___ is . . .' and '. . . + ___ = ...', where the blanks are filled by English number-words and Arabic numerals respectively. 'Sixty-eight plus fifty-seven is one hundred fifteen', 'sixty-eight plus fifty-seven is one hundred twenty-five', '68 + 57 = 115', and '68 + 57 = 125' are addition sentences in this sense. Third, an *addition assertion* is any assertion made by *using* an addition sentence.

Let us try to highlight our feeling that our grasp of the truth conditions of our *addition assertions* mirrors the linguistic structures of our *addition problems* and *sentences*. Assume that my number-words, Arabic numerals, 'is', and '=' have the usual meanings. If 'plus' and '+' denote the plus function, as we ordinarily assume, then all addition problems and sentences have the standard meanings, and our grasp of the truth conditions of addition assertions will involve our grasp of a rule for calculating the plus function. But suppose counterfactually that the expressions 'plus' and '+' denoted the *plush* function, defined so that, for all numbers x and y, x *plush* $y = (x + y) - 10$. Then all addition problems and sentences would have nonstandard meanings, and our grasp of the truth conditions of addition assertions would involve our grasp of a rule for calculating the *plush* function. In particular, when in this counterfactual situation I utter the sentence 'sixty-eight plus fifty-seven is one hundred fifteen', I thereby assert that sixty-eight *plush* fifty-seven is one hundred fifteen. Once we grasp a rule for calculating the plush function we can understand this assertion, and see that it's true. The difference between what I mean by 'plus' and '+' in the actual and counterfactual situations mirrors a difference in the truth conditions of my addition assertions in those two situations.

Here then is a framework within which to place and clarify Kripke's sketchy remarks about meaning: the meaning of an expression is its contribution to the truth conditions of (our assertions of) sentences in which the expression occurs; to grasp the meaning of an expression we must grasp its contribution to the truth conditions of our assertions; and so our grasp of the (linguistic) link between our expressions and their meanings *mirrors* our grasp of the (nonlinguistic) truth conditions of (our assertions of) sentences in which those expressions occur.

8. The Rule Determines My Answer

Kripke is primarily interested in the nonlinguistic role of our grasp of rules; he questions whether we can grasp rules at all, not how we link our supposed grasp of rules to particular linguistic expressions. When he writes that "the rule for addition . . . determines my answer for indefinitely many new sums that I have never previously considered," he is reminding us of our impression that when we grasp the rule for addition we thereby predetermine the truth conditions of an indefinite number of addition assertions. At the restaurant, for example, I felt that my grasp of the rule for addition determined the truth value of my assertion that sixty-eight plus fifty seven is one hundred fifteen *before* I discovered my mistake.

The same impression is evoked by Wittgenstein's example of a pupil who writes '1000', '1004', '1008', '1012', and so on, after he is ordered to continue the series +2 beyond 1000.[13] When we imagine ourselves giving this pupil the order to continue the series +2 beyond 1000, we feel that we *already have in mind* that he should write '1002' after '1000', '1004' after '1002', and so on:

> your idea was that that act of meaning the order had in its own way already traversed all those steps: that when you meant it your mind as it were flew ahead and took all the steps before you physically arrived at this or that one.

Thus you were inclined to use such expressions as: "The

steps are *really* already taken, even before I take them in writing or orally or in thought." And it seemed as if they were in some *unique* way pre-determined, anticipated—as only the act of meaning can anticipate reality.[14]

Similarly, we feel that our grasp of the plus function had "in its own way already traversed" all the steps and determined the truth conditions of all possible addition assertions.

The sense that the steps are determined in advance is also illuminated by the counterfactual comparison of §7. Suppose again that my expressions 'plus' and '+' denote the *plush* function, where x *plush* $y = (x + y) - 10$. Then all addition problems and sentences have nonstandard meanings, and my grasp of the truth conditions of addition assertions will involve my grasp of a rule for calculating the plush function. When we compare this counterfactual situation to the actual one, it is tempting to think that in the counterfactual case my grasp of a rule for calculating the plush function must be what determines in advance the truth conditions of all my (actual and potential) assertions of addition sentences. In the actual situation my grasp of a rule for calculating the plus function seems to determine the steps that are "already taken" when I assert one of my addition sentences, and in the counterfactual situation my grasp of a rule for calculating the plush function seems to determine the different steps that are "already taken" when I assert one of my addition sentences.

This counterfactual comparison highlights our feeling that our grasp of the plus function reaches out to cases we have not yet considered—that the truth conditions of addition assertions are "already present" in the rules we learn for calculating them. Kripke believes that this feeling is fundamental to our ordinary understanding of meaning, and that to make sense of the feeling we must suppose that something present to our minds predetermines the truth conditions of our addition assertions. In §195 of *Philosophical Investigations* Wittgenstein rejects this interpretation of our feeling that meaning predetermines truth conditions:

"But I don't mean that what I do now (in grasping a sense) determines the future use causally and as a matter of experience, but that in a *queer* way, the use itself is in some sense present."—But of course it is, 'in some sense'! Really the only thing wrong with what you say is the expression "in a queer way." The rest is all right; and the sentence only seems queer when one imagines a different language game from the one in which we actually use it.

Wittgenstein suggests that we are confused if we think that meaning requires mysterious mental powers that enable us to have present to mind an infinity of steps. But Kripke sides with the interlocutor of §195:

> Yet (§195) "in a *queer* way" each ... case is "in some sense present." (Before we hear Wittgenstein's skeptical argument we surely suppose—unreflectively—that something like this is indeed the case. Even now I have a strong inclination to think this somehow must be right.)[15]

Kripke insists that this "strong inclination" reflects our common-sense view of meaning, for the success of his dialectical skepticism about meaning depends on it: to abandon the idea that "in a queer way" something in our minds predetermines the truth conditions of our assertions is, he thinks, to abandon the very *idea* of meaning.[16]

9. Following and Being Guided by a Rule

Kripke says that "when we consider a mathematical rule such as addition, we think of ourselves as *guided* in our application of it to each new instance," and that "in computing '68 + 57' as I do ... I follow directions ... that uniquely determine that in this ... instance I should say '125'." We have the impression that when we make and evaluate assertions we are guided by and try to follow independently existing rules. This impression is inextricable from our impression (§8) that the rules we grasp predetermine the truth conditions of indefinitely many assertions.

Both of these impressions inform our commonsense ideas about making and evaluating assertions. When we make an assertion we think of ourselves as aiming to be in accord with the truth conditions anticipated by the rules we grasp. I felt I was trying to follow the steps already determined by the rule for addition when I asserted that sixty-eight plus fifty-seven is one hundred fifteen.

When I discovered my mistake I felt I was discovering my failure to match the steps predetermined by the rule I grasped; I realized that your assertion that sixty-eight plus fifty-seven is one hundred twenty-five was faithful to the predetermined steps of the addition rule, and mine was not.

Our sense that we follow rules encourages and reinforces the impression that the rules we are attempting to follow are in some sense fully present to our minds. Wittgenstein evokes this impression in §138 of *Philosophical Investigations:* "we *understand* the meaning of a word when we hear or say it; we grasp it in a flash, and what we grasp in this way is surely something different from the 'use' which is extended in time!"[17] Sparked by such thoughts, Kripke feels there must be something in our minds that guides us when we grasp a rule: "Even now as I write I feel confident that there is something in my mind—the meaning I attach to the 'plus' sign— that *instructs* me what I ought to do in all future cases."[18] To make sense of our feeling that we are intimately acquainted with the rules we grasp, we feel we must suppose that something in our minds instructs us what we ought to do in all future cases. So according to the "natural and correct understanding"[19] of meaning, to make and evaluate assertions at all we must suppose that something fully present in our minds predetermines the truth conditions of an indefinite number of assertions we have never encountered before.

10. The Normativity of Assertion and Meaning

Kripke's claim that when I grasp the addition function, I "instruct myself what I *ought* to do to conform to [that] meaning" reflects his elusive thesis that *meaning is normative.* To understand this thesis we must see its links to supposed norms that govern our assertions, and to Kripke's view (§§8–9 above) that the truth conditions of our assertions are determined by the rules we grasp.

When Kripke says that our answers to addition problems are correct or incorrect, he is in effect saying that *to make an assertion or judgment we must aim at the truth.*[20] This is displayed in our ordinary practices of making and evaluating assertions. We feel compelled to withdraw an assertion if we discover that it's false, and we feel we mustn't make an assertion unless we have some reason for believing that it's true.

We have seen (§§8–9) that according to Kripke the truth conditions of our assertions are determined by the rules we grasp. So in grasping rules we *predetermine* the truth conditions of our assertions, thereby committing ourselves to making assertions in accordance with those truth conditions. It was *because* I grasped the addition function that when I uttered the sentence 'sixty-eight plus fifty-seven is one hundred fifteen' I asserted that sixty-eight plus fifty-seven is one hundred fifteen, thereby committing myself to evaluating the sentence in light of my grasp of the rule for addition, and to withdrawing it when I discovered that I forgot to carry the '1'.

Kripke thinks that meaning is normative because he believes that *our grasp of rules is inextricably linked to our aim of asserting and judging in accordance with the truth.* The links go in both directions: we can't strive to make true assertions unless we can grasp rules that determine the truth conditions of our assertions, and we can't grasp rules that determine the truth conditions of our assertions unless we strive to make true assertions. So in Kripke's view, to see ourselves as making assertions and judgments we must presuppose that we can grasp rules that determine the truth conditions of our assertions, and thereby can grasp what we must do to obey the "norms" for evaluating, withdrawing, and revising our assertions. If we abandon this presupposition, we feel unable to make assertions, to think or to reason at all.

11. Normativity, Past Intentions, and Future Use

Kripke emphasizes that "my past intentions regarding addition determine a unique answer for indefinitely many new cases in the future." He often expresses this temporal point metalinguistically: "Given my past intentions regarding the symbol '+', one and only one answer is indicated as the one appropriate to '68 + 57'." Some of Kripke's temporal formulations create the impression that the relation between past intentions and future answers is *essential* to his thesis that meaning is normative: "if I intend to accord with my past meaning of '+', I *should* answer '125'.... The relation of meaning and intention to future action is *normative*, not *descriptive*."[21] Here Kripke seems to suggest that I can be right or wrong about how to apply a rule at a given time only if I committed myself to following that rule at some earlier time.

But Kripke's talk of "past intentions" and "future answers" is misleading. For it is fundamental to Kripke's view of rule-following that the truth conditions of the assertions I make at a given time are determined by the rules I grasp *at that time*.[22] If what I now mean by '+' and 'plus' is different from what I meant by '+' and 'plus' in the past, then the addition assertions I make now may be correct even if they are not correct relative to what I meant by '+' and 'plus' in the past.[23] So Kripke doesn't think that I can be right or wrong about how to apply a rule at a given time *only if* I committed myself to following that rule at some earlier time. What then is the role of Kripke's temporal formulations of the normativity of meaning?

One role of Kripke's temporal formulations of the normativity of meaning is to extend our present understanding of the normativity of meaning to the past. According to Kripke, our impression that meaning is normative (§10) is rooted in our present understanding of what we must do to obey the norms for making, evaluating, and withdrawing assertions. If we assume that we now mean by our words what we meant by them in the past, then we can extend our present understanding of the normativity of meaning to the past. But once we have extended our present understanding of the normativity of meaning to the past, we can see that the relationship between past intentions and future use is not essential to Kripke's thesis that meaning is normative. For if our words were meaningful in the past, then we were committed to standards for correctly applying them, whether or not the meanings of our words have changed.

I conclude that there are three essential strands to Kripke's understanding of meaning. First, by grasping rules we predetermine and anticipate the truth conditions of indefinitely many assertions and judgments (§8). Second, to make and evaluate assertions at all we must suppose that something present in our minds instructs us what we ought to do (§9). And third, our grasp of rules is inextricably linked to our aim of asserting and judging in accordance with the truth (§10).

12. Kripke's Skeptical Strategy

If Kripke's temporal formulations are not essential to his interpretation of the normativity of meaning, why then does he place such emphasis on them? The central role of the temporal formulations is to enable Kripke to challenge our ordinary assumptions about meaning without directly questioning the present meaningfulness of our words. To understand his temporal formulations we must understand his skeptical strategy.

Kripke's skeptical strategy is reflected in one of the "ground rules" of his formulation of the skeptical problem:

> I am supposing that the skeptic, provisionally, is not questioning my *present* use of the word 'plus'; he agrees that, according to my *present* usage, '68 plus 57' denotes 125. Not only does he agree with me on this, he conducts the entire debate with me in my language as I *presently* use it. He merely questions whether my present usage agrees with my past usage, whether I am *presently* conforming to my *previous* linguistic intentions. The problem is not "How do I know that 68 plus 57 is 125?" which should be answered by giving an arithmetical computation, but rather "How do I know that '68 plus 57', as I *meant* 'plus' in the *past*, should denote 125?"[24]

In this passage Kripke announces his provisional supposition that we and the skeptic share a language in which to express our doubts. The reason for this supposition is more clearly expressed in another passage: "if I use language at all, I cannot doubt coherently that 'plus', as I now use it, denotes plus! Perhaps I cannot (at least at this stage) doubt this about my *present* usage. But I can doubt that my *past* usage of 'plus' denoted plus."[25] Here Kripke observes that we can't coherently use our words and *simultaneously* doubt that they are meaningful. This is the key to understanding his skeptical strategy.

Suppose someone asks me to justify my presupposition that my word 'plus' means plus not plush (§7). I may try to express this question by asking myself, "How do I know that my word 'plus' denotes plus, not plush?" But when I use that sentence I take for granted that 'plus' means plus, not plush. I can't question whether my word 'plus' now denotes plus without presupposing that it *does* now denote plus. If I try to question whether my word 'plus' now denotes plus, I find myself in the pragmatically incoherent position of trying to use my word 'plus' to express a doubt that undermines my confidence that I can use my word 'plus' to make assertions or to express any doubts at all.

In short, a dialectical skeptic can't start by directly challenging our ordinary assumption that our words are presently meaningful, since we can't at the start make any sense of its not being true. To undermine our ordinary assumption that our words are meaningful, a dialectical skeptic must begin with commonsense assumptions that (we feel) we can coherently doubt.

This is why Kripke focuses on the relationship between past meaning and future use. We feel we can coherently doubt our commonsense presuppositions about what we meant in the past. If we find these doubts compelling, we are drawn in by the skeptic's challenge to explain how our commonsense presuppositions about what we meant in the past could be true. If we are convinced by the skeptic's arguments that nothing determines what we meant in the past, then we will feel driven to conclude that nothing determines what we mean in the present either. So we arrive by an indirect route at a conclusion that at first seems simply incoherent.

To illustrate Kripke's skeptical strategy suppose again that I said to you, "Sixty-eight plus fifty-seven is one hundred fifteen—the total is one hundred fifteen." I take for granted that when I uttered that sentence, by 'plus' I meant plus, and so I committed myself to standards relative to which I was wrong. The skeptic's strategy is to challenge me to say what would make it true that I meant plus, and not some other function that determines a different answer for the addition problem 'sixty-eight plus fifty-seven'.

The skeptic grants that in our ordinary practice of ascribing meanings, we see no reason to doubt that I meant plus by 'plus', or to think that perhaps by 'plus' I meant plush. But he still insists that I tell him what determined that my expression 'sixty-eight plus fifty-seven' meant sixty-eight plus fifty-seven and not sixty-eight *plush* fifty-seven. He notes that if I meant plush by 'plus' when I said, "Sixty-eight plus fifty-seven is one hundred fifteen," then I committed myself to standards relative to which I was right. Thus the skeptic's question directs our attention to our commonsense assumption that by 'plus' I meant plus, not plush, and that I committed myself to standards relative to which I was wrong. The skeptic challenges us to say how this assumption could be true, and since the challenge seems to make sense, we feel obliged to meet it, even though there is no *ordinary* reason to doubt that by 'plus' I meant plus.

Kripke argues that nothing determines what we meant in the

past. He concludes that we did not mean anything at all in the past, even though it *seemed* to us that we did. And "if there can be no fact about which particular function I meant in the *past*, there can be none in the *present* either."[26] So if we are convinced by Kripke's skeptical arguments, we must conclude that our words are meaningless at any time, past or present. We can't coherently accept this conclusion, but we can't simply reject it either, since it looks like an inevitable consequence of our commonsense ideas about meaning.

13. Kripke's Skeptical Challenge

We are finally in a position to begin clarifying Kripke's skeptical challenge. Suppose I am presented with the addition problem '68 + 57' and I answer '125'. Later I reflect on this, and conclude that '125' was the correct answer, because by '68 + 57' I meant 68 plus 57, and 68 plus 57 is 125. All this usually goes without saying. But now suppose I encounter a skeptic who claims that my answer was wrong. This skeptic claims that the correct answer was '5', not '125', because by '+' I did not mean plus, but *quus*, where x quus y = x + y, if both x and y are less than 57, and 5 otherwise. My first reaction is that this skeptical hypothesis is crazy, since I *feel certain* that I meant plus not quus.

As I already emphasized, however, the skeptic *grants* that in our ordinary practice of ascribing meanings, we see no reason to doubt that I meant plus by 'plus', or to think that by 'plus' I meant quus. He nevertheless presses me to say what determined that I meant plus. I feel confident that there is something about my past usage or mental state that determined that I meant plus. Kripke's skeptical hypothesis is designed to evoke this feeling of confidence: "such a bizarre hypothesis as the proposal that I always meant quus is absolutely wild. Wild it indubitably is, no doubt it is false; but if it is false, there must be some fact about my past usage that can be cited to refute it. For although the hypothesis is wild, it does not seem to be *a priori* impossible."[27] We can distinguish two important stages in my acceptance of this skeptical challenge. In the first stage I feel compelled to rule out the skeptic's hypothesis in order to justify my presupposition that I meant plus not quus. In the second stage I feel that the only way to justify my presupposition is to cite a fact about my past that determines that I meant plus. I'll discuss the first stage in this section and the second stage in the next.

The first stage is facilitated by Kripke's interpretation of our ordinary understanding of meaning. In his view it is natural and correct for me to think that if my symbol '+' meant *plus* in the past, then the rule for addition was present to my mind, guided my answers to addition problems, and predetermined the truth conditions of my (actual and potential) addition assertions. It is also natural and correct for me to think that if my symbol '+' meant *quus* in the past, then the rule for quaddition was present to my mind, guided my answers to addition problems, and predetermined the truth conditions of my (actual and potential) addition assertions.

The key point is that I associate both my ordinary presupposition that I meant *plus* by '+' and the skeptical hypothesis that I meant *quus* by '+' with *different mental states*. I think that perhaps in the past the quus rule was present to my mind and this convinces me that the skeptical hypothesis may actually be true. I then see that this possibility would undermine my ordinary presupposition that I meant plus by '+', and so I feel compelled to find something about my past mental state that shows that I did not have the quus rule in mind.

Warren Goldfarb has criticized this stage of our supposed acceptance of Kripke's skeptical challenge on the grounds that the skeptical hypothesis would not be taken seriously in ordinary life:

> It is hard to see any force in the challenge. The ascription of meaning with which we start is supposed to be jeopardized by noting a possibility that it might turn out to be mistaken. Yet that there is such a possibility is less evident than Kripke assumes. . . . We do, after all, engage in elaborate and articulated practices of ascribing meanings to people; we can and do justify our ascriptions when the need arises, we clear up obscurities, and so on. This is our position from the start. To have force, any challenge to our ascriptions must have weight enough to move us from our present, ordinary, position . . . a skeptical problem cannot be assumed to arise just from the logical possibility of error.[28]

In my view this criticism underestimates the force of our feeling that we understand the skeptical hypothesis.

According to Kripke our feeling that we understand the skeptical hypothesis is an inevitable consequence of our idea that what we mean is determined by the directions we have in mind and try to follow when we apply our words. Kripke explains that the "bizarre hypothesis . . . [is] in a sense merely a dramatic device. The basic point is this. Ordinarily, I suppose that, in computing '68 + 57' as I do, I do not simply make an unjustified leap in the dark. I follow directions I previously gave myself that uniquely determine that in this new instance I should say '125'. What are these directions?"[29] The idea that we had in mind directions for calculating either the plus function or the quus function is a natural reflection of our ordinary understanding of meaning, according to Kripke, and not an illusion fabricated by the skeptic. Working dialectically from our ordinary ways of thinking and talking about meaning, we naturally feel that we can make sense of the idea that in the past when we used the symbol '+' we had in mind the directions for calculating the quus function, even though it is not part of our ordinary practices either to raise or to rule out the skeptical hypothesis. Thus we naturally associate both our ordinary presupposition that we meant *plus* by '+' and the skeptical hypothesis that we meant *quus* by '+' with different mental states. We think that perhaps in the past the quus rule was present to our minds and this convinces us that the skeptical hypothesis may actually be true. We then see that this possibility would undermine our ordinary presupposition that we meant plus by '+', and so we feel compelled to find something about our past mental state that shows that we did not have the quus rule in mind.[30]

14. The Challenge to Cite Facts That Determine What We Meant

In the second stage of our acceptance of Kripke's challenge we feel that the only way to justify our ordinary presupposition that we meant plus by '+' is to cite a fact that determines that we meant plus by '+'. Goldfarb argues that this part of Kripke's challenge

rests on ontological considerations. It questions whether, if everything there is were laid out before us, we could read off the correct ascriptions of meaning to people. That is why

Kripke is content with raising bare possibilities of deviant ascriptions. If nothing in the world settles an issue between one or another possibility, then we may conclude that there is nothing to be settled; issues of whether there are any particular grounds for doubting an ascription simply do not enter. Thus it is the notion of fact, of "everything there is," that is to provide the ground of the challenge.[31]

But as I see it the challenge to cite a fact that determines that by '+' we meant plus is an inevitable consequence of Kripke's interpretation of our commonsense ideas about meaning. If his dialectical skepticism is successful, it does not ultimately rest on a prior conception of "everything there is," even though, as we'll see, we must accept some minimal constraints on what counts as a fact if we are to find the skeptic's reasoning convincing.

On my reconstruction of Kripke's skeptical challenge, our search for a fact that determines that by '+' we meant plus is a natural result of his interpretation of our commonsense ideas about meaning. We begin by feeling sure that in the past when we used the symbol '+' we had present to mind the directions for calculating the plus function. When we encounter the skeptical hypothesis, we feel we must concede that it is *possible* that when we used the symbol '+' we had present to mind the directions for calculating the quus function, even though this "possibility" doesn't arise and wouldn't be taken seriously in ordinary life. But we still feel sure that by '+' we meant plus not quus. So when the skeptic challenges us to justify our ordinary presupposition that by '+' we meant plus not quus, we feel that there must be some fact about our previous mental state that *determined* that when we used the symbol '+' we had present to mind the directions for calculating the plus function. On this reconstruction, as I'll now attempt to show, Kripke's challenge to cite a fact that determines that by '+' we meant plus is not motivated by a general conception of "everything there is."

Kripke emphasizes that "there are no limitations . . . on the facts that may be cited to answer the skeptic."[32] He explicitly disavows any behavioristic limitations:

The evidence is not to be confined to that available to an external observer, who can observe my overt behavior but not my internal mental state . . . whatever 'looking into my mind' may be, the skeptic asserts that even if God were to do it, he still could not determine that I meant addition by 'plus'.[33]

The way the skeptical doubt is presented is not behavioristic. It is presented from the 'inside'. Whereas Quine presents the problem about meaning in terms of a linguist, trying to guess what someone else means by his words on the basis of his behavior, Wittgenstein's challenge can be presented to me as a question about *myself:* was there some past fact about me—what I 'meant' by plus—that mandates what I should do now?[34]

In these passages Kripke asserts that there are no limits on what facts we may cite in our attempts to answer the skeptic; in particular, we may cite any facts available from our first-person point of view. And in an earlier passage he asserts that "neither the accuracy of my computation nor of my memory is under dispute."[35]

These assertions seem incompatible, since it seems that ordinarily I directly *remember* that I meant plus by 'plus'. If the skeptic thinks I can't cite a fact that determines that I meant plus, he must think that I can't simply *remember* that I meant plus not quus. And if the skeptic is not questioning my memory, but he is challenging my assumption that I remember that I meant plus by 'plus', it appears that he must implicitly impose limits on the nature of the facts themselves, just as Goldfarb says.[36]

This appearance is misleading. To see why, consider Kripke's reply to the disarmingly simple suggestion that "meaning addition by 'plus' is . . . simply a primitive state, not to be assimilated to sensations or headaches or any 'qualitative' states, nor to be assimilated to dispositions, but a state of a unique kind of its own."[37] The accuracy of our memory is not in question, so the skeptic must grant that if there is a primitive mental state of meaning plus by 'plus' we can remember whether or not we were in that mental state. As I see it, Kripke rejects this simple answer *without* imposing general limitations on the kinds of facts we can cite in answer to the skeptic. He observes that the simple answer "may in a sense be irrefutable . . . But it seems desperate: it leaves the nature of this postulated primitive state—the primitive state of 'meaning addition by "plus'"—completely mysterious."[38] Once we accept Kripke's view of our ordinary understanding of meaning, we should agree that the idea of a primitive state of meaning addition by 'plus' is "completely mysterious." For we have seen that according to Kripke when we ask ourselves what determines that by 'plus' we meant plus, we are asking what determines that when we used 'plus' we had in mind directions for calculating addition, and we thereby determined the truth conditions of all our (actual and potential) addition assertions. To accept the simple answer to this question, we must posit a primitive mental state that determines that in the past we had such directions in mind. We feel that if there were a primitive mental state of meaning plus by 'plus', it would have to be *fully present* at the times when we mean plus. As Kripke says, "such a state would have to be a *finite object*, contained in our finite minds."[39] But we have no idea how a "finite object, contained in our finite minds," could predetermine the truth conditions of our addition assertions.

This is not a dogmatic dismissal of the very idea of primitively meaningful mental states, but an inevitable consequence of Kripke's interpretation of our commonsense ideas about meaning. We have seen that to accept the skeptic's challenge to cite a fact that determines what we meant in the past, we must first take for granted that we can make sense of the skeptic's hypothesis that we meant quus by 'plus', even though this possibility never arises in ordinary linguistic practice. But when we accept that we can make sense of the skeptic's hypothesis, we unwittingly cut all ties between our practices of ascribing meaning to our past uses of words and the facts that supposedly determine what our words meant. In this dialectical context, we are left with no resources for contextualizing and clarifying the supposition that the meanings of our words are determined by primitive meaning states that are fully present to our minds. Without any ways to link the idea of primitive meaning states with our ordinary practices of ascribing meanings to our words, we find the idea utterly mysterious.

Kripke's rejection of the proposal that what we mean is determined by primitive mental states is inspired by Wittgenstein's descriptions of our temptation to posit superfacts that determine what we mean. In §§191–192 of *Philosophical Investigations* Wittgenstein investigates our talk of "grasping" the meaning of a word "in a flash," and notes our temptation to "explain" this by positing a primitive mental state:

191. "It is as if we could grasp the whole use of the word in a flash." Like *what* e.g.?—Can't the use—in a certain sense—be grasped in a flash? And in *what* sense can it not?—The point is, that it is as if we could 'grasp it in a flash' in yet another and much more direct sense than that.—But have you a model for this? No. It is just that this expression suggests itself to us.
192. You have no model of this superlative fact, but you are seduced into using a super-expression.

Inspired by these ideas, Kripke insists that according to our ordinary understanding of meaning we can grasp the directions for calculating addition "in a flash." This seduces us into positing primitive mental states that somehow make our ordinary presuppositions about what we meant true. If we accept Kripke's ordinary understanding of meaning, we end up in the puzzling position described by Wittgenstein in §197 of *Philosophical Investigations:* "we are led to think that the future development must in some way already be present in the act of grasping the use and yet isn't present."[40] We feel driven to embrace these muddled and contradictory requirements for meaning, and so we can't make sense of the idea that there are primitive mental states that satisfy them.

Yet the untenability of primitive meaning states has been questioned. Paul Boghossian asserts that Kripke's rejection of primitive meaning states is not convincing:

Kripke's ... objection to the anti-reductionistic suggestion is that it is utterly mysterious how there could be a finite state, realized in a finite mind, that nevertheless contains information about the correct applicability of a sign in literally no end of distinct situations. But, again, this amounts merely to insisting that we find the idea of a contentful state problematic, without adducing any independent reason why we should. We *know* that mental states with general contents are states with infinitary normative characters; it is precisely with that observation that the entire discussion began. What Kripke needs, if he is to pull off an argument from queerness, is some substantive argument, distinct from his anti-reductionist considerations, why we should not countenance such states. But this he does not provide.[41]

Given my reading of Kripke's dialectical skepticism, however, there is no need for further argument in support of Kripke's rejection of primitive mental states: our rejection of such primitive meaning states follows inevitably from Kripke's understanding of what would be required for meaning. I agree with Boghossian that Kripke's discussion begins by noting our commonsense idea that the meanings of our words are determined by directions in our minds. But Boghossian misses the dialectical progression of Kripke's skeptical reasoning, and hence fails to see the force of Kripke's charge that the idea of primitive meaning facts is mysterious.

Like Goldfarb and Crispin Wright, Boghossian sees Kripke's rejection of primitive meaning facts as the reflection of a general "anti-reductionistic" bias. But I have tried to show that Kripke's reasons for rejecting primitive meaning facts do not stem from such a bias. Instead, on my reading, Kripke starts with the commonsense idea that the meanings of our words are determined by directions in our minds. This idea seems innocent at first, since we naturally take for granted our ordinary procedures for ascribing meaning and evaluating assertions. Once we have accepted that Kripke's skeptical hypothesis makes sense, however, we have effectively severed all links between the facts that are supposed to determine what we mean and our ordinary practices of ascribing meaning to our words. This leaves us with no resources to connect our idea of primitive meaning facts with our actual ascriptions of meaning. Given Kripke's understanding of meaning, if there were primitive meaning facts, they would have to be fully present at each moment when we grasp a rule, and they would have to reach out to all future cases, predetermining the truth conditions of our assertions. Our idea of such meaning facts is muddled and contradictory— "the future development must in some way already be present in" such primitive meaning facts, "and yet isn't present."[42] Thus I disagree with Boghossian when he concludes that "in the context of Kripke's dialectic, the anti-reductionist suggestion emerges as a stable response to the skeptical conclusion, one that is seemingly untouched by all the considerations adduced in the latter's favor."[43] On the contrary, if we work through Kripke's dialectic, starting with the apparently innocent feeling that the meanings of our words are determined by directions in our minds, we should see that no primitive meaning facts can satisfy the requirements on meaning evoked by Kripke's skeptical challenge.[44]

I conclude that Kripke's dialectical skepticism about meaning does not rest on a prior conception of what the facts are. It is an inevitable consequence of Kripke's view of our ordinary understanding of meaning. For we have seen that if we accept Kripke's view of meaning we will feel that we can make sense of the skeptical hypothesis, we will feel obliged to cite a fact that determines that we meant plus not quus, and yet on reflection we will be unable to make sense of the idea that what we meant was determined by a primitive mental state that was somehow fully present whenever we meant plus.

15. Kripke's Skeptical Arguments

We are now in a position to understand Kripke's skeptical arguments for the conclusion that nothing about me—neither my previous linguistic behavior nor any of my past mental states—determines that I meant plus by 'plus'. These arguments take the form of skeptical replies to several different attempts to answer the skeptical challenge.

One might at first think that the meaning of 'plus' is shown by the answers we have already given to addition problems.[45] The skeptic's reply to this commonsense answer is straightforward. He reminds us that there is a number larger than any we have yet encountered in an addition problem.[46] Suppose that 57 is one such number. Then the skeptic challenges us to say what determines that we meant plus by 'plus', and he points out that every application we have made of 'plus' is compatible with the hypothesis that we meant quus: "We can put the problem this way: When asked for the answer to '68 + 57', I unhesitatingly and automatically produced '125', but it would seem that if previously I never performed this computation explicitly I might just as well have answered '5'. Nothing justifies a brute inclination to answer one way rather than another."[47] The fundamental idea behind this skeptical reply is that my past answers to addition problems are compatible with an indefinite number of alternative hypotheses about what I meant by 'plus'.

We may distinguish two versions of this reply. The first version is that even if I assume that all my past answers to addition problems were correct, there remain countless alternative functions that accord with these answers but diverge for addition problems I did not yet answer. So my past answers to addition problems do not by themselves determine what I meant. The assumption that all my past answers were correct creates the impression that the reply essentially depends on the relationship between past and future use. But even if some of my past answers to addition problems were incorrect, they are all compatible with an indefinite number of alternative hypotheses about what I meant by 'plus'. So a better version of the reply is that my past answers to addition problems can be viewed as the results of my attempt to calculate any number of different functions that agree on many though perhaps not all of my past answers.[48] This version highlights the basic problem: my past answers to addition problems don't by themselves determine what I meant by 'plus'.

A second attempt to answer the skeptic reflects our idea that in learning to add we learn directions for calculating sums.[49] Suppose, for example, that when I calculate addition problems I picture myself manipulating marbles. To find the value of m plus n I follow directions that look like this: "Join m marbles with n marbles, and then count the total number of marbles in the resulting heap." These directions are "engraved on my mind as on a slate."[50] When I calculate addition problems I simply "read" these directions and then apply them.

To understand Kripke's reply to this second answer, we must keep in mind that we have already rejected the proposal that there are primitive mental states, fully present in our minds, that determine what we mean. Whatever "mental directions" are, they are not primitive self-interpreting mental states. Any "directions" I may have in mind can be interpreted in a number of different ways. Take, for example, the word 'count', which occurs in the "directions" displayed above:

I applied 'count', like 'plus', to only finitely many past cases. Thus the skeptic can question my present interpretation of my past usage of 'count' as he did with 'plus' . . . he can claim that by 'count' I formerly meant *quount*, where to 'quount' a heap is to count it in the ordinary sense, unless the heap was formed as the union of two heaps, one of which has 57 or more items, in which case one must automatically give the answer '5' . . . the point is perfectly general: if 'plus' is explained in terms of 'counting', a non-standard interpretation of the latter will yield a non-standard interpretation of the former.[51]

This reply is decisive. If we accept Kripke's interpretation of our commonsense ideas about meaning, and we reject the idea that there are primitive self-interpreting mental states, we can't insist that the skeptic's nonstandard interpretations of what we meant are ruled out by "directions engraved in our minds as on a slate."

We have seen that neither our past applications of the word 'plus' nor "directions" we had in mind when we used 'plus' determined that by 'plus' we meant plus not quus. Another answer Kripke considers suffers the same fate as the first two. One might hold that " 'meaning addition by "plus' " denotes an irreducible experience, with its own special quale, known directly to each of us by introspection."[52] The apparent virtue of this proposal is that if meaning were such an experience, then we could understand how we can know immediately what we mean. All we would have to do is introspect—the quality of our experience would indicate to us exactly what we mean. The problem with this suggestion is also obvious once we give up the idea that there are primitive self-interpreting mental states: "No internal impression, with a *quale*, could possibly tell me in itself how it is to be applied in future cases. Nor can any pile up of such impressions, thought of as rules for interpreting rules, do the job. . . . if there were a special experience of 'meaning' addition by 'plus' analogous to a headache, it would not have the properties that a state of meaning addition by 'plus' ought to have—it would not tell me what to do in new cases."[53] We can express the same basic point by saying that any internal impression I had while using the word 'plus' is compatible with the skeptic's hypothesis that I meant quus not plus. So no such experience can determine that I had present to mind the rule for addition not quaddition. My internal impressions can't predetermine the truth conditions of my assertions.

These three commonsense answers to the skeptical challenge all fail because they can't block the skeptic's alternative hypotheses about what we meant by 'plus'. Kripke also considers two *philo-*

sophical answers to the skeptic. The first of these is that the theory that I meant plus is more likely to be true because it is *simpler* than the theory that I meant quus. Kripke's reply is that to answer the skeptical challenge we must show how it *could* be true that I meant plus. An appeal to simplicity can't by itself establish that I meant anything at all, and so we can't meet the skeptical challenge by insisting that the simplest theory of what we meant is true.[54]

The second philosophical answer to the skeptical challenge is that what we meant by 'plus' was determined by our *dispositions* to give certain answers when presented with addition problems. In its simplest form the dispositional answer is that

> to mean addition by '+' is to be disposed, when asked for any sum '$x + y$' to give the sum of x and y as the answer (in particular to say '125' when queried about '68 + 57'); to mean quus is to be disposed when queried about any arguments, to respond with their *quum* (in particular to answer '5' when queried about '68 + 57'). . . . To say that in fact I meant plus in the past is to say—as surely was the case!—that had I been queried about '68 + 57', I would have answered '125'. By hypothesis I was not in fact asked, but the disposition was present none the less.[55]

Many commentators have found this the most promising kind of answer to the skeptical challenge. But now that we have clarified Kripke's interpretation of our commonsense ideas about meaning (§§6–11) and his skeptical challenge (§§12–14), we can see that a dispositional account of meaning "misconceives the sceptic's problem".[56]

> [The dispositionalist claims that] " '125' is the response you are disposed to give, and . . . it would also have been your response in the past." Well and good, I know that '125' is the response I am disposed to give (I am actually giving it!), and maybe it is helpful to be told—as a matter of brute fact—that I would have given the same response in the past. How does any of this indicate that—now *or* in the past—'125' was an answer *justified* in terms of instructions I gave myself, rather than a mere jack-in-the-box unjustified and arbitrary response?[57]

Kripke's basic point is that the dispositional answer fails as an analysis or justification of our ordinary idea that the meanings of our words predetermine the truth conditions of our assertions and judgments. According to Kripke, to grasp a rule is to have in mind directions that determine in advance the truth conditions of our assertions and judgments. We strive to follow the rules to which we are committed, and thus to make true assertions. We may cite a speaker's causal dispositions to *explain* or *predict* her linguistic responses in various circumstances. But her causal dispositions can't indicate which directions she *ought* to be following, so they don't determine what her words mean, or predetermine the truth conditions of her assertions. The dispositional answer therefore fails to meet the skeptic's challenge.

16. Kripke's Skeptical Conclusion

There is no need to consider more attempts to answer Kripke's skeptical challenge, for we are now in a position to see that it can't be met on its own terms. If we accept Kripke's view of our ordinary understanding of meaning, we must concede that our words are meaningless, and that we can't commit ourselves to standards relative to which our "assertions" are correct or incorrect.

We arrived at this incredible conclusion indirectly, using Kripke's skeptical strategy. We saw (§12) that we can't directly doubt that our words are now meaningful. But we feel we can make sense of the skeptical hypothesis that in the past we meant quus by 'plus'. At first we are confident that there must be some fact that determined that we meant plus by 'plus'. Yet once we see that there are no primitive self-interpreting mental states, we soon find that any fact we could cite about our past is compatible with countless skeptical hypotheses about what we meant. We feel compelled to conclude that our words were meaningless in the past. In the final step of the skeptical strategy, we infer that our words are meaningless in the present too. For if there are no facts that determine what I meant in the past, there are none that determine what I mean in the present either.[58] The skeptic's reasoning undermines our starting "assumption" that our words are meaningful.

By this indirect route we come to distinguish between the *feeling* that our words are now meaningful and their actually *being* meaningful. After going through the skeptic's reasoning, it seems that "although I may *feel* (now) that something in my head corresponding to the word 'plus' mandates a determinate response to any new pair of arguments, in fact nothing in my head does so."[59] So we are now apparently able to distinguish between our first-person "subjective" experience of taking our words at face value—accepting such sentences as " 'plus', as I now use it, denotes plus"—and the "objective" question of whether our words have any meaning.

By focusing our attention on the question of whether our words were meaningful in the past we can avoid the pragmatic incoherence of directly doubting that our words are now meaningful. Nevertheless, our indirect skeptical strategy eventually forces us into an incoherent position. For if our words are meaningless, then we can't make assertions, draw inferences, or reason at all. For Kripke these are all activities that make sense to us only against the background of the ordinary assumption that our grasp of rules predetermines the truth conditions of our assertions and judgments. So we can't simultaneously accept the skeptical conclusion and indulge our "subjective" experience that we are asserting, judging, and reasoning. But neither can we simply reject the skeptical conclusion, since it is apparently an inevitable consequence of our ordinary understanding of meaning. Kripke's skeptical arguments ultimately push us to a paradox.

17. Kripke's Objectifying Move

We have seen that Kripke's skepticism about meaning begins by taking for granted that our words are now meaningful, that we can make assertions that are objectively true or false, and ends with the paradoxical conclusion that our words are meaningless and that all our "assertions" are subjective. The argument is designed to show us that our ordinary understanding of meaning and assertion inevitably leads us to this skeptical conclusion. Kripke's talk of "facts" at times suggests that an independent ontological bias drives his skepticism, especially when he rejects the idea of primitive mental states that determine what we mean. But we saw in §13 that once we accept Kripke's understanding of meaning and his skeptical challenge, we feel driven to conclude that there are no primitive mental states that rule out the skeptic's alternative hypotheses about what we meant in the past. So I disagree with Goldfarb when he writes: "Kripke's is not a purely skeptical challenge, in the sense that it does not operate by pushing on ordinary conceptions from within. Rather, it proceeds from a sophisticated notion of the limits of the objective world, and so relies on a substantial assumption."[60] On the contrary, if Kripke's argument is successful it shows that skepticism about meaning arises from within our ordinary ways of thinking and talking about meaning. Kripke's argument stands or falls with his understanding of meaning, and is not motivated by a general conception of "everything there is."

Nevertheless, Kripke's dialectical skepticism about meaning involves what I call an *objectifying move*. His account of our ordinary understanding of meaning, together with his skeptical strategy of considering whether or not there is an objective fact about what I meant in the past, leads us to adopt an external perspective on our own assertions and judgments, treating them as objects of our metaphysical investigation. When our own assertions and judgments are viewed in this way, they appear to us as lifeless signs that can be interpreted in a number of different ways. We then seem to be faced with a dilemma. Either we posit some "superfacts" that give them life, or we conclude that our ordinary presupposition that they are meaningful is illusory. Neither option is acceptable and so we end in a skeptical paradox.

We saw (§13) that if we accept Kripke's understanding of meaning, we feel we understand the skeptical hypothesis that in the past we meant quus by 'plus'. Our feeling that we understand the skeptical hypothesis leads us to look for mental or physical facts that determined what we meant in the past. This objectifying move cuts the vital links between meaning and our ordinary linguistic practices, and inevitably leads to Kripke's skeptical conclusion.

Our tendency to make this objectifying move is like our tendency to see a physical machine as a self-interpreting symbol.[61] If we look at an engineer's drawing of a mechanism with gears that transfer motion from one drive shaft to another, for example, we seem to see the possibilities of the motion in the parts of the machine depicted by the drawing. We picture the ideal operation of such a machine by imagining how it *would* operate if none of its gears ever lost a tooth and the drive shafts never slipped. And it seems that our picture of the ideal movements of the parts must portray properties that somehow inhere in the parts of the physical machine itself.

In a similar way, when we ask what facts about our previous mental state determine that we meant plus not quus, we may imagine that there is some mechanism in our minds, the ideal operation of which would lead us to give correct answers to addition problems. The ideal calculations of addition problems we think of as in a mysterious sense present in our minds. Mistakes are explained by noting factors that lead us to deviate from the ideal calculation. Perhaps we were not concentrating, and some random psychological factor interfered with our ideal performance. This picture suggests that in the past there was some ideal causal or quasi-causal mechanism in our minds that determined that we meant plus not quus. But when we try to make sense of this picture, we find that we do not understand how our past temporally bounded mental states can "contain within them" or in any other way determine the ideal steps we ought to take when we calculate addition problems. And so it seems that "the entire idea of meaning vanishes into thin air."[62]

18. Kripke's Metaphysical Realism

The objectifying move reflects Kripke's metaphysical picture of the conditions under which we are able to say something objectively true or false. If we accept the skeptical argument, we will feel sure that this metaphysical picture was always implicit in our ordinary understanding of meaning.

By working through the skeptical argument, we "discover" the metaphysical picture lurking within our ordinary understanding of meaning. In retrospect it seems that before we considered the skeptic's reasoning, we had unknowingly imposed this metaphysical picture on our subjective impression that we were making assertions, and so we failed to distinguish between the picture and the impression. We assumed that we could simply use our sentences to express our understanding of the "objective" conditions under which our assertions are true or false. But by means of the skeptical argument we have apparently come to see that we can't make "objective" assertions. We feel that we have "discovered" a sharp distinction between our "subjective" impression of making assertions and the "objective" requirement for making assertions: that we have in our minds something that predetermines the truth conditions of our assertions.

But this sense of "discovery" is short-lived. For after we go through the skeptic's reasoning, we can no longer take our ordinary use of our sentences to express the metaphysical truth conditions we picture, and so we are unable to articulate the "objective" standards that our assertions fail to express. In the course of the skeptic's reasoning, we come to see that our metaphysical picture of an "objective" assertion is completely divorced from anything we can do or say. The same reasoning that reveals our attraction to this metaphysical picture undermines our confidence that we understand it.

We are left with no "discovery," no coherent understanding of meaning, and the sense that something went wrong. Yet Kripke flatly rejects the possibility that the skeptical paradox stems from his own misunderstanding. He thinks it is obvious that his is the only "natural and correct" understanding of our common assertions about meaning, and he insinuates that any philosopher who "offers his own analysis of the relevant common assertions, one that shows that they do not really say what they seem to say," is dishonest or deluded. He defends his own analysis of meaning by casting suspicion on any philosopher who claims that our common assertions about some topic "do not really say what they seem to say": "What the claimant calls a 'misleading philosophical misconstrual' of the ordinary statement is probably the natural and correct understanding. The real misconstrual comes when the claimant continues, 'All the ordinary man really means is . . .' and gives a sophisticated analysis compatible with his own philosophy."[63] Since Kripke is confident that any alternative to his picture of meaning would be a distortion of common sense, he sees no way to avoid his skeptical conclusion.

T W O

Quine's Scientific Skepticism about Meaning

19. Dialectical Skepticism Contrasted with Scientific Skepticism

We have seen that Kripke's skepticism about meaning is *dialectical:* starting with his interpretation of our commonsense idea that meaning must predetermine the truth conditions of our assertions, Kripke argues that we are implicitly committed to requirements for meaning that can't be met. He concludes that our words are meaningless, and that we can't make assertions, despite our subjective impression that we can. In contrast, Quine's skepticism about meaning is *scientific:* starting with an austere scientific description of our linguistic behavior, he argues that our commonsense assumption that there is only one correct translation of our words is unfounded. In Quine's view, our sentences are associated with other sentences and linked to impacts at our nerve endings by the mechanism of conditioned response. It is irrelevant to Quine's scientific skepticism that our commonsense judgments about meaning do not implicitly commit us to this austere scientific description of our linguistic behavior. Whether or not we implicitly accept Quine's behavioristic picture of language, our commonsense assumption that there is only one correct translation of our words is unfounded, according to Quine, because "manuals for translating one language into another can be set up in divergent ways, all compatible with the totality of speech dispositions, yet incompatible with one another."[1] We may be tempted to think that if the facts don't uniquely determine what we mean, then we can't make assertions, despite our subjective impression that we can. But in Quine's view our ability to use the sentences of science to make assertions is untouched by his scientific rejection of our commonsense assumption that there is only one correct translation of our words.

In this chapter I reconstruct Quine's naturalistic view of science and meaning. His scientific naturalism is a systematic articulation of the attractive idea that only the mature sciences describe the world as it "really" is. A sustained effort to see meaning from Quine's perspective cultivates our attraction to scientific naturalism, loosens the grip of Kripke's picture of meaning, and helps us to see how our conception of the proper starting point and task for philosophy can shape our thinking about the relationship between meaning and assertion.

20. Quine's Scientific Naturalism

Scientific naturalism—the unifying principle of Quine's philosophy—is "the recognition that it is within science itself, and not in some prior philosophy, that reality is to be identified and described."[2] Science is so fundamental for Quine that it can't be defined; it can only be *displayed* in the doctrines of mature disciplines like physics, chemistry, and biology.[3] Since science gives us our only grip on "reality," all legitimate descriptions—even of the relation between science and "reality"—must be expressed from within science itself.

The role of science in Quine's framework is reflected in his disquotational view of truth. A disquotational truth predicate enables us to attribute truth to any sentence we can understand. Disquotational ascriptions of truth follow a lucid pattern:

'_____' is true if and only if _____.

Properly restricted to avoid the semantical paradoxes, a disquotational truth predicate for a language L has "every bit as much clarity, in any particular application, as is enjoyed by the particular expressions of L to which we apply it. Attribution of truth in particular to 'Snow is white', is every bit as clear to us as attribution of whiteness to snow."[4] Moreover, an attribution of truth to a sentence is *only* as clear to us as the sentence itself. Since for Quine only the sentences of science are clear, they are the only ones that can sensibly be called 'true'.[5]

The same attitude toward the sentences of science is reflected in Quine's claim that "factuality, like gravitation and electric charge, is internal to our theory of nature."[6] The expression 'it is a fact that' is "vacuous" according to Quine: he treats 'it is a fact that snow is white' as equivalent to 'snow is white'.[7] Thus it makes sense to use sentences of the form 'It is a fact that S' only when we *understand* S, and so, given naturalism, only when S is "couched in the terms of" and "seen from within" a scientific theory we accept.

Quine's view that there can be no perspective higher or firmer than science sets limits on the legitimate tasks for philosophy. One such task is to simplify and clarify "logical theory"—to find a suitable "canonical notation" that clarifies ontology and facilitates the application of logical laws to the sentences of science:

> Each reduction that we make in the variety of constituent constructions needed in building the sentences of science is a simplification in the structure of the inclusive conceptual scheme of science. Each elimination of obscure constructions or notions that we manage to achieve, by paraphrase into more lucid elements, is a clarification of the conceptual scheme of science. The same motives that impel scientists to seek ever simpler and clearer theories adequate to the subject matter of their special sciences are motives for simplification and clarification of the broader framework shared by all the sciences. Here the objective is called philosophical, because of the breadth of the framework concerned; but the motivation is the same. The quest of a simplest, clearest overall pattern of canonical notation is not to be distinguished from a quest of ultimate categories, a limning of the most general traits of reality.[8]

Thus "philosophy . . ., as an effort to get clear on things, is not to be distinguished in essential points of purpose and method from good and bad science."[9]

The work of clarification is not restricted to our choice of a canonical notation; it also involves the rejection of murky sentences. Among the murky sentences are those used to ascribe propositional attitudes—sentences such as 'Ralph believes Cicero denounced Cataline' and 'Bernard hopes it won't rain tomorrow'. In Quine's view, the facts don't uniquely determine how such sentences are to be applied, and so we can't use them to "describe reality": "If we are limning the true and ultimate structure of reality, the canonical scheme for us is the austere scheme that knows . . . no propositional attitudes but only the physical constitution and behavior of organisms."[10] Quine's talk of "limning the true and ultimate structure of reality" is just ornamental: he accepts no perspective higher or firmer than science from which we could question how science itself is related to "reality." The point of the passage is that our choice of a canonical scheme reflects our judgments about which sentences are clear and which ones obscure. Quine finds the sentences ascribing propositional attitudes obscure, and so he recommends that we exclude them from our canonical scheme.

But does this say more about Quine than about the sentences we use to ascribe propositional attitudes? It may seem that unless there is an "independent" criterion of truth and factuality, our choice of canonical scheme can't be taken to reflect the "the true and ultimate structure of reality." The reply from Quine brings us back to the bedrock of his naturalism: there can be no criterion of factuality or truth that is independent of our own best sense, shaped by the disciplines of science, of what is clear and what is not. To hanker after such a criterion is to abandon scientific naturalism, and lapse into empty philosophical speculation.

21. Naturalized Epistemology

For scientific naturalism all legitimate descriptions—including descriptions of the relationship between "theory" and "evidence"—must be expressed from within science. This forces us to redefine the task of epistemology. The task can't be to reconstruct the rational foundations of scientific claims from a perspective *independent* of science, for there is no such perspective. Instead the task of epistemology must be to describe the relationship between "theory" and "evidence" from within science itself.

What distinguishes Quine's naturalized epistemology from foundational empiricism is that for naturalized epistemology "the motivating insight, viz. that we can know external things only through impacts at our nerve endings, is itself based on our general knowledge of the ways of physical objects—illuminated desks, reflected light, activated retinas."[11] To develop and clarify this "motivating insight" we must use our best scientific theories to describe the relationship between the impacts at our nerve endings and the sentences we affirm when prompted by those impacts. Given this new task,

> epistemology, or something like it, simply falls into place as a chapter of psychology and hence of natural science. It studies a natural phenomenon, viz., a physical human subject. This human subject is accorded a certain experimentally controlled input—certain patterns of irradiation in assorted frequencies, for instance—and in the fullness of time the subject delivers as output a description of the three-dimensional external world and its history. The relation between the meager input and the torrential output is a relation that we are prompted to study for somewhat the same reasons that always prompted epistemology; namely, in order to see how evidence relates to theory, and in what ways one's theory of nature transcends any available evidence.[12]

Quine recasts epistemology by sketching a scientific picture of "evidence" and "theory" and the relationship between them. "Evidence" is described in terms of impacts at our nerve endings, and "theory" in terms of the linguistic "output" that subjects "deliver" when prompted by those impacts.

Viewed naturalistically, a scientific theory is a fabric of sentences variously associated with one another and linked to impacts at our nerve endings by the mechanism of conditioned response.[13] To study these associations, Quine focuses on individual human subjects, seen as complex physical mechanisms that produce sentences upon receiving various triggerings of their neural receptors. The task of naturalized epistemology is to describe and analyze the associations between sentences and stimulation that are embodied in these physical mechanisms. Quine analyzes these associations by describing a subject's *dispositions* to assent to or dissent from a sentence under various prompting stimulations. He thinks such descriptions are naturalistically acceptable; just as we can identify the fragility of glass or the solubility of sugar with structural traits of glass and of sugar, so, Quine thinks, we can identify a subject's behavioral dispositions with some (unknown) structural traits of the subject's body.[14]

To capture the empiricist idea of an intersubjectively checkable observation, Quine constructs his definition of an *observation sentence*. For Quine an *observation sentence* is a sentence that has the same *stimulus meaning* for all members of a given linguistic community.[15] The stimulus meaning of a sentence S for a given speaker A (at time t) is the ordered pair comprising the class of all irradiation patterns of the eye (and other sense modalities) that would prompt A's assent to S (at t), and the class of all the irradiation patterns that would prompt A's dissent from S (at t). Observation sentences are the sentences most directly associated with sensory stimulation. A subject's assent to (or dissent from) other sentences is always mediated by dispositions associating sentences with sentences. Quine gives an example:

> someone mixes the contents of two test tubes, observes a green tint, and says 'There was copper in it.' Here the sentence is elicited by a non-verbal stimulus, but the stimulus depends for its efficacy upon an earlier network of associations of words with words; viz., one's learning of chemical theory ... the verbal network of an articulate theory has intervened to link the stimulus with the response.
>
> The intervening theory is composed of sentences associated with one another in multifarious ways not easily reconstructed even in conjecture.[16]

The "multifarious" links between sentences "must finally be due to the conditioning of sentences as responses to sentences as stimuli."[17] A subject's present complex of associations between sentences—associations of theoretical sentences with other theoretical ones, and between theoretical sentences and observation sentences—makes up his theory of nature.

Only observation sentences have intersubjective "empirical meaning" when considered in isolation from the rest of a theory. In contrast, theoretical sentences have no direct associations with sensory stimulation. To describe the empirical contribution of theoretical sentences, we must describe the entire complex of dispositions that link them with sensory stimulation. In practice our total theory seems like a loose association of empirically independent chunks.

But some of our dispositions—in particular, our dispositions to assent to sentences that express the laws of logic and mathematics—are so fundamental that if they were altered, all current links between theoretical sentences and sensory stimulation would change. Quine's naturalism about the relationship between "theory" and "evidence" therefore leads him to conclude that "the unit of empirical significance is the whole of science."[18]

22. Posits and Reality

When we *use* our scientific theories, we *quantify over objects*—stones, tables, and electrons. But viewed naturalistically, according to Quine, the "objects" over which we "quantify" are "cultural posits," part of our "man-made fabric" of scientific theory, "devices for working a manageable structure into the flux of experience."[19] How can this be?

The puzzle we feel is the result of viewing scientific theories, including our own, from the naturalistic point of view: "We are studying how the human subject of our study posits bodies and projects his physics from his data, and we appreciate that our position in the world is just like his. Our very epistemological enterprise, therefore, and the psychology wherein it is a component chapter, and the whole of natural science wherein psychology is a component book—all this is our own construction or projection from stimulations like those we were meting out to our epistemological subject."[20] While using our scientific theories we express our robust realism about objects, a realism that appears irreconcilable with the idea that viewed naturalistically the "objects" we "posit" are "constructions" or "projections" from sensory stimulation.

Yet according to Quine there are no *scientific* grounds for our feeling that the realism we express when using our theories is in conflict with naturalized epistemology. And since "we can never do better than occupy the standpoint of some theory or other, the best we can muster at the time," we must not "look down on the standpoint of [our] theor[ies] as make-believe."[21] From within Quine's systematic naturalism there is no legitimate perspective from which to raise a general challenge to the robust realism about objects expressed in our scientific inquiries. Our realism does not rest on any foundation firmer than science itself, and no description of science from within science can undermine it.

23. From Naturalized Epistemology to Indeterminacy of Translation

The starting point for Quine's critique of our ordinary ideas about meaning is his assumption that linguistic meaning is determined by associations of sentences with shared sensory stimulation: "Language is socially inculcated and controlled; the inculcation and control turn strictly on the keying of sentences to shared stimulation. Internal factors may vary *ad libitum* without prejudice to communication as long as the keying of language to external stimuli is undisturbed. Surely one has no choice but to be an empiricist so far as one's theory of linguistic meaning is concerned."[22] Given this assumption, "epistemology . . . becomes semantics,"[23] and the totality of speech dispositions linking sentences with one another and to shared sensory stimulation exhausts the natural facts relevant to both.

Quine's definition of an observation sentence, for example, is central both to naturalized epistemology and to his account of what is objective in linguistic meaning. In "Epistemology Naturalized" he is explicit about the dual role of observation sentences:

> The observation sentence is the cornerstone of semantics. For it is . . . fundamental to the learning of meaning. Also, it is where meaning is firmest. Sentences higher up in theories have no empirical content they can call their own; they confront the tribunal of sensory evidence only in more or less inclusive aggregates. The observation sentence, situated at the very periphery of the body scientific, is the minimal verifiable aggregate; it has an empirical content all its own and wears it on its sleeve.[24]

Here Quine emphasizes the relevance for linguistic meaning of a point noted earlier (§21): only observation sentences have intersubjective "empirical meaning" when considered in isolation from the rest of a scientific theory. Other sentences are linked to sensory stimulations indirectly. There is no hope of isolating the empirical contribution of these sentences, for their empirical consequences are mediated by their links to other sentences. In Quine's view this naturalistic holism of empirical meaning establishes his thesis that translation is objectively indeterminate.

The indeterminacy thesis is a direct challenge to our common-sense ideas about meaning. In ordinary contexts we see no difficulty in telling when two sentences are alike or different in meaning, and we feel that our commonsense standards of similarity and difference in meaning show that there is only one correct translation of our words. According to Quine's indeterminacy thesis, however, "manuals for translating one language into another can be set up in divergent ways, all compatible with the totality of speech dispositions, yet incompatible with one another. In countless places they will diverge in giving, as their respective translations of a sentence of the one language, sentences of the other language which stand to each other in no plausible sort of equivalence however loose."[25] The alternative manuals are "all compatible with the totality of speech dispositions," yet they give what are by commonsense standards "inequivalent" translations. If we are convinced that translation is indeterminate in this sense, then we must concede that contrary to common sense, there is more than one acceptable translation of our words.

Quine's naturalistic empiricism about linguistic meaning sets his standard for what is objective in translation: "The sort of meaning that is basic to translation, and to the learning of one's own language, is necessarily empirical meaning and nothing more."[26] In light of this assumption, to make his indeterminacy thesis plausible Quine must convince us that between any two languages we can construct inequivalent manuals of translation that are compatible with "the totality of speech dispositions" linking sentences with sensory stimulation. We have already seen that in Quine's view only observation sentences have empirical meaning when viewed in isolation; other sentences "have no empirical content they can call their own." He argues that this holism, properly viewed, establishes his indeterminacy thesis: "The crucial consideration behind my argument for the indeterminacy of translation [is] that a statement about the world does not always or usually have a separable fund of empirical consequences that it can call its own."[27] The first step of Quine's argument for indeterminacy is that two (or more) manuals of translation for a language are equally "correct" if they preserve the "net empirical implications" of the language taken as a whole.[28] The second step is that if empirical meaning can be assigned only to languages taken as wholes, then *there must be* alternative manuals of translation which yield the same net empirical implications, yet systematically diverge in their translations of sentences that are not associated directly with sensory stimulation.[29] Quine spends little time on the first step—he thinks it is an undeniable consequence of naturalism. In his view the second step is the substantial one. To convince us that inequivalent manuals of translations can have the same net empirical implications, Quine constructs his celebrated thought experiment involving "radical translation."

24. Collateral Information and Stimulus Meaning

One central aim of Quine's reflections about "radical translation" is to show that for most sentences there is no naturalistic basis for the commonsense distinction between "meaning" and "collateral information." This commonsense distinction plays a role even in the first stages of translation, as we can see by reflecting on Quine's imaginary field linguist, who tries to come up with a manual for translating a "hitherto untranslated" language into English. The linguist has observed that a native assents to 'Gavagai?' when and only when there is a rabbit in the native's visual field, and so he translates 'Gavagai' as 'Rabbit'. Despite the obviousness of this opening translation, there may in fact be subtle differences between the stimulus meanings of these two sentences:

> The difficulty is that an informant's assent to or dissent from 'Gavagai?' can depend excessively on prior collateral information as a supplement to the present prompting stimulus. He may assent on the occasion of nothing better than an ill-glimpsed movement in the grass, because of his earlier observation, unknown to the linguist, of rabbits near the spot. Since the linguist would not on his own information be prompted by that same poor glimpse to assent to 'Rabbit?', we have here a discrepancy between the present stimulus meaning of 'Gavagai' for the informant and that of 'Rabbit' for the linguist.[30]

The linguist nevertheless confidently translates 'Gavagai' as 'Rabbit', and so differences between the stimulus meanings of 'Gavagai' and 'Rabbit' must be viewed as differences between the linguist's and the native's collateral information about rabbits.[31]

In the case of 'Gavagai' and 'Rabbit' the differences in stimulus meaning are so slight that the translation of 'Gavagai' as 'Rabbit' seems fully objective. But for sentences that are not as closely keyed to sensory stimulation the problem of distinguishing between meaning and collateral information is more serious. Consider, for example, the one-word sentence 'Bachelor', whose stimulus meaning varies widely among English speakers. Common sense tells us that the meaning of 'Bachelor' is the same for all English speakers, and so we would ordinarily attribute differences in stimulus meaning to differences in collateral information about who is married and who isn't. Yet our speech dispositions do not justify our assumption that 'Bachelor' has the same meaning for all English speakers.

These examples show that the commonsense distinction between "meaning" and "collateral information" does not reflect an objective distinction in our speech dispositions. As Quine puts it, there is no "experimental sense" to be made of "a distinction between what goes into [a speaker's] learning to apply an expression and what goes into his learning supplementary matters about the objects concerned."[32] Hence for all sentences not directly associated with sensory stimulation, there must be more than one way to "solve" the problem of collateral information—more than one coherent overall description of what each speaker means and believes. So long as these alternative descriptions preserve the net empirical implications of the speaker's sentences, "there can be no ground for saying which . . . is right."[33]

25. Inscrutability of Reference

For observation sentences, whose stimulus meanings are the same for all members of a community, sameness of stimulus meaning is sufficient for sameness of empirical meaning.[34] But sameness of stimulus meaning does not guarantee that two observation sentences have the same meaning by our commonsense standards. The sentences 'Rabbit', 'Undetached rabbit-part', and 'Rabbit stage' each have the same stimulus meaning for all English speakers, yet by commonsense standards they have markedly different meanings.

The discrepancy between the objective empirical meaning of observation sentences and our commonsense standards for sameness and difference in meaning is a symptom of what Quine calls the inscrutability of reference.

Quine's argument for the inscrutability of reference has two stages. First, he points out that the stimulus meaning of 'Gavagai', for example, does not uniquely determine how we are to translate the *term* 'gavagai': "a whole rabbit is present when and only when an undetached part of a rabbit is present; also when and only when a temporal stage of a rabbit is present. If we are wondering whether to translate a native expression 'gavagai' as 'rabbit' or as 'undetached rabbit part' or as 'rabbit stage', we can never settle the matter simply by ostension—that is, simply by repeatedly querying the expression 'gavagai' for the native's assent or dissent in the presence of assorted stimulations."[35] The crucial consideration here is that such sentences as 'Rabbit', 'Undetached rabbit-part', and 'Rabbit stage' have the same stimulus meanings. Second, Quine argues that the translations of the particles and constructions that make up the speaker's "apparatus" of individuation[36]—plural endings, pronouns, numerals, the 'is' of identity, the words 'same' and 'other'—are not determined by speech dispositions either. Translation of the particles and constructions of individuation involves "analytical hypotheses" that go beyond speech dispositions, and reflect the translator's own biases:

> if one workable overall system of analytical hypotheses provides for translating a given native expression into "is the same as," perhaps another equally workable but systematically different system would translate that native expression rather into something like "belongs with." Then when in the native language we try to ask "Is this *gavagai* the same as that?" we could as well be asking "Does this *gavagai* belong with that?" Insofar, the native's assent is no objective evidence for translating "gavagai" as "rabbit" rather than "undetached rabbit part" or "rabbit stage."[37]

Appropriately generalized, this reasoning shows that a speaker's dispositions do not fix the translations of his terms, and so reference is inscrutable.

26. The Limits of Objective Translation

We have now seen two ways in which translation is not determined by speech dispositions. Whole sentences whose stimulus meanings are not the same for all members of the community must be translated without benefit of any clear basis in natural fact (§24). And the translation of terms of a language reflects "analytical hypotheses" that go beyond anything implicit in the natives' conditioned associations of sentences with sensory stimulation (§25). Quine's aim in going into these details is to *show* us that translation is indeterminate. His observations are meant to bring out the gap between our translation practices and speech dispositions.

When our translations go beyond what can be gleaned from stimulus meaning, they reflect our "analytical hypotheses"—our decisions as to how to segment sentences into "words," and how to translate these words by expressions of our own language. The only objective test for a system of analytical hypotheses is whether or not the resulting translation conforms to the totality of speech dispositions. Quine's reflections about "radical translation" are designed to convince us that for each language there *must be* alternative systems of analytical hypotheses compatible with all speech dispositions. He is explicit about what he expects us eventually to see:

> one has only to reflect on the nature of the possible data and methods to appreciate the indeterminacy. Sentences translatable outright, translatable by independent evidence of stimulatory occasions, are sparse and must woefully underdetermine the analytical hypotheses on which the translation of all further sentences depends. To project such hypotheses beyond the independently translatable sentences at all is in effect to impute our sense of linguistic analogy unverifiably to the native mind.[38]

Quine takes for granted that a satisfactory set of analytical hypotheses must give *systematic* mappings of words and sentences from the native language to the translator's language. Yet our previous reflections on the indeterminacy of translation for whole sentences focused on sentence by sentence translation (§24). We noted that stimulus meaning provides no basis for drawing the distinction between meaning and collateral information. Now we can add that even when we take into account the systematic contribution of words to our translations of sentences, we must conclude that the translations of sentences are indeterminate:

There can be no doubt that rival systems of analytical hypotheses can fit the totality of speech behavior to perfection, and can fit the totality of dispositions to speech behavior as well, and still specify mutually incompatible translations of countless sentences insusceptible of independent control.[39]

Two such translations might even be patently contrary in truth value, provided there is no stimulation that would encourage assent to either.[40]

Quine has never given an example of the indeterminacy of the truth values of whole sentences. Recently he has explained why: "the full or holophrastic indeterminacy of translation draws too broadly on a language to admit of factual illustration."[41] Thus the full weight of Quine's indeterminacy thesis must be borne by his theoretical reflections about the relationship between sentences and sensory stimulation.

27. Underdetermination and Indeterminacy

Quine takes his reflections to show both that the associations between sentences and sensory stimulation don't uniquely determine translation and that there is nothing beyond the associations between sentences and sensory stimulation for our translations to be right or wrong about. His thesis that translation is indeterminate goes beyond the observation that translation is underdetermined— that more than one translation manual is compatible with all the evidence. In Quine's view, even our best scientific theories are underdetermined by all possible evidence, yet we assume that they can be objectively right or wrong. So what grounds Quine's sharp distinction between indeterminacy of translation and underdetermination of theories by all evidence? Nothing does, according to Noam Chomsky:

there can be no doubt that Quine's statement about analytical hypotheses is true, though the question arises why it is important. It is, to be sure, undeniable that if a system of "analytical hypotheses" goes beyond evidence then it is possible to conceive alternatives compatible with the evidence, just as in the case of Quine's "genuine hypotheses" about stimulus meaning and truth-functional connectives. Thus the situation in the case of language, or "common-sense knowledge," is, in this respect, no different from the case of physics.[42]

In reply to this objection, Quine explains that his distinction between indeterminacy and underdetermination rests on scientific naturalism:

> In respect of being under-determined by all possible data, translational synonymy and theoretical physics are indeed alike ... Where then does the parallel fail?
>   Essentially in this: theory in physics is an ultimate parameter. There is no legitimate first philosophy, higher or firmer than physics, to which to appeal over physicists' heads.[43]

Here Quine emphasizes once again that science is the bedrock of his philosophy. Our best scientific theories set our "ultimate parameter," and it is only through them that we can identify and describe reality at all (§20). Yet working from *within* our best theories of nature, including a behavioristic theory of linguistic behavior, we can see that translation is not merely underdetermined, but indeterminate.[44]

Quine's naturalistic distinction between underdetermination and indeterminacy may still appear unstable, even incoherent. For it seems that if we accept indeterminacy of translation and reference, we must deny that we objectively refer to objects, and so we must give up our attitude of robust realism about the objects of our scientific theorizing. But if science is our "ultimate parameter," as Quine says, then we must take the attitude of robust realism toward the objects of our scientific theorizing. So it seems we can't simultaneously hold that science is our ultimate parameter and that reference and translation are indeterminate.[45]

Quine's answer to this objection is flatly to deny that scientific naturalism commits us to the determinacy of reference. From within Quine's naturalistic framework no general challenge to the robust realism about objects expressed in our scientific inquiries can be raised (§22). The indeterminacy thesis does not undermine our use of sentences to make assertions, and in Quine's view those who insist that it does are just "whistling in the dark."[46]

28. Inscrutability of Reference and Acquiescing in Our Mother Tongue

Despite Quine's denial that his robust realism is incompatible with the indeterminacy of reference, it remains puzzling how these two positions can be reconciled. For if we accept Quine's indeterminacy thesis, it seems that reference makes no sense even from *within* our own language. It is instructive to see how how this concern arises, and how Quine avoids the paradoxical conclusion that we can't use our sentences to make assertions.

At the start of chapter 2 of *Word and Object* Quine formulates his indeterminacy thesis for a given speaker's language: "the infinite totality of sentences of any given speaker's language can be so permuted, or mapped onto itself, that (a) the totality of the speaker's dispositions to verbal behavior remains invariant, and yet (b) the mapping is no mere correlation of sentences with *equivalent* sentences, in any plausible sense of equivalence however loose."[47] This formulation of the indeterminacy thesis directly supports Quine's claim that "radical translation begins at home."[48] Typically we "translate" our fellow English speakers' words "homophonically," but according to Quine there are in principle countless other "translations" that would capture the linguistic meaning of our utterances equally well. In its purest form, the claim is that a given speaker's language can be mapped onto *itself* in a variety of ways, each preserving all of his speech dispositions.

To understand this claim we must keep in mind that for Quine a speaker's "language" consists in his "present dispositions to verbal behavior."[49] The verbal dispositions of speakers of the same natural language "have perforce come to resemble one another,"[50] but are never exactly alike, since any difference in belief is also a difference in verbal dispositions. Thus a speaker's "language" is not identical to the natural language he speaks. Let's reserve the word "language" for natural languages such as English, French, or German, and use the word "idiolect" for what Quine calls a "speaker's language," which consists in the speaker's dispositions to verbal behavior.

Recast for idiolects, Quine's indeterminacy thesis is that every speaker's idiolect can be systematically "mapped onto" ("translated into") *itself* in a number of different ways, each compatible with all the speaker's dispositions to verbal behavior.[51] This version of the indeterminacy thesis forces us to confront our feeling that we can't use our words to make assertions unless their references are (somehow) uniquely determined. To see why, we must understand Quine's view of the relationship between translation and reference.

Translation is a relation between linguistic expressions, and reference is a relation between words and things; yet the two relations are intimately linked, according to Quine, for we are each in a position to specify the references of our own words *disquotationally.* In his paper "Notes on the Theory of Reference," Quine endorses the following paradigm:

(R) '___' is true of every ___ thing and nothing else.[52]

I can apply this disquotational paradigm to any term I am in a position to use, thereby specifying its reference. For instance I can affirm:

(r) 'rabbit' is true of every rabbit and nothing else.

And to affirm (r) is just to say 'rabbit' refers to rabbits. I'll say that a speaker accepts a *disquotational reference scheme* for his idiolect if he accepts all the instances of (R) applied to the terms of his idiolect—the terms he is in a position to *use* in the second blank of (R).

Now if radical translation begins at home, then we are each in a position to formulate alternative reference schemes for our fellow English speakers. Suppose for example that Oscar is an English speaker whose speech dispositions are virtually the same as mine. I can extend my own disquotational reference scheme to Oscar's words via translation. For instance, relative to a systematic homophonic manual that translates Oscar's word 'rabbit' by my word 'rabbit', I can say that Oscar's word 'rabbit' refers to rabbits. And relative to a systematic nonhomophonic manual that translates Oscar's word 'rabbit' by my phrase 'undetached rabbit-part', I can say that Oscar's word 'rabbit' refers to undetached rabbit-parts.

I can apply the same reasoning to my own words, since my speech dispositions are just like Oscar's in all relevant respects. All I need is to "translate" my idiolect into itself. My idiolect can be systematically "mapped onto" ("translated into") *itself* in a number of different ways, each of which is compatible with all my speech dispositions. One of these is the homophonic mapping, but there are nonhomophonic mappings of my idiolect onto itself, just as there are nonhomophonic mappings of Oscar's idiolect onto mine. Now if I accept a "homophonic" mapping, nothing changes—my disquotational reference scheme remains as before, and I say that 'rabbit' refers to rabbits. But if I accept a systematic nonhomophonic manual that translates 'rabbit' as 'undetached rabbit-part', then my disquotational reference scheme may be extended to yield a *nondisquotational reference scheme* for my own words. According to this nondisquotational reference scheme my word 'rabbit' refers to undetached rabbit-parts.

Reflecting on my own idiolect, I see that I can use a disquotational reference scheme, or any number of nondisquotational reference schemes, each of which is based in a "translation" that preserves all my speech dispositions. So it seems that nothing determines that my word 'rabbit' refers to rabbits and not to undetached rabbit-parts. This shakes my confidence: perhaps I can't distinguish between rabbits and undetached rabbit-parts, despite my feeling that I can. This leads me to "the absurd position that there is no difference on any terms, interlinguistic or intralinguistic, objective or subjective, between referring to rabbits and referring to rabbit-parts."[53] Yet I must take for granted that I can distinguish between rabbits and undetached rabbit-parts even to say that it *seems* that I can't distinguish between rabbits and undetached rabbit-parts. Thus when indeterminacy is applied to our own terms, we seem driven to the paradoxical conclusion that we both can and can't use our words to refer to objects.

The paradox is only apparent, since ascriptions of reference make sense only *relative* to a manual of translation. This is implicit in a passage in Quine's *Word and Object* about the nature of the conflict between rival manuals of translation: "When two systems of analytical hypotheses fit the totality of verbal dispositions to perfection and yet conflict in their translations of certain sentences, the conflict is precisely one of parts seen without the wholes."[54] The apparent conflict between my assertion that my word 'rabbit' refers to rabbits and my assertion that my word 'rabbit' refers to undetached rabbit-parts is "one of parts seen without the wholes." I should not say that my word 'rabbit' refers to rabbits and to undetached rabbit-parts, for this would miss the relativity of reference to a whole system of analytic hypotheses incorporated into a particular manual of translation.

Inscrutability does not upset the complex interconnections between my own words, and so when I simply *use* my words, I can distinguish between rabbits and undetached rabbit-parts: "begin by picturing us at home in our language, with all its predicates and auxiliary devices. . . . In these terms we can say in so many words that this is a formula and that a number, this a rabbit and that a rabbit part, this and that the same rabbit, and this and that different parts. *In just those words.*"[55] Thus the apparent puzzle about the inscrutability of reference results from a failure to distinguish carefully between the *use* and *mention* of our own words. To *use* our words is simply to "acquiesc[e] in our mother tongue and tak[e] its words at face value."[56] The inscrutability of reference does not undermine our ability to say, for example, that 'rabbit' refers to rabbits, not undetached rabbit-parts.

Once we've chosen a "manual of translation" for our own idiolect—a systematic mapping of words to words that preserves all our speech dispositions—we can simply *use* our words to state a reference scheme for our idiolect. By extending my disquotational reference scheme across a nonhomophonic mapping from my idiolect onto itself, I can specify a nondisquotational reference scheme for my own idiolect. My disquotational reference scheme specifies that my word 'rabbit' refers to rabbits, whereas a systematic nondisquotational reference scheme might specify that my word 'rabbit' refers to undetached rabbit-parts. These alternative ascriptions of reference to my word 'rabbit' may at first *appear* incompatible, but this appearance dissolves once the alternative ascriptions are seen in the context of the alternative reference schemes that include them.

Despite the compatibility of alternative reference schemes, many philosophers[57] still *feel certain* that we can't use our words to state reference schemes for our own idiolects unless the references of our words are (somehow) uniquely determined. But in Quine's view this feeling should be dismissed, for there is no scientific perspective from which to question whether we can use the sentences of science to make assertions. Here again we reach the bedrock of Quine's scientific naturalism.

29. Logic, Disquotation, and Indeterminacy

If our use of sentences to make assertions does not require that reference be determinate, then why should we care about reference at all? Why not just bar such constructions as (R) from our canonical notation? Quine's answer is that logic is part of our total theory of nature, that the laws of logic can't be formulated without semantic ascent, especially disquotational truth, and that we need disquotational reference to define disquotational truth for formalized languages. We must now ask whether indeterminacy of translation undermines Quine's use of disquotational truth to state the laws of logic.

From Quine's naturalistic point of view a central task for philosophy is to develop a "canonical notation" that clarifies ontology and facilitates the application of logical laws to the sentences of science (§20). A closely related task is to clarify the status of the laws of logic themselves. In Quine's view (a) the laws of logic are schematic, and (b) we must use a disquotational truth predicate to formulate them. I will sketch his reasons for (a) and (b) in turn.

To formulate the laws of physics or chemistry we need not mention sentences or words at all; but to formulate the laws of logic, in Quine's view, we must generalize over sentences:

> We can generalize on 'Tom is mortal', 'Dick is mortal', and so on, without talking of truth or of sentences; we can say 'All men are mortal'. We can generalize similarly on 'Tom is Tom', 'Dick is Dick', '0 is 0', and so on, saying 'Everything is itself'. When on the other hand we want to generalize on 'Tom is mortal or Tom is not mortal', 'Snow is white or snow is not white', and so on, we ascend to talk of truth and of sentences, saying 'Every sentence of the form 'p or not p' is true', or 'Every alternation of a sentence with its negation is true'.... We ascend only because of the oblique way in which the instances over which we are generalizing are related to one another.[58]

The need for semantic ascent in our formulations of the logical laws stems from Quine's naturalism. In particular, the indeterminacy of translation shows that there can be no propositions, construed as the meanings of sentences. Quine argues that "if there were propositions, they would induce a certain relation of synonymy or equivalence between sentences themselves: those sentences would be equivalent that expressed the same proposition. . . . [But] . . . the appropriate equivalence relation makes no objective sense at the level of sentences."[59] We have already seen why Quine thinks that "the appropriate equivalence relation makes no objective sense at the level of sentences"—his indeterminacy thesis encapsulates this conclusion. So to state the laws of logic we cannot quantify over propositions. The only plausible course left to us is to formulate logical laws as generalizations over linguistic expressions.

To formulate these generalizations we need a truth predicate that applies to sentences. Moreover, our applications of this truth predicate must be transparent, so that our use of semantic ascent to state the logical laws does not depend on the empirical results of a special science. For according to Quine logic is "the handmaiden of all the sciences," and it has "universal applicability."[60] If our applications of the truth predicate used to formulate the logical laws were dependent on special empirical inquiries, then we could not treat logic as "the handmaiden of all the sciences." Only the disquotational truth predicate has the kind of transparency needed for the formulation of schematic laws with "universal applicability"— applicability to all subjects treated within our total theory of nature, as expressed in sentences we are able to use.[61]

But it seems that the indeterminacy of translation undermines the transparency of the disquotational truth predicate. Applied to the sentences of our own idiolect, the indeterminacy of translation enables us to construct countless alternative truth predicates for our own language. Beginning with our disquotational truth predicate, we can extend our ascriptions of truth to our sentences in different ways, depending on which mappings of our language onto itself we accept. The homophonic mapping leaves our disquotational truth predicate unchanged. But the nonhomophonic mappings enable us to extend our disquotational truth predicate to define nondisquotational truth predicates for our own sentences. Some of these predicates do not have the same extension as our disquotational predicate, since rival manuals of translation can disagree on the truth values of sentences. Reflecting on these consequences of Quine's indeterminacy thesis, we might be tempted to conclude that our application of a disquotational truth predicate is dependent on substantive assumptions about our speech dispositions. If so, we lose our privileged grip on disquotational truth, and so we can't take our application of the laws of logic to our own sentences to be more transparent than our application of the laws of logic to anyone else's sentences.

This reasoning overlooks the special role of disquotational truth in our ascriptions of truth to our own sentences. The disquotational truth predicate is our primary device for semantic ascent. We can by extension define truth for our own sentences nondisquotationally, but only via a nonhomophonic manual of translation. So the existence of nondisquotational truth predicates defined by means of nonhomophonic manuals of translation does not undermine the special transparency of disquotational truth. For Quine we are always in a position to apply the disquotational truth predicate to our own sentences without investigating our speech dispositions, and so we can directly apply the laws of logic to any subject treated with our total theory of nature. Despite appearances, the indeterminacy thesis does not undermine Quine's view of the "universal applicability" of the laws of logic.

30. Quine's Objectifying Move

We have seen (§20) that the starting point for Quine's rejection of our commonsense assumption that there is only one correct translation of our words is his scientific naturalism—"the recognition that it is within science itself, and not in some prior philosophy, that reality is to be identified and described."[62] Naturalism sets the framework for Quine's clarification of epistemology and semantics. For Quine the "motivating insight" behind empiricism is that "we can know external things only through the impacts on our nerve endings."[63] The task of epistemology is to describe and clarify the links between sentences and sensory stimulation (§21). Moreover, "one has no choice but to be an empiricist so far as one's theory of linguistic meaning is concerned,"[64] and so our speech dispositions exhaust the natural facts relevant to both epistemology and meaning (§23). Since there are inequivalent "translations" from one idiolect into another, and from each idiolect into itself, that "preserve all speech dispositions," translation and meaning are indeterminate (§§24–27).

Quine's naturalism challenges our ordinary evaluations of sameness or difference in meaning between speakers (§23), even speakers of the "same" natural language (§28). The commonsense standards are only legitimate to the extent that they can be reconstructed or justified in terms of a naturalistic description of language use: "For naturalism the question whether two expressions are alike or unlike in meaning has no determinate answer, known or unknown, except insofar as the answer is settled in principle by people's speech dispositions, known or unknown. If by these standards there are indeterminate cases, so much the worse for the terminology of meaning and likeness of meaning."[65] From Quine's naturalistic perspective our expressions appear as meaningless signs linked by the mechanism of conditioned response to triggerings of our nerve endings.

Quine's *objectifying move* is to suppose that this austere picture of language use portrays the "objective reality" on which all similarities and differences in meaning must be based. There is no way to reconstruct likeness of meaning in terms of speech dispositions linking sentences with sensory stimulation. In the glare created by Quine's behavioristic picture of language use all ordinary talk of meaning looks flimsy and obscure.

The bedrock of Quine's naturalism is our use of sentences of our own idiolects to identify and describe reality. We have seen (§28) that despite our sense that meaning vanishes when we describe our linguistic behavior in Quine's naturalistic terms, we can each use the expressions of our own idiolects to make assertions. Even though nothing determines whether my word 'rabbit' refers to rabbits or to undetached rabbit-parts, I can *use* my word 'rabbit' to say that *a rabbit is not an undetached rabbit-part*. According to Quine's indeterminacy thesis, there are countless empirically equivalent "translations" of our idiolects into themselves. This undermines our feeling that we can't use the words of our own idiolects to make assertions unless the "translations" of our idiolects into themselves are uniquely determined. But we can easily dismiss this feeling, since to use the words of our own idiolects we needn't (even tacitly) "choose" from among the countless empirically equivalent "translations" of our idiolects into themselves. Intrasubjectively, our ordinary discriminations between rabbits and undetached rabbit-parts remain untouched by Quine's indeterminacy thesis.

Quine's objectifying move poses a more radical challenge to commonsense assumptions about communication. In our ordinary use of language to communicate with our fellow English speakers, we typically take their utterances at face value, with no thoughts about how to "translate" them. From Quine's behavioristic perspective, such linguistic interactions appear to rest on our "choice" of a homophonic "translation" between idiolects. According to the indeterminacy thesis, any two "translations" that would in principle facilitate fluent interaction between two speakers are equally "correct" from a behavioristic point of view. Some of these "translations" are radically different from the commonsense homophonic one. Thus in Quine's view, ordinary linguistic interactions between speakers reflect their (tacit) "choice" of one of countless inequivalent ways of "translating" each other's words.

31. Quine's Objectifying Move Contrasted with Kripke's

We have seen that Quine's objectifying move casts doubt on meaning, and yet requires that we take our own words at face value. Quine's skepticism about meaning arises *within* science, and he insists that it does not undermine scientific naturalism. Once we accept Quine's scientific naturalism, we feel compelled to describe language use in austere dispositional terms, and to think that speech dispositions exhaust all the "facts" relevant to meaning. This inevitably leads us to conclude that our ordinary standards for likeness of meaning reflect our ungrounded "choice" of one of countless equally "correct" ways to "translate" our fellow speakers' words. There are also countless empirically equivalent "translations" of our idiolects into themselves, but to use the words of our own idiolects we needn't (even tacitly) "translate" them. Hence, according to Quine, indeterminacy does not undermine our use of sentences of our own theories of nature to identify and describe reality.

In contrast, Kripke's objectifying move is an inevitable consequence of his understanding of meaning. If we accept Kripke's understanding of meaning, we feel obliged to accept his challenge to find "facts" that determine what our words meant in the past. The challenge to find such facts leads us to take an external perspective on our own assertions and judgments, treating them as objects of our investigation into meaning. Once we accept this objectifying move, we are well on our way to Kripke's radical and self-defeating conclusion that the presuppositions for meaning and assertion can't be satisfied, and that consequently we can't make assertions or judgments at all, despite our feeling that we can.

Underlying these objectifying moves are two fundamentally different philosophical perspectives: Quine's scientific naturalism and Kripke's metaphysical realism. In different ways, Quine and Kripke view our linguistic behavior from perspectives external to our ordinary linguistic practices. Quine's austere scientific perspective is incompatible with the commonsense assumption that there is only one correct translation of our words. Kripke's metaphysical realism *seems* compatible with our ordinary assumptions, until we see that we can't meet his metaphysical requirements for meaning.

There is a tendency to think that scientific naturalism presupposes metaphysical realism. The idea is that science can tell us how things "really are" only if the sentences of science have "robust" truth conditions.[66] It is therefore instructive to see that Quine's scientific naturalism does not presuppose metaphysical realism; the two philosophical perspectives can be distinguished, and their consequences for meaning articulated separately. In Chapter One we saw that Kripke's dialectical skepticism does not rest on any substantive scientific picture of linguistic behavior, but purports to uncover requirements for meaning that are implicit in our commonsense judgments about meaning. In this chapter we saw that Quine's indeterminacy thesis is a pure and systematic expression of Quine's scientific naturalism. In striving to clarify and distinguish between these two kinds of skepticism, we begin to see how our philosophical assumptions systematically shape the way we look at meaning and assertion.

THREE

The Very Idea of a Participant Perspective

32. Toward a New Way of Looking at Meaning and Assertion

In Chapters One and Two I articulated two fundamentally different views of meaning and assertion. I explained why Kripke concludes that nothing determines what our words mean, so we can't make assertions, and why Quine thinks we can make assertions, even if the meanings of our words are not uniquely determined. One of my aims in this book is to show that both of these perspectives on meaning and assertion prevent us from properly describing our linguistic practices.

To move beyond these two entrenched perspectives, I propose that we describe the relationship between meaning and assertion from our perspective as participants in our rule-following practices. The idea itself is not new. In "Wittgenstein on Following a Rule,"[1] for example, John McDowell tries to resist Kripke's and Quine's ways of looking at meaning and assertion by sketching an interpretation of Wittgenstein's enigmatic remark that "there is a way of grasping a rule which is *not* an *interpretation*, but which is exhibited in what we call 'obeying a rule' and 'going against it' in actual cases."[2] As a first step toward developing a new way of looking at meaning and assertion from our perspective as participants in our linguistic practices, in this chapter I examine McDowell's interpretation of Wittgenstein's remarks on rule-following.

My point in this chapter is methodological. I show that McDowell's arguments can't by themselves change the way we look at meaning and assertion, since they rest on elusive and unconvincing claims about what is required for our "intuitive" notions of meaning and assertion to have a "real application." From the failure of McDowell's arguments we learn that it is fruitless to try to resist Kripke's and Quine's views unless we can articulate a different way of looking at meaning and assertion.

I begin by drawing a metaphilosophical moral from the contrast between Kripke's and Quine's views of meaning and assertion (§§33–36), then present McDowell's transcendental argument for an alternative perspective on meaning and assertion (§§37–40), and show that this argument fails to come to terms with metaphysical realism and scientific naturalism (§§41–45). I end with a sketch of my own strategy for working through and moving beyond both metaphysical realism and scientific naturalism (§§46–47).

33. A Metaphysical Critique of Scientific Naturalism

We saw in Chapter One that after we go through Kripke's skeptical reasoning we are apparently able to distinguish between our first-person "subjective" experience of making assertions and the "objective" question of whether we really are making assertions when we "use" our sentences. Kripke's dialectical skepticism evokes our ordinary feeling that if our words are not "objectively" meaningful, we can't really make assertions or judgments at all. We come to feel that it is an "objective" matter whether or not our words are meaningful, and so our "subjective" impression that they are meaningful does not justify our ordinary assumption that they are meaningful. We then feel that we can make sense of Kripke's conclusion that our ordinary use of language rests on the *illusion* that we are able to make assertions.

Kripke's skeptical reasoning fosters the feeling that we have "discovered" metaphysical requirements for the "objectivity" of meaning and assertion. In Kripke's view, reflection on our commonsense ideas about meaning shows that our words are "objectively" meaningful only if our mental states *predetermine* the truth conditions of our assertions. Kripke argues that nothing about us predetermines the truth conditions of our assertions, and concludes that our words are meaningless and so we can't make any assertions or judgments at all.

Kripke acknowledges that his skeptical conclusion is "self-defeating," since to express it we must take for granted that it isn't true. But he suggests this is a *pragmatic* problem that stems from our contingent need to use language to state the conclusion. He thinks that once we have grasped his general distinction between the appearance and the reality of making assertions, we can grasp his skeptical conclusion even if our attempts to state it are self-defeating. He doesn't think his account of the "objective" require- ments for making assertions is called into question by the incoherence of our attempts to state his skeptical conclusion.

There is no way to draw a general distinction between the appear- ance and the reality of making assertions without presupposing that our grasp of the "objective" requirements for making asser- tions is in principle independent of *all* our ordinary and scientific procedures for identifying and evaluating assertions. For this reason Kripke's picture of the "objective" requirements for making assertions deserves to be classified as a kind of *metaphysical realism*. This will become important when we consider McDowell's tran- scendental argument against Kripke's skeptical conclusion. It is also crucial for understanding why Kripke could not accept Quine's view of the relationship between meaning and assertion.

As we saw in Chapter Two, for Quine there is no legitimate perspective from which to raise a general doubt about whether we can use our sentences to make assertions. Metaphysical realists are baffled by this rejection of their appearance-reality distinction for assertions. From a metaphysical realist's perspective, it seems that Quine conflates the *appearance* with the *reality* of making an asser- tion, and thereby embraces a radically subjective kind of linguistic idealism.

34. The Fallacy of Subtraction

For Quine there are no metaphysical requirements for the objec- tivity of our assertions, since there is no perspective higher or firmer than science, and no legitimate question of whether it is "really" possible for us to use the sentences of science to make assertions. All clear questions begin and end with the use of sentences in science, and we can't make sense from within science of the ques- tion of whether or not we can really use our sentences to make assertions. We may find it *unsettling* to think that the meanings of our words are not uniquely determined by the facts, but this is a

psychological reaction without scientific or philosophical significance. Quine disregards our feeling that if the meanings of our
words are indeterminate we can't make assertions. From his point
of view, metaphysical realists like Kripke read too much into their
feeling that our words must have a determinate meaning if we are
to make assertions.

The metaphysical realist maintains that if a sentence does not
have determinate truth conditions, then it is not possible to use that
sentence to make an objective assertion. Quine calls this the "fallacy
of subtraction":

> The want [for sentences to have determinate truth conditions]
> has been felt so strongly as to encourage philosophers to
> defend a notion of sentence synonymy such as the identity of
> propositions demands, and to defend it by flimsier arguments
> than they might have permitted themselves if no preconcep-
> tions had been at stake. One of those arguments involves the
> fallacy of subtraction: it is argued that if we can speak of a
> sentence as meaningful, or as having meaning, then there must
> be a meaning [truth condition] that it has, and this meaning
> will be identical with or distinct from the meaning [truth con-
> dition] that another sentence has.[3]

Quine takes for granted that our sentences are "meaningful," in the
sense that we can use them to make assertions, but he challenges
the metaphysical realist's claim that if we can use a sentence to
make an assertion, then it has a determinate meaning or truth condition. In contrast, metaphysical realists take for granted that we
can "subtract" the "presupposition" that a sentence can be used to
make an assertion from our "subjective" experience of using it to
make an assertion. This reflects the metaphysical realist's assumption that there is a general distinction between the appearance and
the reality of making an assertion. From Quine's perspective, this
metaphysical assumption looks like a desperate attempt to defend
an unscientific feeling that should be dismissed.

35. Is Quine's Scientific Naturalism a Kind of Idealism?

Naturally, a metaphysical realist will not accept that his view is
based in a simple fallacy. He will attempt to *justify* his assumption
that we can't make objective assertions unless our sentences have

determinate truth conditions. He will argue that Quine's natural-istic account of language leaves us with no objective distinction between the correct or incorrect use of our sentences. The objec-tivity of an assertion, he will claim, depends on its being correct or incorrect independently of our *subjective inclination* to say that it is "correct" or "incorrect." He will insist that if we accept Quine's naturalism, then we must conclude that there are no objective stan-dards for us to be faithful to, and so it is impossible for us to make objective assertions at all.

There is a simple and instructive reply to this charge: Quine never attempts to *define* truth in terms of what we are inclined to say. For Quine truth is disquotational. When confronted with the charge that on his view we can't distinguish between *feeling* that we are right and *being* right, Quine would simply point out that our *inclination* to affirm the sentence 'Sixty-eight plus fifty-seven is one hundred twenty-five', for example, does not *make it true* that sixty-eight plus fifty-seven is one hundred twenty-five. If the metaphysical realist presses Quine to say why this does not follow on his view, Quine will give the obvious answer: the ques-tion whether sixty-eight plus fifty-seven is one hundred twenty-five is part of elementary arithmetic, and in no way depends on whether or not the *sentence* 'Sixty-eight plus fifty-seven is one hundred twenty-five' has a determinate truth condition. So Quine's view does not reduce the question of whether sixty-eight plus fifty-seven is one hundred twenty-five to the merely psycho-logical question of whether we are all inclined to affirm the sen-tence 'sixty-eight plus fifty-seven is one hundred twenty-five', and he does not think the question of whether sixty-eight plus fifty-seven is one hundred twenty-five is dependent on or can be analyzed in terms of our psychological reactions.

The impression that on Quine's view truth is subjective rests on a failure to distinguish between use and mention. When Quine gives behavioristic descriptions of the relationship between sentences and sensory stimulation, he is mentioning, not using, those sentences. When we use our sentences to make assertions, according to Quine, the question of what makes our asser-tions true or false does not arise. For Quine, to use our sentences to make and evaluate assertions is not to explain their truth in terms of our psychological inclinations, or in any other terms at all.

36. A Metaphilosophical Moral

The contrast between Kripke's metaphysical realism and Quine's scientific naturalism is instructive, even if we find that we can't accept either point of view. For in our struggle to understand the contrast between their views, we must learn to suspend our own presuppositions long enough to catch a glimpse of how things look to each of them.

We have seen that Kripke's general appearance-reality distinction for assertions rests on his metaphysical picture of what is required for making an objective assertion, and that Quine's rejection of any metaphysical requirements for making assertions reflects his view that there is no perspective higher or firmer than natural science. These differences reflect different conceptions of the starting point and tasks of philosophy. Kripke assumes that philosophy begins with "intuitions" and aims to analyze the concepts expressed by these intuitions.[4] Quine, on the other hand, sees philosophy as continuous with natural science. Philosophy clarifies the ontology and logical structure of our scientific claims, as well as the epistemology of scientific theories. These tasks are all to be achieved from within science by using the clear vocabulary and methods of science. There is no unquestioned reliance on our "intuitions." Many of our intuitions must simply be ignored, according to Quine, since they do not contribute to a clarification of science from within science.

These differences between Kripke's and Quine's conceptions of the starting point and task of philosophy show why there is no neutral perspective from which to evaluate arguments offered on behalf of either Kripke's or Quine's views of meaning and assertion. For Quine, Kripke's intuitions don't count as compelling reasons to accept metaphysical realism about assertion. And for Kripke, Quine's rejection of a perspective higher or firmer than our use of the sentences of science amounts to a radically subjective kind of linguistic idealism.

Seeing these radical differences between Kripke's and Quine's points of view should help to loosen the grip of our own unquestioned assumptions, and to begin a search for the proper starting points and methods in philosophy. In the next few sections I consider John McDowell's argument that we should reject both

Kripke's and Quine's frameworks for thinking about meaning and assertion. Inspired by Wittgenstein's remark that "there is a way of grasping a rule which is *not* an *interpretation*, but which is exhibited in what we call 'obeying a rule' and 'going against it' in actual cases,"[5] McDowell sketches a version of what I call the *participant perspective* on meaning and assertion. In §§37–40 I present McDowell's argument and his characterization of the participant perspective. I then argue (§§41–43) that McDowell's "transcendental" argument is unconvincing, and so his attempt to elucidate the participant perspective fails to loosen the hold of scientific naturalism and metaphysical realism. I trace the failure of McDowell's argument to a flawed philosophical methodology (§46), and then sketch my own method for developing a new way of looking at meaning and assertion (§§46–47).

37. A First Look at McDowell's Strategy

In "Wittgenstein on Following a Rule" John McDowell in effect argues that there *must* be an alternative to Kripke's and Quine's views on meaning and assertion. According to McDowell, Kripke's skeptical conclusion results from his mistaken assumption that to follow a rule we must grasp an *interpretation* of it. McDowell also rejects Crispin Wright's view that at the basic level of language use—when we use such sentences as 'That's yellow', 'That's a rabbit'—speakers are disposed to assent to and dissent from sentences under the same circumstances, but there is no real content to the idea of investigation-independent patterns of application for their words. In rejecting this view of the basic level of language, McDowell in effect also rejects Quine's austere behavioristic picture of meaning and translation.

McDowell portrays Wittgenstein's view of meaning as "the indispensable middle course" between two unacceptable positions:

> Wittgenstein's problem is to steer a course between a Scylla and a Charybdis. Scylla is the idea that understanding is always interpretation. The idea is disastrous because embracing it confronts us with the ... choice between the paradox that there is no substance to meaning, on the one hand, and the fantastic mythology of the super-rigid machine, on the other.

We can avoid Scylla by stressing that, say, calling something
'green' can be like crying 'Help!' when one is drowning—
simply how one has learned to react to this situation. But then
we risk steering on to Charybdis—the picture of a basic level at
which there are no norms; if we embrace that . . . then we
cannot prevent meaning from coming to seem an illusion. . . .
the key to finding the indispensable middle course is the idea
of a custom or practice.[6]

I won't directly address the question of whether this is a good
interpretation of Wittgenstein. Instead I'll present McDowell's
account of "Scylla" (§38) and "Charybdis" (§39), and his "transcendental" argument for the "the indispensable middle course"
(§40). I'll then evaluate his argument for and characterizations of
the middle course (§§41–43).

The key to McDowell's argument for the middle course is that
both Scylla and Charybdis undermine our "familiar intuitive notion
of objectivity":

> The idea at risk is the idea of things being thus and so anyway,
> whether or not we choose to investigate the matter in question,
> and whatever the outcome of any such investigation. That idea
> requires the conception of how things could correctly be said
> to be anyway—whatever, if anything, we in fact go on to say
> about the matter; and *this notion of correctness can only be the
> notion of how the pattern of application that we grasp, when we come
> to understand the concept in question, extends, independently of the
> actual outcome of any investigation, to the relevant case.*[7]

McDowell's imagery apparently supports a general distinction
between the conditions required for objectivity, on the one hand,
and the impression that we have met these conditions, on the other.
And McDowell argues that "if the notion of investigation-
independent patterns of application is to be discarded, then so is
the idea that things are, at least sometimes, thus and so anyway,
independently of our ratifying the judgment that that is how they
are. It seems fair to describe this extremely radical consequence as
a kind of idealism."[8] Thus McDowell's central criticisms of both
Scylla and Charybdis, and the crucial move in his "transcendental
argument" for the middle course, rest on his insight into what is

required for the "objectivity" of assertion—an insight inspired, he suggests, by his reading of Wittgenstein. Unfortunately, McDowell's "transcendental argument" for the middle course fails to show us how to move beyond scientific naturalism and metaphysical realism. To see why, we must first take a sympathetic look at McDowell's reasons for rejecting Kripke's and Wright's views about meaning.

38. McDowell's Critique of Kripke

McDowell asserts that the "intuitive conception of objectivity" for assertions involving a given concept like *plus* requires that there be a "pattern of application that we grasp, when we come to understand the concept in question, [a pattern that] extends, independently of the actual outcome of any investigation, to the relevant case."[9] Hence, in McDowell's view, if it is impossible for us to "grasp" such patterns of application, as Kripke maintains, then we are unable to make "objective" assertions, and so we fall into an "abyss" of subjective idealism from which there is no way to "claw ourselves back."[10]

McDowell argues that Kripke's skeptical conclusion rests on his mistaken assimilation of understanding and meaning to *interpretation*. As we saw in Chapter One, Kripke's skeptical challenge tempts us to think that our words are meaningful only if there are temporally bounded mental or physical states that predetermine the truth conditions of our assertions. In light of this reconstruction, we can accept McDowell's rough reconstruction of Kripke's skeptical reasoning:

> What could constitute my understanding, say, the 'plus' sign in a way with which only certain answers to given addition problems would accord? Confronted with such questions we tend to be enticed into looking for a fact that would constitute my having put an appropriate *interpretation* on what I was told and shown when I was instructed in arithmetic. Anything we hit on as satisfying that specification contents us only 'for a moment'; then it occurs to us that whatever we have hit on would itself be capable of interpretation in such a way that acting in conformity with it would require something quite

different. So we look for something that would constitute my having interpreted the first item in the right way. Anything we come up with as satisfying that specification will in turn content us only 'for a moment'; and so on: 'any interpretation still hangs in the air along with what it interprets, and cannot give it any support'.[11]

McDowell offers this skeptical reasoning as an elaboration, on Kripke's behalf, of one aspect of the paradox Wittgenstein summarizes at the start of §201 of *Philosophical Investigations:* "This was our paradox: no course of action could be determined by a rule, because every course of action can be made out to accord with the rule. The answer was: if everything can be made to accord with the rule, then it can be made out to conflict with it. And so there would be neither accord nor conflict here."[12] If we accept that meaning requires interpretation, according to McDowell, we then face an unacceptable dilemma: either we conclude that every interpretation satisfies us only for a moment, and so face the recently described regress, each step of which "hangs in the air along with what it interprets," or we must posit a "superfact"—a self-interpreting mental or physical state. And "the irresistible upshot of this [second horn of the dilemma] is that we picture following a rule as the operation of a super-rigid yet . . . ethereal machine."[13]

In McDowell's view, Kripke is right to conclude that if meaning requires interpretation, our words are meaningless, but wrong to conclude that Wittgenstein is a skeptic about meaning. McDowell points out that in the second paragraph of §201 Wittgenstein explicitly disavows the assumptions that lead to skepticism about meaning:

> It can be seen that there is a misunderstanding here from the mere fact that in the course of our argument we give one interpretation after another; as if each one contented us at least for a moment, until we thought of yet another standing behind it. What this shows is that there is a way of grasping a rule which is *not* an *interpretation,* but which is exhibited in what we call "obeying the rule" and "going against it" in actual cases.[14]

McDowell concludes that Kripke is wrong about Wittgenstein. But worse than that, according to McDowell, Kripke's skeptical reasoning leads to the "extremely radical" conclusion that our ordinary feeling that our assertions are objective is an *illusion.*[15]

39. McDowell's Critique of Wright

McDowell also rejects Crispin Wright's interpretation of Wittgenstein's remarks on rule-following. Wright's account of rule-following is McDowell's Charybdis—the view that at the most basic level of language use there are no "norms," only "human beings vocalizing in certain ways in response to objects, with this behavior (no doubt) accompanied by such 'inner' phenomena as 'feelings' of constraint, or convictions of rightness of what they are saying."[16] McDowell's objection is that on Wright's account we are under "the *illusion* of being subject to norms,"[17] and our intuitive notions of meaning and objectivity have no real application. As we have seen, McDowell believes that to give up these intuitive notions is to fall into an "abyss" of subjectivity, and so he rejects Wright's account of rule-following.

As McDowell sees it, Wright begins by rejecting the idea that our "grasp" of "patterns" of application for our words is essentially *idiolectical.* Wright reasons that if I adopt the essentially idiolectical picture of understanding, then *"whatever* sincere applications I make of a particular expression, when I have paid due heed to the situation, will seem to me to conform with my understanding of it. There is no scope for a distinction here between the fact of an application's seeming to me to conform with the way in which I understand it and the fact of its really doing so."[18] So Wright is driven to find another way to understand the difference between correct and incorrect application of our rules. He tries to understand the difference by appeal to a linguistic community, relative to which an individual's application of words is called "correct" or "incorrect." But Wright insists that there is no independent standard for the linguistic community to follow, any more than there is in the case of an isolated idiolect. The community does not go right or wrong, "it just goes."[19] So according to Wright's interpretation of Wittgenstein, to say that our use of language is "correct" or "incorrect" is just to say that our use of language is in accord or out of step with the linguistic activities of other members of our linguistic community. Wright concludes that the very idea of "ratification-independent patterns" for the application of our words must be abandoned.

The central problem with this position, according to McDowell, is that it leaves out the *normativity* of meaning. He tries to bring out the point as follows: "it would be a serious error ... not to make a radical distinction between the significance of, say, 'This is yellow' and the significance of, say, 'This would be called "yellow" by (most) speakers of English' ... and ... Wright's [position] seems to leave it mysterious, at best, why this distinction should be so important."[20] The danger, according to McDowell, is that Wright's analysis will not draw a sufficiently "radical" distinction between being in accord (or out of step) with other speakers, on the one hand, and saying something true (or false), on the other. McDowell concedes that Wright has an apparently satisfactory answer to this concern: "It may appear that the answer is both obvious and readily available to Wright: 'To say that "This would be called 'yellow' by speakers of English" would not be to call the object in question "yellow", and that is what one does when one says "This is yellow".' "[21] The key consideration is that, for Wright, the point of saying that the community itself "just goes" is not to *define* truth in terms of what the community agrees on at any given time, but to reveal the emptiness of our picture of rules as rigid rails that in our use of language we try to track.[22] According to McDowell, however, "this ... merely postpone[s] the serious question: does Wright's reading of Wittgenstein contain the means to make it intelligible that there should so much as be such an action as calling an object 'yellow'?"[23] This question leads to the heart of McDowell's argument that Wright's account fails to give real application to our intuitive notions of meaning and assertion.

McDowell's criticism of Wright's account centers on the question of how we are to understand the "basic level" of language use, where our justifications come to an end. Our ordinary use of a word like 'green' brings us to this basic level, according to Wittgenstein:

How do I know that the color I am now seeing is called "green"? Well, to confirm it I might ask other people, but if they did not agree with me, I should become totally confused and should perhaps take them or myself for crazy. That is to say: I should either no longer trust myself to judge, or no longer react to what they say as to a judgment.

If I am drowning and I shout "Help!", how do I know what the word Help means? Well, that's how I react in this situation.—Now *that* is how I know what "green" means as well as also know how I have to follow the rule in the particular case.[24]

Here Wittgenstein is showing us that at this level of language use our justifications come to an end. We do not grasp meanings, we just act, and "it is our *acting* which lies at the bottom of the language-game."[25] McDowell's objection is that at the basic level of language, on Wright's picture, "there is nothing but verbal behavior and (no doubt) feelings of constraint. Presumably people's dispositions to behavior and associated feelings match in interesting ways; but at this ground-floor level there is no question of shared commitments—everything normative fades out of the picture."[26] McDowell thinks that if this is the way things look in Wright's picture of the "basic level" of language use, then Wright's picture is ultimately unable to accommodate our intuitive notions of meaning and objectivity. Wright claims to replace our partly confused intuitive notion of the normativity of meaning with a communal account of correct and incorrect application of our words. But McDowell thinks this is not enough to give real application to our intuitive notions of meaning and objectivity.

He claims that to accommodate these intuitive notions, we must preserve a sense in which our use of language can be correct or incorrect even at the most basic level of language use, where our justifications come to an end. The crux of McDowell's criticism is that on Wright's account at the basic level our use of language can be no more than "mere brute meaningless sounding off."[27] Having acknowledged that this is how things are at the basic level, McDowell argues, we are no longer able to see normativity in our language use:

Wright hopes to preserve a foothold for a purified form of the normativeness implicit in the contractual conception of meaning, by appealing to the fact that individuals are susceptible to communal correction. *It is problematic, however, whether the picture of the basic level, once entertained as such, can be prevented from purporting to contain the real truth about linguistic behavior. In that case its freedom from norms will preclude our attributing any genuine substance to the etiolated normativeness that Wright hopes to preserve.* The problem for Wright is to distinguish the position he attributes to Wittgenstein from one according to which the possibility of going out of step with our fellows gives us the *illusion* of being subject to norms, and consequently the *illusion* of entertaining and expressing meanings.[28]

The two italicized sentences constitute the heart of McDowell's argument against Wright. McDowell offers another formulation of essentially the same argument in a later passage:

> the trouble is . . . that the denial of ratification-independence, by Wright's own insistence, yields a picture of the relation between the communal language and the world in which norms are obliterated. And once we have this picture, it seems impossible simply to retain alongside it a different picture, in which the openness of an individual to correction by his fellows means that he is subject to norms. The first picture irresistibly claims primacy, leaving our openness to correction by our fellows looking like, at best, an explanation of our propensity to the illusion that we are subject to norms.[29]

Thus McDowell tries to show that Wright's picture of the basic level of language use undermines our confidence in the intuitive idea that "the openness of an individual to correction by his fellows means that he is subject to norms."

McDowell's diagnosis of Wright's failure to understand the normativity of meaning is that Wright endorses antirealism, a particular conception of the epistemology of understanding:

> According to that conception, the behavior that counts as manifesting understanding to others must be characterizable, in such a way as to display its status as such a manifestation, without benefit of a command of the language in question. Without that proviso, the 'manifestation challenge' that 'antirealists' direct against the truth-conditional conception of meaning would be trivialized. The challenge would hold no fears for the truth-conditional conception if one were allowed to count as satisfying the requirement of manifestation by such

behavior as saying—manifestly, at least to someone who understands the language one is speaking—that such and such is the case. So the distinctive manifestations allowed by 'anti-realism' consist, rather, in such behavior as assenting to a sentence in such and such circumstances.[30]

McDowell's claim is that once Wright assumes this picture of the epistemology of understanding, he can't find any place for norms in our use of language. The key problem, according to McDowell, is that "our characterization of the manifesting behavior is not allowed to exploit understanding of the language in question."[31] We must "extrapolate" from the "evidence," using "inductive" reasoning alone, "which means that if we accept the requirement that understanding be fully manifested in behavior, no extrapolation is licensed at all."[32] McDowell concludes that Wright finds no real application for our intuitive notions of meaning and truth, and so Wright steers us into Charybdis, a deadly vortex of subjective idealism.

40. McDowell's Transcendental Argument and the Middle Course

McDowell assumes that our "intuitive notion of objectivity" *must* have an application, so he offers a transcendental argument against the kind of antirealism he attributes to Wright: "a condition for the possibility of finding real application for the notion of meaning is that we reject 'anti-realism'."[33] This same transcendental argument works against Kripke's assumption that meaning requires interpretation. So, according to McDowell,

> the transcendental argument shows that there *must* be a middle position. Understanding is grasp of patterns that extend to new cases independently of our ratification, as required for meaning to be other than an illusion (and—not incidentally—for the intuitive notion of objectivity to have a use); but the constraints imposed by our concepts do not have the platonistic autonomy with which they are credited in the picture of the super-rigid machinery.[34]

McDowell's transcendental argument is driven by his assumption that what he calls our "intuitive notion of objectivity" *must* have a real application. We have seen that in McDowell's view the intuitive notion of objectivity requires that we be able to grasp patterns that predetermine the truth conditions of our assertions. His central criticism of both Wright and Kripke is that there is no room left in their views for any substantive notion of "patterns" that predetermine the truth conditions of our assertions.

McDowell believes that "the key to finding the indispensable middle course is the idea of a custom or practice."[35] Only by viewing our linguistic behavior from within the framework of an established custom or practice of using words meaningfully can we avoid the twin perils of assimilating meaning to interpretation and of collapsing into Wright's naturalistic antirealism. For only from within a custom or practice can we see our use of language, even at the "basic level," as involving "shared commitments," which are essential to our grasp of "ratification-independent patterns of use." This links directly with §201, where Wittgenstein writes "there must be a way of grasping a rule which is *not* an *interpretation*, but which is exhibited in what we call 'obeying a rule' and 'going against it' in actual cases." For according to McDowell, "we have to realize that obeying a rule is a practice if we are to find it intelligible that there is a way of grasping a rule which is not an interpretation."[36] Thus the notion of a practice or custom is supposed to show us how to apply our intuitive notions of meaning and objectivity.

As I see it, the fundamental move behind McDowell's middle position is the rejection of the antirealist picture of the epistemology of understanding I discussed earlier (§39). McDowell maintains that the intuitive notion of objectivity has no real application unless speakers of a language can share linguistic commitments to "ratification-independent patterns." The Wittgensteinian notions of custom and practice are meant to show us how this sharing of patterns is possible: "The essential point is the way in which one person can know another's meaning without interpretation. . . . it is only because we can have what Wright calls 'a reflective knowledge of features of others' understanding of a particular expression' that meaning is possible at all."[37] Here again we have the language of McDowell's transcendental argument: what makes meaning (and the intuitive notion of objectivity) *possible* is that "one person can know another's meaning without interpretation."

McDowell's picture of our shared linguistic practices emerges in contrast with Wright's "anti-realist" picture of understanding, according to which what a speaker means by his words must be gleaned from his behavior, described in terms that do not presuppose our mastery of the language he speaks. McDowell rejects this picture of the epistemology of understanding: "If . . . we reject the 'anti-realist' restriction on what counts as manifesting one's understanding, we entitle ourselves to this thought: *shared membership in a linguistic community* is not just a matter of matching in aspects of an exterior that we present to anyone whatever, but *equips us to make our minds available to one another, by confronting one another with a different exterior from that which we present to outsiders.*"[38] But McDowell's talk of "confronting one another with a different exterior from that which we present to outsiders" is elusive. Unfortunately, all of McDowell's descriptions of his alternative to Wright's picture are similarly elusive. For example, he writes, "*shared command of a language* equips us to know one another's meaning without needing to arrive at that knowledge by interpretation, because it *equips us to hear someone else's meaning in his words* . . . a linguistic community is conceived as bound together, not by a match in mere externals (facts accessible to just anyone), but by *a capacity for a meeting of minds.*"[39] These characterizations are supposed to show us that our "intuitive notion of objectivity" has "real application." McDowell thinks that if we view our linguistic practices as he suggests, we can avoid both Charybdis—Wright's picture of our linguistic behavior as free of any real normative constraints—and Scylla—the platonistic picture of super-rigid patterns that exist independent of human nature.

To explain how the appeal to shared linguistic commitments avoids Scylla, McDowell writes that "a particular performance, 'inner' or overt, can be an application of a concept—a judgment or a meaningful utterance—only if it owes allegiance to constraints that the concept imposes. And being governed by such constraints is not being led, in some occult way, by an autonomous meaning (the super-rigid machinery), but acting within a communal custom."[40] In his effort to contrast his middle position with the platonistic conception of ratification-independent patterns of use, McDowell writes that "we have to give up that picture of genuine truth, in which the maker of a true judgment can shrink to a point of pure thought, abstracted from anything that might make him distinctively and recognizably one of us."[41] McDowell's middle position is a "recoil from the extreme form of the thesis that the facts are not up to us, not from that thesis in any form whatever." For McDowell, meaning and objectivity are not "wholly autonomous," as they are supposed to be on the platonistic picture. His criticism of platonism is that "we can find this picture of genuine truth compelling only if we either forget that truth-bearers are such only because they are meaningful, or suppose that meanings take care of themselves, needing, as it were, no help from us."[42] So to distinguish his picture from the platonistic one, McDowell feels the need to say that meanings are not "wholly autonomous"—they need "help from us." McDowell wants us to see that it is only in the framework of a custom or practice that normativity—the idea of ratification-independent patterns of application—can have any real application. To see this, he thinks, we must be willing to acknowledge that in some sense our "human nature" enters into the very fabric of these "ratification-independent patterns."

McDowell recognizes that someone attracted to the platonistic thesis will find this middle position like a kind of antirealism, and he grants that in some sense it is a rejection of realism. Yet for two reasons he insists that his middle position deserves to be considered a picture of "investigation-independent patterns" of use. The first reason is that his middle position

> has nothing to do with the rejection of the truth-conditional conception of meaning, properly understood. That conception has no need to camouflage the fact that truth conditions are necessarily given by us, in a language that we can understand. When we say " 'Diamonds are hard' is true if and only if diamonds are hard," we are as much involved on the right-hand side as the reflections on rule-following tell us that we are.[43]

The second reason is that McDowell's middle position amounts to a "recoil from an extreme form of the thesis that the facts are not up to us, not from that thesis in any form whatever. What Wittgenstein's polemic against the picture of the super-rigid machine makes untenable is the thesis that possession of a concept is grasp of a pattern of application that extends *of itself* to new cases."[44] The intuitive notion of meaning and objectivity are given "real application" only when viewed in the context of our shared customs and practices, according to McDowell, so meanings need "help from us" and cannot be thought to extend "of themselves" to new cases.

41. Two Problematic Assumptions of McDowell's Argument

It might appear that McDowell provides a compelling argument that there must be a middle course between Kripke's metaphysical realism and Quine's scientific naturalism. One might hope to find in McDowell's suggestive remarks the beginnings of a new way of looking at meaning and assertion, rooted in our perspective as participants in our rule-following practices. Unfortunately, however, the appearance is misleading and the hope is unfounded.

In §§42–44 I consider how Kripke, Wright, and Quine should reply to McDowell's transcendental argument. McDowell's transcendental argument depends on two problematic assumptions: (1) to abandon what McDowell calls our "intuitive conception of meaning and objectivity" is to collapse into an extreme form of idealism, and (2) only McDowell's middle course can give proper application to this intuitive conception. In §§42–43 I provisionally assume that (1) is correct, and show that neither a metaphysical realist nor Wright should find (2) convincing. In §44 I explain why a scientific naturalist like Quine would flatly reject (1). In §§46–47 I draw a philosophical moral from the failure of McDowell's transcendental argument, and sketch a new strategy for developing a participant perspective on meaning and assertion.

42. A Metaphysical Realist Critique of McDowell's Arguments and His Middle Course

McDowell claims that we must give up the idea that meanings are "wholly autonomous" and need no "help from us." The metaphysical realist's reply to this claim can mimic McDowell's argument against Wright:

> McDowell's picture only gives us the *illusion* of meaning. Since McDowell is giving up the idea of genuinely independent patterns of application, he is abandoning the notion of normativity altogether. Of course, McDowell—just like Wright—aims

to respect our intuition that meaning is 'normative,' and that our use of language is faithful to shared standards. McDowell's talk of a "meeting of minds," of "confronting each other with a different exterior," and of "making our minds available to one another," may make us *feel* that we can share normative commitments, but they do nothing to address the serious questions of how there can so much as *be* such a thing as correct or incorrect application of our words. The difficulty for McDowell is to say how such talk can show that we are able to grasp genuinely independent patterns, instead of merely having the subjective *feeling* that we grasp them, a feeling that we can only "share" when we think of ourselves as initiated into the same custom or practice.

Starting with this reply to McDowell, the metaphysical realist can produce his own "transcendental argument" for the conclusion that there *must* be a viable form of *platonism*. Using the same pattern of argument McDowell uses against Wright, the metaphysical realist can argue as follows:

We can't abandon the intuitive conception of meaning and objectivity without collapsing into an 'abyss' of subjectivity. But of course we can't think of meaning as an interpretation, in the way that Kripke does, for that leads to skepticism about meaning. And we can't accept either McDowell's position or Wright's, since these positions both fail to capture the intuitive notions of meaning and truth, which require that there be genuine ratification-independent patterns of application for our words. To reject this intuitive notion is to collapse into an extremely radical kind of idealism. So there *must* be a way we grasp 'wholly autonomous' meanings, and hence objective truth conditions, without interpretation. This grasp is *fundamental* to our use of language—the bedrock of our reasoning at all. We must come to see that it is not problematic, even though it is easy to become confused about what is required for such a grasp of truth conditions.

McDowell would surely claim that this transcendental argument rests on the fantasy of super-rigid rules, independent of our application. But the metaphysical realist's reply to this claim is all too easy: we come to "grasp" autonomous truth conditions when we learn our language, and become fully initiated into a linguistic community. McDowell might ask how our grasp of these wholly autonomous patterns of application is "manifested" in our linguistic behavior. But McDowell himself has no independent means of saying what can or can't be "manifest" in our behavior. If McDowell objects that the realist's transcendental argument invokes mysterious faculties of "grasping" truth conditions, the realist should reply that McDowell's own talk of "meeting of minds" and "making our minds available to each other" is no better.

Thus a metaphysical realist can construct a transcendental argument for platonism that is just as compelling—and hence just as empty—as McDowell's transcendental argument for his participant perspective on meaning and assertion.

43. A Reply from Wright

Let us continue to grant, provisionally, that to abandon our "intuitive conception of meaning and objectivity" is to collapse into an extreme form of idealism. To evaluate McDowell's reasons for rejecting Wright's interpretation of Wittgenstein, we must evaluate McDowell's assumption that if at the basic level of language use there is no real application for our intuitive idea that our use of language can be subject to "correction," then our intuitive conceptions of meaning and objectivity have no real application. As a first step toward evaluating this assumption, consider the following reply to McDowell:

> Wright does not equate truth with what everyone in the linguistic community agrees on; he just notes that our familiar feeling that our use of language is constrained by independent conceptual commitments is really just a result of our openness to correction by our fellow speakers. Thus at the basic level of language, our use of words is like our cry of 'Help' when we feel we are drowning: we just act. The actions at the basic level of language use are reflections of our natural dispositions, and nothing more. Nevertheless, when we say something is yellow we do not mean that everyone calls it yellow, or is disposed to

call it yellow—Wright does not *define* truth as what we all agree on. We must give up the platonic fantasy of standards independent of our linguistic community, relative to which our collective use can be forever wrong. But McDowell's concern that Wright's position gives us at best the *illusion* of being subject to norms is itself simply a reflection of McDowell's allegiance to an illusory metaphysical picture of what is required for our intuitive conception of objectivity to have a "real" application. Properly understood our intuitive conception of objectivity does not rest on any metaphysical picture at all.

McDowell would not be persuaded by this reply. As we have seen, McDowell argues that Wright's picture of language use leaves out "norms":

> the trouble is that the denial of ratification-independence, by Wright's own insistence, yields a picture of the relation between the communal language and the world in which norms are obliterated. And *once we have this picture, it seems impossible simply to retain alongside it a different picture, in which the openness of an individual to correction by his fellows means that he is subject to norms.* The first picture irresistibly claims primacy, leaving our openness to correction by our fellows looking like, at best, an explanation of our propensity to the illusion that we are subject to norms.[45]

McDowell's reasoning here has two parts. First, he argues that according to Wright's picture, "norms are obliterated" at the basic level of language use, and so there is no real application for our intuitive conception of objectivity at this level. And second, he claims that if we accept Wright's picture of the basic level of language use, then we will fail to find a "real" application for our intuitive notions of meaning and objectivity even at nonbasic levels of language use.

The trouble with the first claim is that McDowell offers us no independent means of assessing it. Wright would agree that at the basic level of language use there is no application of our intuitive idea that our use of language is subject to "correction." But Wright should not agree with McDowell that this *by itself* shows that there is no application for our intuitive conception of objectivity at the basic level of language. The reason is that Wright's picture of language is compatible with our use of a disquotational truth predicate. Wright can say, for example, that 'It is yellow' is true of a given object *x* if and only if *x* is yellow. So in reply to McDowell's first claim, Wright could say that at the basic level the "objectivity" of our assertions may only be expressed disquotationally. There is no reason for Wright to agree that if there is no application of our intuitive idea that our use of language is subject to "correction" at the basic level, then our intuitive idea of the objectivity of assertions has no application at this level.

As we have already seen, McDowell rejects this move. He claims that an appeal to disquotational truth would "merely postpone the serious question: does Wright's [picture of language use] contain the means to make it intelligible that there should so much as *be* such an action as calling an object 'yellow'?"[46] But what *is* required "to make it intelligible that there should so much as be such an action as calling an object 'yellow' "? Apart from his rejection of Wright's picture, McDowell has no substantive answer to this question. McDowell's appeals to our "customs" or "practices" of following rules add no independent content to his criticism of Wright, since the proper understanding of these "customs" or "practices" is exactly what is at issue between them.

The trouble with McDowell's second claim—that Wright's picture of the basic level of language use implies that our intuitive notions of meaning and objectivity have no real application even at nonbasic levels of language use—is that it begs the question in an unilluminating way. Wright should insist that at nonbasic levels of language use we can give real application to our intuitive idea that our assertions are subject to "correction," even if we can't give application to this idea at the nonbasic level of language use. As I urged two paragraphs ago, Wright should not accept McDowell's tacit assumption that the question whether we can give real application to our intuitive idea that our assertions are subject to "correction" is the same as the question whether we can give real application to our intuitive idea that our assertions are "objective." The latter idea can be expressed disquotationally, and might not rest on a general application, for all our assertions, of the idea that they are subject to "correction."

McDowell's argument against Wright's picture of language use is driven by McDowell's own convictions about what is required for our "intuitive notions of meaning and objectivity" to have "real application." Since he offers no independent constraints on our understanding of these notions, his claims about what they require are unconvincing.

44. A Reply from Quine

We've now seen that McDowell's transcendental argument for his participant perspective is unconvincing even if we accept the first assumption discussed in §41—that to abandon what McDowell calls our "intuitive conception of meaning and objectivity" is to collapse into an extreme form of idealism. But why should we accept this assumption? It is like the metaphysical realist's assumption that we can't make assertions if the meanings of our words are not uniquely determined. As we saw in Chapter Two, Quine flatly rejects this assumption. Quine would also dismiss McDowell's assumption that unless there are substantive norms for language use, we can at best be under the illusion that we can use our words to make objective assertions.

McDowell, in turn, would certainly reject Quine's idea that all we have to go on in translating another's words are his speech dispositions. In this respect McDowell's rejection of Wright's antirealism carries over to Quine: McDowell would say that Quine makes no room for "norms," since Quine views linguistic behavior in purely dispositional terms. McDowell would urge that the only way to make sense of normativity of meaning is to accept that when we are initiated into a language, we "make our minds available to one another, by confronting one another with a different exterior from that which we present to outsiders."[47]

For Quine this metaphorical talk is irrelevant, since all that matters to translation is objective empirical meaning, which can be preserved by countless inequivalent manuals of translation. Like most of us, McDowell may prefer to use the homophonic manual of translation for most fellow English speakers. In Quine's view, there is nothing wrong with this preference, so long as one accepts that it is compatible with his indeterminacy thesis. McDowell is clearly convinced that for Quine our use of language can be no more than "mere brute meaningless sounding off."[48] But Quine would dismiss this feeling as unscientific. McDowell's transcendental argument is useless against Quine's principled scientific naturalism.

45. Do These Criticisms Rest on a Misunderstanding of McDowell?

I conclude that McDowell's transcendental argument for the participant perspective is ineffective against both metaphysical realism and scientific naturalism. The argument depends on two problematic claims: (1) to abandon what McDowell calls our "intuitive conception of meaning and objectivity" is to collapse into an extreme form of idealism, and (2) only McDowell's middle course can give proper application to this intuitive conception. We have seen (§§42–43) that even if we take (1) for granted, McDowell offers no compelling grounds for (2). Moreover, (1) is also questionable (§44).

In light of these weaknesses in McDowell's transcendental argument, one might suggest that his central aim in "Wittgenstein on Following a Rule" is not to *argue* against metaphysical realism and scientific naturalism, but to show us a different way of looking at our linguistic practices. McDowell briefly suggests a similar reading of Wright's picture of truth: "In Wittgenstein's eyes, as I read him, Wright's claim that 'for the community itself there can be no authority, so no standard to meet' can be, at very best, an attempt to say something that cannot be said but only shown. It may have some merit conceived in that light; but attributing it to Wittgenstein as a doctrine can yield only distortion."[49] Perhaps McDowell's own characterizations of his middle course are best viewed as "an attempt to say something that cannot be said but only shown." One might think that when McDowell rejects the platonist's picture of meanings as "wholly autonomous" and "not up to us," for example, he is trying to *show* us a new way of looking at meaning and assertion.

Apart from these elusive characterizations of the platonist's picture, however, McDowell does not cite or discuss any examples that could be used to show that the platonic conception has no real application. Similarly, apart from McDowell's claim that Wright's picture of language use undermines our intuitive conceptions of meaning and objectivity, McDowell makes no attempt to show us that Wright's picture is unacceptable. Since McDowell's elusive remarks don't by themselves change the way we look at things, his criticisms of platonic realism or Wright's antirealism can't plausibly be interpreted as attempts to say what can only be shown. Thus I see no viable alternative to my reconstruction of the role of McDowell's transcendental argument for the participant perspective.

46. The Methodological Moral

Bringing together our metaphilosophical reflections (§36) with our presentation (§§37–40) and criticisms (§§41–44) of McDowell's transcendental argument for a participant perspective on meaning and assertion, we are now in a position to see that McDowell's failure to loosen the hold of metaphysical realism and scientific naturalism stems from a fundamentally flawed philosophical methodology. The methodological moral is that we should not attempt to resist metaphysical realism or scientific naturalism unless we can articulate an alternative. In particular, we should not try to construct transcendental arguments based on our intuitions about what meaning and assertion require.

I recommend a different approach. In my view, to understand rule-following and other central topics in the philosophy of language, we should start from our perspective as participants in our linguistic practices, and try to identify and neutralize philosophical assumptions that prevent us from properly describing these practices. In later chapters I will show in detail how this conception of the starting point and task of the philosophy of language can help us to move beyond metaphysical realism and scientific naturalism.

Coming on the heels of my criticisms of McDowell's transcendental argument, this brief characterization of my method might be taken to suggest that in my view we are free to adopt any philosophical perspective we like, and that there are no rational grounds for choosing one way of looking at things over another. Worries about philosophical relativism evaporate, however, when we see that some ways of looking at things are better than others, and that we can do no better than to occupy some standpoint or other, the best one we can articulate at the time. One of my aims here is to show that while many philosophical pictures of our linguistic practices provide useful dialectical material, they must ultimately be left behind. In particular, I'll explain why metaphysical realism and scientific naturalism lose their interest when seen in the light of the alternative picture I sketch in Parts II and III of this book.

47. My Strategy in the Rest of the Book

My strategy for finding and articulating a new way of looking at meaning and assertion falls roughly into two stages. The challenge of the first stage is to learn to see the roots of our own perspective as participants in rule-following practices, despite the attractions of entrenched frameworks from which our participant point of view looks unimportant. In the second stage, I develop more detailed descriptions of our linguistic practices from the participant point of view, and show that these descriptions are at odds with both metaphysical realism and scientific naturalism.

Part II of this book is devoted to the first stage. Our strong attractions to metaphysical realism and scientific naturalism prevent us from taking the participant perspective seriously. The current hegemony of metaphysical realism and scientific naturalism can be traced back to our collective rejection of the logical positivists' analytic-synthetic distinction. Quine made the case for his scientific naturalism with his powerful and relentless criticisms of Carnap's analytic-synthetic distinction. And Putnam's influential criticisms of the logical positivists' analytic-synthetic distinction and verificationism led to a new tide of enthusiasm for metaphysical realism. So one way to begin to clarify and come to terms with scientific naturalism and metaphysical realism is to reexamine their roots in Quine's and Putnam's rejections of the analytic-synthetic distinction.

Carnap proposed that we replace our vague intuition that we can share standards for evaluating our assertions with formally precise specifications of rules for evaluating our assertions, and he developed the clearest account ever given of the analytic-synthetic distinction. But Quine's impressive criticisms fostered the widespread impression that Carnap's project is hopelessly unclear. And it is tempting to assume that if Carnap's rigorous attempt to clarify meaning rests on obscure notions, then we must dismiss the very *idea* of a systematic philosophical framework based on our common participation in rule-following practices. But these prejudices reflect deep-seated misunderstandings of the issues at stake between Carnap and Quine. I'll argue that Quine's criticisms of Carnap's analytic-synthetic distinction stem from Quine's rejection of Carnap's view of the task and starting point of philosophy. To see how Quine systematically rejects Carnap's philosophical framework is to take a first step toward uncovering the roots of an alternative to Quine's scientific naturalism.

The second step of Part II is to show that Putnam's reasons for rejecting both Carnap's analytic-synthetic distinction and his verificationism are fundamentally different from Quine's, and stem from our perspective as participants in ongoing ordinary and scientific inquiries. I present a systematic and radical reconstruction of Putnam's arguments against the analytic-synthetic distinction. Using this reconstruction I show that Putnam's rejection of Carnap's analytic-synthetic distinction and Putnam's arguments for realism are rooted in our participation in ordinary and scientific inquiries. To understand the fundamental contrast between Putnam's and Quine's reasons for rejecting Carnap's analytic-synthetic distinction is to take a big step toward developing a new way of looking at meaning and assertion. I end Part II with a first glimpse of this new way, and a preliminary sketch of how to clarify it.

In Part III I turn to the second stage of the project: I fill in the details of the new picture sketched in Chapter Six, and show how it undermines metaphysical realism and scientific naturalism. I explain how Putnam's rejections of the analytic-synthetic distinction naturally lead to a deflationary version of anti-individualism, and show that Burge's developments of anti-individualism may be seen as further articulations of the same deflationary picture of our linguistic practices. My systematic reconstruction of Putnam's and Burge's arguments clarifies the realism implicit in anti-individualism, and undermines the widespread view that anti-individualism is a kind of metaphysical realism. To explore some of the deepest consequences of this new picture of anti-individualism, I address and allay standard doubts and confusions about self-knowledge and the relationship between thought and language. After I have filled in the new picture, I use it to criticize and reject Kripke's and Quine's skepticism about meaning.

Once we trace metaphysical realism, scientific naturalism, and anti-individualism back to their roots in Quine's and Putnam's rejection of the logical positivists' analytic-synthetic distinction, we begin to see that the participant perspective is the source of some of the most persuasive and influential arguments of the last forty years of analytic philosophy. My aim is to show how far this perspective can be taken, and to understand exactly how it differs from metaphysical realism and scientific naturalism.

II

—

THE ANALYTIC-SYNTHETIC DISTINCTION

F O U R

Carnap's Analytic-Synthetic Distinction

48. Carnap's Project: The Codification of a Methodology for Rational Inquiry

To come to terms with scientific naturalism and metaphysical realism, I propose that we investigate Quine's and Putnam's rejections of Carnap's analytic-synthetic distinction. We can appreciate the fundamental and illuminating differences between Quine's and Putnam's criticisms of Carnap's analytic-synthetic distinction only once we have learned to see the analytic-synthetic distinction from Carnap's point of view.

Carnap's analytic-synthetic distinction is integral to his project of codifying criteria for evaluating assertions and resolving disagreements. The project is rooted in Carnap's conviction that there is a sharp contrast between the controversies of traditional metaphysics and the clear questions that arise within mathematics, logic, and the empirical sciences:

> Even in the pre-Vienna period, most of the controversies in traditional metaphysics appeared to me sterile and useless. When I compared this kind of argumentation with investigations and discussions in empirical science or in the logical analysis of language, I was often struck by the vagueness of the concepts used and by the inconclusive nature of the arguments. I was depressed by disputations in which the opponents talked at cross purposes; there seemed hardly any chance of mutual understanding, let alone of agreement, because there

was not even a common criterion for deciding the controversy
... I came to hold the view that many theses of traditional
metaphysics are not only useless, but even devoid of cognitive
content.[1]

Carnap's attitude toward the controversies found in traditional
metaphysics reveals his motivating insight that if investigators are
to agree or disagree at all, they must share criteria for evaluating
their assertions.

Carnap's project is radical: he proposes that we drop all unclear
ways of talking, and use logical and mathematical methods to
specify precise criteria for evaluating our assertions.[2] Carnap holds
that a sentence S of a precisely specified language L is *analytic* (or
contradictory) if it is true (or false) solely in virtue of the rules for
using expressions of L; otherwise it is *synthetic*. Carnap takes for
granted that his proposed methods for specifying the rules of a
language L are so clear that his explications of the analytic-synthetic
distinction need no metaphysical or epistemological support.[3]

In this chapter I present a systematic reconstruction of the
analytic-synthetic distinction from Carnap's point of view. Although Carnap frequently changed his views about important
details, the central features of his project were present in *The Logical
Syntax of Language (1937)*, and remained substantially unchanged
for the rest of his career.[4] I begin (§§49–51) with an overview of
these central features, then add detail and correct common misunderstandings. My central goal is to uncover the roots of Carnap's
perspective on the analytic-synthetic distinction.

49. Pure and Descriptive Semantics, Explicit Rules, and Language Systems

Carnap assumes that to specify criteria for evaluating assertions we
must state rules for the use of linguistic expressions, both sentences
and the expressions that occur in them. For Carnap, whenever one
is specifying rules for the use of expressions one is in effect distinguishing between an *object language* to which the expressions belong
and a *metalanguage* in which the rules for the proper use of the
object language expressions are stated. Precise statements of such
rules can be valuable even if the metalanguage *contains* the object

language, since one may use the transparent formal, arithmetical, and semantical vocabulary of a language L to specify rules for using the expressions of L.[5]

The task of *pure* syntax and semantics is to specify rules for using expressions and to investigate the consequences of adopting particular systems of rules. To investigate the relationship between a precisely specified language L and the speech behaviors of an individual or a group, we must decide how the terms used in our specification of L are to be correlated with those speech behaviors. Such investigations and decisions are made within *descriptive* syntax and semantics.[6] Carnap holds that the specifications of rules made within pure syntax and semantics are completely independent of and prior to any assumptions or stipulations made within descriptive syntax and semantics. As we will see, the distinction between pure and descriptive syntax and semantics is crucial to Carnap's view that the analytic-synthetic distinction is independent of all metaphysical and epistemological assumptions.

To specify the rules of a given language L we must state *formation rules,* which tell us which strings of symbols count as sentences of L, and define the *logical consequence* relation for L. In Carnap's view the logical consequence relation varies considerably from language to language, for it depends on which sentences are taken as primitive truths. Together with the other rules of a language L, sentences taken as primitive truths of L behave like axioms, generating further sentences that are true solely in virtue of the rules of L.[7] A complete set of rules for using expressions of a language fixes what Carnap called a *language system,* or *linguistic framework.* In his view it is only in the context of a language system that we are able to make assertions that can be properly evaluated as true or false.

50. The Principle of Tolerance

Carnap's interest in constructing and comparing language systems grew out of his puzzlement over controversies about the foundations of mathematics, especially the debate over whether to allow constructive or nonconstructive methods of proof when formalizing mathematics. Both approaches seemed legitimate to him, and yet constructivists and nonconstructivists thought they were making incompatible assertions about the nature of logic. Carnap came to believe that the controversy between constructivism and nonconstructivism is based in a misunderstanding. The two alternative logics are not in conflict; they are the results of different conventions for setting up rules for using the expressions of a language.

To make this conventionalist view of logic clear, in *Logical Syntax* Carnap described two language systems: Language I, in which the logical consequence relation is restricted in the way recommended by the constructivists, and Language II, in which the logical consequence relation is unrestricted, as in nonconstructive classical mathematics. The key point for Carnap was that these language systems are both legitimate. The constructivists and nonconstructivists in effect make different *proposals* as to which language system to use; these proposals are neither true nor false, and so the constructivist and the nonconstructivist do not genuinely disagree. In his "Intellectual Autobiography," Carnap elaborates on his aims in *Logical Syntax:*

> in the controversy about the foundations of mathematics, the conception of intuitionism may be construed as a proposal to restrict the means of expression and the means of deduction of the language of mathematics in a certain way, while the classical conception leaves the language unrestricted. I intended to make available in syntax the conceptual means for an exact formulation of controversies of this kind. Furthermore, I wished to show that everyone is free to choose the rules of his language and thereby his logic in any way he wishes.[8]

In *Logical Syntax* this attitude toward the apparent dispute between constructivism and nonconstructivism in logic was expressed by Carnap's principle of tolerance: "*In logic, there are no morals.* Everyone is at liberty to build up his own logic, i.e. his own form of language, as he wishes. All that is required of him is that, if he wishes to discuss it, he must state his methods clearly, and give syntactical rules instead of philosophical arguments."[9] Carnap continued to affirm his principle of tolerance even though he often changed his views about the metatheoretical resources available for describing language systems.[10] Tolerance was fundamental for him. He valued particular metatheoretical methods for constructing language systems only insofar as he believed that they would prove useful in clarifying assertions and resolving philosophical disputes.

Yet it may seem that the principle of tolerance merely masks Carnap's own dogmatism about the limits of cognitively meaningful language. On one tempting reading, Carnap holds that there is only one correct metalanguage for constructing language systems: Although he *sounds tolerant*, since he allows conventional choices to be expressed within this universal metalanguage, *in fact he is dogmatic*, since he dismisses the very possibility of language systems that cannot be specified within his universal metalanguage.

But this reading misses the *pragmatism* of Carnap's philosophy. Carnap treated his own descriptions of metalanguages for constructing language systems as *proposals*, even when he was not himself able to specify any clear alternative to them. And there is a crucial distinction between saying that one does not understand a given use of language and saying that it does not make any sense. Carnap restricted himself to the first kind of claim, and remained open-minded about the prospects of coming to understand assertions he found puzzling. Mainly he hoped that his proposed metalanguages would help philosophers clarify their questions and resolve their disputes.[11] The paradigm example of this was Carnap's attempt to show that constructivists and nonconstructivists were not really in disagreement, but adopted different conventions for using their expressions. Carnap believed he could use the syntax metalanguage to convince constructivists and nonconstructivists that they were in effect talking past each other.

Throughout his career Carnap was hopeful that his proposed metalanguages would be useful in resolving and clarifying all important philosophical puzzles and controversies, yet he did not to try to show that there is a universal language past whose boundaries we cannot go. To view the principle of tolerance as masking an underlying dogmatism about how to construct language systems is to miss Carnap's pragmatism about what it takes to clarify rules of rational inquiry.[12]

51. A First Sketch of the Pragmatic Roots of Carnap's Analytic-Synthetic Distinction

Carnap's pragmatism about what it takes to clarify rules of rational inquiry is the key to understanding his analytic-synthetic distinction. As noted above (§49), for Carnap a sentence S of a language system L is *analytic* (or *contradictory*) if it is true (or false) solely in virtue of the rules for using expressions of L; otherwise it is *synthetic*. To understand the analytic-synthetic distinction, we must understand the problem it is designed to solve.

In his "Intellectual Autobiography," Carnap describes the view he shared with members of the Vienna Circle:

> we arrived at the conception that all valid statements of mathematics are analytic in the specific sense that they hold in all possible cases and therefore do not have any factual content.
>
> What was important in this conception from our point of view was the fact that it became possible for the first time to combine the basic tenet of empiricism with a satisfactory explanation of the nature of logic and mathematics. Previously, philosophers had only seen two alternative positions: either a non-empiricist conception, according to which knowledge in mathematics is based on pure intuition or pure reason, or the view held, e.g., by John Stuart Mill, that the theorems of logic and of mathematics are just as much of an empirical nature as knowledge about observed events, a view which, although it preserved empiricism, was certainly unsatisfactory.[13]

Carnap reports that he and the other members of the Vienna Circle believed that: "the rationalists had been right in rejecting the old empiricist view that the truth of '2 + 2 = 4' is contingent upon the observation of facts, a view that would lead to the unacceptable consequence that an arithmetical statement might possibly be refuted tomorrow by new experiences."[14] So the problem was to show that investigators can have nonempirical knowledge of logic and mathematics without positing a special faculty of pure intuition. For Carnap this problem was exacerbated by his acceptance of a number of apparently incompatible logical and mathematical systems, such as classical mathematics and intuitionism.

Carnap proposed to solve the problem by drawing the distinction between analytic and synthetic sentences of a language system. The logical and mathematical sentences of a language system L are *analytic*—true in virtue of the rules of L—or *contradictory*—false in virtue of the rules of L; and so, Carnap claimed, *we can know the truth values of these sentences without appealing to evidence of any kind, empirical or nonempirical*. In contrast, to know the truth values of the *synthetic* sentences of L—those whose truth values are not determined by the rules of L—we must appeal to evidence. Thus Carnap hoped to reconcile our nonempirical knowledge of the truth values of logical and mathematical sentences with the basic tenet of empiricism—that all *evidence* for the truth or falsity of sentences is *empirical* evidence.

But what is the status of the methods and rules themselves? Do we need a special faculty of intuition to know which methods to use in specifying the rules of our language systems, or to know how to follow those rules? If so, we do not make any real progress over the rationalist's account of our knowledge of logic and mathematics. If Carnap's analytic-synthetic distinction is to solve the positivist's problem, there must be a way of understanding rules that does not rest on pure intuition or empirical evidence.

For Carnap, the question of whether there is a way of understanding rules that does not rest on pure intuition or empirical evidence is answered by finding logical and mathematical techniques that are transparent to those who use them. He was interested not in providing a philosophical *theory* of what makes logical and mathematical truth *possible*,[15] but in proposing methods for codifying rules, methods that investigators could take for granted in their inquiries. In Carnap's view, we need not make any metaphysical or epistemological assumptions in order to get on with the work of codifying inquiry and resolving disputes, and so there is no *point* in saying that such codifications "depend" on metaphysical or epistemological assumptions. The ultimate criterion for the legitimacy of a proposed method for codifying rules and drawing the analytic-synthetic distinction is its *usefulness* in resolving disputes and articulating the methodological role of assertions. I'll elaborate and defend this view of Carnap's analytic-synthetic distinction in the rest of this chapter.

52. Quine's Criticism of the Thesis That Logic Is True by Convention

According to Carnap's principle of tolerance it is a matter of *choice* which set of rules one adopts. Because of the existence of alternative rules, and Carnap's principle of tolerance, its seems natural to say that on Carnap's view logical truths are *true by convention*. But this formulation is misleading. To see what Carnap means by saying that logical and mathematical truth is analytic, and to distinguish this from the claim that logic is true by convention, it is helpful to consider Quine's objections (in "Truth by Convention"[16] and "Carnap and Logical Truth"[17]) to what Quine calls the "linguistic doctrine of logical truth."

The positivist's claim that logic and mathematics are true by convention should be broken down into two theses: first, the logicist thesis that mathematics is a conventional transcription of logic, and second, the thesis that logic is true by convention.[18] The first claim, though it is important to the strategy of fitting logic and mathematics with empiricism, is to be evaluated on technical, not philosophical grounds, and Quine does not question it.[19] On the assumption that mathematics can be viewed as a conventional transcription of logic, the *philosophically* important work is done by the positivist's account of the epistemological status of logic.

Quine's objection to the thesis that logic is true by convention begins with the observation that there are infinitely many valid truth-functional schemata. This means that we cannot hope to list them all. An axiomatization of the valid truth-functional schemata must employ rules of inference. A typical axiomatization employs *modus ponens* and a *substitution rule*, according to which the results of uniform substitutions of schemata for schemata in any valid schema may be accepted as valid as well.[20]

The heart of Quine's criticism is that the *explicit* adoption of a particular set of axioms for truth-functional logic cannot be the basis for logical truth, since we must use logic to derive consequences from the axioms. Quine summarizes the objection as follows: "logical truths, being infinite in number, must be given by general conventions rather than singly; and logic is needed then to begin with, in the metatheory, in order to apply the general conventions to individual cases."[21] Much earlier, Lewis Carroll made what was at root the same point with his parable of Achilles and the Tortoise.[22] Each time Achilles gets the Tortoise to accept a sentence corresponding to the inference rule *modus ponens,* he finds that the Tortoise will not draw the proper inferences from that sentence, conjoined with other sentences he already accepts. The Tortoise shows us that inference rules cannot be adopted by an explicit convention, but are needed to draw inferences from explicitly adopted conventions.

In "Truth by Convention," where Quine first presented this criticism, he concedes that one may avoid the regress by maintaining that logic is true in virtue of *implicit* conventions that we may subsequently make explicit. He describes this possibility as follows:

> It may be held that we can adopt conventions through behavior, without first announcing them in words; and that we can return and formulate our conventions verbally afterward, if we choose, when a full language is at our disposal. It may be held that the verbal formulation of conventions is no more a prerequisite of the adoption of the conventions than the writing of a grammar is a prerequisite of speech; that explicit exposition of conventions is merely one of many important uses of a completed language. So conceived, the conventions no longer involve us in a vicious regress.[23]

Quine claims that while this position may enable us to avoid the regress, it has no "explanatory force": "In dropping the attributes of deliberateness and explicitness from the notion of linguistic convention we risk depriving the latter of any explanatory force and reducing it to an idle label. We may wonder what one adds to the bare statement that the truths of logic and mathematics are a priori, or to the still barer behavioristic statement that they are firmly accepted, when he characterizes them as true by convention in such a sense.[24] We may sum up Quine's objection to the thesis that logic is true by convention as follows. The thesis has "explanatory force" only if logic is true by *explicit* convention. But logical truths cannot be based solely in explicit conventions, since rules of inference must be presupposed in the metalanguage if we are to draw the consequences of any explicitly adopted axioms for generating the logical truths.[25]

53. Carnap's Pragmatic Approach to Codifying Rules for Inquiry

In his reply to Quine's paper "Carnap and Logical Truth," Carnap writes that his view of the status of logic is not well expressed by the thesis that logic is based in linguistic conventions.[26] We saw earlier (§51) that Carnap proposed a middle course between the nonempiricist view that knowledge of logical truths is based on pure intuition, and the old empiricist view that ultimately our acceptance of the theorems of logic can only be justified by empirical observation. To answer Quine's criticisms of the thesis that logic is true by convention, we must say more about how Carnap understood this middle course.

I suggest that the key to understanding the middle course is Carnap's pragmatic approach to codifying rules for inquiry. In any given context of inquiry, investigators may wish to clarify the rules by which they evaluate statements and resolve disputes. As a practical aid in such clarification, they may settle on an explicit account of the rules governing the proper use of the expressions of a language. They can then agree that some of their assertions are true solely in virtue of these rules. From Carnap's deflationary pragmatic perspective, this can only mean that in their context of inquiry, given the rules they have agreed on, if they are to continue using the language according to those rules, they must acknowledge that the truth of some sentences and the falsity of others is completely settled by the rules they laid down, and so no new empirical investigation is needed to justify their acceptance of those sentences. For Carnap this is *not* a metaphysical claim: to understand it one need only acknowledge that investigators can share metalanguages with which they can communicate about and agree on explicit rules for evaluating statements and resolving disputes. That investigators *can* communicate about and agree on explicit rules for evaluating statements and resolving disputes is obvious to anyone familiar with modern logic, mathematics, or any of the mature physical sciences. From this pragmatic perspective, Quine's Lewis Carroll point is simply irrelevant to the thesis that logical truth is analytic. If investigators can communicate at all, they are always in a position to take for granted some rules of inference (or other) in their shared metalanguage, and so there is no need for explicit conventions for deriving consequences from axioms they agree to adopt.

One might think that Carnap's view of logical truth rests on the metaphysical claim that the rules of a language are what *make* the logically true sentences of that language true. But given Carnap's explicitly antimetaphysical stance, and what I am calling his pragmatism about codifying rules for inquiry, this metaphysical reading is wrong. Quine's criticism of the linguistic doctrine of logical truth depends on the assumption that Carnap's aim is to *explain* what makes the laws of logic true. But once we adopt Carnap's pragmatic perspective on codifying rules for inquiry, it is difficult to see how anyone could be bothered by his claim that logic is true "in virtue of" rules.

Carnap disavows any interest in explaining what *makes* the truths of logic true. Rejecting the idea that the laws of logic are true by linguistic convention, he writes: "the logical truth of the sentence 'All black dogs are dogs' is not a matter of convention . . . Once the meanings of the individual words in a sentence of this form are given (which may be regarded as a matter of convention), then it is no longer a matter of convention or of arbitrary choice whether or not to regard the sentence as true; the truth of such a sentence is determined by the logical relations holding between the given meanings."[27] Here one must again be careful not to read a metaphysical ambition into Carnap's talk of the truth of a sentence being "determined by the logical relations holding between the given meanings." Read it as follows: given the rules set down for the use of the expressions, we may deduce, with no appeal to empirical observation of any kind, that certain sentences are true. This seems harmless, if it is relativized to particular contexts in which investigators have come to an agreement on rules for using their language. Then there is no temptation to think that Carnap is offering a metaphysical explanation of the truths of logic. Thus Quine's criticism, which depends on the assumption that Carnap is attempting to provide such an explanation, is irrelevant from Carnap's point of view.[28]

54. Mistakes and Discoveries in Logic and Mathematics

One might still have misgivings. Why does Carnap say that the truth of some sentences is "determined by the logical relations holding between the given meanings"? This seems to show that he thinks there is some explanatory work being done by the specification of rules for a given context of inquiry. How are we to understand this if not metaphysically, as the attempt to say what *makes* these statements true?

The answer is that Carnap thinks it is the task of his account of logical and mathematical truth to clarify what it is for an investigator to make *mistakes* and *discoveries* in logic and mathematics.[29] It is a commonplace that an individual who knows the rules of his language can make mistakes about whether a given logically true sentence is true, or whether a given sentence in mathematics is true. I gave a very simple example of this in §4 of Chapter One. In that example I mistakenly believe, after a hasty calculation, that sixty-eight plus fifty seven is one hundred fifteen. My mistake is easily discovered, by using simple rules for calculating sums, rules to which I was committed when I made my mistake. Carnap offers a deflationary, nonmetaphysical account of such mistakes. The foundation of his account is that investigators specify explicit rules for using the expressions of their language. He does not develop his precise logical frameworks in order to *explain* how this is possible; instead he presents them as tools with which investigators construct and codify rules for inquiry. He is trying to further mutual understanding by offering investigators resources for constructing languages whose rules are more precise than the ones they often use. He does not think that we can coherently question whether it is *possible* to follow the rules we specify. This is the kind of question that simply can't arise if one adopts Carnap's proposals for clarifying rational inquiry.

The motivating assumption behind Carnap's deflationary view is that instead of trying to *explain* logical and mathematical truth, we must *codify* the epistemological role of sentences that express logical and mathematical truths.[30] As we will see, to codify for Carnap in effect meant to *replace* vague uses of language with more precise languages. For Carnap no clear question can be raised about whether the codifications we use rest on metaphysical or epistemological assumptions, since if we do not find a purported codification of rules transparent, we can't *use* it to codify our rules.

55. 'Analytic in L' in Terms of State Descriptions

We've seen (§§52–54) that Quine's objection to Carnap's view that logic is true by convention is based in a misunderstanding of Carnap's pragmatic criterion for codifying rules for inquiry. To see just how deflationary Carnap's project really is, we must look more closely at his proposed methods for specifying language systems and defining analyticity.

After learning of Alfred Tarski's method of defining truth for formalized languages, Carnap settled on a semantical explication of 'analytic in L' based in a Tarski-style truth definition for L. In his "Intellectual Autobiography" he reports his enthusiasm for the semantical explication of analyticity, and relates it to his search for a definition of logical truth:

> To me it had always seemed to be one of the most important tasks . . . to construct a definition of logical truth or analyticity. In my search for an explication I was guided, on the one hand, by Leibniz' view that a necessary truth is one which holds in all possible worlds, and on the other hand, by Wittgenstein's view that a logical truth or tautology is characterized by holding for all possible distributions of truth-values. Therefore the various forms of my definition of logical truth are based in either the definition of logically possible states or on the definition of sentences describing those states (state-descriptions). I had given the first definition of logical truth in my book on syntax. But now I recognized that logical truth in the customary sense is a semantical concept. The concept which I had defined was the syntactical counterpart of the semantical concept. There-fore, using some of Tarski's results, I defined L-truth in seman-tics as an explication for the familiar concept of logical truth, and related concepts such as L-implication and L-equivalence. In this way, the distinction between logical and factual truth, which had always been regarded in our discussions in the Vienna Circle as important and fundamental, was at last vin-dicated.[31]

Carnap's pragmatic attitude toward shared formal and semantical rules becomes clearer when we see how he uses state descriptions to explicate the "familiar concept of logical truth."

It is crucial to see that for Carnap the class of sentences that are true in virtue of meaning, or analytic, is larger than the class of strictly logical truths like 'All black dogs are dogs', which are, we might loosely say, true in virtue of the meanings of logical words such as 'all', 'not', 'if', 'then'. Carnap also thinks that there are sentences, such as 'All bachelors are unmarried', which are true in virtue of the meanings of their predicates, together with the mean-ings of the logical words. This wider class of sentences includes all the logical truths, plus all the sentences that result from the logical truths when the meaning relationships between the predicates, such as 'bachelor' and 'unmarried', are taken into account.

In this section I briefly sketch the semantical explication of 'analytic in L' that Carnap offers in chapter 1 of *Meaning and Necessity*, and show why it fails as an explication of the wider class of analytic statements. In the next section (§56) I sketch a later refinement that shows how thin Carnap's notion of analyticity really is.

To examine the basic idea behind Carnap's semantical explications of 'analytic in L', consider L_1, a first-order quantificational language without identity, none of whose sentences contains free variables. The logical expressions of L_1 are confined to a universal quantifier, '(x)', and three truth-functional expressions, '$\sim$' , '$\rightarrow$', and '$\leftrightarrow$', all with the usual meanings. L_1 has a number of names and predicates, and includes clauses that specify how those names and predicates are to be interpreted. For example, in L_1 there are the names 'a' and 'b', which denote Carnap and Quine respectively, and the predicates 'F', 'G', 'H', interpreted as follows:

'F' is true of an object x if and only if x is human.
'G' is true of an object x if and only if x is a rational animal.
'H' is true of an object x if and only if x is a logician.

As a comment on his interpretation of L_1, Carnap writes: "The English words here used are supposed to be understood in such a way that 'human being' and 'rational animal' mean the same."[32] Thus in effect Carnap assumes that '$(x) (Fx \leftrightarrow Gx)$' is *analytic* in L_1, since it is true in virtue of the interpretations we gave for the predicates 'F' and 'G'. It will become clear that this assumption plays an important informal role in Carnap's intended explication of 'analytic in L_1'.

On the basis of the interpretations of the predicates and names of L_1, Carnap assumes that we have defined a Tarski-style truth predicate for L_1, in the usual way. The details need not concern us here.[33] The important point is that we know we can construct a definition of 'true in L_1' on the basis of the interpretations of the predicates and constants of L_1. Carnap explicates 'analytic in L_1' by constructing a definition of '*L-true* in L_1' that meets the following constraint:

Convention   A sentence S of language-system L is *L-true* in L if and only if S is true in L and S's truth can be established on the basis of the semantical rules of L, without any reference to extra-linguistic facts.[34]

This is just a vague informal hint of how '*L-true* in L_1', Carnap's proposed replacement for 'analytic in L_1', is supposed to be understood.[35]

In *Meaning and Necessity* Carnap's strategy for defining '*L-true*' depends on his concept of a *state description*. A state description for language L_1 is a class that contains, for every atomic sentence (consisting of a predicate with a name in each of its argument places) of L_1, either that sentence or its negation, but not both. Carnap suggests that each state description expresses one possible "state of the universe," as complete a description of that possible state as one could give in L_1. But his talk of "possible states of the universe" plays no important role in his semantical definition of 'analytic in L_1'.

Finally, we come to Carnap's explication of 'analytic in L_1'. He defines the central concept, *L-true* for a language system L, as follows:

A sentence S is *L-true* (in language-system L) if and only if S holds in all state descriptions (of L).

Applied to L_1, this definition of '*L-true*' explicates what I have called "logical truth," which is determined by the meanings of the logical constants '(x)', '$\sim$', '$\rightarrow$', and '$\leftrightarrow$': such logically true sentences as '$(x)(Fx \rightarrow Fx)$' come out *L-true* in L_1.[36]

But there is an obvious problem with thinking of this preliminary definition of '*L-true*' as an explication of the broader category of analytic truths of L_1, which supposedly includes such sentences as '$(x)(Fx \leftrightarrow Gx)$', whose predicates, according to Carnap, "mean the same." The problem is that Carnap's unrestricted syntactic definition of the state descriptions of L_1 cannot mirror any supposed *meaning relations* between the predicates of L_1. For example, by Carnap's definition, there is a state description that includes the sentences 'Fb' and '$\sim$Gb', which mean that *Quine is human* and *Quine is not a rational animal*, respectively. I noted earlier that under the interpretation given, the predicates 'F' and 'G' are supposed to "mean the same," and at a minimum this requires that they have the same extensions in all state descriptions. Thus at one point, on the basis of his earlier supposition that the predicates 'F' and 'G' "mean the same," Carnap asserts that the sentence '(x) $(Fx \leftrightarrow Gx)$' is *L-true* in L_1.[37] But if we accept Carnap's unrestricted specification of the state descriptions of L_1, then we must accept that the truth values of all of the atomic sentences of L_1 are *independent* of each other; in particular, we must accept that there is a state description that includes both 'Fb' and '$\sim$Gb'. And if there is such a state description, then the sentence '(x) $(Fx \leftrightarrow Gx)$' is not *L-true* in L_1. So it seems that Carnap's definition of '*L-true*' does not explicate the wider class of analytic sentences of L_1.[38]

56. 'Analytic in L' in Terms of State Descriptions and Meaning Postulates

It is tempting to think that this failure of '*L-true*' as an explication of 'analytic in L_1' stems from the vagueness of the idea of synonymy, or sameness of meaning. It looks as though the formal aspects of the explication at best characterize logical truth for L_1, and that the wider class of so-called analytic truths can't be explicitly specified. We could put arbitrary syntactic restrictions on what counts as a state description. But it seems that such restrictions would reflect our prior decisions as to what states are "possible." And since our judgments about what state descriptions are "possible" depends on our judgments as to whether various statements are analytic, this procedure is circular. Thus it seems that there can be no legitimate semantical explication of the wider class of analytic truths.

From Carnap's point of view this objection is based in a misunderstanding of the goal of his explications of analyticity. This is clear from Carnap's use of meaning postulates to give a precise explication of the wider notion of analyticity in terms of state descriptions and meaning postulates.

Carnap's explication of analyticity is based in the definition of '*L-true*' given above. He distinguishes between the language system L_1 and a more restricted language system L_2, the set of whose state descriptions is smaller. The state descriptions for L_2 are the state descriptions of L_1 in which the *meaning postulates* of L_2 are true. For example, to make it true in virtue of the semantical rules of L_2 that 'F' and 'G' are synonymous, Carnap includes the sentence

'(x) $(Fx \leftrightarrow Gx)$' among the meaning postulates of L_2. The restriction of the state descriptions of L_1 is done as follows. Let M be the conjunction of all the meaning postulates of L_2, and assume that x is a state description of L_2 if and only if x is a state description of L_1 in which M is true. Given this characterization of what counts as a state description of L_2, Carnap can explicate the wider notion of analyticity in terms of '*L-true*' as follows:

> A sentence S is *L-true* in L_2 if and only if S holds in all state description of L_2.

Thus the strategy is to start with the unrestricted syntactic characterization of the state descriptions of language system L_1 and, with the addition of meaning postulates, to specify the state descriptions of another language system, in this case L_2. Carnap's explication of 'analytic in L_2' is then given by '*L-true* in L_2'.[39]

In reply to the objection that this explication presupposes that we already know which state descriptions are "possible," Carnap points out that we can choose meaning postulates for a language without even knowing what the predicates denote. We need not already know what is "possible" to explicate a precise notion of analyticity for a language system.[40]

The resulting explication of analyticity is clear but trivial. It reflects Carnap's deflationary attitude toward talk of "meaning relations" and the convention that "analytic truths" are "true in virtue of meaning." These phrases give the misleading impression that Carnap is attempting to "explain" how some sentences could be true independently of any verifying or falsifying experience. But there is nothing more to his talk of sentences that are "true in virtue of meaning" than meets the eye in his particular explications of the phrase, and these explications don't provide any insight into or explanation of what *makes* such sentences true.

So according to Carnap whether or not a sentence is "true in virtue of meaning" is to be trivially determined by a decision as to which language system one is using. He skirts the vexed question of how an individual comes to know whether or not two predicates are synonymous:

> Suppose that an author of a system wishes the predicates 'B' and 'M' to designate the properties Bachelor and Married,

respectively. How does he know that these properties are incompatible and that therefore he has to lay down [the] postulate $[(x)(Bx \rightarrow \sim Mx)]$? This is not a matter of knowledge but of decision. His knowledge or belief that the English words 'bachelor' and 'married' are always or usually understood in such a way that they are incompatible may influence his decision if he has the intention to reflect in his system some of the meaning relations of English words.[41]

The central point is that the strict explications of analyticity that can be given in particular language systems of the sort Carnap constructs are not intended to capture some language-system–independent relationship of synonymy. Consistent with Carnap's framework-relative conception of truth and falsity, there are and can only be *pragmatic* criteria for choosing one set of meaning postulates over another: "it cannot be the task of the logician to prescribe to those who construct systems what postulates they ought to take. They are free to choose their postulates, guided not by their beliefs concerning facts of the world but by their intentions with respect to the meanings, i.e., the ways of use of the descriptive constants."[42] So if we grant Carnap's starting assumption that investigators can find common ground from which to articulate and follow rules for evaluating their assertions, we can also accept his explication of analyticity in terms of logical truth and meaning postulates. Our first thought that he is using obscure notions gives way to the realization that Carnap's explications are precise, yet trivial and philosophically empty—exactly as he intends them to be.

57. Pure and Descriptive Semantics

We are now in a position to see that Carnap's method of defining analyticity in terms of *L-true* guarantees that, as he puts it, "the analytic-synthetic distinction can be drawn always and only with respect to a language-system, i.e., a language organized according to explicitly formulated rules, not with respect to a historically given natural language."[43] Together with Carnap's pragmatic perspective on rule-following, this passage should allay the concern that his explications of analyticity rest on a framework-independent understanding of the idea that some sentences are "true in virtue of meaning." But does this mean that Carnap's analytic-synthetic distinction does not apply to sentences of a natural language?

To answer this question we must distinguish between pure and descriptive semantics.[44] In pure semantics we construct and investigate language systems, and since we are not aiming to describe the semantical properties of languages already in use, our work is independent of empirical observations about language users. In contrast, the task of descriptive semantics is to describe the semantical properties of languages already in use. For example, in descriptive semantics we may study a natural language L as used by a person X. One hypothesis of descriptive semantics might be:

(H) The sentence "All ravens are black" is analytic in language L.[45]

We can evaluate this claim only if we investigate the speech behavior of person X. According to Carnap the empirical content of such semantical descriptions of natural languages is fixed by conventional decisions about how to correlate the basic expressions of a language system with the expressions of a natural language. So a preliminary answer to our question is that in Carnap's view we can meaningfully describe sentences of a natural language L as L-true (analytic) or L-indeterminate (synthetic) once we have *correlated* expressions of L with expressions of a particular language system within which the analytic-synthetic distinction is precisely drawn.

Carnap is vague about how the expressions of a natural language are to be correlated with expressions of a language system, but he offers a suggestive analogy: "Both in semantics and in syntax the relation between the pure and the descriptive field is *perfectly analogous* to the relation between pure or mathematical geometry, which is part of mathematics and hence analytic, and physical geometry, which is a part of physics and hence empirical."[46] Throughout his career Carnap endorsed Hans Reichenbach's account of the relationship between pure and physical geometry. Let us now see if Reichenbach's account of the role of coordinative definitions in physical geometry can help us understand Carnap's view of the relationship between pure and descriptive semantics.

58. Reichenbach's Coordinative Definitions

Reichenbach introduced his notion of a coordinative definition to solve a problem he posed about how we can determine the geometry of physical space. The problem arose as a result of the mathematical discovery that there are consistent non-Euclidean geometries. Before the discovery of consistent non-Euclidean geometries, physicists did not know of any alternatives to Euclidean geometry, and so simply assumed that physical geometry is Euclidean. But after this discovery, it could no longer be assumed without evidence that the geometry of physical space is Euclidean.

The problem Reichenbach set out to solve is that the interpretation of our measurements of physical space apparently depends on unverifiable assumptions. When we use measuring rods to determine whether one path through space is the same length as another, Reichenbach reasoned, our measurements typically presuppose that there are no "universal forces" acting on all bodies, including our measuring rods, causing them systematically to "shrink" or "increase" in length in some regions but not in others. The problem is that we have no empirical means of determining whether there are any such universal forces, and if so, which regions of space they affect, and how much they distort our measurements. It seems that any measurements we actually make are compatible with an infinite number of different universal forces, and hence an infinite number of different physical geometries. Since there is no other empirical method for determining the shape of space, it seems that we must conclude that we can never know what geometry our physical space actually has.

Suppose there are points A and B in region R of our space, and points C and D in a different region R'; the length AB matches the length of our measuring rod when it is transported to region R; and the length of CD matches the length of our measuring rod when it is transported to R'. The problem is to determine whether AB = CD. We cannot directly infer that AB = CD, since there may be "universal forces" that cause our measuring rods to expand or shrink in region R or R'. To determine whether AB = CD, we must first determine whether our measuring rod retains its length when it is moved from region R to region R'. But according to Reichenbach, "there is no way of knowing whether a measuring rod retains its length when it is transported to another place; a statement of this kind can only be introduced by a definition."[47] So we can discover the physical geometry of space only if we have adopted *coordinative definitions* that fix both the standard for measurement and the congruence relation between lengths in different regions of space. After choosing our measuring rod, we can define the congruence relation by stipulating that the rod retains its length wherever it is transported. This coordinative definition in effect sets the "universal forces" equal to zero. Given the congruence of our measuring rod with both AB and CD, we can then conclude that AB = CD, even though these lengths are measured in different regions of space.

Once we decide on a coordinative definition for our measurements, it then becomes an empirical question whether the geometry of physical space is Euclidean or non-Euclidean. Suppose that when we set the "universal forces" equal to zero, we discover that our physical space is Euclidean. If we had chosen a different coordinative definition the same measurements would establish that our physical space is non-Euclidean. Suppose for example that we decide that in region R' there are "universal forces" that cause everything uniformly to "expand." Then even though our measuring rod is congruent in region R' with CD, this does not show that AB = CD; since everything *expands* in region R', length CD is greater than length AB, and the sum of the angles of all triangles in region R' is greater than 180 degrees. Reichenbach concludes that "the question of the geometry of real space . . . cannot be answered before the coordinative definition is given which establishes the congruence for this space."[48] Reichenbach also holds that the choice of coordinative definition is "arbitrary," since even though we may *implicitly* presuppose that our measuring rod has the same length wherever it is transported, there are other coordinative definitions that could be used to investigate the geometry of our space. In Carnap's terminology, such coordinative definitions are "analytic": their "truth" follows from our choice of explicit rules for using our words.[49]

59. The Analogy between Physical Geometry and Descriptive Semantics

As we have seen, Carnap says that the relationship between pure and descriptive semantics is "perfectly analogous" to the relationship between pure and physical geometry. So he thinks that just as we need coordinative definitions to link the concepts of mathematical geometry to measuring rods, so we need coordinative definitions to link the concepts of pure semantics to speech behaviors. And just as different coordinative definitions in geometry lead us to different conclusions about the shape of physical space, so different coordinative definitions in descriptive semantics lead us to different conclusions about the semantical properties of a given natural language. The coordinative definitions of both disciplines are analytic, and by the principle of tolerance we are therefore free to choose whatever coordinative definitions we like, so long as the resulting frameworks are useful for investigating physical space or the semantical properties of natural languages.

To see how the analogy is supposed to apply to a particular case, let us look at one of Carnap's own sketches of how the concept of analyticity might be applied to a natural language. In descriptive semantics we may study a natural language L as used by a person X. I noted earlier (§57) that one hypothesis of descriptive semantics might be:

(H) The sentence "All ravens are black" is analytic in language L.

Suppose two linguists are trying to evaluate (H). They must link (H) to the observable speech behaviors of person X. Carnap supposes that "the two linguists agree on the basis of previous experience that X uses the words 'all' and 'are' in the ordinary sense, and that S has repeatedly affirmed the sentence ["All ravens are black"] and hence presumably regards it as true."[50] The two linguists ask person X the following question: "Mr. Smith told us that he had found a raven which is not black but white, and that he will show it to you tomorrow. Will you then revoke your assertion of 'All ravens are black' "? Carnap imagines two different responses to this question from person X:

(R1) "I would never have believed that there are white ravens; and I still do not believe it until I see one myself. In that case I shall, of course, have to revoke my assertion."

(R2) "There cannot be white ravens. If a bird is not black, then I just would not call it a raven. If Mr. Smith says that his raven is not black, then (assuming that he is not lying or joking) his use either of the word 'raven' or of the word 'black' must be different from my use."

Carnap claims that (R1) is disconfirming evidence for (H), and that (R2) is confirming evidence for (H). Carnap takes this story to show that (H) "can be tested by observations of the speaking behavior of X."[51]

Carnap is remarkably casual about the question of how the concepts of pure semantics are correlated with empirical observations. His story leaves it unclear what coordinative definitions would have the consequence that (R1) and (R2) could be used as evidence against or for (H).[52] Obviously, Carnap sees no difficulty in principle for his view that descriptive semantics is possible. He takes for granted that we can and do give empirical content to semantical descriptions of natural languages, and so there *must* be a way explicitly to state coordinative definitions that give precise empirical content to hypotheses like (H). Since it is only a matter of convention which coordinative definitions we adopt, we are free to fiddle with our coordinative definitions until we come up with a language system that gives content to hypotheses like (H). This language system will presumably be a precise replacement for the looser languages already used by linguists for testing hypotheses about what speakers mean. But Carnap apparently thinks that nothing hangs on exactly how we state the coordinative definitions that give content to our empirical descriptions of the semantical properties of natural languages. So in his view it is enough just to sketch the kinds of evidence to which we might appeal once we have given an explicit reconstruction of the empirical content of such semantical descriptions.

A comparison of Carnap's and Quine's attitudes toward the scientific status of descriptive semantics sheds light on Carnap's lack of concern about the coordinative definitions that give empirical content to the assertions of descriptive semantics. We saw in Chapter Two that according to Quine, translation—hence descriptive semantics—is unscientific. Quine observes that if we choose our "analytical hypotheses" carefully, alternative inequivalent manuals of translation between two languages can be constructed in such a way that each manual is compatible with the totality of speech dispositions. In Quine's view, there is "no fact of the matter" about which of these alternative manuals is correct, and so translation—and meaning itself—is objectively indeterminate.

Given Carnap's view that descriptive semantics is "perfectly analogous" to physical geometry, Carnap would not be surprised or disturbed by Quine's observation that we can construct alternative manuals of translation compatible with all speech dispositions. From Carnap's perspective, Quine's thought experiments about translation merely show that different coordinative definitions will yield different conclusions about the semantic properties of natural languages. When Quine insists that nothing determines which of the alternative "analytical hypotheses" we should adopt, from Carnap's perspective this merely shows that we have not yet specified the coordinative definitions that give descriptive semantics empirical content. Since our choice of coordinative definitions is not constrained by any "external" facts, nothing determines which of these definitions we should accept.[53] But the same is true for physical geometry—nothing determines the congruence relation across regions of physical space, and yet once we define the congruence relation, we can make measurements to discover the shape of space. Analogously, Carnap would reply, once we decide which coordinative definitions to adopt, we can formulate and test hypotheses about the semantical properties of natural languages.

Quine would of course dismiss this reply from Carnap. For Quine, the mature sciences constitute our "ultimate parameter," despite being underdetermined by all evidence. So physical geometry—as part of physics—is objective, even though underdetermined. Quine would reject Carnap's claim that descriptive semantics is "perfectly analogous" to physical geometry. They are analogous from an *epistemological* point of view, but "theories" in descriptive semantics are not and should not be included in our "total theory of nature." Unlike physical geometry, "theories" in descriptive semantics are not only underdetermined but indeterminate.[54]

From Carnap's point of view, however, our understanding of what makes a scientific claim "objective" is given to us only from *within* the science of logic, the core of which is pure semantics. We must use the resources of pure semantics to construct language systems for descriptive semantics. So there is no reason to worry about the precise details of how pure semantics is related to empirical evidence. Using the logical resources of pure semantics, we can look at actual empirical investigations of language, and then propose various language systems for descriptive semantics. We are free to alter our language systems until we find one that gives precise empirical content to semantical descriptions of natural languages. Thus Carnap is puzzled and unconvinced by Quine's assertions that descriptive semantics is unscientific.[55]

60. Beth's Criticism of Pure Semantics

Carnap believed that the concepts of pure semantics are transparent, and hence free of any epistemological or metaphysical assumptions. When Quine challenged Carnap to clarify the concepts of "analyticity" and "L-truth" by relating them to linguistic behavior, Carnap was puzzled. In "Meaning and Synonymy in Natural Languages," Carnap attempts to address Quine's concerns by sketching what he calls "a practical vindication of semantical intension concepts." As Carnap sees it, "Quine's criticism does not concern the formal correctness of the definitions in pure semantics; rather, he [Quine] doubts whether there are any clear and fruitful corresponding pragmatical concepts which could serve as *explicanda*. That is the reason why he demands that these pragmatical concepts be shown to be scientifically legitimate by stating empirical, behavioristic criteria for them."[56] Carnap goes on to say that he does not think the concepts of pure semantics are useful only if there is a corresponding pragmatical concept that they explicate. He believes we can use the resources of pure semantics to construct and adopt new language systems, without any concern about how the language systems are to be correlated with speech dispositions.

But just at this fundamental level, Quine refuses to accept Carnap's pragmatic approach to codifying semantical rules for inquiry. Quine argues that since a speaker's dispositions to verbal behavior do not uniquely determine which semantical rules the speaker follows, the very idea of a semantical rule is obscure and unscientific.[57] As we have seen, Carnap's motivating insight is that if investigators are to agree or disagree at all, they must share criteria for evaluating their assertions. The starting point for his work in pure semantics is that investigators can use shared metalanguages to discuss and codify semantical rules. Quine rejects this starting point—the heart of Carnap's philosophy.

Without taking on Quine's challenge directly, I will now begin to develop an answer to it from Carnap's perspective. I will approach the issue by considering a related but weaker objection raised by E. W. Beth.[58] In Chapter Five I will address Quine's more systematic and trenchant objections to Carnap's project.

Beth's objection begins with the idea that when Carnap tries to clarify the use of expressions of a language by giving explicit rules for the use of its expressions, he takes for granted a particular interpretation of the metalanguage in which those rules are stated. Beth points out that if Carnap's metalanguage ML were "interpreted" differently, the syntactic rules given in *Logical Syntax* would fail to explicate concepts of L-determinacy and L-indeterminacy for Carnap's language II. So if two investigators wish to use ML to explicate these concepts, they must both interpret ML in the same way. The investigators could use Carnap's syntactical methods to specify precise rules for the expressions of ML, but to do so they would have to use a meta-metalanguage MML, and interpret MML in the same way. If the investigators insist on asking, for each metalanguage they use, whether they interpret that metalanguage in the same way, they will embark on a potentially infinite regress of metalanguages, and never agree about how to codify rules for their joint inquiry. Hence to apply Carnap's method of codifying rules for their joint inquiry, they must find a way to avoid this regress.

In Beth's view the only way investigators can avoid the regress is to use a metalanguage whose interpretation they simply take for granted. Beth concludes that to use Carnap's method of codifying rules for inquiry, investigators must adopt a "mystical attitude" about language: they must *blindly trust* that they both interpret their metalanguage in the same way.

61. Carnap's Reply to Beth

In his reply to Beth, Carnap emphasizes that when two or more investigators use the resources of pure semantics and syntax, they must use the same metalanguage to state the rules they propose to use:

Since the metalanguage ML serves as a means of communication between author and reader or among participants in a discussion, *I always presupposed, both in syntax and in semantics, that a fixed interpretation of ML, which is shared by all participants, is given.* This interpretation is usually not formulated explicitly; but since ML uses English words, it is assumed that these words are understood in their ordinary senses. *The necessity of this presupposition of a common interpreted metalanguage seems to me obvious.*[59]

True to his motivating insight, Carnap takes for granted that for investigators to agree, disagree, and resolve their disputes, they must share criteria for evaluating their assertions. To discuss and codify criteria for their inquiries, investigators should use the clearest common fragment of the clearest language they share. When the clearest language they share is an ordinary unformalized one like English, they must take special care to minimize vagueness and ambiguity: "It is of course not quite possible to use [an] ordinary language with a perfectly fixed interpretation, because of the inevitable vagueness and ambiguity of ordinary words. Nevertheless it is possible at least to approximate a fixed interpretation to a certain extent, e.g., by a suitable choice of less vague words and by suitable paraphrases."[60] This reflects Carnap's pragmatism about what counts as clear enough to be useful in explicating the rules of a language. What Carnap offers in pure semantics are the tools for working from such contexts of partial agreement toward a situation in which investigators have clarified all issues of common interest to them. The starting point for this kind of work is that the participants already take for granted a common core of clear terms in which to discuss and codify semantical rules.

For Carnap it is a confusion to try to "justify" this starting point. Justification is framework relative: the intersubjective criteria for justifying a statement S of language system L are fixed by the semantical rules of L. To understand and evaluate a proposed justification of S, we must be able to communicate about the semantical rules of L. Thus we have no understanding of justification apart from some codification (or other) of rules for inquiry.

Similarly, for Carnap it is a confusion to speak of an implicit "interpretation" of the metalanguages of pure semantics. All inter-

pretations are expressed in some metalanguage (or other): to interpret the expressions of a language L is to use a metalanguage ML
to specify semantical rules for L. For Carnap, our ultimate parameter for codifying intersubjective criteria for inquiry is set by our
use of shared metalanguages. There is no higher or firmer perspective from which to question whether investigators "really" share
the metalanguages whose expressions they find clear. Hence there
is no sense to Beth's objection that to use the methods of pure
semantics investigators must indulge in "mystical attitudes" about
language, blindly trusting that they "interpret" their metalanguages in the same way.

To combat Beth's confusion about pure semantics, Carnap
emphasizes that the best antidote to "mystical attitudes" about
language is to use the methods of pure semantics to codify rules for
inquiry: "I doubt whether Beth is correct when he says that [inves-
tigations in pure syntax and semantics] . . . might countenance mystical attitudes with regard to natural [unformalized] languages. I
rather think that *any empirical investigation, in any field, especially if it
is careful in its method and clear in the choice of the concepts used, is the
best antidote against mystical attitudes.*"[61] Thus Carnap urges Beth to
replace his confused ideas about understanding and interpretation
with transparent specifications of semantical rules.[62]

It may seem that this reply to Beth hides an inconsistency in
Carnap's position. For even if Beth's idea that speakers implicitly
"interpret" their own words does not make sense within *pure*
semantics, it apparently *does* make sense within what Carnap calls
descriptive semantics. It is natural to suppose that two speakers
implicitly "interpret" their own words in the same way only if their
words have the same meanings. Within descriptive semantics we
can choose coordinative definitions that give empirical content to
the question of whether speakers' words have the same meanings.
If in addition we suppose that investigators *share* a language only if
their words have the same meanings, then within descriptive
semantics we can give empirical content to the question of whether
two speakers share a language. The trouble is that, by Carnap's
own standards, a speaker's linguistic behavior does not *uniquely*
determine what semantical rules she is following: there is more
than one coherent set of coordinative definitions, hence more than
one coherent semantical description of her linguistic behavior. This
apparently undermines Carnap's starting assumption that investi-

gators can share a metalanguage within which to codify semantical rules.

To see why, suppose that investigators A and B begin by taking for granted that they share metalanguage ML. Later they use meta-metalanguage MML to lay down coordinative definitions relative to which they formulate and test semantical interpretations of expressions of ML. To make sense of their assumption that they shared ML, they at first suppose that their past speech behaviors determined that their implicit "interpretations" of the expressions of ML were the same. After reflecting on Carnap's analogy of descriptive semantics with physical geometry, however, they realize that in Carnap's view there is more than one way to interpret their past uses of the expressions of ML. They are naturally inclined to choose coordinative definitions relative to which their utterances of ML had the *same* meanings. But this does not justify their assumption that they implicitly "interpreted" ML in the same way, since it does not rule out other coordinative definitions, relative to which their past utterances of expressions of ML had *different* meanings. For instance, they could choose to describe A's use of ML relative to one set of coordinative definitions, and B's use of ML relative to a different set of coordinative definitions. These coordinative definitions could be deliberately chosen to yield inequivalent semantical descriptions of their past utterances of expressions of ML. So if two speakers share a language only if their linguistic behaviors determine that their words have the same meanings, then Carnap's assumption that we can share metalanguages within pure semantics is inconsistent with his view that there is more than one way to interpret a speaker's utterances.

This "problem" stems from a subtle but serious misunderstanding of both pure and descriptive semantics. For Carnap an empirical description of the semantical properties of a speaker's utterances is not a description of how the speaker implicitly "interprets" her words. Empirical discoveries about the semantical properties of a speaker's utterances can neither *undermine* nor *justify* agreements reached within pure semantics, since such agreements set the ultimate parameters for our inquiries. In this sense there is no legitimate perspective higher or firmer than pure semantics from which to question our use of the shared metalanguages to codify rules for inquiry.

F I V E

Quine's Reasons for Rejecting Carnap's Analytic-Synthetic Distinction

62. A Strategy for Clarifying Quine's Dispute with Carnap

In Quine's presentation of his objections to Carnap's analytic-synthetic distinction, he takes care to avoid giving the impression that he and Carnap are talking past each other. But Quine rejects the core of Carnap's philosophy, and it often seems that Quine just refuses to understand Carnap's point of view.[1] In this chapter I show that the dispute between Quine and Carnap about analyticity is rooted in their rival conceptions of the starting point and task of philosophy, and that Quine does not undermine Carnap's analytic-synthetic distinction on Carnap's own terms.

Quine's and Carnap's contrasting conceptions of philosophy shape their views of the task of logic. For Carnap the central task of logic is to codify intersubjective rules for evaluating assertions, whereas for Quine the task of logic is to provide explanatory generalizations that clarify the conceptual scheme of natural science. In Carnap's view, rules for intersubjective evaluations of our assertions are specified within the science of pure logic, and hence built into language itself. But in Quine's view, Carnap's proposals for specifying rules for evaluating our assertions have no explanatory role, and hence make no contribution to logical theory. Moreover, according to Quine, the indeterminacy thesis shows that there are no intersubjective semantical rules in Carnap's sense. So Quine concludes that Carnap's analytic-synthetic distinction is scientifically meaningless.

My reconstruction of Quine's objections is important to my argument for several reasons. First, Quine's criticisms are standardly taken to undermine Carnap's analytic-synthetic distinction on its own terms. This shows that philosophers are now almost blind to Carnap's conception of the starting point and task of philosophy. To reopen our eyes to Carnap's perspective on philosophy, I explain why it is not vulnerable to Quine's criticisms. Second, many philosophers think that we can accept Quine's central arguments against Carnap's analytic-synthetic distinction without embracing Quine's indeterminacy thesis.[2] I argue that this is a mistake. Once these standard misunderstandings of Quine and Carnap have been exposed, I go on in Chapter Six to reconstruct Putnam's reasons for rejecting Carnap's analytic-synthetic distinction. A thorough understanding of the contrasts between Carnap's, Quine's, and Putnam's views of the starting point and task of philosophy helps to loosen the hold of scientific naturalism and metaphysical realism.

I begin (§63) with a puzzling exchange between Carnap and Quine about what constitutes a language, and then sketch their contrasting conceptions of language, logic, and interpretation (§§64–65). This sketch sets a framework for my clarifications of Quine's central objections to Carnap's attempts to characterize the analytic-synthetic distinction in purely logical terms (§§66–70). I then argue that Quine's objections to Carnap's characterizations of the analytic-synthetic distinction are not complete unless they are supplemented with Quine's argument for the indeterminacy of translation (§§71–73). I conclude by contrasting Carnap's methodological conception of science with Quine's scientific naturalism (§74).

63. A Puzzling Exchange between Carnap and Quine

As Carnap was preparing his reply to Quine's paper "Carnap and Logical Truth," Carnap asked Quine for a clarification of Quine's use of the term "language": "The question is, which of your discussions are meant to refer to (a) natural languages, and which to (b) codified languages (i.e., language-systems based on explicitly formulated rules) . . . The distinction is of great importance for my discussion, because from my point of view the problems of analyticity in the two cases are quite different."[3] Quine replied as follows:

You ask whether I mean "(a) natural languages" or "(b) codified languages . . . based on explicitly formulated rules." Now
here I suppose you mean codified languages to carry explicit
"semantical rules" with them—i.e., outright specification of
the so-called analytic sentences. If so, then (b) is not what I am
talking about . . . But I do not mean to limit myself to (a) either.
It is indifferent to my purpose whether the notation be traditional or artificial, so long as the artificiality is not made to
exceed the scope of "language" ordinarily so-called, and beg
the analyticity question itself.[4]

Quine does not want Carnap to beg the analyticity question by
stipulating that some languages have explicitly codified rules. Yet
from Carnap's point of view, Quine begs the analyticity question by
refusing to take for granted that some languages have explicitly
codified rules. Each seems unable to avoid begging the question
against the other.

64. Carnap and Quine on Language and Logic

The dispute between Carnap and Quine about analyticity can't be
separated from their fundamentally different conceptions of language, and their corresponding views of the starting point and task
of logic.

For Carnap a language should be viewed primarily as "an instru-
ment of communication."[5] His starting point is that if speakers are
to agree or disagree they must share rules for evaluating their
assertions. So a language is a "system of signs and of rules for their
use,"[6] not a theory (or "a system of assertions about objects"). The
rules of a language fix the intersubjective standards relative to
which assertions of sentences of the language can be evaluated as
true or false. It is the task of logic to analyze and facilitate communication about objective matters by specifying the intersubjective
content, or truth conditions, of sentences.

In contrast, for Quine a language should be viewed primarily as
a *theory*. Our starting point in applying logic is our use of sentences
of our own idiolect or theory, not our agreement or disagreement
with others about how to use our words. The explanatory task of
logic is to simplify and clarify the logical structure and conceptual
commitments of our own theory. In Quine's view, we continue the

work of natural science when we paraphrase our sentences into a canonical idiom that facilitates deductions and clarifies our conceptual commitments: "The same motives that impel scientists to seek ever simpler and clearer theories adequate to the subject matter of their special sciences are motives for simplification and clarification of the broader framework shared by all the sciences. . . . The quest of a simplest, clearest overall pattern of canonical notation is not to be distinguished from a quest of ultimate categories, a limning of the most general traits of reality."[7] Thus Quine's conception of the task of logic is a further expression of his scientific naturalism: "the recognition that it is within science itself, and not in some prior philosophy, that reality is to be identified and described."[8]

Just as it is not the task of natural sciences like physics or biology to further communication, so for Quine is it not the task of logic to codify intersubjective standards for evaluating our assertions. Any clarification of the intersubjective "contents" of our sentences must be given in terms of speech dispositions that link sentences and sensory evidence, and logic is silent about these dispositions. In Quine's view, "communication" between two individuals must be understood in terms of the "meshing" of their speech dispositions.[9] As we will see in detail, Quine's indeterminacy thesis directly opposes Carnap's "motivating insight" that if investigators are to agree or disagree they must share rules for evaluating their assertions.

65. Carnap and Quine on the Interpretation of Artificial Notations

Carnap's and Quine's rival conceptions of language and of the starting point and task of logic are reflected in their different views of how the artificial notations of symbolic logic are interpreted.

Carnap conceives of a language as a system of *shared* rules for using symbols. Thus he thinks that to interpret a language is to *agree* on how to use its expressions—to specify the rules that are to be shared by those who use the language. As we have seen, for Carnap the task of logic is to codify intersubjective rules for using symbols of artificial languages. *To interpret symbols of an artificial notation is to agree with others about how they are to be used.* In general, for Carnap, to interpret an expression is say how that expression contributes to the truth conditions of sentences in which it occurs.

To interpret the symbols of an artificial notation, we must *agree* on what their contribution to the truth conditions of sentences is to be. For example, Carnap writes: "Specification of truth-conditions for a connective consists in an *agreement* which fixes the conditions under which a compound sentence (formed by means of the connective and the sentences that enter as components) is to be considered true in terms of the truth or falsity of its components."[10] To come to an explicit agreement with another speaker about how we shall use our words, we must of course share a metalanguage within which to express our agreement. As we saw in Chapter Four, Carnap is tolerant and pragmatic about what counts as a suitable metalanguage for formulating our agreements about how we shall use our words.

For Quine the task of logic is not to codify intersubjective rules, but to simplify and clarify logical theory. *To interpret symbols of an artificial notation is just to use them to further one's own evolving theoretical purposes.* An individual *interprets* a sentence S' of an artificial notation when he uses it *in place of* an unformalized sentence S of his idiolect. The relationship of S' to S is just that "the particular business that the speaker was on that occasion trying to get on with, with help of S among other things, can be managed well enough to suit him by using S' instead of S."[11] Quine carefully avoids any essential reference to agreements with other speakers in his account of the interpretation of an artificial notation. He emphasizes that "the speaker is the one to judge whether the substitution of S' for S in the present context will further his present or evolving program of activity to his satisfaction."[12] An individual's use of artificial notations is just an extension of his everyday intrasubjective departures from ordinary idioms, departures that help him to clarify and simplify his evolving "theory." For Quine our use of the artificial notations of modern logic is motivated by our quest for simple and clear theories of nature, and not primarily by a desire to facilitate communication.

66. Quine on Truth by Convention Again

We are now in a position to see that Quine's objection to the thesis that logic is true by convention reflects Quine's fundamental rejection of Carnap's view of language, logic, and interpretation.

As we saw in §52, Quine asserts that the thesis that logic is true by convention has "explanatory force" only if logic is *made true* by the explicit adoption of conventions for the use of logical words. He observes that we must presuppose rules of inference in our meta-language if we are to derive consequences from any explicitly adopted axioms for generating the logical truths. He concludes that logic is not made true by the explicit adoption of conventions for the use of logical words, and so the thesis that logic is true by convention is empty.

In §53 we saw that from Carnap's point of view this objection is irrelevant. According to Carnap, the central task of logic is to codify intersubjective rules for using the symbols of artificial languages. Since our specifications of the rules of an object language L always presuppose a shared metalanguage, we can't *explain* why the *L-true* sentences of L are true. But in Carnap's view we can nevertheless show that in any given context of inquiry in which investigators share a metalanguage, they can specify rules relative to which the *L-true* sentences of an object language L are "empty of empirical content." In this deflationary way Carnap solves the positivists' problem of showing that our knowledge of logical and mathematical truths is not dependent on evidence of any kind.

Why did Quine fail (or refuse) to see this?[13] The answer lies in Quine's view of the starting point and task of logic. We have seen that for Quine the central task of logic is to provide explanatory generalizations that clarify the conceptual scheme of natural science. Logical theories are to be evaluated in the same way as theories in other sciences like physics and biology.[14] But in the sciences we aim at truth; there is no scientific theory whose primary purpose is to facilitate communication. So when Quine tries to understand the thesis that logic is true by convention, he views it as an explanatory hypothesis, which we must evaluate on scientific grounds. From Quine's point of view, Carnap's proposals for clarifying logical truth amount to the recommendation that we derive the logical truths from explicitly adopted axioms and inference rules. But Carnap's proposed axioms and inference rules merely *reorganize* our knowledge of the logical truths; they do not yield new truths or explain old ones. So by Quine's standards, Carnap's linguistic doctrine of logical truth makes no contribution to logical theory. To understand this fundamental rejection of Carnap's view of logical truth, we must carefully reconstruct Quine's critique of Carnap's proposals for explicating the analytic-synthetic distinction.

67. Preliminaries for Understanding Quine's Critique of Analyticity

Quine's objections to analyticity are of a piece with his objections to the thesis that logic is true by convention.[15] In this section I sketch a framework for my reconstructions (in §§68–70) of Quine's objections to analyticity. My aim is to show that Quine's objections to analyticity are rooted in his view that the task of logic is to facilitate deduction and clarify our conceptual commitments.

Let us begin by considering Quine's distinction between logical truth and analyticity. An example of what Quine calls a "logical truth" is: "No unmarried man is married." Quine characterizes logical truth as follows: "If we suppose a prior inventory of *logical* particles, comprising 'no', 'un-', 'not', 'if', 'then', 'and', etc., then in general a logical truth is a statement which is true and remains true under all reinterpretations of its components other than the logical particles."[16] The "second class" of "analytic truths" is exemplified by: "No bachelor is unmarried." This class includes any statement that "can be turned into a logical truth by putting synonyms for synonyms."[17] Quine draws an important distinction between his characterizations of logical truth and analyticity: "We still lack a proper characterization of this second class of analytic statements, and therewith of analyticity generally, inasmuch as we have had in the above description to lean on a notion of 'synonymy' which is no less in need of clarification than analyticity itself."[18] At this point in "Two Dogmas of Empiricism" Quine leaves the notion of logical truth behind, and begins his critique of analyticity.

But to see the roots of Quine's critique of analyticity, we must first see why he thinks logical truth is a *clear* and *explanatory* notion, whose proper characterization eschews all links to Carnap's project of codifying intersubjective rules for evaluating our assertions.

To define logical truth for sentences we can use, we need only paraphrase sentences of our ordinary language into a suitable artificial notation, specify the "logical particles," and define in syntactical terms what counts as an admissible reinterpretation of the nonlogical components of sentences in the notation.[19] We can then define a logical truth as a true sentence (of the notation) that remains true under all admissible reinterpretations of its nonlogical components. This definition is as clear as the notion of truth. When truth is defined disquotationally, any application of truth to a sentence is as clear as the sentence itself. So whether or not we care about codifying intersubjective rules for evaluating our assertions, we can each use Quine's method intrasubjectively to define a notion of logical truth that is as clear to us as the sentences of our own idiolects.

For Quine the "explanatory value" of a proposed characterization of a logical notion should be judged by its contribution to logical theory, whose task is to facilitate deduction and clarify our conceptual commitments. Quine's characterization of logical truth simplifies the theory and practice of deduction, and it clarifies our total theory of nature by enabling us to frame general truths that hold for all subjects. Thus whether or not we care about codifying intersubjective rules for evaluating our assertions, we are each in a position intrasubjectively to see that a definition of logical truth makes an important contribution to our own evolving theories of nature.

The burden of §§2–4 of "Two Dogmas of Empiricism" is to show that in contrast with logical truth, the notion of analyticity cannot be clarified or explained in purely logical terms. This is a direct challenge to Carnap's view that the notion of analyticity is available within pure logic,[20] independent of any special empirical investigations. Quine examines two strategies for clarifying or explaining analyticity in purely logical terms for sentences of languages we already use. The first strategy, discussed in §§2–3, is to give a purely logical clarification of the notion of *cognitive synonymy*. If we had such a clarification, we could clarify the "second class" of analytic truths as those sentences that become logical truths on substitution of synonyms for synonyms. The second strategy, discussed in §4, is to use the notion of a semantical rule to explicate analyticity. Carnap uses the second strategy, as Quine well knows. Quine's discussion of the first strategy is designed to prepare us for his rejection of the second strategy, and therewith of Carnap's explications of analyticity in terms of semantical rules.

In the next three sections I reconstruct Quine's critique of both of these strategies for characterizing analyticity in purely logical terms. I start (in §68) with Quine's criticisms of the first strategy, next turn (in §69) to Quine's rejection of the second strategy, focusing on Carnap's use of the notion of a semantical rule. I then continue my discussion of the second strategy (in §70) by examining Quine's objection to Carnap's idea that we can use "postulates" to determine primitive truths of a language system.

68. Definition and Interchangeability

Pursuing the first strategy, Quine considers attempts to clarify cognitive synonymy by the use of formal *definitions* (§2), and in terms of *interchangeability salve veritate* (§3). He argues that both attempts fail to clarify or explain cognitive synonymy in purely logical terms. Quine's arguments in §§2–3 leave open the possibility that we can clarify cognitive synonymy in psychological terms, perhaps using Quine's favored concept of a speech disposition. But even if we could clarify cognitive synonymy in terms of speech dispositions, this would not show that the notion of analyticity is part of logical theory, and so it would not vindicate Carnap's assumption that he can clarify the notion of analyticity without presupposing any concepts of an empirical science. With this in mind, let us now turn to Quine's arguments.

Consider the naive proposal that the cognitive synonymy of 'bachelor' and 'unmarried man' is based in a *definition*. Quine points out that although our dictionaries define 'bachelor' as 'unmarried man', the definition is actually a report on usage, and so it is not available independent of empirical observations: "The lexicographer is an empirical scientist, whose business is the recording of antecedent facts; and if he glosses 'bachelor' as 'unmarried man' it is because of his belief that there is a relation of synonymy between those forms, implicit in general or preferred usage prior to his own work."[21] Thus the definitions that appear in dictionaries do not show that the notion of cognitive synonymy can be explained solely in logical terms, without appeal to any special science.

A more sophisticated proposal is that within pure logic we can give *explications*—precise definitions of terms whose prior use was vague—and thereby avoid the charge that our definitions are mere reports of preexisting usage. But this proposal fares no better:

even explication, though not merely reporting a preexisting synonymy between definiendum and definiens, does rest nevertheless on *other* preexisting synonymies. The matter may be viewed as follows. Any word worth explicating has some contexts which, as wholes, are clear and precise enough to be useful; and the purpose of explication is to preserve the usage of these favored contexts while sharpening the usage of other contexts. In order that a given definition be suitable for purposes of explication, therefore, what is required is not that the definiendum in its antecedent usage be synonymous with the definiens, but just that each of these favored contexts of the definiendum, taken as a whole in its antecedent usage, be synonymous with the corresponding context of the definiens.[22]

Against this one might reply that all we require of an explication is that it further our present theoretical purposes, not that it preserve a preexisting synonymy relation. The trouble with this reply is that the only reason to adopt an explication is that it captures what is cognitively important to us about a preexisting usage.

Out of desperation one might insist that no understanding of what is cognitively important to us about a preexisting usage is needed for explication. But then one's purposes should be just as well served by mere definitional abbreviations of terms already in use. This is the third proposal Quine considers, and he finds it clear enough: "Here the definiendum becomes synonymous with the definiens simply because it has been created expressly for the purpose of being synonymous with the definiens. Here we have a really transparent case of synonymy created by definition; would that all species of synonymy were as intelligible."[23] Quine's point is that this is the only kind of definition that does not presuppose that we already understand cognitive synonymy. With this cryptic observation, he concludes that we cannot clarify or explain cognitive synonymy by giving definitions.

To test Quine's conclusion, suppose someone stipulates that by "cognitive synonymy" he just means the kinds of synonymies based in trivial definitional abbreviations for terms already in use. Can he then make sense of analyticity, as logical truth plus definitional abbreviations? In "Two Dogmas of Empiricism" Quine does not consider this question, but it is important to see that in his view the answer is "No." Even an *attenuated* notion of analyticity resists clarification in terms of logical truth plus definitional abbreviations. The reason is that a mere stipulation of a definitional abbreviation by itself does nothing to clarify the difference between a revision in our beliefs and a change in our language. To explicate this difference, as we have seen, Carnap relies on the notion of an explicit semantical rule. In Quine's view the acceptance of definitional abbreviations does not amount to the specification of semantical rules for the expressions thus defined, and so it cannot by itself bridge the gap between Quine's schematic characterization of logical truth and the positivists' idea of analyticity.[24]

In §3 of "Two Dogmas of Empiricism" Quine examines the proposal that two expressions of a language L are cognitively synonymous if in all their logically significant occurrences in sentences of L they are interchangeable *salve veritate*. Quine observes that to make this proposal precise one has to specify the language for which it is given. If the language contains a sentential operator that has the same meaning as the English word 'necessarily', then interchangeability *salve veritate* is sufficient for cognitive synonymy. The problem is that the word 'necessarily' is as much in need of clarification in logical terms as 'analytic'. So we make no real progress by assuming that we understand necessity and by defining cognitive synonymy in terms of interchangeability in all sentences *salve veritate*. If on the other hand we begin with an extensional language, then interchangeability *salve veritate* is not sufficient for cognitive synonymy. A proper characterization of cognitive synonymy should enable us to distinguish between synthetic truths and truths based in meaning alone, but so far we have seen no way to draw this distinction without presupposing that we understand necessity or cognitive synonymy itself.

In Quine's view, if we are to accept a notion as part of our logical theory, we must be able to show that it facilitates the theory and practice of deduction or clarifies our conceptual commitments. We saw earlier that Quine's characterization of logical truth passes this test, and we have recently seen why neither definition nor the criterion of interchangeability *salve veritate* can similarly vindicate analyticity. Worse than that, Quine's discussion of definition shows that analyticity is closely linked to our ordinary notion of cognitive synonymy, whose proper clarification awaits empirical investigations of preexisting usage. So by the end of Quine's discussions of the first two proposals we are still without any proper characterization of analyticity, and we have reason to suspect that there are serious obstacles to finding one.

69. Semantical Rules

In §4 of "Two Dogmas of Empiricism" Quine finally turns to an explicit discussion of Carnap's proposal that we clarify analyticity in terms of semantical rules. Quine's aim is to show that Carnap's talk of semantical rules and language systems makes no meaningful contribution to logical theory—that such talk is explanatorily empty. What drives Quine's criticisms is his view that the task of logical theory is to facilitate deduction and clarify our conceptual scheme.

Quine's criticisms of analyticity are a natural extension of his rejection of Carnap's view that logical truths are "true in virtue of rules." We saw (§65) that for Quine there is no explanatory value to reorganizing our body of logical truths by showing that they can be derived from a set of explicitly adopted axioms. Quine sees no explanatory value to Carnap's assumption that for each precisely characterized language there is a unique set of rules for using its expressions, and so Quine sees no point in saying that logical truths are "true in virtue of rules." His central criticism of the notion of analyticity is that there is no way to specify the analytic truths of a language without using the "scientifically meaningless" notion of a semantical rule. Quine concludes that unlike logical truth, analyticity makes no explanatory contribution to logical theory.

The essential dependence of Carnap's characterization of analyticity on his notion of a semantical rule is illustrated by Carnap's explication of analyticity in terms of state descriptions. We saw (§§55–56) that for Carnap a sentence is *L-true* if it is true in all state descriptions, where a *state description* for the language L_1 is a class that contains, for every atomic sentence (consisting of a predicate with a name in each of its argument places) of L_1, either that sentence or its negation, but not both. When state descriptions of a language L are characterized in this unrestricted syntactic way, Carnap's notion of *L-truth* is extensionally equivalent to what Quine calls logical truth.[25] Yet as we have seen, Carnap explicates analyticity in terms of *L-truth* by placing further restrictions on what counts as a state description. Carnap calls these restrictions "meaning postulates." From Quine's point of view, the trouble is that to make sense of "meaning postulates" we must assume with Carnap that for each precisely characterized language there is a unique set of semantical rules for using its expressions.

Quine begins §4 by assuming that we are each able to use sentences in an artificial notation, and he asks how we could clarify or explain Carnap's idea that some of these sentences are analytic. We could arbitrarily stipulate that a certain class of sentences of L are to be called "analytic." But this leaves us in the dark about the explanatory value, if any, of such a stipulation—we might as well just say that this is the class of sentences of kind K.

We know that "analytic" sentences are supposed to be true, so we can add this information to our understanding of K. Suppose then that we give a recursive specification of a set of true sentences of our language, and call them "K-truths." What is the explanatory value for logical theory of defining a set of K-truths? Once we have a Tarski-style truth definition for a language L, we can define arbitrary subsets of the true sentences of L. For example, we can define the set of true sentences of L that begin with the letter 'K'. This set of sentences obviously has no explanatory value for logical theory. Quine's question is how the set of "analytic" sentences is to be distinguished in point of explanatory value from the countless arbitrary sets of true sentences we could define.

According to Carnap, the difference between the "analytic" sentences of a language L and arbitrary sets of true sentences of L is that the former but not the latter are true "in virtue of the semantical rules of L." Thus the whole weight of his explication of analyticity rests on the notion of a semantical rule. From Quine's point of view, until we are given some clear explanation of how talk of "semantical rules" contributes to logical theory, we simply do not understand the difference between a set of sentences that are true "in virtue of semantical rules," on the one hand, and any arbitrary set of true sentences, such as those true sentences whose first letter is 'K', on the other. As Quine puts it: "Semantical rules are distinguishable, apparently, only by the fact of appearing on a page under the heading 'Semantical Rules'; and this heading is itself then meaningless."[26] We could paraphrase this as follows: "rules that specify the set K are distinguishable only by the fact of appearing on a page under the heading 'rules that specify the set K'; this heading is itself then just an indication that we have made an arbitrary selection of true sentences." Carnap's appeal to semantical rules does not show that sentences labeled "analytic" have any explanatory value. From an explanatory point of view, the heading 'Semantical Rules' is arbitrary, hence scientifically meaningless.

Carnap agrees that within pure semantics the question "What are the semantical rules of L?" makes no sense for languages whose semantical rules are not precisely specified. For Carnap, within pure logic the analytic-synthetic distinction can only be drawn for a language system with precisely formulated rules.[27] So from Carnap's point of view, Quine's objections to the application of the notion of semantical rules to languages whose semantical rules are not precisely specified are irrelevant to the question of whether the analytic-synthetic distinction can be precisely drawn within pure logic.

Quine was well aware that Carnap would make this reply. The central point of §4 is to try to show that Carnap's idea of a "language-system" is of no use in clarifying analyticity. In the third paragraph of §4 Quine writes: "It is often hinted that the difficulty in separating analytic statements from synthetic ones in ordinary language is due to the vagueness of ordinary language and that the distinction is clear when we have a precise artificial language with explicit 'semantical rules.' This, however, as I shall now attempt to show, is a confusion."[28] By the end of Quine's discussion of artificial languages without precisely formulated semantical rules, Quine takes himself to have shown that the very idea of a "semantical rule" is scientifically meaningless, even for what Carnap calls "language-systems." Quine argues that Carnap's stipulations that some rules are to count as the "semantical rules" of a language system L does no more than specify a particular set of true sentences of L. Mere stipulation that some subset of the true sentences of a language L are called "analytic" does not show that there is any explanatory value in distinguishing between the "analytic" sentences and other true sentences of L. So the claim that semantical rules are built into Carnap's idea of a language system does not tell us why the notion of analyticity is of any scientific interest.[29] Quine concludes that Carnap's specifications of language systems add no content to the idea of semantical rules, or of analyticity.

Early in §4 Quine characterizes his skeptical challenge to Carnap's notion of analyticity as follows: "The notion of analyticity about which we are worrying is a purported relation between statements and languages: a statement S is said to be *analytic for* a language L, and *the problem is to make sense of this relation generally, that is, for variable 'S' and 'L'.*"[30] Carnap replies that it is impossible to give a precise explication of analyticity for variable 'S' and 'L', but that in this respect analyticity is no worse off than other concepts used in logic.[31] As we have seen, Quine argues that Carnap's explications do not show that the concept of analyticity has any scientific interest. To explain the interest of the notion of analyticity, we would have to say what different definitions of 'S is analytic in L' have in common, for variable S and L. For Quine this is not a *general* condition on all definitions used in logic, but a consequence of our failure to understand the notion of a "semantical rule" on which Carnap's explications of analyticity depend.[32] Since according to Quine we do not understand the notion of a semantical rule, all we can glean from Carnap's explications is that a sentence S is analytic in L if and only if S is a member of some subset of true sentences of L, and this is not enough to show that the notion of analyticity has any explanatory value.

70. Postulates, Semantical Rules, and the Task of Logic

We have now seen that given Quine's view of the task of logic, Carnap's explications of analyticity are arbitrary and hence without logical interest. But do Quine's criticisms rest on an arbitrary definition of 'logic'? This question becomes especially pressing when Quine compares postulates with semantical rules.

> Relative to a given set of postulates, it is easy to say what a postulate is: it is a member of the set. Relative to a set of semantical rules, it is equally easy to say what a semantical rule is. But given simply a notation, mathematical or otherwise, and indeed as thoroughly understood a notation as you please in point of the translations or truth conditions for its statements, who can say which of its true statements rank as postulates? Obviously the question is meaningless—as meaningless as asking which points in Ohio are starting points.[33]

The contrast between Carnap's and Quine's views of the task of logic emerges clearly when Quine concedes that a choice of postulates can be of methodological significance, but insists that this does not show that a choice of postulates or semantical rules has any significance for logical theory:

> The word 'postulate' is significant only relative to an act of inquiry; we apply the word to a set of statements just in so far as we happen, for the year or the moment, to be thinking of those statements in relation to the statements which can be reached from them by some set of transformations to which we have seen fit to direct our attention. Now the notion of semantical rule is as sensible and meaningful as that of postulate, if conceived in a similarly relative spirit—relative, this time, to one or another particular enterprise of schooling unconversant persons in sufficient conditions for truth of statements of some natural or artificial language L. But from this point of view no one signalization of a subclass of the truths of L is intrinsically more a semantical rule than another; and, if 'analytic' means 'true by semantical rules', no one truth of L is analytic to the exclusion of another.[34]

Carnap would agree that independent of our interest in a precise codification of rules for evaluating our statements "no one signalization of a subclass of the truths of L is intrinsically more a semantical rule than another." But in Carnap's view, the task of logic is the codification of the methodology of the sciences. Relative to this task, our specification of semantical rules is as clear as our use of postulates in a given act of inquiry. Thus Carnap should reply that the selection of a particular set of semantical rules makes sense relative to his project of codifying the methodology of the sciences.

In the paragraph just quoted Quine concedes that the notion of a postulate makes sense relative to an act of inquiry. So why does Quine refuse to accept Carnap's use of semantical rules to codify the methodology of science?[35]

Part of the answer is that for Quine the task of logic is not to codify the methodology of science. Logic is itself a natural science, whose business is truth, not method. From Quine's point of view, Carnap has confused epistemology with logic. What Carnap takes to be part of logic makes no sense when viewed as an explanatory theory, and hence it is meaningless from a scientific point of view.

But this apparently leaves us at an impasse. Given Carnap's view that the task of logic is to codify rules for rational inquiry, he can agree with Quine that analyticity has no "explanatory value" for logical theory[36] without giving up the claim that analyticity is important to "logic," if that term encompasses the methodology of science. Quine must go beyond his preliminary arguments in "Two Dogmas of Empiricism" if he is to show that Carnap's idea of a codification of rules for inquiry makes no scientific sense.[37]

71. Indeterminacy and Carnap's Analytic-Synthetic Distinction

We saw (§64) that Quine's conception of the starting point and task of logic is of a piece with his scientific naturalism: "the recognition that it is within science itself, and not in some prior philosophy, that reality is to be identified and described."[38] Quine's arguments in §§1–4 of "Two Dogmas of Empiricism" show the consequences of Quine's scientific naturalism about logic. The reason that Carnap's idea of a codification of rules for inquiry makes no sense, according to Quine, is that from a naturalistic point of view Carnap's methodological perspective on science is unscientific.

Carnap maintains that the use of logical and mathematical techniques to construct precise languages for use in scientific work is itself part of science: it is the "logic of science," a part of logic, which is among the rigorous and clear sciences Carnap endorses. But Quine does not accept Carnap's logic of science as part of science. Quine sees Carnap's methodological conception of science as an illegitimate attempt to view science from a perspective higher and firmer than science.

In Quine's view, Carnap's unscientific methodological perspective on science must be replaced with naturalized epistemology. As we saw in Chapter Two, the motivating insight of naturalized epistemology is that "we can know external things only through impacts at our nerve endings."[39] Quine recasts epistemology by sketching a scientific picture of "evidence" and "theory" and the relationship between them. "Evidence" is described in terms of "impacts at our nerve endings," and "theory" in terms of the linguistic output that subjects deliver when prompted by triggerings of their neural receptors. Viewed naturalistically, a scientific theory is a fabric of sentences variously associated with one another and linked to impacts at our nerve endings by the mechanism of conditioned response.[40]

These links between sentences and impacts at our nerve endings exhaust the natural facts relevant to "cognitive meaning," and this leads to Quine's indeterminacy thesis, according to which the totality of speech dispositions does not uniquely determine how idiolects are to be "translated." To take another investigator's words at face value is (in effect) to "choose" a homophonic manual of translation for his words, but there are many radically different manuals that preserve all his speech dispositions. Translation manuals are not like scientific theories: in addition to being underdetermined by all evidence, they are also indeterminate.

From Quine's naturalistic point of view, this shows that Carnap's methodological perspective on science is unscientific. Within pure semantics, according to Carnap, investigators use the same words when they specify the "semantic rules" of a language. But the indeterminacy thesis shows that it is an illusion—mere "make-believe"[41]—to think that the "semantical rules" articulated from the perspective of Carnap's pure semantics are scientifically legitimate. By taking for granted the homophonic translation manuals for their "shared" metalanguages, the perspective of pure semantics creates the illusion of scientific objectivity. But since the assumption of a homophonic translation manual is arbitrary from a scientific point of view, the perspective of pure semantics is illegitimate. Carnap's explications of the analytic-synthetic distinction can be understood only from the perspective of pure semantics, where investigators must use the same same words when specifying "semantic rules" for using expressions of an object language. Like the perspective on which its explication depends, Carnap's analytic-synthetic distinction is arbitrary and unscientific.

72. Does Carnap Need a Criterion of Analyticity?

Quine's arguments in "Two Dogmas of Empiricism," together with naturalized epistemology and the indeterminacy thesis, show that from within Quine's naturalistic framework Carnap's analytic-synthetic distinction makes no sense. But Quine never succeeded in convincing Carnap that he should accept Quine's naturalistic framework. For Carnap pure semantics is part of the science of logic, and since he understands science from within pure semantics, he cannot make sense of Quine's naturalistic point of view. Thus on the reading I have presented, Quine does not show on Carnap's terms that the analytic-synthetic distinction makes no sense.

According to Thomas Ricketts, however, Quine's objections to Carnap's analytic-synthetic distinction undermine Carnap's position from within.[42] Ricketts reconstructs Quine's reasoning as follows:

> Quine's challenge to analyticity . . . begins with a concern about the applicability of th[is] notion to the theorizing of investigators, be they real scientists or idealized types thereof. *In order to judge the rationality of the theorizing of an investigator, we must be in a position to ascertain independently of such judgments what frameworks, what rules, the investigator has adopted. Unless we epistemic judges can apply this distinction, an investigator will always be able to escape criticism altogether by pleading he has been misunderstood.* We need then a criterion for attributing a linguistic framework to an investigator, what I shall call a *criterion of analyticity.* Without such a criterion, we have no bench from which to deliver our epistemic judgments, and so find ourselves caught in a position of epistemic solipsism destructive of the very ideal of rationality Carnap wants to articulate and vindicate.[43]

According to Ricketts, Quine's indeterminacy thesis shows that there can be no criterion of analyticity, and so Carnap's analytic-synthetic distinction cannot be drawn; "the mere acknowledgement" that Carnap must provide a criterion of analyticity "vitiates Carnap's conception of rational reconstruction."[44]

There are two ways of reconstructing Ricketts's reasons for asserting that Carnap must have a criterion of analyticity. On the most natural reconstruction, Ricketts reasons that investigators cannot evaluate each other's assertions until they first justify their assumption that they share a linguistic framework. This requires that they agree on a criterion by which they can find out whether they share a linguistic framework, and if so, which one.[45] I shall call this the *epistemological requirement.* Ricketts also seems to think that Carnap needs to show that an investigator's speech dispositions, austerely conceived, uniquely determine what semantical rules he is following, whether or not investigators are required to cite uninterpreted speech dispositions as "evidence" for their presupposition that they understand each other.[46] I shall call this the *metaphysical requirement.*

Ricketts does not clearly distinguish between these two requirements, but I will discuss them separately. As I see it, Carnap does not and should not accept either one.

Despite its air of plausibility, the epistemological requirement automatically leads to an infinite regress, without any help from Quine's arguments for indeterminacy. To see why, suppose A and B take for granted that they share a language, and propose a criterion of analyticity using this language. In order to justify their assumption that this "criterion" provides them with a "common bench before which to litigate their differences," they must find some independent justification for their initial assumption that they share the language they used to state the "criterion" itself. Thus if Ricketts's first challenge were legitimate, A and B would have to meet a second challenge. They would need to find a second criterion of analyticity for justifying their assumption that they understand the first criterion of analyticity in the same way. Suppose they seem to agree on a second criterion for understanding the first criterion. How can they be sure that they understand the second criterion in the same way? Presumably they must agree on a third criterion for understanding the second criterion for understanding the first criterion in the same way. And so on. We cannot avoid the regress by claiming that there is a stage at which A and B need not justify their assumption that they share a criterion of analyticity, for this would lead both A and B to "a position of epistemic solipsism destructive of the very ideal of rationality Carnap wants to articulate and vindicate."[47]

Carnap does not and should not accept any requirement that leads automatically to an infinite regress. As we saw at length in Chapter Four, Carnap has a pragmatic attitude toward the languages investigators use to codify rules for rational inquiry. In practice there is no need for an epistemological criterion of analyticity; it is enough that investigators use a common language whose words they find clear.

Ricketts might reply that Carnap needs to show that an investigator's speech dispositions uniquely determine what semantical rules he is following. This would not automatically lead to an infinite regress, since A's and B's speech dispositions might uniquely determine that they share a linguistic framework whether or not they could *justify* this to each other. If Carnap accepts this requirement, then Quine's indeterminacy thesis would directly challenge Carnap's conception of pure semantics and the analytic-synthetic distinction.

But Carnap does not accept Ricketts's metaphysical requirement either. As we saw in §§57–60, Carnap has a coherent defense of the claim that pure semantics makes no presuppositions about how linguistic behaviors are related to semantical rules. He says that pure semantics is related to descriptive semantics just as pure geometry is related to applied geometry. This means that an investigator's speech dispositions do not by themselves uniquely determine what semantical rules he is following. To describe the relationship between speech dispositions and semantical rules, we must first choose an appropriate set of coordinative definitions. For Carnap pure semantics is a science in its own right, not in need of any independent scientific or metaphysical support.

I conclude that Carnap does not need a criterion of analyticity to vindicate pure semantics and the analytic-synthetic distinction. Ricketts's epistemological and metaphysical "requirements" both rest on a misunderstanding of Carnap's project, and so Ricketts fails to show that Quine's arguments undermine Carnap's view of rational inquiry from within.

73. Holism and the Analytic-Synthetic Distinction

So far I have focused on §§1–4 of "Two Dogmas of Empiricism." But Christopher Hookway thinks Quine's central argument against Carnap's analytic-synthetic distinction occurs in §5 of "Two Dogmas of Empiricism," where Quine observes that "our statements about the external world face the tribunal of sense experience not individually but only as a corporate body."[48] In Hookway's view, this observation contains the seeds of a powerful objection to Carnap's analytic-synthetic distinction.

Hookway claims that Carnap introduced the analytic-synthetic distinction "to explain why scientists agree about the bearing of observations and experiments upon their hypotheses."[49] The basic idea is that "shared rules determine which experiences refute, and which confirm, the claims made by scientists."[50] Statements whose truth values are determined solely by the rules are analytic or contradictory, whereas statements whose truth values also depend on evidence are synthetic.

The main difficulty for Carnap's analytic-synthetic distinction, according to Hookway, is that a scientific hypothesis is never tested in isolation. In 1906 Pierre Duhem noted that if a given hypothesis, in conjunction with our total theory of nature, entails an observation sentence that is apparently in conflict with our experience, this does not tell us which theoretical or observational beliefs to revise.[51] Carnap believed he could accommodate Duhem's thesis by distinguishing

> between two kinds of readjustment in the case of a conflict with experience, namely, between a change in the language, and mere change in, or addition of, a truth-value ascribed to an indeterminate statement, (i.e. a statement whose truth-value is not fixed by the rules of language, say by the postulates of logic, mathematics, and physics). A change of the first kind constitutes a radical alteration, sometimes a revolution, and it occurs only at historically decisive points in the development of science. On the other hand, changes of the second kind occur every minute.[52]

There are no rules for making changes of the first kind, since these changes involve conventional choices of rules for a new language, and only pragmatic considerations can be relevant to such choices. In contrast, changes in the truth value ascribed to an indeterminate or synthetic sentence are governed by the semantical rules of the framework. So, in Carnap's view, Duhem's thesis amounts to the observation that in case of a conflict with experience, we are free to change our linguistic framework, or to change our ascription of truth values to some of our synthetic statements. Properly understood, Duhem's thesis does not undermine the analytic-synthetic distinction.

Against this, Hookway argues that if we accept Duhem's thesis, Carnap's analytic-synthetic distinction "loses its explanatory force."[53] Hookway assumes that if Carnap's analytic-synthetic distinction is to have explanatory force, we must be able to distinguish between two kinds of "mechanisms" of belief revision, corresponding to Carnap's distinction between pragmatic changes in language systems and the reevaluation of truth values from within a language system: "Experience can prompt changes in our body of beliefs: systematic considerations of simplicity and fruitfulness have a role in deciding how to make these adjustments. There simply seems no basis for discerning two different mechanisms. The puzzle is less why Quine made this move than why Carnap didn't."[54] Hookway concludes that we must give up Carnap's analytic-synthetic distinction, since "there is nothing for the distinction of two different mechanisms to explain."[55]

There are several problems with this reconstruction of Quine's reasons for rejecting Carnap's analytic-synthetic distinction. The first and most serious problem is that Carnap did not introduce the analytic-synthetic distinction to provide a psychological or mechanistic explanation of "why scientists agree about the bearing of observations and experiments upon their hypotheses." As we have seen at length, the analytic-synthetic distinction is part of pure semantics, and hence independent of any empirical assumptions. Once this distinction is drawn, we can introduce coordinative definitions relative to which we can describe an investigator's sentences as analytic or synthetic. But Carnap does not assume that such descriptions posit the existence of rule-following "mechanisms" that determine an investigator's linguistic behavior. It is better to think of descriptive semantics as licensing redescriptions of a speaker's linguistic behavior in terms of semantical rules. For Carnap there is no further question of what "really" underlies a speaker's use of one language system rather than another. We understand all there is to this idea when we adopt coordinative definitions that give empirical content to the claims of descriptive semantics.

The second problem is that Carnap does not think that we must define the analytic-synthetic distinction directly in terms of sensory experience. For Carnap there can be no analytic-synthetic distinction at all unless we first specify, from within pure semantics, the rules of the language system we intend to use. These rules determine which sentences of the language system are synthetic, and how these sentences are to be evaluated in light of empirical evidence. In Carnap's view, Duhem's thesis amounts to the observation that it is only in conjunction with our substantive beliefs that the rules of the language system we are using tell us what the empirical consequences of a given statement are. Carnap uses the analytic-synthetic distinction to *clarify* Duhem's thesis, and this shows that for Carnap the analytic-synthetic distinction is more fundamental than the question of whether scientific statements can be tested in isolation.

This second problem is linked with a third: Hookway misunderstands the role of Quine's argument in §5 of "Two Dogmas of Empiricism." Quine understood Carnap's views well enough to know that the points in §5 would not directly engage Carnap. As I see it, Quine's aim in §5 was to show that if we do not *already* have a clarification of the analytic-synthetic distinction from within pure logic or semantics, we cannot define the distinction in experiential terms. Carnap would surely agree with this. Yet from Carnap's point of view, Quine's argument in §5 is beside the main point, which is whether the notion of a semantical rule is a purely logical one. For Carnap the central arguments in "Two Dogmas of Empiricism" are in §4, where Quine attempts to show that the notion of a semantical rule is scientifically meaningless. Taken by itself, Quine's observation in §5 that there is a holism of theory testing does not challenge Carnap's analytic-synthetic distinction.[56]

74. Carnap's Method versus Quine's Doctrine

In §§62–70 I explained why none of Quine's arguments in §§1–4 of "Two Dogmas of Empiricism" shows that we cannot use the notion of a semantical rule to codify rules for inquiry. To establish this strong conclusion, given his own starting point, Quine needs to show that the very idea of a codification of rules for inquiry is scientifically meaningless. For this he needs his indeterminacy thesis. But Quine's indeterminacy thesis does not undermine Carnap's position from within; instead it shows that Quine's scientific naturalism is fundamentally at odds with Carnap's conception of the starting point and task of philosophy. Whereas Carnap takes for granted that in the context of constructing language systems investigators use shared metalanguages to specify intersubjectively binding semantical rules, for Quine the perspective of investigators who take themselves to "share" language lies outside of natural science, and so the notion of an "intersubjectively binding semantical rule" that Carnap defines from this perspective is unscientific and illusory.

This clash of alternative points of view is reflected in Carnap's and Quine's contrasting views of the relationship between semantical descriptions of a speaker's utterances, on the one hand, and her speech dispositions, on the other. For Carnap, as we have seen (§§57–59), the relationship is mediated by our choice of coordinative definitions that relate concepts of pure semantics to linguistic behaviors. Carnap can agree with Quine that nothing determines which coordinative definitions we must use for descriptive semantics. But Carnap thinks we can use the methods of pure semantics to specify coordinative definitions that give empirical content to the claims of descriptive semantics. Carnap's conception of descriptive semantics is untouched by Quine's reflections about radical translation.

Quine's scientific naturalism fosters a fundamentally different view of what is objective about meaning. For Quine the cognitive content of a speaker's idiolect is exhausted by her dispositions to assent to and dissent from sentences under various prompting stimulations. The only objective constraint on a "translation" of one speaker's idiolect, or "theory," into another's, or even into itself, is that it "preserve the totality of speech dispositions."[57] According to Quine's indeterminacy thesis, there are many translation manuals that "preserve" the total pattern of associations between sentences and sensory stimulation, and hence capture the "empirical content" of sentences equally well. When two speakers of the same natural language use a homophonic manual of translation between their idiolects, they are in effect "choosing" one manual over countless others that would also "preserve" the total pattern of associations between their sentences and sensory stimulations.

In Quine's view the only transparent semantical notions are disquotational. We are each in a position to use disquotational paradigms to ascribe truth or reference to the sentences and predicates of our own idiolect, if we "choose" the homophonic mapping from our idiolect onto itself. It is only for our own idiolects that we can take the homophonic manual for granted without danger of empirical error, and use disquotational truth and reference. All ascriptions of truth or reference to another speaker's words rest on "hypotheses" about how to "translate" her idiolect, even if we both speak the "same" ordinary language, such as English. For Quine each individual has her own language, or idiolect, and what we ordinarily call "language," such as English or French, is a more or less loose association of idiolects linked together by entrenched but scientifically arbitrary assumptions about how to "translate" between them.

In contrast, the "ultimate parameter" for Carnap's methodological conception of science is set by our use of a common metalanguage to specify syntactical and semantical rules for the proper use of linguistic expressions. Since for Carnap our only understanding of scientific content and method is given by our specifications of semantical rules for using expressions of a shared language, empirical discoveries cannot challenge the scientific utility and clarity of the notion of a semantical rule.

These fundamentally opposed views of language and semantics reflect Carnap's and Quine's different conceptions of the starting point and task of philosophy. Carnap's perspective is pragmatic and methodological: he aims to clarify and thereby help to resolve the agreements and disagreements of practicing scientists. Quine's perspective is naturalistic and doctrinal: all there is to science is explanation and prediction. Since for Quine the notion of a semantical rule has no explanatory or predictive value, Quine concludes that Carnap's analytic-synthetic distinction is scientifically meaningless.

Ultimately, Quine's "argument" against Carnap's analytic-synthetic distinction is that we must reject Carnap's conception of the starting point and task of philosophy, and replace it with scientific naturalism. Quine's impressive rhetoric, combined with what seems to be a blindness to Carnap's point of view, gives his "argument" the flavor of a demonstration that Carnap is wrong. But we can now see why Carnap was always puzzled by Quine's insistence that pure semantics makes no sense: it is impossible to state Quine's objections to Carnap's analytic-synthetic distinction in Carnap's own terms.

S I X

Putnam's Reasons for Rejecting Carnap's Analytic-Synthetic Distinction

75. Putnam and the Participant Perspective

In this chapter I recast Putnam's central arguments in "The Analytic and the Synthetic"[1] as criticisms of Carnap's analytic-synthetic distinction. On my reconstruction, Putnam starts by taking our linguistic practices at face value; using examples from the history of science, and sketching new ways of thinking about belief and reference, Putnam shows that the analytic-synthetic distinction prevents us from properly describing our linguistic practices.

My reconstruction highlights fundamental differences between Putnam's and Quine's reasons for rejecting the analytic-synthetic distinction. As I see it, Putnam's conception of the starting point and task of philosophy is fundamentally at odds with Quine's scientific naturalism and indeterminacy thesis. Working from Putnam's starting point, I explain why Quine's scientific naturalism prevents us from properly describing our linguistic practices. If we start by taking at face value our actual practices of agreeing, disagreeing, evaluating assertions, and resolving disputes, and we gradually remove obstacles to our understanding of these practices, we may eventually overcome the attractions of entrenched frameworks from which our participant perspective looks philosophically unimportant. My aim in this chapter is to begin this gradual process.

76. The Roots and Strategy of Putnam's Arguments

Before we look at details, it will help to discuss the roots and strategy of Putnam's arguments against the analytic-synthetic distinction.

We saw in Chapter Four that Carnap designed his analytic-synthetic distinction to solve the positivists' problem of reconciling our knowledge of logic and mathematics with empiricism (§51). Carnap's "solution" to the positivists' problem was shaped by his "motivating insight" that if investigators are to agree or disagree at all, they must share precise rules for evaluating their assertions. Once the rules for a language L are precisely specified, the truth values of some of the sentences of L may be deduced from the rules alone, whereas the truth values of the other sentences of L can be discovered only through empirical investigation. The former sentences are either analytic or contradictory, and the latter are synthetic. Carnap proposed that we view logical and mathematical truths as among the analytic or contradictory sentences of language systems we are free to adopt. Since the truth values of analytic and contradictory sentences of a language can be deduced from the rules of that language, we can evaluate such sentences without appeal to empirical evidence or a special faculty of pure reason.

In this "solution" of the positivists' problem, Carnap took for granted that if the truth of a sentence S can be deduced from the rules for L, it is reasonable to accept S without any empirical evidence, and to hold S immune from disconfirmation by all empirical evidence. In Carnap's view, investigators are free to adopt any rules they like, and thereby to commit themselves to accepting without evidence any statement whose truth can be deduced from those rules. Once we have adopted a set of rules for a language system L in which the truth of a given sentence S may be deduced without appeal to any evidence, to know that S is true is just to see that S follows from the rules of L.

Unlike Quine, Putnam does not directly question this aspect of Carnap's "solution" to the positivists' problem. Putnam finds the notion of a semantical rule for an artificial language unproblematic, and he accepts that if we specify rules for using the expressions of a language L, some of the sentences of L may be said to be true in virtue of those rules.[2]

Putnam's central arguments in "The Analytic and the Synthetic" may be seen as criticisms of Carnap's view that if a sentence of a language L is not true in virtue of the rules of L, then it is *synthetic*—true or false in virtue of "empirical" observations. To understand this aspect of Carnap's analytic-synthetic distinction, it is important to keep in mind that for Carnap there is no conception of empirical evidence apart from a precise statement of the rules for using sentences of a language system. The reason is that Carnap's "motivating insight"—that if investigators are to agree or disagree they must share precise rules for evaluating their assertions—together with his proposals for codifying rules of language systems, determines what counts in any given language system as "empirical" confirmation or disconfirmation. So built into Carnap's "solution" to the positivists' problem is the principle that if a sentence is not true in virtue of rules, then its truth or falsity *must* be open to "empirical" confirmation or disconfirmation. In other words, in Carnap's view *it is reasonable to hold a sentence S of language L immune from disconfirmation by all empirical evidence only if S is true in virtue of the rules for L.* I call this *Carnap's empiricist principle.*

To challenge Carnap's empiricist principle, Putnam exhibits false sentences that physicists at one time held immune from disconfirmation by all empirical evidence. These sentences are not analytic, since they are false, nor should they be understood as synthetic in Carnap's sense, since reasonable investigators held them immune from empirical disconfirmation. Putnam's examples apparently undermine Carnap's empiricist principle: we must either give up this principle, or redescribe Putnam's examples.

As we will see, however, Putnam's descriptions of his examples are compelling enough to raise serious questions about Carnap's analytic-synthetic distinction. The reason is that the descriptions are rooted in our perspective as participants in ongoing ordinary and scientific inquiries. From the participant perspective, we take at face value our actual practices of agreeing, disagreeing, evaluating assertions, and resolving disputes. If we take seriously this participant point of view, we may agree with Putnam that the most important task for philosophy is to remove obstacles to the proper description of these practices.[3] We are then in position to see the force of Putnam's claim that the positivists' analytic-synthetic distinction should be rejected because it prevents us from attaining a clear view of our inquiries.[4]

From Carnap's point of view, of course, Putnam's purported counterexamples to the empiricist principle look unconvincing. To remain faithful to the "motivating insight" that if investigators are to agree or disagree they must share precise rules for evaluating their assertions, Carnap would reject Putnam's descriptions of our everyday and scientific inquiries.

But anyone who is not dogmatically committed to Carnap's "motivating insight" should be convinced by Putnam's counterexamples. I agree with Putnam that one important goal of philosophy is to remove obstacles to our understanding of our actual practices of agreeing, disagreeing, evaluating assertions, and resolving disputes. In my view, Putnam's counterexamples and descriptions show that Carnap's analytic-synthetic distinction prevents us from properly describing these practices. Once we appreciate these points, Carnap's analytic-synthetic distinction loses whatever initial appeal it may have had for us.

77. Changes in Belief versus Changes in Reference

In "The Analytic and the Synthetic" Putnam discusses a number of examples that challenge Carnap's empiricist principle. I will focus on Putnam's discussion of the methodological role of definitions of energy in pre-relativistic and relativistic physics.

Putnam observes that before Einstein '$e = \frac{1}{2}mv^2$', the pre-relativistic equation for kinetic energy, might have seemed true by definition:

> Certainly, before Einstein, any physicist might have said, "'$e = \frac{1}{2}mv^2$', that is just the definition of 'kinetic energy'. There is no more to it than that. The expression 'kinetic energy' is, as it were, a sort of abbreviation for the longer expression 'one-half the mass times the velocity squared'."[5]

Let us now briefly consider how Carnap might reconstruct the methodological role of '$e = \frac{1}{2}mv^2$' in pre-relativistic physics. The equation '$e = \frac{1}{2}mv^2$' is expressed in the language of physics, which Carnap would count as a "natural" language, since the rules for the correct use of its expressions are not explicitly stated in one of his formalized language systems. To reconstruct the methodological role of $'e = \frac{1}{2}mv^2{}'$ we must then specify precise semantical rules for using $'e = \frac{1}{2}mv^2{}'$, together with coordinative definitions that correlate the semantical rules with the linguistic behaviors of the physicists who accepted $'e = \frac{1}{2}mv^2{}'$. The description of the methodological role of the equation rests on coordinative definitions, and so more than one reconstruction is compatible with all the physicists' speech behaviors. But since we would naturally say that the physicists treated the equation as immune from disconfirmation, the obvious choice would be to describe the equation as a *definition* of the term 'e' (or as a logical consequence of other definitions). This could be done by treating $'e = \frac{1}{2}mv^2{}'$ as a postulate of the language system in which the reconstruction is given. Relative to this reconstruction $'e = \frac{1}{2}mv^2{}'$ is true in virtue of the rules of the language system.

Putnam notes that to accommodate Einstein's principle that all physical laws must be Lorentz-invariant a different equation was required: "Einstein ... changed the definition of kinetic energy. That is to say, he replaced the law $'e = \frac{1}{2}mv^2{}'$ by a more complicated law. If we expand the Einstein definition of energy as a power series, the first two terms are $'e = mc^2 + \frac{1}{2}\ mv^2 + \ldots'$."[6] Since physicists now treat this equation as immune from disconfirmation, the obvious choice for Carnap would be to describe the new equation as a new definition of the term 'e' (or as a logical consequence of other new definitions). On this reconstruction $'e = mc^2 + \frac{1}{2}\ mv^2 + \ldots'$ is also true in virtue of the rules of the language.

Putnam argues that if we view these two equations as true in virtue of the rules of the language, we will misunderstand the actual role of the term *energy* in the language of physics as we use it. He observes that "whatever the status of the energy definition may have been before Einstein, in revising it, *Einstein treated it as just another natural law*. . . . Among the equations that had to be revised . . . was the equation $'e = \frac{1}{2}mv^2{}'$."[7] To see the the equation $'e = \frac{1}{2}mv^2{}'$ as just another natural law is to see that the scientists who revised $'e = \frac{1}{2}mv^2{}'$ *disagree* with those who accepted it. From within the evolving language of physics, this change in belief is signaled by a change in the equation for 'e', and by the continued use of the same term 'e' to refer to *energy*.

Putnam's central objection, then, is that if we accept Carnap's analytic-synthetic distinction, we will not see that the scientists who accept the relativistic equation disagree with those who accepted the earlier one. The problem may be traced to Carnap's empiricist principle that it is reasonable to hold a sentence S immune from disconfirmation by all empirical evidence only if S is true in virtue of the rules for L. Since prior to Einstein it was reasonable to hold '$e = \frac{1}{2}mv^2$' immune from disconfirmation by all empirical evidence, Carnap's empiricist principle leads him to view the equation as true in virtue of the rules. For the same reason, he will also view the relativistic equation as true in virtue of the rules. But an unblinkered look at our use of these two equations shows that they make conflicting claims about *energy*. We must therefore reject Carnap's empiricist principle, and with it the analytic-synthetic distinction from which it stems: "to speak of Einstein's contribution as a redefinition of kinetic energy is to assimilate what actually happened to a wholly false model."[8]

78. Law-cluster Concepts and Terms

To make sense of the actual evolution of our theories of kinetic energy, Putnam reminds us that it is natural to see 'e' as referring to the same quantity in both '$e = \frac{1}{2}mv^2$' and '$e = mc^2 + \frac{1}{2}mv^2 + \ldots$'. To remind us of this familiar aspect of our linguistic practices, Putnam offers the following sketch of a commonsense alternative to Carnap's view of the role of the term 'e': "The extension of the term 'kinetic energy' has not changed. If it had, the extension of the term 'energy' would have to have changed. But the extension of the term 'energy' has not changed. The forms of energy and their behavior are the same as they always were, and they are what physicists talked about before and after Einstein."[9] To help make sense of this alternative Putnam introduces the notion of a "law-cluster concept."[10]

Law-cluster concepts are expressed by law-cluster terms. Such terms occur in statements of many different scientific laws, any of which may be given up without changing the concept expressed by that term. Once we view 'e' as a law-cluster term, we can accept that the reference of the term 'e' did not change when the old equation was given up, and we can view our acceptance of the new relativistic definition of energy as reflecting a change in our beliefs about energy.[11] This new model of the semantic role of terms like 'e' helps us to see that those who accept the relativistic energy equation disagree with those who accepted the earlier one.

79. Framework Principles and the Contextually A Priori

If we accept Putnam's description of the role of terms like 'e', we can no longer view '$e = \frac{1}{2}mv^2$' as true in virtue of rules, and so we can no longer accept Carnap's account of why it was reasonable for physicists to hold '$e = \frac{1}{2}mv^2$' immune from empirical disconfirmation. Putnam's alternative is rooted in his descriptions of our actual practices of evaluating and revising beliefs. By reminding us of how physicists respond to empirically wrong answers and false predictions, Putnam tries to persuade us that it was reasonable for physicists to hold '$e = \frac{1}{2}mv^2$' immune from empirical disconfirmation because they did not know of a plausible alternative.

Putnam takes for granted that we have no grasp on what is reasonable or unreasonable apart from our actual practices of evaluating and revising beliefs. So to support his alternative to Carnap's views about what is reasonable or unreasonable, Putnam reminds us of what we actually say and do in response to unexpected observations. He observes that

> if a physicist makes a calculation and gets an empirically wrong answer, he does not suspect that the mathematical principles used in the calculation may have been wrong (assuming that those principles are themselves theorems of mathematics) nor does he suspect that the law '$f = ma$' may be wrong. Similarly, he did not frequently suspect before Einstein that the law '$e = \frac{1}{2}mv^2$' might be wrong ... These statements, then, have a kind of preferred status. They can be overthrown, but not by an isolated experiment. They can be overthrown only if someone incorporates principles incompatible with those statements in a successful conceptual system.[12]

Here Putnam describes how physicists *actually* revise their beliefs, and hints at a way of making sense of these revisions. He observes that a physicist does not revise his mathematical theorems when he "makes a calculation and gets an empirically wrong answer." In Putnam's view, this shows that it is reasonable in those circumstances to hold the theorems immune from disconfirmation. Similarly, if a physicist knows of no plausible alternatives to '$e = \frac{1}{2}mv^{2}$' he will not reject it even if he gets a false prediction from the theory that contains it. In Putnam's view this is enough to show that it is reasonable in these circumstances to continue accepting '$e = \frac{1}{2}mv^{2}$' despite a false prediction.

This deflationary view of when it was reasonable for physicists to hold '$e = \frac{1}{2}mv^{2}$' immune from empirical disconfirmation may be extended to hold for what Putnam calls "framework principles":

> there are many, many principles—we might broadly classify them as 'framework principles'—which have the characteristic of being so central that they are employed as auxiliaries to make predictions in an overwhelming number of experiments, without themselves being jeopardized by any possible experimental results. This is the classical role of the laws of logic; but it is equally the role of certain physical principles, e.g. '$f = ma$', and ... the law '$e = \frac{1}{2}mv^{2}$', at the time when those laws were still accepted.[13]

By reminding us of how physicists respond to empirical results, Putnam aims to persuade us that it is reasonable to hold framework principles immune from empirical disconfirmation.

We can summarize these points by saying that framework principles are *contextually a priori* and *revisable*. To say that a statement S is contextually a priori is to say that S is "necessary relative to a body of knowledge": "when we say that a statement is necessary relative to a body of knowledge, we imply that it is included in that body of knowledge and that it enjoys a special role in that body of knowledge. For example, one is not expected to give much of a reason for that kind of statement. But we do not imply that the statement is necessarily *true*, although, of course, it is thought to be true by someone whose knowledge that body of knowledge is."[14] In Putnam's view, if S is contextually a priori it is reasonable to hold S immune from disconfirmation even if S is not analytic.

80. An Objection from Carnap's Point of View

As a step toward further clarification of Putnam's alternative, let us consider an objection from Carnap's point of view. We saw in Chapter Four that for Carnap there is no conception of "empirical evidence" apart from a precise statement of the rules for using sentences of a language system, and that this reflects Carnap's "motivating insight" that investigators can agree or disagree only if they share rules for evaluating their assertions. Taking Carnap's "motivating insight" for granted, I'll develop an objection on Carnap's behalf to Putnam's description of the methodological status of $'e = \frac{1}{2}mv^2{}'$. The objection amounts to an argument for the following claim: *if we accept Putnam's description of the methodological status of $'e = \frac{1}{2}mv^2{}'$, then two investigators might disagree about whether $'e = \frac{1}{2}mv^2{}'$ is true even though they do not agree about how to settle their dispute.* Given the "motivating insight," this claim reduces Putnam's position to absurdity in Carnap's eyes.

To see the source of the argument, recall that according to Putnam it was reasonable for physicists to hold $'e = \frac{1}{2}mv^2{}'$ immune from disconfirmation because they did not know of any plausible alternative. Built into this historical example is the fact that physicists now agree that relativistic physics is more plausible than pre-relativistic physics, and so they accept the relativistic energy equation and reject $'e = \frac{1}{2}mv^2{}'$. The objection I have in mind is based in the thought that on Putnam's view this agreement seems to be just an accident of history. For all Putnam says, it seems that there could be two investigators who disagree about which of these alternative theories is more plausible, and who therefore disagree about $'e = \frac{1}{2}mv^2{}'$, even though they do not agree about how to settle their dispute.

To illustrate this possibility, suppose that investigator A finds pre-relativistic physics more reasonable than relativistic physics, and investigator B takes the opposing view. They reach conflicting verdicts on the sentence $'e = \frac{1}{2}mv^2{}'$: A affirms it, and B rejects it. Suppose also that A and B know that their disagreement is not due to a mistake in deductive reasoning, or to a disagreement about any empirical observation. For instance, A agrees with B that if relativistic physics is true, then $'e = \frac{1}{2}mv^2{}'$ is false, and B agrees that if pre-relativistic physics is true, then $'e = \frac{1}{2}mv^2{}'$ is true. They realize that their disagreement comes down to a dispute about which physical theory it is more reasonable to accept. But they do not agree about how to resolve this dispute. Putnam's picture commits us to accepting that under these circumstances A and B genuinely *disagree* about whether $'e = \frac{1}{2}mv^2{}'$ is true.

For Carnap this is unacceptable. If under these circumstances A and B assume that they disagree, each will *feel* he is right, even though he knows that the other does not agree with him about how to settle the dispute. As we saw in Chapter Four, this is exactly the kind of situation Carnap deplores, both in traditional metaphysics and in contemporary debates in the foundations of mathematics. In his view, to suppose that there are "disagreements" of this kind leads to obscurity and confusion. His "motivating insight" is that investigators can disagree with each other only if they share rules for *settling* their disagreement. From the start Carnap rejects the *very idea* of "disagreements" between investigators who do not agree about how to decide whether their assertions are true or false.

We may sum up what I shall call *Carnap's objection* as follows: Putnam's picture is unacceptable because it allows for the possibility of intersubjectively irresolvable disagreements between investigators.

81. A Reply from Putnam's Point of View

There is no neutral position from which to evaluate this objection. From Putnam's point of view, Carnap's "motivating insight" keeps Carnap from seeing that investigators can disagree even if they do not share precise rules for settling their disagreement. If we accept Putnam's starting point and his view of the task of philosophy, we will conclude that Carnap's central mistake is to decide in advance what can count as agreement and disagreement.

Properly viewed, Putnam's kinetic energy example shows that *we often commit ourselves to the outcome of investigations into the truth of a given sentence S even when we don't know of any precise rules for discovering the truth value of S*. To appreciate this aspect of our actual practices of agreeing and disagreeing, we must take seriously the evolution of our beliefs as a result of investigations that extend over time; we must take a *diachronic* view of inquiry, not merely a *synchronic* one. Carnap's synchronic view of inquiry supports his motivating insight that investigators can agree or disagree only if they share precise rules for evaluating their assertions. All changes in our procedures for evaluating statements are then seen as merely pragmatic, and considered irrelevant to the reconstruction of how our statements are evaluated. From this synchronic point of view, Carnap can't see the shared commitments that are expressed in our continuing participation in an evolving inquiry over a long stretch of time.

In our illustration of Carnap's objection, we supposed that A and B disagree about whether it is reasonable to accept $'e = \frac{1}{2}mv^2'$, even though they agree that if relativistic physics is true, then $'e = \frac{1}{2}mv^2'$ is false. Since A knows of the relativistic alternative, it is not reasonable for A to dismiss B's reasons for rejecting $'e = \frac{1}{2}mv^2'$. Nevertheless A is not *convinced* that B's alternative is more plausible, nor is B convinced that A's alternative is more plausible. Carnap assumes that in such a situation A's and B's dispute will always degenerate into pointless bickering.

But Carnap overlooks the possibility that through discussion and further inquiry, A may *persuade* B or vice versa. As a result of ongoing discussion and inquiry, our beliefs often evolve in unexpected ways. Since Putnam views our inquiries diachronically, he sees such changes in belief as rational, not merely pragmatic.[15]

Naturally, Putnam's diachronic picture of shared commitments can't rule out sheer *stubbornness*. An investigator may insist on accepting a given statement even after hearing a very convincing case for giving it up. If he is unable to give any reasons for not rejecting the disputed statement, his stubbornness becomes an obstacle to further inquiry. If his stubbornness survives all criticism, it will effectively isolate him from other investigators. In some rare and extreme cases we would no longer say that he disagrees with the other investigators. This is the grain of truth behind Carnap's objection.

There is of course a difference between being merely stubborn and having the courage of one's convictions. An authoritative and unyielding personality may persuade others of his views by claiming the high ground, and refusing to take their alternatives seriously. But to remain persuasive an investigator must be open to other points of view; he will not remain persuasive for long if he dogmatically refuses to reevaluate his views.

Simply put, the answer to Carnap's objection is that despite his "motivating insight," we often disagree about the truth value of a given statement even when we don't agree on precise rules for settling our dispute.

82. Analyticity and One-Criterion Words

Despite these arguments against Carnap's empiricist principle and motivating insight, Putnam thinks there are analytic sentences in natural languages. He starts with a paradigm example of an "analytic" sentence—'Bachelors are unmarried men'—and offers a "rationale" for saying that such sentences are analytic.[16] His rationale is that the subject terms of analytic sentences are "one-criterion words," not law-cluster terms: since analytic sentences contain no law-cluster terms, we can't give them up without changing the subject. For example, the word 'bachelor' is true of x if and only if x is an unmarried human adult male. In fact there is no other criterion for being a bachelor, and so if we give up this criterion, we change the meaning of 'bachelor'.

From this description it might seem that unlike framework principles such statements as *Bachelors are unmarried men* could serve as paradigms of knowledge based solely on meaning, independent of any substantive "empirical" beliefs. These paradigms could then help us to "solve" the positivists' problem of reconciling our knowledge of logic and mathematics with empiricism. In Putnam's view, however, when we judge that 'Bachelors are unmarried men' is analytic, we take for granted that there are no *laws* about bachelors, and that 'bachelor' is a one-criterion word. So ordinary "analytic" statements like *Bachelors are unmarried men* are not paradigms of belief based solely on meaning. Like framework principles, these ordinary "analytic" statements also provide counterexamples to Carnap's empiricist principle that it is reasonable to hold a sentence S immune from disconfirmation only if S is true in virtue of the rules for L, independent of any substantive "empirical" beliefs.

In Putnam's view, we have good reason to believe, for example, that 'bachelor' is a one-criterion word, and that the sentence 'Bachelors are unmarried men' is an "analytic definition." But these beliefs goes beyond the positivists' picture of truths based on meaning, independent of "empirical" fact. For instance, we can imagine that unknown to us there are empirical laws about bachelors, currently under investigation by an obscure group of experimental psychologists. If this seems too implausible, we can also imagine a possible future in which psychologists discover such laws.[17] In this imagined future, philosophers familiar with

Putnam's distinction between one-criterion and law-cluster terms would say, "Just as physicists used to think that the kinetic energy definition was true by definition, so they used to think that 'Bachelors are unmarried men' was true by definition. In both cases they were wrong, for 'kinetic energy' and 'bachelor' are law-cluster terms."

Despite these possibilities, when we classify a sentence as analytic in Putnam's sense, as he says, "we use what we know." Putnam's point is better expressed in terms of belief: it is because we believe that there are and will be no laws about bachelors, and that 'bachelor' is a one-criterion word, that we classify 'Bachelors are unmarried men' as analytic.[18]

This is an inevitable consequence of Putnam's starting point. On my reconstruction, Putnam begins by taking our actual linguistic practices at face value. Our participation in these practices—hence any satisfactory description of the methodological role of both framework principles and analytic statements—always presupposes a background of beliefs.

83. The Method behind Putnam's Criticisms

I have proposed that we view Putnam's criticisms of the analytic-synthetic distinction as attempts to show that the distinction prevents us from properly describing our linguistic practices. To prepare for the next section, in which I explain why Putnam's and Quine's criticisms of the analytic-synthetic distinction are incompatible, I will now consolidate and summarize my view of the method behind Putnam's criticisms.

Putnam invites us to engage in a three-stage process of reflecting about how we should describe our use of language. In the first stage Putnam uses examples to remind us of familiar aspects of our use of language; in the second he explains why these aspects seem mysterious if we are in the grip of the analytic-synthetic distinction; and in the third he sketches a new way of looking at the examples, showing us how to describe them in a broader context within which we find their familiar aspects clear and unproblematic.

For instance, Putnam invites us to engage in a three-stage process of reflecting about how we should describe the change in our theoretical beliefs about kinetic energy. In the first stage he reminds us that prior to Einstein's theory of relativity it was reasonable for physicists to hold '$e = \frac{1}{2}mv^2$' immune from disconfirmation, even though we now believe the equation is false. In the second stage Putnam notes that if we are in the grip of the positivists' analytic-synthetic distinction, we feel compelled to describe this equation as true in virtue of meaning. He points out that if we describe the equation as true in virtue of meaning, we fail to see that '$e = \frac{1}{2}mv^2$' is false, and that the physicists who accept the relativistic energy equation *disagree* with the scientists who accepted '$e = \frac{1}{2}mv^2$'. To help us make sense of this aspect of the kinetic energy equations, in the third stage Putnam proposes that we view 'e' as a law-cluster term—a term that expresses a law-cluster concept. Once we view 'e' as a law-cluster term, we can describe the revision of '$e = \frac{1}{2}mv^2$' as the linguistic expression of a radical change in our beliefs about kinetic energy. This description is further clarified when we view '$e = \frac{1}{2}mv^2$' as what Putnam calls a "framework principle"—a statement that is so central to a body of beliefs that it is held practically immune from disconfirmation. So in the third stage of his reflections about how to describe the kinetic energy equations, Putnam tries to demystify the natural thought that our acceptance of the new relativistic definition of energy marked a change in our beliefs about kinetic energy. The effect of Putnam's third stage is to show that a commitment to Carnap's analytic-synthetic distinction would prevent us from properly describing the evolution in our theoretical beliefs about kinetic energy.

Putnam's discussion of the bachelor example may also be seen as an attempt to persuade us that the analytic-synthetic distinction prevents us from properly describing our use of language. In the first stage Putnam reminds us of such statements as 'Bachelors are unmarried men', which seem analytic. In the second stage we recall that positivists would view such statements as true solely in virtue of meaning, completely independent of "empirical" facts. In the third stage Putnam offers an alternative description of such statements as 'Bachelors are unmarried men'. He agrees that they are "analytic," in the sense that we cannot give them up without changing the subject, but he denies that our judgment that we can't give them up without changing the subject is completely independent of our background beliefs about bachelors. The reason we can't revise the statement *Bachelors are unmarried men* without changing the subject is that the only criterion for x's being a bachelor is that x be an unmarried man, and so 'bachelor' is what

Putnam calls a "one-criterion" word. When we see that 'bachelor' is a "one-criterion" word, we can see why we find it natural to say that 'Bachelors are unmarried men' is analytic. Yet our judgment that "bachelor" is a one-criterion word reflects our "empirical" belief that there are no natural laws about bachelors. Putnam concludes that a commitment to Carnap's analytic-synthetic distinction would prevent us from properly describing the methodological role of trivial analytic statements like 'All bachelors are unmarried'.

To highlight the method behind these arguments, it is helpful to compare Carnap's analytic-synthetic distinction with framework principles such as $'e = \frac{1}{2}mv^2'$. Putnam emphasizes that framework principles "can be overthrown only if someone incorporates principles incompatible with those statements in a successful conceptual system."[19] Carnap's analytic-synthetic distinction is like a framework principle in the sense that we can overthrow it only if we incorporate rival descriptions of our language use into a coherent system. Unlike a framework principle, however, Carnap's analytic-synthetic distinction is not part of a scientific theory and so we should not think of it as true or false. To discredit Carnap's philosophical picture of inquiry it would be enough to sketch a more plausible philosophical picture.

But Putnam goes further than this: he presents his alternative as a clarification of what in a sense we *already knew* about how our language works. To "overthrow" Carnap's analytic-synthetic distinction Putnam tries to remind us of familiar ways in which ordinary aspects of our use of language fit together in a natural and coherent system. Putnam's talk of "law-cluster concepts," "framework principles," and "one-criterion words" highlights aspects of our use of language that we can't see clearly if we are under the spell of Carnap's analytic-synthetic distinction. In this way Putnam aims to break the spell of the analytic-synthetic distinction, and to change the way we look at our linguistic practices.

84. Why Putnam's Critique of the Analytic-Synthetic Distinction Is Incompatible with Quine's

We are now in a position to see that despite superficial similarities, Putnam's and Quine's criticisms of Carnap's analytic-synthetic distinction are incompatible.

Let's start with the similarities. The most important one is that both Putnam and Quine challenge Carnap's descriptions of our ordinary and scientific practices. As we saw in Chapter Five, Quine's scientific naturalism leads him to reject Carnap's notion of a semantical rule and, with it, Carnap's analytic-synthetic distinction. And in §§75–83 we have seen that Putnam's descriptions of our actual practices of agreeing, disagreeing, evaluating assertions, and resolving disputes challenge Carnap's motivating insight that investigators can agree or disagree with each other only if they share precise rules for evaluating their assertions.

A related similarity is that Quine and Putnam both highlight pragmatic aspects of our acceptance and revision of statements. In "Carnap and Logical Truth,"[20] Quine claims that there is no important methodological distinction to be drawn between statements that were introduced by acts of legislative definition or postulation,[21] on the one hand, and well-attested hypotheses, on the other:

> Suppose a scientist introduces a new term, for a certain substance or force. He introduces it by an act either of legislative definition or of legislative postulation. Progressing, he evolves hypotheses regarding further traits of the named substance or force. Suppose now that some such eventual hypothesis, well attested, identifies this substance or force with one named by a complex term built up of other portions of his scientific vocabulary. We all know that this new identity will figure in the ensuing developments quite on a par with the identity which first came of the act of legislative definition, if any, or on a par with the law which first came of the act of legislative postulation. Revisions, in the course of further progress, can touch any of these affirmations equally. Now I urge that scientists, proceeding thus, are not thereby slurring over any meaningful distinction. Legislative acts occur again and again; on the other hand a dichotomy of the resulting truths themselves into analytic and synthetic, truths by meaning postulate and truths by force of nature, has been given no tolerably clear meaning even as a methodological ideal.[22]

On the surface this passage appears compatible with Putnam's observation that the languages we use in our everyday and scientific inquiries include "law-cluster" terms that occur in a large number of laws, many of which can be revised without a change in subject. A passage from chapter 2 of Quine's *Word and Object* strengthens the impression that Quine's and Putnam's descriptions of our scientific inquiries are compatible:

> in theoretical science, unless as recast by semantics enthusiasts, distinctions between synonymies and "factual" equivalences are seldom sensed or claimed. Even the identity historically introduced into mechanics by defining 'momentum' as 'mass times velocity' takes its place in the network of connections on a par with the rest; if a physicist subsequently so revises mechanics that momentum fails to be proportional to velocity, the change will probably be seen as a change of theory and not particularly of meaning. [Here Quine cites the passage I just quoted from "Carnap and Logical Truth".] Synonymy intuitions do not emerge here, just because the terms are linked to the rest of language in more ways than words like 'bachelor' are.[23]

To add to the appearance of compatibility, Quine endorses Putnam's observation that 'Bachelors are unmarried men' is analytic because 'bachelor' is a one-criterion word: "One looks to 'unmarried man' as semantically anchoring 'bachelor' because there is no socially constant stimulus meaning to govern the use of the word; sever its tie with 'unmarried man' and you leave it no very evident social determination, hence no utility in communication."[24] Quine cites Putnam's paper "The Analytic and the Synthetic," and endorses Putnam's account of what Quine calls "the synonymy intuition" that 'Bachelors are unmarried men' is analytic: "My account fits with [Putnam's] and perhaps adds to the explanation."[25] So it appears that Quine's and Putnam's reasons for rejecting Carnap's analytic-synthetic distinction are compatible.

This appearance is misleading. For Quine's methodological reflections in the passages just quoted are of a piece with his scientific naturalism and his "motivating insight" that "we can know external things only through impacts at our nerve endings." When Quine claims in the passage from §X of "Carnap and Logical Truth" that the analytic-synthetic distinction "has been given no tolerably clear meaning even as a methodological ideal," he takes for granted that the only "meaningful distinctions" to be found in our actual scientific practices are those that are determined by speech dispositions. We have already seen that for Quine "the question whether two expressions are alike or unlike in meaning has no determinate answer, known or unknown, except insofar as the answer is settled in principle by people's speech dispositions, known or unknown."[26] By these standards there is an indeterminacy of translation. In Quine's view, our habitual use of homophonic "translations" of our fellow English speakers merely reflects our subjective preference for one of many inequivalent "translations" that preserve all speech dispositions, and hence capture all there is to meaning.

In contrast, Putnam's criticisms are inextricably linked to our commonsense view that the references of words of a public language are the same for all competent speakers of the language. In the kinetic energy case, for instance, Putnam takes for granted our ordinary judgments that the two equations make incompatible statements about kinetic energy, and that 'e' has the same reference in both equations. From our perspective as participants in ongoing inquires, these judgments look secure. But from Quine's point of view, these judgments rest on our scientifically arbitrary "choice" of the homophonic translation manual between idiolects.[27]

Quine would say that Putnam's observation that the term 'e' has the same reference in both equations reflects Putnam's "choice" of a homophonic translation between his idiolect and those of the physicists who accepted '$e = \frac{1}{2}mv^2$'. In Quine's view, this homophonic translation is not the only acceptable one. We may choose to map the earlier physicists' term 'e' to an entirely different term of the later physicists' vocabulary; if this mapping is part of a systematic "translation" that preserves all speech dispositions, then by Quine's standards we are not "slurring over any meaningful distinction."[28] So when Quine observes that "if a physicist subsequently so revises mechanics that momentum fails to be proportional to velocity, the change will probably be seen as a change of theory and not particularly of meaning,"[29] he is just saying that the "translation" between the earlier and later physical theories will probably in practice be close to homophonic, with the differences between the two theories viewed as differences in belief, not meaning.

One might be tempted to see this as just like Putnam's observations that the physicists' revisions of the pre-relativistic kinetic energy equation reflect a change in belief, not reference. But this temptation reflects a misreading of either Quine or Putnam. For Quine's main point in chapter 2 of *Word and Object,* where this discussion of Putnam appears, is that for sentences that are not firmly tied to sensory stimulation, our "intuitive" distinctions between changes in belief and changes in meaning merely reflect our preference for one of many empirically adequate "translations" between speakers. Strictly speaking, for Quine, the physicists' speech dispositions do not determine that they should use the homophonic manual between the earlier and later physical theories, since "unless pretty firmly and directly conditioned to sensory stimulation, a sentence S is meaningless except relative to its own theory; meaningless intertheoretically."[30] Mappings between the sentences and terms of earlier and later physical theories always reflect our tacit "choice" of one set of "analytical hypotheses" over another empirically adequate set.

So despite superficial similarities between Putnam's and Quine's rejections of the analytic-synthetic distinction, their conceptions of the starting point and task of philosophy are incompatible. Starting from our perspective as participants in actual linguistic practices, Putnam shows that the analytic-synthetic distinction prevents us from properly describing our ordinary and scientific inquiries. In contrast, Quine's scientific naturalism inevitably leads to his indeterminacy thesis, according to which there are many inequivalent ways to "mesh" our dispositions with those of other investigators. Hence for Quine the *actual* evolution of our theoretical beliefs illustrates just one of many inequivalent ways in which our dispositions would "mesh" with those of previous investigators.

85. Against Indeterminacy

But Quine's indeterminacy thesis cuts both ways, depending on whether one starts with Quine's scientific naturalism or with our perspective as participants in actual inquiries. Quine's scientific naturalism is inextricable from his "motivating insight" that "we can know external things only through impacts at our nerve endings," and this "insight" underlies Quine's indeterminacy thesis. But there is no more reason to embrace Quine's naturalistic empiricist than there is to embrace Carnap's analytic-synthetic distinction.

Defenders of Quine's indeterminacy thesis typically focus on the question of whether there are facts that determine how our words are to be translated.[31] Some philosophers accept Quine's naturalistic picture, and so they feel they must find such facts.[32] In my view this approach is fruitless. Instead of looking for facts that determine how our words must be translated, we should examine Quine's reasons for thinking that there are countless radically different "translations" that capture all that is objective to meaning. If we abandon the assumptions that lead Quine to this conclusion, there is no need to find facts that determine how our words are to be translated. Without any special reason to question our actual linguistic interactions, both *within* natural languages and *between* them, we have no reason to accept Quine's indeterminacy thesis.

Quine's "insight" that "we can know external things only through impacts at our nerve endings" underlies his naturalized epistemology and his view of what is objective in translation. The same "insight" is reflected in Quine's claim that the objective empirical meaning of a sentence S of a speaker's idiolect is determined by his dispositions to assent to and dissent from S and other sentences under various prompting stimulations. Since between any two idiolects there are countless different translations that "preserve the totality of speech dispositions," Quine concludes that between any two idiolects there are countless different manuals of translation. Almost all of these "translations" would be automatically ignored or dismissed from our perspective as participants in actual linguistic practices. Quine nevertheless insists that any manual of "translation" that preserves the totality of speech dispositions thereby preserves what is "objective" in linguistic meaning. The result is indeterminacy.[33]

Although Putnam wrote "The Analytic and the Synthetic" before Quine first published his argument for the indeterminacy of translation,[34] when properly viewed Putnam's examples can help to disarm Quine's indeterminacy thesis. To "overthrow" Carnap's analytic-synthetic distinction, Putnam reminds us of familiar ways in which ordinary features of our use of language fit together in a natural and coherent system. Once we take our participant view of language seriously, we can no longer accept Carnap's "motivating insight" that if investigators are to agree or disagree they must share precise rules for evaluating their assertions. Similarly, to "overthrow" Quine's indeterminacy thesis, we may appeal to

Putnam's examples, together with his talk of "law-cluster concepts," "framework principles," and "one-criterion words," to show how our ordinary judgments about agreement, disagreement, sameness and difference of reference fit together. From our perspective as participants in actual linguistic practices, there is no good reason to accept Quine's "motivating insight" that "we can know external things only through impacts at our nerve endings,"[35] or his thesis that between any two speakers there are countless radically different "translations" that capture all that is objective to meaning.[36]

Like Putnam's rejection of the analytic-synthetic distinction, this rejection of Quine's indeterminacy thesis is only as convincing as Putnam's alternative descriptions of our linguistic practices. The only way to evaluate Putnam's alternative is to investigate and refine his picture of how familiar aspects of our use of language fit together when they are described from the participant perspective. Now that we have a strategy for resisting Carnap's and Quine's "motivating insights" about how our scientific inquiries *must* be described, we are in a position to take our participant perspective more seriously, and to begin to develop a new way of looking at our use of language in science and ordinary life.

86. Four Preliminary Concerns

My aim in this chapter has been to uncover the roots of our perspective as participants in rule-following practices and to sketch a strategy for resisting the attractions of entrenched frameworks from which our participant perspective looks unimportant. To consolidate central themes and prepare for further developments, I will end by addressing four preliminary concerns about my methods and conclusions.

The first may be expressed as follows: "Putnam's talk of 'agreement', 'disagreement', 'law-cluster concepts', 'framework principles', and 'one-criterion terms' is imprecise and unscientific. We can't be sure that this talk is free of obscure metaphysical assumptions unless we recast it in terms of an appropriate special science such as psychology. Yet it seems unlikely that Putnam's examples and descriptions could be recast in scientific terms. For example, there is apparently no scientific method for determining whether one speaker 'disagrees' with another.[37] We may feel that we understand Putnam's descriptions of our language use, but if we can't make them scientifically precise, we should not take them seriously."

My reply has two parts. First, Putnam's preliminary sketches of our participant perspective play a useful role in Putnam's argument against the analytic-synthetic distinction even though these sketches can't by themselves prevent obscure metaphysical ideas from distorting our thinking about language. The crucial point of Putnam's argument against the analytic-synthetic distinction is that if we want to understand how we evaluate our assertions in science and everyday life, we must take seriously our actual judgments about whether or not a belief is reasonable, when two investigators disagree, and when they are talking past each other. Putnam's talk of "agreement," "disagreement," "law-cluster concepts," "framework principles," and "one-criterion terms" reminds us of how we actually evaluate our assertions, and thereby helps us to see that Carnap's analytic-synthetic distinction prevents us from properly describing our everyday and scientific inquires. Once reminded, we are in a position to address any misunderstandings fostered by Putnam's own descriptions of our inquiries.

Second, sciences such as psychology may help us to understand how we evaluate our assertions, but Putnam's arguments strongly suggest that scientific descriptions can't *replace* the descriptions we give from our perspective as participants in actual inquiries. To understand how we actually evaluate our assertions, we must understand the difference in practice between agreement and disagreement. This distinction can be drawn properly only from our perspective as participants in actual inquires. If we restrict ourselves to descriptions couched solely in scientific terms, we in effect abandon the participant perspective, and thereby prevent ourselves from seeing how we evaluate our assertions.

Putnam's view of inquiry rests on judgments we make from our perspective as participants, judgments about what it is reasonable for an investigator to believe in a given context of inquiry. For example, Putnam reminds us that it was reasonable for physicists before Einstein to hold '$e = \frac{1}{2}mv^2$' immune from disconfirmation, since they did not know of a plausible alternative. He thinks we must take these judgments seriously even if we can't describe in precise scientific terms when it is reasonable to hold a particular belief immune from disconfirmation.

These observations may prompt a second concern: "In Putnam's view, we must take seriously our judgments about what it is 'reasonable' for an investigator to believe in a given context of inquiry even if those judgments can't be redescribed or justified in purely scientific terms. So in Putnam's view, our judgments about whether a belief is 'reasonable' are higher and firmer than the standards expressed in natural science. But there are no legitimate standards higher or firmer than those expressed in natural science. Hence Putnam's view is unacceptable."

This objection is based in a mistake. Putnam aims to remove obstacles to the proper description of our actual practices of agreeing, disagreeing, evaluating assertions, and resolving disputes. In his view, we have no understanding of what is reasonable or unreasonable apart from our actual practices of evaluating our assertions in science and everyday life, and there is no legitimate perspective from which to proclaim that one of these entrenched practices is higher and firmer than any other.

Yet it may seem too restrictive to say that we have no understanding of what is reasonable or unreasonable apart from our actual practices of evaluating our assertions in science and everyday life. We should be able to question even our most deeply entrenched beliefs. This idea may foster a further concern about Putnam's view: "We should not rule out the possibility that an entire group of investigators cling irrationally to statements they ought to give up. But in Putnam's view, we are never in a position to question whether it is reasonable to hold a deeply entrenched belief immune from disconfirmation. This radical *conservatism* guts the very idea of reasonable standards for evaluating assertions."

This objection rests on the mistaken assumption that in Putnam's view if every member of a given linguistic community holds a statement S immune from disconfirmation, then it is reasonable to hold S immune from disconfirmation. In some contexts it is *unreasonable* to hold a statement immune from disconfirmation, even if no one actually recognizes this.

Putnam's observations about "framework principles" show that our judgments of whether or not a statement S is contextually a priori are based in subtle evaluations of whether it is reasonable for an investigator to treat S as contextually a priori given her other beliefs, and her evaluation of the plausibility of available alternatives. To accept an individual's judgment that a statement S is contextually a priori, it is not enough for us to see that from her point of view S looks more plausible than other alternatives she is aware of. We must also determine whether her assessment of the plausibility of those alternatives is itself reasonable, and whether she has spent a reasonable amount of time and energy trying to discover alternatives. If her assessment of the alternatives is unreasonable, or her failure to become acquainted with alternatives is based in psychological needs and biases that by her own standards she should master and overcome, then it is not reasonable for her to treat S as contextually a priori. But if by her own standards the beliefs she holds immune from disconfirmation are in fact contextually a priori, then there are no legitimate grounds for criticizing her acceptance of those beliefs. Putnam's view leaves room for both of these possibilities. His descriptions of our actual practices of evaluating our assertions always leave open the possibility of doubting or revising even our most deeply entrenched beliefs.

This strongly suggests that Putnam is committed to metaphysical realism, where truth is "correspondence" and the "external world" is conceived completely independently of any of our beliefs. This may lead to another objection: "On Putnam's view we can make sense of the possibility that even our most deeply entrenched beliefs may be false. This requires that we think of truth in terms of 'correspondence' with an 'external' world, conceived independently of any of our beliefs. So even though Putnam starts by taking seriously the judgments we make as participants in actual inquiries, he ends up with an obscure metaphysical picture of truth and objectivity."

Some philosophers are happy to embrace metaphysical realism. They would say that this last "objection" is not really an objection at all. These philosophers are inclined to reconstruct Putnam's argument against positivism as follows: "Truth is one thing, and reasonable belief is another. We must reject Carnap's analytic-synthetic distinction, because it conflates truth with reasonable belief."

But in my view, this is not how Putnam criticizes the analytic-synthetic distinction. His criticism is not based in a free-floating "intuitive" understanding of truth and reasonable belief. Instead he uses examples to show that in our actual linguistic practices we distinguish between truth and contextually a priori belief. In Putnam's view, we have no understanding of truth and reasonable belief apart from these practices.

In Chapters Seven and Nine I will argue that, properly viewed, Putnam's descriptions of our practices of agreeing, disagreeing, evaluating assertions, and resolving disputes actually *undermine* the persistent idea that we can conceive of an "external" world completely independently of any of our substantive beliefs. For now I just want to emphasize that Putnam's criticisms of the analytic-synthetic distinction are more subtle and complex than the stripped-down version sketched two paragraphs ago. To understand the relationship between truth and reasonable belief, we must carefully investigate our actual practices. As we work through the details and consequences of our participant perspective on meaning and assertion, we should not take for granted that we can even *make sense* of the metaphysical realist's idea that our statements are true if and only if they "correspond" with an external world conceived independently of any of our beliefs.

III

Anti-Individualism

SEVEN

From the Rejection of the Analytic-Synthetic Distinction to Anti-Individualism

87. The Participant Perspective and Anti-Individualism

I will now begin to develop a more systematic description of the participant perspective whose roots we glimpsed in Chapter Six. For Putnam, as I read him, the most important task for philosophy is to remove obstacles to the proper description of our linguistic practices. To undermine Carnap's analytic-synthetic distinction, Putnam reminds us that reasonable physicists have in the past held false statements immune from disconfirmation. For example, at one time physicists held '$e = \frac{1}{2}mv^2$' immune from disconfirmation because they knew of no plausible alternative. Yet we now take for granted that our revision of '$e = \frac{1}{2}mv^2$' reflects a radical change in our theoretical beliefs about *energy*. To make sense of this change, Putnam proposes that we think of 'energy' as a "law-cluster term" whose reference remains the same despite radical changes in our beliefs.

In the period between "The Analytic and the Synthetic" (1962) and "The Meaning of 'Meaning'" (1975) Putnam came to see that just as our languages include terms such as 'energy' whose references remain the same despite radical *changes* in our beliefs, so they include terms whose references are the same for all competent members of our linguistic community despite radical *differences* between our beliefs. The kinetic energy examples illustrate the division of linguistic labor *across time*. The transition from Putnam's rejection of the analytic-synthetic distinction to his anti-individualism is completed in "The Meaning of 'Meaning'," where Putnam presents examples and thought experiments that highlight the division of linguistic labor *at a given time.*

This development was facilitated by Kripke's causal picture of reference, which brought with it a new appreciation of what Putnam calls "the division of linguistic labor" and "the contribution of the environment." More than any other aspect of Putnam's anti-individualism, his talk of "the contribution of the environment" seems to presuppose a metaphysical picture of how the references of our words are determined. But I will argue that our understanding of the contribution of the environment is rooted in the division of linguistic labor, and so we can't give any content to the standard metaphysical picture of how the references of our words are determined.

This deflationary picture of Putnam's anti-individualism goes against the orthodox interpretation of his position in "The Meaning of 'Meaning'," and conflicts with Putnam's own view of what he believed at the time he wrote that paper. My goal is not to provide a definitive account of what Putnam actually believed when he presented his arguments for anti-individualism. Instead I am using my exegesis of Putnam's arguments to develop my own description of the central features of anti-individualism, and to show how those features help us understand our perspective as participants in everyday and scientific inquiries. In the process I hope to convince those who hold the orthodox interpretation that my version of anti-individualism is better.

I begin by summarizing (§88) and deflating (§89) Putnam's early attempts to show that our languages contain terms whose references may remain the same despite radical changes in our beliefs. I then present crucial aspects of Kripke's causal picture of reference (§90) and of Putnam's adaptation of Kripke's causal picture of reference (§91), distinguish two roles for the causal picture of reference (§92), and link these roles to what Putnam calls "the division of linguistic labor" and "the contribution of the environment" (§93). I explain why talk of "the contribution of the environment" is standardly understood in metaphysical terms (§§94–95), and then argue that properly described, the contribution of the environment is rooted in the division of labor across time (§§96–99). Finally, I argue that Putnam's descriptions of the division of linguistic labor, both at a given time and across time, show that there is no hope for developing a substantive theory of reference (§§100–101).

88. Sameness of Reference despite Radical Changes in Belief

Before Kripke's introduction of the causal picture of reference, Putnam had two ways of showing that our languages contain terms whose references remain the same despite radical changes in our beliefs.

The first is to *find actual cases in which the references of our words have remained the same despite radical changes in our beliefs*. As we saw in Chapter Six, Putnam reminds us that at one time it was reasonable for physicists to hold '$e = \frac{1}{2}mv^2$' immune from disconfirmation. Later they abandoned '$e = \frac{1}{2}mv^2$', and replaced it with an equation compatible with Einstein's relativity theory, thus expressing their disagreement with those who accepted the earlier equation. To make sense of this diachronic aspect of our beliefs about kinetic energy, Putnam proposes that we view 'e' as a law-cluster term. This clarifies both the role of 'e' and our judgment that the physicists who revised the kinetic energy equation disagreed with those who had previously held it immune from disconfirmation. As a result, we see that the reference of the term 'e' remains the same despite the change from '$e = \frac{1}{2}mv^2$' to the revised kinetic energy equation.

Putnam's second way of showing that our languages contain terms whose references remain the same despite radical changes in our beliefs is to *use a term of our language to describe a situation in which we revise or abandon some of the very central beliefs that we use that term to express*. This method is illustrated by a supposition that Putnam uses to undermine Norman Malcolm's criterial theory of meaning:

> Consider the following case: there is a disease, multiple sclerosis, which is extremely difficult to diagnose. The symptoms resemble those of other neurological diseases; and not all of the symptoms are usually present. Some neurologists believe that multiple sclerosis is caused by a virus, although they cannot presently specify what virus. Suppose a patient, X, has a 'par-

adigmatic' case of multiple sclerosis. Then Malcolm's view is that, no matter what we find out later, X *has* multiple sclerosis because that is what we presently mean. In particular, if we later identify a virus as *the* cause of multiple sclerosis, and this patient's condition was not caused by that virus, he *still* had multiple sclerosis.[1]

Here Putnam invites us to suppose that we someday identify a certain virus V as the cause (of all cases) of multiple sclerosis, and find that V is not present in "paradigmatic" patient X. This conflicts with Malcolm's view that if patient X has what we take to be a paradigmatic case of multiple sclerosis, then no empirical inquiry could overturn our belief that X has multiple sclerosis. In Malcom's view, we can't coherently conclude that "paradigmatic" patient X does not have multiple sclerosis; if the term 'multiple sclerosis' is someday used in such a way that it does not correctly apply to patient X, then the term 'multiple sclerosis' no longer refers to multiple sclerosis.[2] Yet when we entertain Putnam's supposition that we someday identify a certain virus as *the* cause of multiple sclerosis, we take for granted that our term 'multiple sclerosis' refers to multiple sclerosis. Despite Malcolm's criterial theory, we naturally and effortlessly conclude that in the circumstances Putnam describes, it turns out that patient X does not have multiple sclerosis, since there is no trace of the virus in his body.

Putnam takes this to show that our term 'multiple sclerosis' would continue to refer to multiple sclerosis even if we discover that some of what we now take to be "paradigmatic" cases of multiple sclerosis are not cases of multiple sclerosis. To invite us to see this, he uses our term 'multiple sclerosis' to describe a situation in which we revise or abandon some of the very central beliefs that we use that term to express. This illustrates Putnam's second early way of showing us that our language contains terms whose reference remain the same despite radical changes in our beliefs.

89. Idiolects, Disquotation, and Changes in Belief

From Quine's perspective, Putnam's early attempts to show that our languages contain terms whose references remain the same despite radical changes in our beliefs presuppose a nondisquotational view of reference. In Putnam's kinetic energy case, for example, Putnam takes for granted that 'e' has the same reference for the scientists who accepted '$e = \frac{1}{2}mv^2$' as it has for those who later revised that equation in light of Einstein's relativity theory. If we are in the grip of Quine's idiolectical picture of language, it will seem that to accept Putnam's conclusions about the kinetic energy case, we must suppose there are facts that uniquely determine how the earlier physicists' term 'e' should be "translated" into the language of contemporary physicists. And to suppose that there are such facts is to suppose that reference is a robust nondisquotational relationship between words and things or kinds. So if we are in the grip of Quine's idiolectical picture of language, it will seem that Putnam's early observations about reference rest on a nondisquotational picture of reference.

Although few contemporary philosophers of language accept Quine's indeterminacy thesis, many agree with Quine that to reject the indeterminacy thesis we must suppose that there are facts that determine how speakers should "translate" each other's words.[3] Hence many would agree with Quine that Putnam's early observations about reference presuppose that reference is a robust nondisquotational relationship between words and things or kinds.

As I explained in Chapter Six, however, in my view the central insight behind Putnam's view of reference is that we can properly describe our linguistic practices only if we abandon the idiolectical picture of language. In this section I sketch my view that if we embrace a nonidiolectical picture of language, we can accept Putnam's early observations that our languages contain terms whose references remain the same despite radical changes in our beliefs *without* committing ourselves to a nondisquotational theory of reference.

As we saw in Chapter Two, Quine emphasizes that when there is no question of what he calls "translation," the disquotational paradigm for reference is philosophically unproblematic. I propose that we accept this aspect of Quine's view, but describe our linguistic practices in such a way that there is no special philosophical question of how two speakers of the same natural language "translate" each other's words. In this chapter I will try to convince you that just as for Quine it is unproblematic to say that two occurrences of the same word within a single person's idiolect have the same reference, so for Putnam it is unproblematic to say that two occurrences of the same word within a single public language have the same reference. There is no neutral way to characterize Putnam's nonidiolectical picture of language. Nevertheless, in the rest of this section I offer a brief preliminary sketch of how one might come to accept Putnam's nonidiolectical descriptions of our linguistic practices.

Suppose we are at first inclined to accept an idiolectical picture of language and a purely disquotational view of reference. Disquotational reference is a notion we can apply to the words of our own idiolects with all the ease and clarity of the disquotational paradigm: '_____' refers to _____. In particular, we are each in a position to apply the disquotational reference paradigm to our own term 'multiple sclerosis'. Even if we are at first inclined to accept an idiolectical picture of language, we can each use our own term 'multiple sclerosis' to describe a case in which we come to revise some of the very beliefs we now express using our term 'multiple sclerosis'.

For instance, suppose that yesterday I sincerely uttered my sentence 'Jones has multiple sclerosis', thus expressing my belief that Jones had a paradigmatic case of multiple sclerosis, and that today I say, "Yesterday I thought that Jones had multiple sclerosis, because he had all the symptoms I associated with that disease. But I have discovered that multiple sclerosis is caused by a virus which is not actually present in Jones at all. I no longer think that Jones has multiple sclerosis." In this story I take for granted that the references of my terms, including 'multiple sclerosis', remain the same despite the change in my belief about Jones. To make sense of the story, I need not embrace a nondisquotational view of reference; it is enough for me to accept as philosophically unproblematic my ordinary judgment that my idiolect has not changed from yesterday to today.[4]

The point of this story is that if we take for granted that our idiolects persist unchanged from moment to moment, we can make sense of our ordinary judgment that the references of our words do not change from one moment to the next without embracing a nondisquotational theory of reference. If we see our own idiolects as persisting through time, then we need not (even tacitly) "translate" our own words to extend our use of disquotation beyond the present moment, to past and future uses of our own words.[5]

But Putnam is not primarily interested in changes of belief expressed within a single speaker's idiolect. In most of his examples and thought experiments, Putnam appeals to our ordinary judgments about whether two speakers agree or disagree and whether their words have the same reference. The force of Putnam's kinetic energy example depends on our judgment that 'e' has the same reference for the scientists who accepted '$e = \frac{1}{2}mv^2$' as it has for those who later revised that equation in light of Einstein's relativity theory. To indicate how it could be that for Putnam these judgments do not rest on any substantive view of reference, I propose that we extend the descriptive strategy displayed in the first story to encompass cases in which a speaker revises, corrects, or disagrees with a statement made by another speaker at some earlier time.

For instance, suppose that yesterday you sincerely uttered the sentence 'Jones has multiple sclerosis', thereby expressing your belief that Jones had a paradigmatic case of multiple sclerosis, and that today I sincerely utter the sentence 'Jones does not have multiple sclerosis', thereby expressing my belief that Jones does not have multiple sclerosis. To make sense of this story, it is enough for us to take for granted that you and I use the same term 'multiple sclerosis' to express our disagreement about whether Jones has multiple sclerosis. We need not also embrace a nondisquotational view of reference, or suppose that our ordinary judgment that you and I use the same term 'multiple sclerosis' to express our disagreement reflects our "analytical hypotheses" about how to "translate" each other's words. Instead I propose that we describe your utterances and mine as utterances of the same term 'multiple sclerosis', part of the public language we both use. It is then unproblematic to note that in *our* language 'multiple sclerosis' refers to multiple sclerosis.

The point of this second story is that if we accept as philosophically unproblematic our ordinary judgment that two different speakers of the same public language can use the same terms to express their beliefs and thoughts, we can make sense of our ordinary judgment that the references of both speakers' words are the same without embracing a nondisquotational theory of reference. Thus I propose that to make sense of Putnam's kinetic energy example it is enough to see the two equations as part of a single language that persists through time, so that the physicists of today can take at face value the utterances of their colleagues from the late nineteenth century. In my view, the point of Putnam's kinetic energy example is to remind us that the two kinetic energy equations are part of a single language that is shared by many individuals and persists through radical changes in belief. In the rest of this chapter I will explain how this deflationary description of Putnam's views of reference can be used to clarify and deflate Putnam's anti-individualism and, in particular, his talk of "the division of linguistic labor" and "the causal theory of reference."

90. Kripke's Causal Picture of Reference

As I see it, Putnam's anti-individualism is a natural development of his two early ways of showing that our languages contain terms whose references remain the same despite radical changes in our beliefs (§88). His assimilation of Kripke's causal picture of reference was an important step in this development. To prepare for my reconstruction of how Putnam assimilated Kripke's causal picture of reference, I will briefly review Kripke's reasons for proposing it.

In *Naming and Necessity* Kripke argues that we should abandon the description theory of proper names, which he attributes to Frege and Russell. According to Frege and Russell, Kripke says, "a proper name, properly used, simply was a definite description abbreviated or disguised."[6] Kripke distinguishes between two versions of the description theory of proper names. On the first version, a description such as 'the teacher of Alexander' *gives the meaning* of a proper name like 'Aristotle'. Kripke understands this to imply that in each possible world the name 'Aristotle' refers to whomever taught Alexander in that world. On the second version, a description *fixes the reference* but does not give the meaning of a name. If the description 'the teacher of Alexander' fixes the reference but does not give the meaning of 'Aristotle', then 'Aristotle' refers in every world to whomever taught Alexander in the *actual* world. When a description fixes the reference but does not give the meaning of a name, we can use the name to refer to the person or thing that satisfies the description in the actual world, even when we are describing possible situations in which the description is not true of that person or thing.

Kripke appeals to our modal intuitions to argue against the theory that descriptions give the meaning of a proper name. For example, we accept that *Aristotle might not have taught Alexander*. But if we assume that the description 'the teacher of Alexander' gives the meaning of 'Aristotle', then when we assert 'Aristotle might not have taught Alexander' we are in effect asserting that there is a possible world in which there is a man who is the unique teacher of Alexander and who is not a teacher of Alexander. But the latter assertion is inconsistent. Kripke argues that since we accept that Aristotle might not have taught Alexander, we should conclude that the description 'the teacher of Alexander' does not give the meaning of the name 'Aristotle'. He uses similar arguments to show that *no* description gives the meaning of the name 'Aristotle'. For any definite description or disjunction of descriptive predicates that we believe to hold uniquely of Aristotle, Kripke thinks we can make sense of saying that Aristotle might not have uniquely satisfied that description or any of those descriptive predicates. So Kripke concludes that our modal intuitions undermine the theory that descriptions give the meaning of proper names.

But Kripke's modal intuitions do not undermine the theory that descriptions fix the reference but do not give the meaning of proper names. For instance, we may without contradiction suppose that the description 'the teacher of Alexander' picks out Aristotle in the actual world, even while we assert that Aristotle might not have taught Alexander. To undermine the theory that descriptions fix the reference but do not give the meaning of proper names, Kripke uses a different strategy: he highlights aspects of our use of proper names that suggest that their references are not *in fact* determined by descriptions we associate with them. His strategy is illustrated by his Schmidt-Gödel example:

Let's suppose that someone says that Gödel is the man who discovered the incompleteness of arithmetic . . . In the case of Gödel that's practically the only thing many people have heard about him—that he discovered the incompleteness of arithmetic. Does it follow that whoever discovered the incompleteness of arithmetic is the referent of 'Gödel'? . . . Suppose that Gödel was not in fact the author of the theorem. A man named 'Schmidt' whose body was found in Vienna under mysterious circumstances many years ago, actually did the work in question. His friend Gödel somehow got hold of the manuscript and it was thereafter attributed to Gödel. On the view in question, then, when our ordinary man uses the name 'Gödel', he really means to refer to Schmidt, because Schmidt is the unique person satisfying the description, 'the man who discovered the incompleteness of arithmetic'. . . . So, since the man who discovered the incompleteness of arithmetic is in fact Schmidt, we, when we talk about 'Gödel', are in fact always referring to Schmidt. But it seems to me that we are not. We simply are not.[7]

Kripke uses this example to show that there is a conflict between our ordinary judgment that our name 'Gödel' refers to Gödel and the theory that descriptions fix the reference of our proper names. Kripke points out that if *in fact* Gödel did not prove the incompleteness theorem, then according to the description theorist in his example, our name 'Gödel' actually refers to Schmidt. But this conflicts with our ordinary judgment that our term 'Gödel' actually refers to Gödel. For any definite description we associate with a name, according to Kripke, we can coherently suppose that the reference of the name does not *in fact* uniquely satisfy the description. Kripke concludes that it is neither necessary nor sufficient for x to be the reference of proper name N that x satisfy some uniquely identifying description that we associate with N.

When Kripke says, "Suppose that Gödel was not in fact the author of the theorem,"[8] he is using the name 'Gödel' to refer to Gödel even while he is saying that Gödel was not in fact the author of the incompleteness theorem. So when we read through the example, *our* understanding of the supposition is that *Gödel was not in fact the author of the incompleteness theorem.* We take for granted, in expressing this supposition, that our name 'Gödel' refers to Gödel. No wonder we accept Kripke's conclusion that even if we are in the supposed situation, our name 'Gödel' refers to Gödel, not Schmidt—the conclusion is built into Kripke's description of the case.

Kripke introduced his celebrated "causal theory of reference" to help us see how it could be that our name 'Gödel' actually refers to Gödel even if the definite descriptions we associate with the name

'Gödel' are not uniquely satisfied by Gödel. His goal is "to present just a *better picture* than the picture presented by the received views,"[9] not to offer a theory of necessary and sufficient conditions for reference. Here is one of his sketches of the new picture:

> A rough statement of a theory might be the following: An initial 'baptism' takes place. Here the object may be named by ostension, or the reference of the name may be fixed by a description. When the name is 'passed from link to link', the receiver must, I think, intend when he learns it to use it with the same reference as the man from whom he heard it. If I hear the name 'Napoleon' and decide it would be a nice name for my pet aardvark, I do not satisfy this condition.[10]

The new idea behind this picture—the reason it is called a "causal" theory of reference—is that minimal competence in the use of a name can be "passed from link to link," one speaker to another. Some kind of contact or interaction with a person who already uses the name is sufficient, provided that he or she is able to use the name, perhaps only in virtue of picking it up from someone else, who picked it up from yet another person, and so on. Ultimately, our ability to use 'Gödel' to refer to Gödel is linked in this way to an individual who was present at an initial "baptism" that settles the reference of the name.

Kripke's causal picture of reference is not a theory of necessary and sufficient conditions for reference. It is meant only as a sketch. Many philosophers have raised counterexamples to Kripke's initial formulation, and proposed refinements of it.[11] I will not discuss these counterexamples or refinements here. My deflationary view of the causal picture of reference will gradually emerge once we see the similarities between Kripke's observations about reference and Putnam's rejection of the analytic-synthetic distinction.

91. Putnam's Assimilation of Kripke's Causal Picture of Reference

In "Explanation and Reference" (1973), written just before "The Meaning of 'Meaning' " (1975), Putnam notes that he is indebted to Saul Kripke "for suggesting the idea of causal chains as the mechanism of reference."[12] In this section I will argue that Kripke's causal picture of reference helps Putnam to see that the *diachronic* observations he used in his arguments against logical positivism are fundamentally linked to corresponding *synchronic* observations about agreement and disagreement in shared languages. Later I will develop the point in more detail, focusing on Putnam's arguments in "The Meaning of 'Meaning'."

To bring out the similarities between Putnam's diachronic and Kripke's synchronic observations about reference, it is helpful to compare Putnam's multiple sclerosis example with Kripke's Schmidt-Gödel example. I noted earlier (§88) that when Putnam asks us to imagine that "we later identify a virus as *the* cause of multiple sclerosis," he uses 'multiple sclerosis' to refer to multiple sclerosis, and thereby tries to show us that the references of the terms in our language are not determined by criteria in the way that Malcolm believes. If we take for granted that Putnam's descriptions of his examples make sense, we will reject Malcolm's criterial view of meaning. This is similar to Kripke's strategy in describing the Schmidt-Gödel case. I noted above that when we use the name 'Gödel' to express Kripke's supposition that Gödel was not in fact the author of the incompleteness theorem, we naturally take for granted that 'Gödel' refers to Gödel. Since we think that even if Kripke's supposition is actually true, our name 'Gödel' refers to Gödel, we conclude that the reference of the name 'Gödel' is not actually fixed by the description 'the man who proved the incompleteness theorems'. Kripke's own description of the supposition is part of what convinces us that the reference of our name 'Gödel' is not fixed by any descriptions we associate with the name. Our conviction that we understand Kripke's supposition that Gödel did not actually prove the incompleteness theorem, and other suppositions like it, undermine our confidence in the description theory.

Even though Putnam's multiple sclerosis example is aimed at showing that we can make sense of *diachronic* changes in beliefs about multiple sclerosis, the example can be adapted to show that at one and the same time, two or more scientists may disagree about what causes multiple sclerosis while still sharing a language in which the term 'multiple sclerosis' refers to multiple sclerosis. All we need suppose is that one group of scientists accepts the theory that multiple sclerosis is caused by virus V, while another group of scientists does not accept this theory. The differences in their beliefs about multiple sclerosis will show up in disagreements about whether particular individuals have multiple sclerosis: Jones's symptoms may lead one group to believe that he has multiple sclerosis, while the other group disagrees, since there is no trace of virus V in his body.

The parallel between this revised version of Putnam's multiple sclerosis example and Kripke's Schmidt-Gödel example is incomplete but instructive. Kripke's aim was to show that the references of our proper names are not determined by definite descriptions we associate with them. His Schmidt-Gödel case suggests a recipe for describing, for each description that is supposed to single out the reference of a name, a situation in which the bearer of the name is not in fact uniquely satisfied by the description. Similarly, my recent synchronic adaptation of Putnam's original multiple sclerosis case suggests a recipe for describing, for almost any belief that is alleged to be part of the "meaning" of a "law-cluster" term that is used to express that belief, a situation in which individuals disagree about whether the belief is true.

Putnam was convinced that his own diachronic examples, together with synchronic extensions of them, show that reference is not settled by descriptions or beliefs we associate with our words. Like Kripke, Putnam believed that we need a new way of thinking about reference. Putnam was trying to sketch a new way of thinking of reference when he introduced his idea of "law-cluster terms." But he saw that Kripke's causal picture of reference was a breakthrough.

In Putnam's view, the insight behind Kripke's causal picture of reference is that language is a "collective" enterprise: "what is important about Kripke's theory is not that the use of proper names is 'causal'—what is not?—but that the use of proper names is *collective*. Anyone who uses a proper name to refer is, in a sense, a member of a collective which had 'contact' with the bearer of the name."[13] Putnam's conclusion is that investigators who share a language are able to use words like 'energy' and 'multiple sclerosis' to refer to energy and multiple sclerosis in virtue of being appropriately connected with the references themselves, or by picking up the use of the name from members of their community who are appropriately connected with the references.

In "Explanation and Reference," Putnam gives an example of the kind of connection he has in mind for the term 'electricity':

> I cannot ... think of anything that *every* user of the term 'electricity' *has* to know except that electricity is ... a physical magnitude of some sort, and, possibly, that 'electricity' (or electrical charge or charges) is capable of flow or motion. Benjamin Franklin knew that 'electricity' was manifested in the form of sparks and lightning bolts; someone else might know about currents and electromagnets; someone else might know about atoms consisting of positively and negatively charged particles. They could all use the term 'electricity' without there being a discernable 'intension' that they all share. I want to suggest that what they do have in common is this: that each of them is connected by a certain kind of causal chain to a situation in which a *description* of electricity is given, and generally a causal description—that is, one which singles out electricity as the physical magnitude *responsible* for certain effects in a certain way.[14]

This sketch of how individuals succeed in referring to electricity with the term 'electricity' helps us see that scientists, taking for granted that their word 'electricity' refers to electricity, may use the term 'electricity' to express substantial theoretical disagreements about what electricity is.

In "Explanation and Reference," Putnam's central aim is to develop a picture of reference that helps us see that scientists years ago used the word 'electricity' to refer to electricity, despite their false and incomplete theories about what electricity is. The causal picture enables Putnam to clarify his observation that terms like 'electricity', which he previously classified as "law-cluster" terms, are "transtheoretical." If the terms are transtheoretical, then it makes sense to say that the languages that contain such terms are transtheoretical. In retrospect, we can see that this was the central point of the diachronic examples Putnam used in his arguments against the logical positivists.[15]

The new picture also leads to a correction of Putnam's earlier account of the role of "law-cluster" terms. Kripke's emphasis on what Putnam calls the "collective" nature of our use of proper names helps Putnam see that it is not required of each individual that he know all the laws in which a term occurs in order to be in a position to use that term to express his agreement or disagreement with other investigators. It is sufficient that he be able to identify the reference by some test, or that he be a member of a community at least some of whose members can identify the reference of the term.[16]

These observations may be summed up as follows. Putnam sees Kripke's causal picture of reference as an important step toward clarifying our understanding of the languages we actually use in our inquiries, and so he easily and gratefully incorporates it into his own project. Putnam's own causal picture of "transtheoretical" terms is a refinement, clarification, and partial correction of his earlier idea of "law-cluster" terms. The picture that begins to emerge once Putnam assimilates Kripke's causal picture of reference is that individuals participate in linguistic practices that persist through radical changes in belief and theory. Our understanding of what an individual means and believes is dependent on our seeing him or her as a member of a "collective" linguistic practice that includes other speakers both at a given time and over long periods of time, during which the beliefs of the members of that "collective body" may fundamentally change.

92. Two Roles for the Causal Picture of Reference

In Kripke's presentation of the causal picture of reference, there is an "initial baptism" that establishes the reference of a term, and "causal chains" that lead from the baptism to other uses of the term. Kripke points out that in many cases the baptism depends on a causal link to the reference of the term.[17] Thus in Kripke's picture causal links play two different roles: they clarify the initial "baptism" event, and they help us see how the reference of a name is "transmitted" from speaker to speaker. Both aspects of Kripke's causal picture of reference are helpful in clarifying Putnam's earlier observation that our languages contain terms whose references remain the same despite radical changes in our beliefs.

In "Explanation and Reference" Putnam describes his view of how reference of the term 'electricity' is fixed as follows:

> suppose I were standing next to Ben Franklin as he performed his famous experiment. Suppose he told me that 'electricity' is a physical quantity which behaves in certain respects like a

liquid . . . ; that it collects in clouds, and that, when a critical point of some kind is reached, a large quantity flows from the clouds to the earth in the form of a lightning-bolt; that it runs along (or perhaps 'through') his metal kite string; etc. He would have given me *an approximately correct definite description* of a physical magnitude. I could now use the term 'electricity' myself. Let us call this event—my acquiring the ability to use the term 'electricity' in this way—an *introducing event*.[18]

This is similar to what Kripke calls an initial baptism, although there is no implication in Putnam's picture that there must be only one introducing event, or indeed only one approximately true description that is employed in an introducing event for the term 'electricity'.

Putnam observes that the reference of a word can be passed from one speaker A to another speaker B, provided that B's use of the word is "causally linked" to A's use of the word and, ultimately, to an "introducing event":

If I teach the word ['electricity'] to someone else by telling him that the word 'electricity' is the name of a physical magnitude, and by telling him certain facts about it which do not constitute a causal description . . .—even if the facts I tell him do not constitute a definite description of any kind, let alone a causal description—still, the word's being in his vocabulary will be causally linked to its being in my vocabulary, and hence, ultimately, to an introducing event.[19]

The point is that a speaker who knows very little about electricity can nevertheless use the word 'electricity' to refer to electricity thanks to his "causal links" to an "introducing event."

Putnam says that an introducing event involves an "approximately true description" of the reference of the term. In the kinetic energy case, for example, we judged that physicists in the nineteenth century had false beliefs about *energy*; in Putnam's view, this shows that we can refer to energy even if not all our beliefs about energy are true. In his clarification of the causal picture of reference, Putnam makes similar observations about our use of 'electricity' to refer to electricity:

Even if the causal description failed to describe electricity, if there is good reason to treat it as a mis-description *of electricity* (rather than a description of nothing at all)—for example, if electricity was described as the physical magnitude with such and such properties which is responsible for such and such effects, where in fact electricity is responsible for the effects in question, and the speaker intended to refer to the magnitude responsible for those effects, but mistakenly added the incorrect information 'electricity has such and such properties' because he mistakenly thought that the magnitude responsible for those effects had those further properties—we still have a basis for saying that both the original speaker and the persons to whom he teaches the word use the word to refer to electricity.[20]

This clarification of the causal picture is continuous with Putnam's earlier observations that there are terms in our languages whose references remain the same despite radical changes in our beliefs.

The approximately true descriptions that Putnam cites in his account of an introducing event mention causal links to the reference of the terms introduced. For example, the user of the term 'electricity' is saying that it refers to whatever *causes* certain effects. The relationship between the cause and the effects is then part of the picture of how we are able to refer to 'electricity'.

A comparison with Kripke's description of the use of proper names may help to bring out the role of causal connection between the language user and the reference in the introducing events. Sometimes proper names of babies are introduced during baptism ceremonies, in which the reference of the name is indicated ostensively. Suppose that during one such ceremony the baptizer points to a certain baby and says, "Let this baby be called 'Oscar'." In this case we think of the act of pointing, and the "causal" connections between the baptizer and the baby, as essential to what makes 'Oscar' a name of that particular baby. For if the same words and gestures had been performed in front of a qualitatively similar but different baby, the name would have referred to that different baby. So the ostensive connection is crucial to settling the reference of a name introduced in a baptism ceremony.

The same is true for such terms as 'electricity'. We can imagine a qualitatively indistinguishable world in which the stuff causally responsible for the effects that we attribute to electricity is not electricity. Inhabitants of that world apply the term 'electricity' to something other than electricity, and so in their language the term 'electricity' does not refer to electricity. This counterfactual suggests that the reference of our term 'electricity' is partly settled by our connection with electricity.

The connections that clarify reference in the introducing events are not the same as the connections that help us see how minimal competence in the use of a word can be passed from speaker to speaker, and ultimately linked to an introducing event. The causal picture of reference is so named primarily in virtue of the second kind of connection involved in reference, and this is the aspect of Kripke's picture that inspires Putnam to say "the use of proper names is *collective.*" Yet both kinds of connection are important to Putnam's assimilation of Kripke's causal picture of reference. In "The Meaning of 'Meaning' " Putnam sketches his picture of reference in more detail, and explicitly distinguishes the two kinds of causal roles. According to Putnam, our failure to see that our use of terms is "collective" has kept us from noticing that there is what he calls a "division of linguistic labor," and our failure to see the importance of the causal connections in introducing events has kept us from noticing what he calls "the contribution of the environment."

93. The Division of Linguistic Labor and the Contribution of the Environment

Putnam introduces the phrases "the division of linguistic labor" and "the contribution of the environment" in "The Meaning of 'Meaning'." In this and the next two sections (§§93–95) I will consider some of the examples that Putnam uses to illustrate these ideas, and sketch the standard metaphysical interpretation of Putnam's view of the relationship between language and the environment. The contribution of the environment is usually thought to be completely independent of the division of linguistic labor. But I will show (§§96–101) that our understanding of the contribution of the environment cannot be independent of the division of linguistic labor; the standard metaphysical interpretation of Putnam's view of the relationship between language and the world—and hence also of Putnam's view of reference—reflects a fundamental misunderstanding of anti-individualism.

To illustrate the division of linguistic labor, Putnam reminds us that even though most of us can't tell an elm from a beech tree, our uses of the words 'elm' and 'beech' pass muster in the community of English speakers. We naturally submit the judgments we make using the words 'elm' and 'beech' to criticism and correction by more knowledgeable members of our linguistic community, and also by encyclopedias, dictionaries, and authoritative books describing the various kinds of trees. These familiar aspects of our linguistic practices show that when we use the word 'elm' we refer to elm trees, and when we use the word 'beech' we refer to beech trees. Moreover, when we sincerely utter sentences containing the word 'elm', we thereby express our beliefs or thoughts about elm trees, and when we sincerely utter sentences containing 'beech', we thereby express our beliefs or thoughts about beech trees. When I sincerely utter the sentence 'Many elm trees in North America died of Dutch Elm disease', for example, I thereby express my belief that *many elm trees in North America died of Dutch Elm disease.*

This example reminds us that some members of our linguistic community have the "job" of knowing about elm and beech trees, and others do not need to know this to be counted as competent users of the words 'elm' and 'beech'. To refer to elms with the word 'elm' and beeches with the word 'beech', and to express beliefs and thoughts about elms and beeches, it is sufficient for the nonexperts to be connected to a community that has experts who are able to distinguish between elms and beeches.

Unlike this example of the division of linguistic labor, Putnam's illustration of the contribution of the environment is fictional. Putnam presents two similar thought experiments to highlight the contribution of the environment. Both of these thought experiments have two steps. In step one of the first thought experiment, we consider Oscar, who lives on Earth, and is competent in the use of the word 'water', despite his ignorance of the molecular structure of water. Oscar displays his competence in two ways: he typically applies the word 'water' to samples of water, and he submits the judgments he makes using his word 'water' to criticism and correction by more knowledgeable members of his linguistic community. Thus Oscar implicitly acknowledges that his own rough and ready criteria for applying 'water' do not by themselves settle what his word 'water' means. Nevertheless, since Oscar is a competent member of his linguistic community, his word 'water' refers to *water*, his sentence 'Water is wet' means that *water is wet*, and when he sincerely assents to the sentence 'Water is wet', he thereby expresses his belief that *water is wet*.

In the second step of the thought experiment we consider Twin Oscar, who has virtually the same physical structure and dispositions to behavior as Oscar. Twin Oscar lives on Twin Earth, which is exactly like Earth, except that where there is water on Earth, there is twin water on Twin Earth. Twin water is in all ordinary contexts indistinguishable from water, but the molecular structure of twin water is XYZ not H_2O, and twin water displays different properties from water at very high and low temperatures. Twin Oscar is a competent speaker of Twin English, the language used on Twin Earth, and his use of the word 'water' passes all the ordinary tests for competence, despite his ignorance of the molecular structure of twin water, the liquid to which the word 'water', as it is used in his community, is correctly applied. Moreover, like Oscar, Twin Oscar submits the judgments he makes using his word 'water' to criticism and correction by more knowledgeable members of his linguistic community. Thus Twin Oscar implicitly acknowledges that his own rough and ready criteria for applying his word 'water' do not by themselves settle when it is correctly applied. Nevertheless, since Oscar is a competent member of the Twin Earth linguistic community, his word 'water' refers to *twin water*, his sentence 'Water is wet' means that *twin water is wet*, and when he sincerely assents to the sentence 'Water is wet', he thereby expresses his belief that *twin water is wet*.

Now let us consider whether this example shows that there is a distinctive contribution of the environment, separate from the division of linguistic labor. Oscar and Twin Oscar are virtually the same when considered independent of their respective environments. Yet Oscar's word 'water' refers to *water*, and Twin Oscar's word refers to *twin water*. The salient difference is that Oscar applies his word 'water' to samples of water, and Twin Oscar applies his word 'water' to samples of twin water. The difference between the meanings of their words is apparently determined by their causal relationships to the different liquids. This illustrates what Putnam calls the contribution of the environment.

In this first thought experiment, we imagined that there are experts on Earth who know that water is H_2O, and experts on Twin Earth who know that twin water is XYZ. By the division of linguistic labor, what Oscar and Twin Oscar mean by their respective uses of 'water' is linked to the way the experts in their linguistic communities use 'water'. So in the first thought experiment, the difference between what Oscar and Twin Oscar mean by 'water' is partly a reflection of what the experts in their respective linguistic communities know.

In the second thought experiment, Putnam highlights the contribution of the environment by considering a time before *anyone* on Earth or Twin Earth knew how to distinguish between water and twin water. Putnam imagines two competent speakers, also called 'Oscar' and 'Twin Oscar', who lived on Earth and Twin Earth in 1750, before the chemists on either planet had discovered the molecular structures of the water and twin water. When we consider the two speakers in abstraction from their respective environments, there is no discernible difference between Oscar's or Twin Oscar's linguistic behavior with regard to the term 'water', nor is there any difference between their linguistic communities, except that they apply the word 'water' to different liquids. Putnam claims that even though Oscar and Twin Oscar can't tell water from twin water, and even though there are no experts in either of their communities who can tell these liquids apart, Oscar's word 'water' means *water*, and Twin Oscar's word 'water' means *twin water*.

But why should we say this, rather than that the word 'water' had the same meaning and reference in both communities? Putnam's answer to this question marks a new development of his causal picture of reference. We saw earlier that according to Putnam there are two ways that a speaker may come to refer to electricity with his term 'electricity': through connections with other speakers who are able to identify the reference of the term, and by means of an "approximately true" description of the reference. We can see that Oscar's word 'water' refers to *water*, and Twin Oscar's word 'water' refers to *twin water*, since Oscar and Twin Oscar have "approximately true" descriptions of the liquids to which they apply their words. They use the same individuating descriptions to fix the references of their respective terms, but these descriptions are indexically applied to the different liquids water and twin water.

According to Putnam, both Oscar and Twin Oscar take for granted a description like the following: "water is the kind of liquid I and other members of my linguistic community find in ponds and streams, the liquid which falls from the sky when it rains, and which we use to wash our dishes, brew our coffee, and so on." Putnam schematizes the description that both Oscar and Twin Oscar use as follows: "water is whatever bears the same$_L$ (same liquid) relation to the stuff which I and other speakers in my linguistic community typically call 'water'." Oscar applies this description to water, whereas Twin Oscar applies the description to twin water.

Putnam argues that these different applications of the description are enough to show that Oscar's word 'water' means *water* not twin water, and that Twin Oscar's word 'water' means *twin water* not water:

> The key point is that the same$_L$ relation is a *theoretical* relation: whether or not something is or is not the same liquid as *this* may take an indeterminate amount of scientific investigation to determine. Moreover, even if a 'definite' answer had been obtained either through scientific investigation or through the application of some 'common sense' test, the answer is *defeasible:* future investigation might reverse even the most 'certain' example. Thus, the fact that an English speaker in 1750 might have called XYZ 'water', while he or his successors would not have called XYZ water in 1800 or 1850 does not mean that the 'meaning' of 'water' changed for the average speaker in the interval. . . . What changed was that in 1750 we would have mistakenly thought that XYZ bore the same$_L$ relation to the liquid in Lake Michigan, while in 1800 or 1859 we would have known that it did not.[21]

According to Putnam, then, in 1750 Oscar's word 'water' and Twin Oscar's word 'water' refer to water and twin water respectively, even though neither they nor any of their contemporaries can tell water from twin water. Putnam presents this second thought experiment in such a way that for *us* the salient difference between Oscar's and Twin Oscar's situations in 1750 is that the liquids they call 'water' are different. Putnam apparently thinks that by itself this difference shows their words have different meanings. I will explain later (§§96–98) why this appearance is misleading. But first (§§94–95) I will sketch and try to motivate the standard interpretation of "the contribution of the environment."

94. The Standard Metaphysical Picture of the Contribution of the Environment

I noted earlier (§92) that in Kripke's causal picture of reference there is a role for causal connections to play in fixing the reference of proper names introduced in baptisms. By pointing we may indicate that a particular baby is to be called 'Oscar', for example. This name-giving act sets up a causal link between the name and the baby. No other baby, however similar he looks, is the reference of our name 'Oscar'. But suppose that simultaneous with our baptism of Oscar, there is a twin baptism of Twin Oscar. On Twin Earth they are saying, "Let this baby be called 'Oscar'." We have no difficulty seeing that on Earth the name 'Oscar' refers to Oscar, whereas on Twin Earth the name 'Oscar' refers to Twin Oscar, even though we would not be able to tell baby Oscar and baby Twin Oscar apart. Putnam's claim that in 1750 our word 'water' refers to water, and the Twin Earthlings' word 'water' refers to twin water, seems based in a similar observation about the role of causal connections in determining the meaning and reference of words like 'water'. Tacit comparisons of Putnam's talk of the contribution of the environment with Kripke's causal picture of how the references of ordinary proper names are settled has led many to embrace a metaphysical picture of the contribution of the environment.

Let's develop the comparison in more detail. On Earth and Twin Earth, during the respective baptisms of Oscar and Twin Oscar, the baptizers utter the sentence "Let this baby be called 'Oscar'." We might in addition suppose that the baptizers of Oscar and Twin Oscar would accept the sentence " 'Oscar' is the name of whatever bears the same$_H$ (same human) relation to *this*" (pointing to the baby). Similarly, we might suppose that in 1750 both Oscar and Twin Oscar would accept the sentence "water is whatever bears the same$_L$ (same liquid) relation to the stuff to which I and other speakers in my linguistic community typically apply 'water'." Ordinarily we have no difficulty distinguishing between human beings, and so it would be odd to think that the same$_H$ (same human) relation is *theoretical* in the way that the same$_L$ (same liquid) relation is, especially in 1750, before the chemical structure of water was discovered.[22] But aside from this difference, the cases look similar.

In both cases we can picture the references of the words 'Oscar' and 'water' as dependent on causal links between actual applications of those words, on the one hand, and independently existing entities (such as *babies*) or natural kinds (such as *water*), on the other. In neither case is the associated description enough by itself, independently of any causal links or pointing gestures, to settle the references of the words 'Oscar' and 'water'. We can imagine that on Twin Earth a qualitatively similar baby is baptized with the name 'Oscar', and that the twin baptizer uses exactly the same descriptions that the baptizer on Earth uses, and yet on Twin Earth 'Oscar' refers to Twin Oscar, the baby with whom the twin baptizer is in causal contact, and on Earth 'Oscar' refers to Oscar, with whom our baptizer is in causal contact. Similarly, in 1750 the descriptions used by Oscar and Twin Oscar don't by themselves fix the references of their respective terms, and yet, if Putnam is right, Oscar's word 'water' refers to water, and Twin Oscar's word 'water' refers to twin water.

When we compare these cases, we naturally take the ordinary name-bearer relation, exemplified here by the relation between the name 'Oscar' and Oscar himself, as the model for understanding the relation between natural kind terms and their references. We then view natural kinds as independently existing entities to which we may be causally related by ostension. We picture water as separated by nature from other kinds of stuff, just as humans are separated by nature from other things.

In this way the name-bearer model leads to the idea that the "contribution of the environment" is to *individuate* the entities to which our terms refer. The environment can "contribute" in this way only if the medium of reference is not primarily our beliefs and descriptions, but our causal connections with independently existing natural entities. It is as if all it takes to refer to a naturally individuated entity is to point at a part or a sample of it; the rest is up to the "external world."

95. Two Versions of the Standard Metaphysical Picture

There are two standard versions of this name-bearer picture of the contribution of the environment. Sometimes these versions are combined, and sometimes not. Each version sketches a metaphysical interpretation of the nature and status of the entities with which we are supposed to be causally related when we use such descriptions as "water is whatever bears the same$_L$ (same liquid) relation to the stuff that I and other speakers in my linguistic community typically call 'water'."

The first version is what I will call *metaphysical realism*. The idea behind metaphysical realism is that we can conceive of the entities and substances and species of the "external" world independently of any of the empirical beliefs and theories we hold or might hold in the future. To accept this picture, we must conceive of the relationship between our words and the "external" world from an "external" perspective. We must imagine that we can completely distinguish between what we believe and think about the things to which we refer, on the one hand, and the pure truth about these things, on the other. In this imagined "external reality," things, species, and substances are individuated by their own natures or constituting principles. This picture generates questions about what these principles of individuation are, and thus drives philosophers to theorize about the metaphysical structure of the things, species, and substances in the "external" world.

We may try to use this metaphysical picture to interpret the name-bearer picture of the reference of natural kind words. Just as the baby exists independently of us and has its own internal principle of individuation, so the substance *water* and a species like *tiger* exist independently of us, each with its own internal principle of individuation. When we introduce a natural kind term like 'water' with the description "water is whatever bears the same$_L$ (same liquid) relation to the stuff which I and other speakers in my linguistic community typically call 'water'," we suppose that the causal connections we have to the "external" world enable us to pick out an independently existing substance with its own internal principle of individuation.

The central idea behind the metaphysical realist picture is that there are principles that individuate the entities and things in the "external" world, and that we conceive of these principles as existing independently of any of our ordinary or scientific beliefs. Our beliefs are true just in case they "correspond" with the way things are in the "external" world. "Correspondence" we picture as a substantive relation between our words and the "external" world, where the relata are conceived independently of each other.

The second version of the name-bearer picture of the contribution of the environment is what I will call *scientific realism*. According to this version, the entities, species, and substances to which we (take ourselves to) refer are the ones we quantify over and describe in our best scientific theories. Our scientific theories may be wrong, so we don't want to say that if our best present science tells us that there are entities of a certain type, these entities certainly exist. But, according to a scientific realist, we have no good reason to think that our words refer to independently existing things unless our best scientific theories commit us to the existence of those things.

Although scientific realism is often combined with metaphysical realism, it need not be. A scientific realist may reject the metaphysical realist's view that truth is "correspondence" with the "external" world. For example, as we saw in Chapter Two, Quine is a scientific realist who eschews the correspondence view of truth, and rejects the idea that we can conceive of the "external" world independently of any of our theories.[23]

Putnam was tempted by both metaphysical and scientific realism when he wrote "The Meaning of 'Meaning'." Yet I will argue that many of his examples and arguments are incompatible with both versions of the name-bearer picture. I will urge that the central arguments in "The Meaning of 'Meaning' " be viewed as extensions of the philosophical project I sketched in Chapter Six. This involves going beyond Putnam's text in many places, using his words to develop a more compelling and unified interpretation of the reasoning that leads to anti-individualism. I discuss metaphysical realism (in §99) after I explain (in §§96–98) what is wrong with the scientific realist's picture of the entities, species, and substances to which we refer.

96. Donnellan's Puzzle

To focus my discussion I will examine a puzzle Keith Donnellan has raised for what he thinks of as the Kripke-Putnam view of natural kind terms. Donnellan's puzzle is based in a sophisticated version of the scientific realist's interpretation of Putnam's view of natural kind terms. Working through Donnellan's puzzle leads to a better understanding of Putnam's picture of reference in "The Meaning of 'Meaning'." Donnellan describes his puzzle as follows:

> I want to imagine two cultures which up to a certain point in their history are as alike as one can make them. In particular, the languages they speak are identical, or, at any rate, there is nothing up to the date mentioned which affords a basis for positing a difference. I want also to imagine that at a certain period in their histories each culture develops a sophisticated science and scientific view of the world and that these are also identical down to the smallest detail. Now let us take one of the terms for kinds which existed in the vernacular language prior to the rise of science. I want to argue that although that term, by hypothesis, would exhibit no linguistic differences in the two languages prior to the rise of science, and although the sciences developed are identical, *the term could come to have a different extension in each culture.*[24]

Donnellan develops his puzzle by imagining a Twin Earth that has the same history as Earth up until a certain time, and then diverges after that time. In his story there is no divergence in their scientific views: Donnellan imagines that scientists in both communities have developed the same periodic table of the elements, and have the same chemical theories of the various properties of the elements.

A crucial detail of this thought experiment is that there are differences in the distribution of isotopes of the various elements on the two planets: "on Twin-Earth not only do elements usually have several isotopes, but also it is a general rule that one of the isotopes of a particular element makes up the bulk of the element as it occurs in nature—the other isotopes being fairly rare."[25] Donnellan emphasizes that in his story these differences between Earth and Twin Earth do not prevent the two communities from developing chemical theories that are "identical down to the last detail."[26]

Donnellan's supposition that on Twin Earth "as a general rule . . . one of the isotopes of a particular element makes up the bulk of the element as it occurs in nature" is fundamental to the plausibility of his description of how the two language communities evolve:

it seems to me not psychologically implausible for my Twin-Earthlings to be more taken with, so to speak, the isotope number of a bit of substance rather than with its atomic number and also not implausible for them to diverge from our practice and to identify the substance designated by some of their vernacular natural kind terms not with a certain element, but with the isotope which makes up the bulk of what had been previously called by that term. Hence, for example, they identify gold, not with the element having atomic number 79, but with a certain isotope number. The rare isotopes of the element having number 79 would then be dismissed as not "really" being gold, although, to be sure, in various ways very much like gold.[27]

This leads Donnellan to the central point of his Twin Earth story: *despite having identical histories up to a certain point, and even though both communities develop exactly the same chemical theories, they "map" their vernacular natural kind term 'gold' onto their identical chemical theories in different ways.* After the development of chemical theory, on Twin Earth the term 'gold' is said to denote a certain isotope of the element it is said to denote on Earth. If the experts on both Earth and Twin Earth are right about the reference of 'gold' in their respective linguistic communities, then two individuals whose linguistic dispositions are identical, one of whom lives on Twin Earth, the other one on Earth, refer to different substances when they use the term 'gold'.

This claim about the references of 'gold' in the two communities is plausible only if there are no grounds for saying that the scientists on Earth or on Twin Earth made a *mistake* when they "mapped" their respective vernacular kind terms onto their chemical theories. Donnellan assumes that under the circumstances he describes both "mappings" are beyond criticism: "there does not seem to be any way of showing that either party is right while the other is wrong."[28] I am not convinced of this, but I accept it provisionally, for the sake of highlighting other aspects of Donnellan's position. Later (in §98) I will question Donnellan's supposition that the Twin Earthlings' term 'gold' refers to an isotope of the element with atomic number 79.

Donnellan draws two conclusions from his thought experiment.

The first is that *science does not by itself determine how the vernacular kind term 'gold' should be mapped onto chemical theory.* He thinks his thought experiment shows that "we can agree with Putnam's theory about how natural kind terms function in ordinary language and still see that we might have done things differently even with the very same scientific results."[29] Donnellan's second conclusion is that *each community's mapping of the vernacular kind term 'gold' onto chemical theory in effect changed the extension of 'gold' in that community.* Donnellan explains this as follows: "If you accept that my story of Earth and Twin Earth contains no inconsistencies or other mistakes, then I do not see how we can accept Putnam's view that it is clear that natural kind terms in ordinary language have the same extension before and after scientific discoveries and the mapping of those terms onto those discoveries."[30] Donnellan highlights his second conclusion with the following example:

> Locke's ring, which he took to be gold, might have been made of the stuff having atomic number 79. In my story, the Earthling Putnam would say that Locke was correct. But suppose his ring were made of one of those rare isotopes, as we would say, of gold. Twin-Earthlings would say the ring wasn't made of gold at all. Putnam's doppelgänger would conclude that Locke was dead wrong. But nothing about language or science explains this difference.[31]

Donnellan acknowledges that from our present perspective, it seems natural to say that Locke's word 'gold' referred to gold, which we now know to have atomic number 79. But Donnellan thinks his story shows that we can't reasonably say that Locke's word 'gold' had the same extension as our word 'gold'. For if it were correct to say that Locke's word 'gold' had the same extension as our word 'gold', which denotes the element with atomic number 79, then it would be equally correct to say that Twin Locke's word 'gold' had the same extension as the Twin Earthlings' word 'gold', which denotes an *isotope* of the element with atomic number 79. This would commit us to saying that the extension of Twin Locke's word 'gold' is different from the extension of Locke's word 'gold'. But, according to Donnellan, "we seem to have no reason to think that their John Locke and ours differed psychologically or linguistically. Or rather, we have none unless we accept what seems to be an outrageously bizarre view of language—that the extensions of one's terms may be determined by the psychological quirks of some people several centuries hence."[32] Donnellan sums up his criticism of Putnam's account of the extensions of vernacular natural kind terms as follows: "we seem either to have to embrace unacceptable views about language or to admit that nature, after all, does not fully determine the extension of vernacular natural kind terms, and science is not wholly responsible for discovering their true extensions."[33] The first horn of the dilemma is presumably the "unacceptable" view that "the extensions of one's terms may be determined by the psychological quirks of some people several centuries hence." Donnellan concludes that Putnam's picture of the reference of natural kind terms is unacceptable: either it rests on the implausible view just described, or we must conclude that Putnam was wrong to suggest that "science is wholly responsible" for discovering the extensions of our vernacular natural kind terms.

On my reading, Donnellan's puzzle presupposes *scientific realism* (§95). Donnellan takes for granted that according to Putnam, science is "wholly responsible" for discovering the "true extensions" of vernacular natural kind terms like 'gold' and 'water'. Donnellan's thought experiment is designed to show that differences in extensions of natural kind terms could evolve in communities whose scientific theories are identical. He takes this to refute the assumption that science is wholly responsible for discovering the extensions of vernacular natural kind terms. Donnellan's own commitment to scientific realism is reflected in his assumption that if science does not wholly determine the extensions of vernacular natural kind terms, then their extensions are settled by the "psychological quirks" of individuals who "map" those terms onto the vocabulary of science. His thought experiment leads him to conclude that science is not wholly responsible for discovering the extensions of vernacular natural kind terms, and that the extensions of our vernacular natural kind terms must therefore be settled by our "psychological quirks." Thus he rejects Putnam's view that our vernacular natural kind terms have the same extensions now that they had centuries ago.

97. Vernacular Natural Kinds and Artifact Terms

But Putnam's discussion of vernacular natural kind words in "The Meaning of 'Meaning' " is more sophisticated than Donnellan's interpretation suggests. In the section titled "Other Senses" Putnam notes that the *same liquid* relation is *interest relative*. There are at least two ways in which it is interest relative. According to Putnam, x is the same liquid as y "just in case (1) x and y are both liquids, and (2) x and y agree in important physical properties."[34] To express and evaluate our judgments as to whether x and y meet Putnam's first condition, we must use the natural kind term "liquid," which is interest relative in the sense I will describe in this section. And whether or not x and y meet Putnam's second condition depends on what Putnam means by "important" physical properties. He emphasizes that what counts as an "important" physical property of the things and substances to which we apply a given natural kind term is partly settled by our entrenched interests in using the term.

Putnam emphasizes that on his view science is *not* "wholly responsible" for discovering the extensions of our vernacular natural kind terms:

> [a] ... misunderstanding that should be avoided is the following: to take the account we have developed as implying that the members of the extension of a natural-kind word necessarily *have* a common hidden structure. It could have turned out that the bits of liquid we call 'water' had *no* important common physical characteristics *except* the superficial ones. In that case the necessary and sufficient condition for being 'water' would have been possession of sufficiently many of the superficial characteristics.[35]

This passage shows that Putnam was not thinking of vernacular natural kind terms in the way that Donnellan assumes. The crucial point is that what counts as an important property of the things to which we apply our natural kind terms depends on our actual practices in applying the terms. If we learn that there are no chemical properties common to the samples to which our community regularly applies a term, we will usually conclude that the extension of the term can't be described in purely scientific terms. Thus in Putnam's view science is not wholly responsible for discovering the extensions of vernacular natural kind terms. Science may help us investigate the extensions of our natural kind terms, but we are guided in such investigations by the entrenched uses of the terms, and hence by the beliefs and interests that are central to our understanding of the references of the terms. Some of these entrenched uses, beliefs, and interests are learned when speakers learn the language, even though typically no single member of a linguistic community learns them all. Viewed collectively, our entrenched uses of terms set the methodological context of our inquiries. Against this evolving background of beliefs, a scientific discovery can give us new insight into what we have been talking about all along, yet no scientific discovery *by itself* can show that we did not mean anything at all by our words.

In "The Meaning of 'Meaning' " Putnam gives several examples that illustrate this aspect of our inquiries. His jade example shows that our vernacular kind terms do not always "map" onto what from a scientific point of view is a single natural kind: "An interesting case is the case of *jade*. Although the Chinese do not recognize a difference, the term 'jade' applies to two minerals: jadeite and nephrite. Chemically, there is a marked difference. Jadeite is a combination of sodium and aluminum. Nephrite is made of calcium, magnesium, and iron. These two quite different microstructures produce the same unique textural qualities!"[36] Here Putnam is emphasizing that the kind term 'jade' has a correct use that reflects our interests in textural qualities we have valued for centuries. The discovery that there are two different microstructures that produce the same textural qualities did not (and should not) undermine our entrenched uses of the term. Putnam argues that "if H_2O and XYZ had both been plentiful on Earth, then we would have had a case similar to the jadeite/nephrite case: it would have been correct to say that there were *two kinds of 'water'*. And instead of saying that 'the stuff on Twin Earth turned out not to really be water', we would say 'it turned out to be the XYZ *kind of water*'."[37] Putnam uses these examples to show that our vernacular natural kind terms should not be viewed from a scientific realist's point of view. We have entrenched practices within which it is relatively clear what counts as a correct application of a vernacular natural kind term. We may criticize and correct some of our entrenched applications of a term; but this doesn't by itself show there is nothing for us to be right or wrong about, even if there is no underlying chemical kind common to all the samples to which we apply the term.

This point is emphasized further by Putnam's discussion of artifact terms like 'pencil' and 'chair'. He argues against the "traditional view" that these words are defined by clusters of properties. On this view, statements like pencils are artifacts would be analytically true, true in virtue of the cluster definition of 'pencil'. Against this, Putnam tells the following story: "Imagine that we someday discover that *pencils are organisms.* We cut them open and examine them under the electron microscope, and we see the almost invisible tracery of nerves and other organs. We spy on them, and we see them spawn, and we see the offspring grown into full-grown pencils. We discover that these organisms are not imitating other (artificial) pencils—there are not and never were any pencils except these organisms."[38] With this thought experiment, similar in structure to the multiple sclerosis story, Putnam wants to show that we can change our beliefs about what pencils are without changing the subject. In the language of "The Analytic and the Synthetic," pencils are not one-criterion words, and so it would be wrong to classify statements about them as analytic. Putnam's story about pencils is also similar to his thought experiment in "It Ain't Necessarily So," where he invites us to imagine we have discovered that cats are robots controlled from Mars.[39] In both cases, he suggests, we would not say that the subject has changed. We would say we discovered that pencils are not artifacts, and that cats are not animals: our beliefs would change, but not the references of our terms 'pencil' and 'cat'.

These examples show that Donnellan's interpretation of Putnam's view of natural kind terms leaves out the fact that we have entrenched practices of using our terms prior to any scientific investigation of what their extensions are. Even if there are no chemical properties common to most samples to which we apply a given term, our understanding of the term is expressed in our actual practices of applying it, and our evolving accounts of its reference. The examples also show that in "The Meaning of 'Meaning'" Putnam rejects the scientific realist's view that if the extensions of our terms are not "wholly determined" by our scientific discoveries, then our use of these terms to group things into kinds just reflects our "psychological quirks." In Putnam's view, our interests in continued use of a term, reflecting entrenched beliefs that can be traced across time within the same linguistic community, set the intersubjective methodological context within which we can distinguish between changes in belief and changes in subject, even if we discover that there is no unified scientific account of what the term refers to.

98. The Division of Linguistic Labor across Time

Donnellan might object that if the samples to which we apply a given vernacular natural kind term do not share any scientifically important properties, then our current use of the term merely reflects our latest *decisions* about how to use the term, not *discoveries* about what the term applies to. On this view, any substantial change in our practices of applying such a term reflects a change in subject, not a change in our beliefs about the same subject. This objection rests on a misunderstanding of several related aspects of our ordinary and scientific practices. First, even when we *are* able to describe the extension of a vernacular natural kind term in purely scientific terms, the process by which we arrive at this description presupposes that we have a practical grasp of how the term is correctly applied. And our actual use of a term is our only guide to how it ought to be applied. We may discover that we can't give a purely scientific description of the extension of a given term. But the fact that such discoveries are possible shows that our practical grasp of the proper application of the term is *not* merely a reflection of our "psychological quirks."

Second, our practical grasp of the proper application of a term enables us to distinguish between changes in belief and changes in subject matter, even over long periods of time. For our use of terms in our language reflects entrenched beliefs and interests that can be individuated over time, from moment to moment and hence over long periods of time within the same community. The continuity of a linguistic practice over long periods of time, even centuries, can be seen as a natural consequence of the moment to moment continuity of our practical grasp of the proper application of our words, and of the long-term stability of our central interests in using them.

Third, and most important, the evolution of our use of words over long periods of time within the same linguistic community illustrates *the division of linguistic labor across time.* Just as we do not think that we must be able to distinguish between gold and fool's gold to express beliefs with such contents as *gold is a valuable metal,* so we should not think that John Locke's word 'gold' referred to gold only if he was in a position to distinguish gold from all qualitatively similar substances. Our view that when John Locke used the word 'gold' he meant what we now mean by 'gold' is not settled solely by Locke's linguistic dispositions. Locke is a member of our (temporally extended) linguistic community, and so he *ought* to defer to our present views as to what gold is, whether or not he *would* do so if he had the opportunity.[40]

Consider how Donnellan's thought experiment looks now that I have highlighted these three aspects of our ordinary and scientific practices. Recall that in Donnellan's story a certain isotope of gold is more prevalent on Twin Earth than it is on Earth.[41] In the situation Donnellan's describes, the Twin Earthlings take themselves to have discovered that the stuff they call 'gold' is this prevalent isotope, just as we take ourselves to have discovered that the stuff we call 'gold' is the element with atomic number 79. As I mentioned earlier, Donnellan emphasizes that "there does not seem to be any way of showing that either party is right while the other is wrong."[42]

But what would it take to show that one party is right while the other is wrong? Suppose that Earthling gold experts are taken to Twin Earth, and they challenge the Twin Earthlings' claim that what they call 'gold' is correctly applied only to the prevalent isotope of the element with atomic number 79. The Earthlings might argue that this identification is wrong, because it misses the importance of many of the entrenched interests and beliefs that shaped the use of the term on Twin Earth for centuries. The Earthlings might be able to convince the Twin Earthlings that their word 'gold' is correctly applied to the element with atomic number 79, despite the fact that on Twin Earth one particular isotope of the element is prevalent. Comparison with the jade case might help the Twin Earthlings to see that there is no good reason for them to view the reference of their word 'gold' as restricted to the isotope. The prevalence of the isotope might even provide a psychological explanation of their mistake. And if Earthlings could make these criticisms of the Twin Earthlings' identification of 'gold' with that isotope, then Twin Earthlings could too.

If the possibility of such criticisms and corrections is left open by Donnellan's description of the case, then the central supposition of Donnellan's thought experiment—that the extension of 'gold' on Earth is different from the extension of 'gold' on Twin Earth—does not bear scrutiny. More important, to make sense of the possibility of such criticisms and corrections is indirectly to acknowledge that entrenched beliefs and interests that shape the proper use of a term can persist in a linguistic community even over long periods of time. Properly described, such patterns of persisting beliefs and interests illustrate what Putnam calls "the division of linguistic labor across time."[43]

To highlight the division of linguistic labor across time, let's suppose that in the circumstances Donnellan describes, due to the salience of a certain isotope on Twin Earth, the term 'gold' on Twin Earth does not refer to the element with atomic number 79. If there are no good grounds for criticizing either our judgment that gold is the element with atomic number 79, or their judgment that what they call 'gold' is a certain isotope of the element with atomic number 79, then the division of labor across time is enough to show that there was no change in reference on either planet. Thus, contrary to Donnellan's intuitions about his story, Twin Locke's term 'gold' and Locke's term 'gold' did not have the same reference, even though in their day no one was able to distinguish twin gold from gold.

The observations in this and the previous section show that in Putnam's view our understanding of "the contribution of the environment" is exhausted by our understanding of possible *discoveries* about the proper application of our terms. We can make discoveries about the proper application of a term only if there is a practical understanding of its use. Practical understanding of the use of our terms reflects entrenched beliefs and interests that can persist from moment to moment and over long periods of time, even centuries. This continuity in our use of terms illustrates what Putnam calls "the division of linguistic labor across time."[44]

Properly described, the division of linguistic labor across time dissolves Donnellan's dilemma about how to interpret Putnam's view of the references of vernacular natural kind terms. In

Putnam's view, science is not "wholly responsible" for determining the extensions of our vernacular kind terms, nor are the extensions of these terms merely a reflection of our "psychological quirks." Hence Donnellan's puzzle poses no problem for Putnam's view that many of our vernacular natural kind terms have the same reference now that they had centuries ago. Like many others, Donnellan fails to see that our understanding of the contribution of the environment is inextricably linked to our understanding of the division of linguistic labor across time.[45]

99. Against Metaphysical Realism

The question remains whether we can accept the metaphysical realist's understanding of the contribution of the environment. The crucial idea behind metaphysical realism is that there is a "correspondence" relation between our words and "external" entities conceived from a point of view completely independent of any of our beliefs or interests. In this section, I will sketch what I take to be the most compelling attempt to give metaphysical realism content from our perspective as participants in ordinary and scientific inquiries, and show why the attempt fails.

In its most sophisticated form, metaphysical realism reflects our grasp of what Bernard Williams and Thomas Nagel call "the absolute conception"[46]—an absolutely objective representation of the world, without any subjective elements, from which all other representations can be understood. Williams and Nagel think we can understand the absolute conception as the limit of a dialectic that begins with our actual inquiries, and progresses through ever-expanding circles of representations.

This dialectic is launched by the truism that our beliefs result from interactions with an independently existing world. From time to time we discover that some of our beliefs are limited or distorted. In the simplest cases we notice that our location affects the way things appear to us—different locations lead us to describe "external" objects differently. The discovery of limits or distortions in our beliefs requires that we form a more encompassing perspective on ourselves and our relationship to the objects we perceive, a perspective that takes into account the cognitive processes that limited or distorted our beliefs.

When this happens locally, within our commonsense or scientific inquiries, it does not lead to the absolute conception. But Williams and Nagel maintain that we can extend our understanding of the dialectical process of overcoming the limitations in our beliefs far beyond any of our beliefs or interests. They think that the dialectic gives content to the idea of an absolutely objective representation of the world, without any subjective elements, from which all other representations can be understood.

The question is whether by itself the dialectic described by Williams and Nagel gives any content to the metaphysical realist interpretation of the contribution of the environment. The answer is that it does not.

Working from our perspective as participants in ordinary and scientific inquiries, described in Putnam's anti-individualistic way, we find that the dialectic described by Williams and Nagel cannot be extended as far as they imagine. The reason is that our understanding of the contribution of the environment is inextricably linked to our understanding of the division of linguistic labor, which reflects the entrenched beliefs and interests that mediate our use of language. Our interests may change, and we may discover that our beliefs are false, as Putnam's kinetic energy example shows. But we can follow the dialectic described by Williams and Nagel from one step to the next only if we can rely on beliefs and interests to give content to the more detached perspective we are allegedly able to grasp. Our understanding of successive steps in the dialectic fades away as we detach ourselves more and more from the beliefs and interests that form the background for our ordinary and scientific inquiries. Eventually we are left with a schema for generating a new step from a previous one, but without any idea of how to apply it. Stripped of all beliefs and interests, we are unable to form any conception of the contribution of the environment. Thus the dialectic described by Williams and Nagel does not give content to the metaphysical realist's interpretation of the contribution of the environment.

I will return to this argument against metaphysical realism in §§124–126. For now it is enough to see that there is no easy progression from Putnam's arguments for anti-individualism to metaphysical realism.

100. Our Linguistic Obligations

In §§96–99 I showed how to resist the standard scientific and meta-physical pictures of the contribution of the environment (described in §§93–95). To complete my deflationary reconstruction of Put-nam's anti-individualism, I will now highlight aspects of the rela-tionship between the division of linguistic labor and our linguistic obligations.

A speaker can share in the division of linguistic labor for a par-ticular term in a given linguistic community only if he is competent in the use of the term. Putnam has no theory of the necessary and sufficient conditions for such competence. In his view, we should start with our own best judgments as to when a person is competent in the use of a term, and remove obstacles to our understanding of these judgments, instead of trying to provide necessary and suffi-cient conditions for such competence. In this section I will use Put-nam's discussion of the "stereotypes" associated with our words to show why there is no hope of finding necessary and sufficient con-ditions for competence in the use of a term. This will shed light on our linguistic obligations, and it will lead us to question the standard interpretation of Putnam's causal picture of reference.

Putnam's observations about the division of linguistic labor remind us that we may be competent in the use of a term, and express beliefs by means of that term, even when we know very little about how the term is to be applied, or when some of our beliefs about how it is to be applied are false. Nevertheless, to partake in the division of linguistic labor for a given term in our language, we must be competent in the use of that term. The min-imal requirements for competence in the use of a term are in effect minimal requirements for participating in a linguistic practice within which one's utterances of sentences containing the term are taken at face value and evaluated accordingly.

Putnam's linguistic "stereotypes" are beliefs that qualify a speaker as minimally competent in the use of a word in her lin-guistic community. An individual is competent in the use of a word if her use of the word "passes muster" in her linguistic community. There is no simple rule for determining whether a person's use of a word passes muster in her community. It is not enough, for example, that members of her community who casually hear her utter the word take her to mean what they do by it. Suppose we hear some passer-by say, "Tigers are dangerous." At first it would be natural to conclude that she believes that tigers are dangerous. But suppose she stops and, while pointing at a snowball, says, "That is a tiger. Tigers are not animals and they do not have stripes." If she shows no signs of insincerity, we will surely conclude that she is not competent in the use of the English word 'tiger'—that her use of the word 'tiger' does not pass muster in the English speaking community. We would revise our previous assumption that she believes that tigers are dangerous. This example reminds us that to treat an individual as competent in the use of a term is simultaneously to take for granted that she has some idea what she is talking about when she uses the term.[47]

In each linguistic community and for each term in the language of that community there are minimal requirements for competent use of a term, but these minimal requirements may vary from community to community.[48] This becomes clear when we see that "the nature of the required minimum level of competence depends heavily upon both the culture and the topic."[49] Putnam notes, for example, that "in our culture speakers are required to know what tigers look like (if they acquire the word 'tiger', and this is virtually obligatory); they are not required to know the fine details (such as leaf shape) of what an elm tree looks like. English speakers are *required by their linguistic community* to be able to tell tigers from leopards; they are not required to be able to tell elm trees from beech trees."[50] In contrast, we can easily imagine a culture in which the ability to tell elms from beeches is very important, perhaps even a life and death matter. It would be natural for members of such a group to hold each other to a higher minimal standard for mastery of their respective words for elms and beeches than we hold ourselves to for mastery of our words 'elm' and 'beech'. We can also imagine a group of people who lack some interests that we have in our community, and who consequently hold members of their community to a lower minimal standard for mastery of, say, their words for *tiger* and *leopard*.

These examples show that we have no understanding of what is required for minimal competence in a given linguistic community apart from the community's entrenched interests in and beliefs about how to use a term; and so there is little hope of stating necessary and sufficient conditions for minimal competence in the use of a term. Instead we must trust the judgments we make from our perspective as participants in linguistic practices. Since such judgments are always inextricably linked to a context of entrenched interests and beliefs, standards for minimal competence may vary from culture to culture, or over time within the same linguistic community.[51]

Despite the inextricability of standards for minimal competence from entrenched interests and beliefs, we take our linguistic obligations seriously. We need no independent philosophical justification for the linguistic obligations we acknowledge as participants in our linguistic practices. Whether or not we have a philosophical theory of our linguistic obligations, "the fact is that we are fully competent speakers of English ourselves, with a devil of a good sense of what our linguistic obligations are."[52] When we look carefully at our linguistic practices from our participant perspective, we see that there is a division of linguistic labor among those speakers whose use of our language meets certain minimal requirements. These requirements reflect evolving beliefs and interests that sustain the division of linguistic labor across time.

I conclude that Putnam's earlier observation that there are terms in our language whose references remain the same despite radical changes in beliefs is part of a larger picture that includes the division of linguistic labor both at a given time and across time. As participants in ongoing linguistic practices, we find we have "a devil of a good sense" of what we are talking about when we agree or disagree with others, and of what counts as a change in belief, not a change in subject. We see that just as there is a division of linguistic labor at any given time, there is a division of linguistic labor across time. The division of linguistic labor, both at a given time and across time, reflects the entrenched beliefs and interests that together constitute our best understanding of what we are talking about.

101. Putnam's Causal Picture of Reference and Anti-Individualism

The heart of Putnam's causal picture of reference is not the idea of an independently specifiable causal relationship between our words and the world, but his observation that there is a division of linguistic labor both at a given time and across time within the same linguistic community.

To see this we must be more explicit about the difference between a *theory* of reference and a *picture* of reference. Following Kripke, I assume that a *theory* of reference is a noncircular statement of necessary and sufficient conditions for a speaker to refer to a particular object with his use of a word.[53] A theory of reference might be given in purely scientific terms, or it might be stated by using nonscientific notions taken from our ordinary practices. The important point is that a theory of reference gives necessary and sufficient conditions, without employing the notion of reference, or any notion that implicitly presupposes the notion of reference. A *picture* of reference, on the other hand, does not state necessary and sufficient conditions for a term to have a particular reference. The point of a picture of reference is to help us see how our beliefs about what we are talking about fit together with other familiar features of our linguistic practices, such as changes in belief, agreement and disagreement, the evaluation of assertions, and the resolution of disputes.

Some philosophers believe that reference is not an objective relation unless there is a scientific theory of reference. In their view, the *criterion* for the objectivity and determinacy of reference is scientific. This is what I call *scientific realism about reference*. From the perspective of scientific realism about reference, there is no value to Putnam's observations about reference unless they can be clarified in purely scientific terms.

But if we accept scientific realism about reference, we must conclude that Putnam's observations about reference are useless. For we have seen (§97) that in Putnam's view science is not wholly responsible for discovering the extensions of our natural kind and artifact terms. Our uses of such terms provide us with an objective understanding of what they apply to independently of our judgments as to whether they pick out chemical or biological natural kinds. Our practical grasp of the uses of our terms reflects entrenched beliefs and interests that can be individuated from moment to moment and over long periods of time, even centuries. This shows (§98) why our understanding of the contribution of the environment is inextricably linked to the division of linguistic labor across time. The references of a speaker's words should be described in the context of the division of linguistic labor, which reflects our practical judgments about who counts as a member of a given linguistic community. But we have also seen (§100) that there is no hope for a noncircular statement of necessary and sufficient conditions for membership in a given linguistic community, even if we do not require that these conditions be expressed in purely scientific terms. Hence there is no hope of finding a noncircular statement of necessary and sufficient conditions for a speaker to refer to a particular object with his use of a word. Putnam's observations about reference can't be developed into a rigorous theory of reference.[54]

This is not surprising once we see that Putnam's causal picture of reference is a natural development of his rejection of the analytic-synthetic distinction. We saw earlier (§82) that Putnam introduces "law-cluster concepts," "framework principles," and "one-criterion words" to highlight aspects of our linguistic practices that we can't see if we accept Carnap's analytic-synthetic distinction. To "overthrow" Carnap's analytic-synthetic distinction Putnam reminds us of familiar ways in which ordinary features of our use of language fit into a natural and coherent system.

Like the talk of "law-cluster concepts," "framework principles," and "one-criterion words," Putnam's causal picture of reference is introduced to help us to see aspects of our use of language that more traditional philosophical pictures of meaning and reference have prevented us from seeing. The heart of this causal picture is the observation that there is a division of linguistic labor both at a given time and across time within the same linguistic community. Putnam's rejection of the analytic-synthetic distinction depends on examples that illustrate the division of linguistic labor across time. Kripke's talk of "causal" links between speakers of the same linguistic community helped Putnam see the significance of the division of linguistic labor, and this led to his investigations of the requirements for membership in a linguistic community. Here again Putnam's aim is not to try to state necessary and sufficient conditions for such membership, but to remove obstacles to our understanding of the requirements for membership expressed in our actual linguistic practices. Finally, Putnam's observations about membership in a linguistic community fit together with his observations about the contribution of the environment, illustrated by discoveries we have made, or may make in the future, about the extensions of our words.

This completes my deflationary sketch of Putnam's anti-individualism. In my view, the heart of Putnam's anti-individualism is his observation that there is a division of linguistic labor both at a given time and across time. My deflationary account of the division of linguistic labor lifts the philosophical weight off the reference relation, and places it on our investigations and elucidations of familiar aspects of our linguistic practices. Earlier (§89) I suggested that if we accept as philosophically unproblematic our ordinary judgment that two different speakers of the same public language can use the same terms to express their beliefs and thoughts, we can make sense of our ordinary judgment that the references of their words are the same without embracing a non-disquotational theory of reference. I have tried to show (§§90–101) that, for Putnam, to view these ordinary judgments as philosophically unproblematic is to acknowledge our linguistic obligations, and to partake in the division of linguistic labor both at a given time and across time.

EIGHT

Participation, Deference, and Dialectic

102. Anti-Individualism from Putnam to Burge

In this chapter I reconstruct Tyler Burge's anti-individualistic descriptions of our linguistic practices.[1] My goal is to add detail to my deflationary picture of anti-individualism by highlighting central aspects of our practices of evaluating our beliefs and thoughts.

As we saw in Chapter Seven, the heart of Putnam's anti-individualism is his discovery that there is a division of linguistic labor both at a given time and across time. Given at least a minimal competence in the use of our language, our words are taken at face value and evaluated accordingly. Since our sincere utterances express our beliefs and thoughts, Putnam's discovery of the division of linguistic labor at a given time and across time shows that in some cases the proper evaluation of our beliefs and thoughts is partly dependent on our social and physical environments.

Tyler Burge has extended and developed Putnam's anti-individualistic picture of our practices of evaluating assertions, beliefs, and thoughts. In my view, despite his use of such terms as 'content', 'notion', and 'necessity', Burge's self-conscious methodology and careful commentary suggest a sophisticated deflationary anti-individualism about how our beliefs and thoughts are evaluated. Yet at crucial moments Burge succumbs to rationalistic rhetoric about the metaphysics of meaning and truth. These moments threaten to spoil Burge's otherwise illuminating descriptions of how we evaluate our beliefs and thoughts. I will explain how we can accept some of Burge's observations without embracing his rationalist rhetoric about the metaphysics of meaning and truth.

My discussion of Burge's view falls into two main parts. In the first part (§§103–107) I use Burge's terminology carefully but uncritically. In preparation for my own deflationary version of Burge's descriptions of how we evaluate our beliefs and thoughts, I reconstruct Burge's arthritis thought experiment and his account of the dialectic of meaning-giving characterizations, clarify his talk of "complete" and "incomplete" understanding, and describe the schematic structure of Burge's arguments for anti-individualism. In the second part (§§108–112) I explain why Burge's terminology and rhetoric seem to commit him to an obscure metaphysics and epistemology of meaning, and I try to show that properly viewed Burge's anti-individualistic descriptions of how we attribute and evaluate our beliefs and thoughts are free of problematic presuppositions.

103. Burge's Starting point, Content Clauses, and Notions

Early in "Individualism and the Mental" Burge writes, "My objective is to better understand our common mentalistic notions. . . . I assume that a primary way of achieving theoretical understanding is to concentrate on our *discourse* about mentalistic notions."[2] "Mentalistic notions" are beliefs, thoughts, fears, desires, and so on. "Discourse about mentalistic notions" includes sentences of the forms 'A believes that S', 'A thinks that S', 'A fears that S', 'A desires that S'—sentences used to attribute beliefs, thoughts, fears, desires, and other "propositional attitudes." Burge aims to elucidate our discourse about mentalistic notions.

He focuses on the role of "that-clauses" embedded in mentalistic discourse. In the sentence 'Bertrand believes that water is fit to drink', the expression 'that water is fit to drink' is a "that-clause"—a linguistic item that may be used to attribute various attitudes to the "content" it expresses.[3] Burge takes for granted that we know how to use sentences of the forms 'A believes that S', 'A thinks that S', 'A fears that S', 'A desires that S' to attribute beliefs, thoughts, desires, and fears. If I am asked what my friend Bertrand believes, I may say that Bertrand believes that water is fit to drink. Here I use the expression 'that water is fit to drink' to "give the content" of

Bertrand's belief—to say what Bertrand believes. In this "ontologically neutral"[4] sense, that-clauses express the "contents" of beliefs and thoughts. In Burge's view, we do not need a *theory* of sameness and difference for contents to have a good implicit understanding of the contents expressed by our sentences. Our understanding of the contents expressed by our sentences is revealed in our actual practices of attributing beliefs and thoughts, agreeing, disagreeing, evaluating assertions, and resolving disputes.

Although Burge intends his use of the term "content" to be "ontologically neutral," he thinks of it as "holding a place in a systematic *theory* of mentalistic language".[5] Later (in §§112) I will offer a deflationary reconstruction of Burge's talk of "content"; I will suggest that to say that two assertions, beliefs, or thoughts have the "same content" is just to say that they should be evaluated in the same way. In my view, the term "content" is only as clear as our actual practices of evaluating assertions, beliefs, and thoughts. Despite my doubts about the clarity and usefulness of the term "content," however, I will sometimes use this term in my preliminary reconstructions (§§103–107) of Burge's descriptions of how we evaluate our beliefs and thoughts.

Burge notes that substitution of coextensive expressions does not always preserve the truth value of ordinary belief attributions. So for example, imagine that Bertrand learns about some of the chemical properties of H_2O, but he does not know that H_2O is water, and he doubts that H_2O is fit to drink. Under these circumstances, we would ordinarily accept (1) and reject (2):

(1) Bertrand believes that water is fit to drink.
(2) Bertrand believes that H_2O is fit to drink.

But the only difference between (1) and (2) is that (2) has an occurrence of 'H_2O' where (1) contains an occurrence of 'water'. So substitution of coextensive expressions like 'H_2O' for 'water' in (1) does not preserve truth. 'H_2O' and 'water' have what Burge calls "oblique occurrence" in (1) and (2).[6] Such terms express what Burge calls "notions": "Just as whole that-clauses provide the content of a person's attitude, semantically relevant components of that-clauses will be taken to indicate notions that enter into the attitude (or the attitude's content)."[7] In Burge's view, we implicitly know what *attitude contents* and *notions* are if we know how to use that-clauses to attribute beliefs and thoughts to individuals. Thus our willingness to say that Bertrand believes that water is fit to drink shows that we think Bertrand understands the notion of water, even though he does not know that water is H_2O. In this "ontologically neutral" sense, according to Burge, terms with "oblique occurrence" express "notions" that "enter into" the "contents" of beliefs and thoughts.

Just as there is no general theory of the minimal requirements for competence in the use of a given term (§100), so there is no general statement of what is required for understanding the notion expressed by a given term. But to have a good implicit understanding of the notions expressed by our terms we do not need a theory of sameness and difference for notions. For Burge our understanding of the notions expressed by our terms is revealed in our actual practices of agreeing, disagreeing, evaluating assertions, and resolving disputes. Later (in §112) I will offer a deflationary reconstruction of Burge's talk of "notions." But despite my doubts about the clarity and usefulness of the term "notion," I will use this term in my preliminary reconstructions (§§103–107) of Burge's descriptions of how we evaluate our beliefs and thoughts.

We may summarize these points as follows. Burge is primarily interested in what he calls the "contents" of our beliefs, thoughts, and desires, and the "notions" that "enter into" these contents. He assumes that our understanding of "contents" and "notions" is expressed in our use of language, including our mastery of mentalistic discourse; and, in this sense, the words "content" and "notion" are labels for what we already implicitly understand. To have a good implicit understanding of "contents" and "notions" we do not need a theory of sameness and difference for them. Burge's aim is to elucidate "contents" and "notions" by investigating our use of language, focusing on our practices of attributing and evaluating beliefs and thoughts.

In the next three sections (§§104–107) I will use Burge's terminology of "contents" and "notions" to present and clarify his thought experiments. I will explain later (in §108) why this terminology and some of Burge's rhetoric encourage obscure metaphysical and epistemological theses about meaning and truth. I will then try to convince you (in §§109–112) that properly viewed, Burge's anti-individualistic descriptions of how we evaluate our beliefs and thoughts are free of problematic metaphysical or epistemological commitments.

104. Step One of Burge's Arthritis Thought Experiment

Burge's arthritis thought experiment is designed to highlight relationships between our social and physical environments and the proper evaluation of our assertions, beliefs, and thoughts. He divides the thought experiment into three steps. In the first step he describes an ordinary situation in which an individual whom I will call "Alfred" believes that he has arthritis in his thigh. In the second step Burge imagines that a twin of Alfred was born and raised in a community in which the word 'arthritis' applies to rheumatoid ailments *including the one in his thigh*. In the third step Burge concludes that Alfred's and his twin's beliefs have different "contents," in the sense that their beliefs should be evaluated differently.

In my view the first step is the most important one. To accept Burge's description of Alfred's beliefs in the first step is to accept Burge's conception of the starting point and method for elucidating our mentalistic discourse. The second and third steps of Burge's thought experiment highlight some of the consequences of what we implicitly accepted in the first. I will reconstruct the first step in this section, and the second and third steps in the next.

In step one Burge describes an ordinary situation in which an individual believes that he has arthritis in his thigh:

> A given person has a large number of attitudes commonly attributed with content clauses containing 'arthritis' in oblique occurrence. For example, he thinks (correctly) that he has had arthritis for years, and that his arthritis in his wrists and fingers is more painful than his arthritis in his ankles, that it is better to have arthritis than cancer of the liver, that stiffening joints is a symptom of arthritis, that certain sorts of aches are characteristic of arthritis, that there are various kinds of arthritis, and so forth. . . . In addition to these unsurprising attitudes, he thinks falsely that he has developed arthritis in the thigh. . . . Generally competent in English, rational and intelligent, the patient reports to his doctor his fear that his arthritis has now lodged in his thigh. The doctor replies by telling him that this

cannot be so, since arthritis is specifically an inflammation of joints. Any dictionary could have told him the same. The patient is surprised, but relinquishes his view and goes on to ask what might be wrong with his thigh.[8]

To highlight Burge's method of elucidating our mentalistic discourse, I will augment this preliminary description of step one.

Burge's method is easier to see if we suppose that our subject, Alfred, sincerely assents to many English sentences containing the word 'arthritis'. Let's assume, for example, that Alfred assents to 'I have arthritis in my ankles', and 'stiffening of the joints is a symptom of arthritis'. Since Alfred is a competent English speaker, his sincere utterances show that he believes that he has arthritis in his ankles, and that stiffening of the joints is a symptom of arthritis. Alfred also sincerely assents to the sentence 'I have arthritis in my thigh'. *We* know that he cannot have arthritis in his thigh, but Alfred does not know this until he sees his doctor. Since he is a competent English speaker, Alfred's sincere assertion of the sentence 'I have arthritis in my thigh' expresses his belief that he has arthritis in his thigh.

Let's also assume that Alfred *willingly defers* to the doctor. He takes for granted that his own beliefs about arthritis do not set the standards by which to evaluate the truth or falsity of his belief that he has arthritis in his thigh. We may even suppose that he is *relieved* to learn that his belief that he had arthritis in his thigh *could not have been true.*

For contrast, consider Bertrand, in whose idiolect the term 'arthritis' is a mere *abbreviation* for the phrase 'rheumatoid ailment that can occur in the joints and muscles'. Suppose that Bertrand sincerely assents to his sentence 'I have arthritis in my thigh', goes to his doctor for help, but does not accept the doctor's "correction," and continues to assent to 'I have arthritis in my thigh' even after the doctor tells him that he cannot have arthritis in his thigh. In these circumstances members of the English-speaking community should not take Bertrand's words at face value. When Bertrand sincerely assents to his sentence 'I have arthritis in my thigh' he does *not* thereby express the belief that he has arthritis in his thigh.

The contrast between Alfred's and Bertrand's situations helps us to see that the English-speaking community's standards for evaluating utterances made using the word 'arthritis' are not simply *imposed* on Alfred. His acceptance of these standards is partly expressed by his willingness to defer to experts and to consult dictionaries and encyclopedias.[9] Burge emphasizes that "the subject's willingness to submit his statement and belief to the arbitration of an authority suggests a willingness to have his words taken in the normal way—regardless of mistaken associations with the word. Typically, the subject will regard recourse to a dictionary, and to the rest of us, as at once a check on his usage and his belief. When the verdict goes against him, he will not usually plead that we have simply misunderstood his views."[10] These observations reinforce Burge's claim that a competent speaker like Alfred may believe that he has arthritis in his thigh, even though one cannot have arthritis in one's thigh.

Against this one might insist that since Alfred does not know the accepted definition of 'arthritis', he does not know what arthritis is, and so he does not have *any* beliefs involving the notion arthritis. Instead Alfred has a false *metalinguistic* belief that 'arthritis' applies to rheumatoid ailments of the joints and muscles. When Alfred accepts the doctor's "correction," then, he is not abandoning the belief that he had arthritis in his thigh (since he never had that belief); he is correcting his false metalinguistic belief that 'arthritis' applies to rheumatoid ailments of the joints and muscles. I will call this the *metalinguistic objection.*

This metalinguistic objection can be recast and generalized with the help of new terminology. Let's say (first) that a *sentence* is "analytically" true or "analytically" false if its truth (or falsity) is settled by the best-known dictionary entries for the terms that occur in it, and (second) that a *belief* is "analytically" true (or false) if the sentence that expresses the "content" of the belief is "analytically" true (or false).[11] To evaluate an "analytically" true (or false) belief one must consult an authoritative dictionary. A rational person can sincerely assent to an "analytically" true sentence whether or not he knows the dictionary entries for all the terms in the sentence. But a rational person sincerely assents to an "analytically" false sentence only if he does *not* know the complete dictionary entry for all of the terms in the sentence.

The key principle of the metalinguistic objection may now be expressed as follows:

(*)   If an individual does not know an authoritative dictionary
       entry for a word, then he is not competent to use the
       word, and he should not be credited with beliefs whose
       contents are specified by *using* that word.

For example, Alfred does not know the dictionary entry for
'arthritis' and so he sincerely assents to 'I have arthritis in my
thigh,' an "analytically" false sentence. If we accept (*) we must
conclude that Alfred is not competent to *use* the word 'arthritis'.
It therefore seems that the content of the belief he expresses
with the sentence 'I have arthritis in my thigh' must be metalinguistic. Alfred assumes that 'arthritis' applies to rheumatoid ailments of the joints and muscles, and when he assents to the
sentence 'I have arthritis in my thigh' he thereby expresses
the metalinguistic belief that 'arthritis' applies to the ailment in
his thigh.

With these points in mind, we may recast and generalize the
metalinguistic objection as follows: *if an individual sincerely assents to
an "analytically" false sentence, the belief he thereby expresses is metalinguistic in form.* Burge flatly denies this claim. Here is how he
sums up his denial:

> Both ... "analytically" true and ... "analytically" false atti-
> tudes are linguistic in the sense that they are tested by con-
> sulting a dictionary or native linguistic intuitions, rather than
> by ordinary empirical investigation. ... The pragmatic focus of
> expressions of these attitudes will be on usage, concepts, or
> meaning. But *it is simply a mistake to think that these facts entail,
> or even suggest, that the relevant contents are metalinguistic in
> form.*[12]

To understand Burge's reply to the metalinguistic objection, we
must see why he rejects (*).

The key to Burge's rejection of (*) is his starting assumption
that we have no grasp of beliefs and thoughts apart from our
mastery of mentalistic discourse. To find out whether an individual should be credited with beliefs that are expressed by using
(not mentioning) a word, we must look carefully at our actual
practices of attributing beliefs and thoughts. When we investigate
these practices we find that "ordinary attributions typically

specify the mental content without qualifications or hesitations."[13] We find that in the circumstances described earlier we would accept the sentence 'Alfred believes that he has arthritis in his thigh'. Since our grasp of beliefs and thoughts is expressed in our mastery of mentalistic discourse, in those circumstances we should conclude that *Alfred believes he has arthritis in his thigh.* Alfred is competent in the use of the term 'arthritis' even though he does not know the complete dictionary entry for the word.

It is instructive to compare the methodology behind Burge's rejection of (*) with Putnam's conception of the starting point and task of philosophy of language. Recall that according to my reconstruction, Putnam starts by taking at face value our practices of agreeing, disagreeing, evaluating assertions, and resolving disputes. The task for philosophy of language is to remove obstacles to our understanding of these practices. Putnam's method is to remind us of familiar ways in which ordinary features of our practices fit together in a natural and coherent system. In particular, he uses examples to show that there is a division of linguistic labor both at a given time and over time. To share in the division of linguistic labor for a particular term in a linguistic community is to be competent in the use of the term, and so minimal requirements for competence in the use of a term are also minimal requirements for participation in a linguistic practice within which one's utterances of sentences containing the term will be taken at face value and evaluated accordingly. Putnam's examples show that an individual may be competent in the use of a term even if he does not know its dictionary entry.

Burge's rejection of (*) reflects his view that if an individual is minimally competent in the use of a term, he can express beliefs whose contents are specified by using that term. By our ordinary standards Alfred is minimally competent in the use of the term 'arthritis', and so when Alfred sincerely assents to the sentence 'I have arthritis in my thigh' he thereby expresses his belief that he has arthritis in his thigh. If we accept Burge's starting point and methodology for elucidating mentalistic discourse, we will naturally accept the first step of Burge's thought experiment: in the circumstances described, Alfred believes that he has arthritis in his thigh.

105. Steps Two and Three of Burge's Arthritis Thought Experiment

The second and third steps of Burge's thought experiment are designed to illuminate aspects of Alfred's situation that were only implicit in the first step.

In the second step Burge describes a counterfactual situation in which someone physically and phenomenologically just like Alfred is born and raised in a community where the term 'arthritis' is conventionally defined to apply to rheumatoid ailments in the limbs as well as the joints. The counterfactual has two easily separable parts. In the first we single out all of the physical and phenomenological features of Alfred that we can describe without any mention of his social or physical environment, and we imagine that there exists a twin of Alfred—another person with exactly the same features. In the second part we imagine an environment in which (one of) Alfred's twin(s) is born and raised.

Burge describes the first part of the second step of his thought experiment in some detail:

> We are to conceive of a situation in which the patient [Alfred's twin] proceeds from birth through the same course of physical events that [Alfred] actually does, right to and including the time at which [Alfred] first reports his fear to his doctor. Precisely the same things (non-intentionally described) happen to [Alfred's twin]. He has the same physiological history, the same diseases, the same internal physical occurrences. He goes through the same motions, engages in the same behavior, has the same sensory intake (physiologically described). His dispositions to respond to stimuli are explained in physical theory as the effects of the same proximate causes. All of this extends to his interaction with linguistic expressions. He says and hears the same words (word forms) at the same time [Alfred] actually does. [Alfred's twin] develops the disposition to assent to 'Arthritis can occur in the thigh' and 'I have arthritis in the thigh' as a result of the same physically described proximate causes. . . . We further imagine that the patient's non-intentional, phenomenal experience is the same. He has the same pains, visual fields, images, and internal verbal rehearsals.[14]

In this first part of the second step we imagine a person who is physically and phenomenologically indistinguishable from Alfred in all ways that could be described without mentioning any events or objects beyond his skin. To imagine Alfred's twin is to see Alfred in a new light, distinguishing his physical and phenomenological features from any features that can't be described without mentioning events or objects beyond his skin.

In the second part of the second step Burge stipulates a crucial respect in which Twin Alfred's linguistic community is different from Alfred's (and our) linguistic community:

> in our imagined case, physicians, lexicographers, and informed laymen apply 'arthritis' not only to arthritis but to various other rheumatoid ailments. The standard use of the term is to be conceived to encompass the patient's actual misuse. . . . We . . . also suppose that this difference and those necessarily associated with it are the only differences between the counterfactual situation and the actual one. (Other people besides the patient [Twin Alfred] will, of course, behave differently.)[15]

We imagine that the linguistic dispositions of members of Burge's counterfactual linguistic community are virtually the same as the linguistic dispositions of members of Alfred's and our actual linguistic community, except that in the counterfactual community 'arthritis' is correctly applied to rheumatoid ailments in the limbs as well as the joints. So our understanding of Burge's *counterfactual* situation is dependent on our implicit understanding of Alfred's (and our) *actual* linguistic practices.

In the third step Burge draws conclusions from his comparisons of the two situations. Alfred and Twin Alfred are competent speakers of English and Twin English, respectively. Just as we take Alfred's words at face value in our community, so the members of Twin Alfred's community take Twin Alfred's words at face value. When Alfred sincerely utters the words 'I have arthritis in my thigh', he thereby expresses the belief that he has arthritis in his thigh. And when Twin Alfred sincerely utters the same words, he thereby expresses whatever belief Twin Earthlings attribute with their sentence 'Alfred believes that he has arthritis in his thigh'.

We supposed that on Twin Earth the word 'arthritis' is correctly applied to rheumatoid ailments of the limbs as well as the joints, so we know that whatever notion 'arthritis' expresses in Twin English—the language used on Twin Earth—it is not the notion expressed by our word 'arthritis'.[16] Taking our ordinary practices of attributing and evaluating beliefs as our best guide to what individuals believe, we see that Alfred and Twin Alfred express different beliefs when they sincerely utter the words 'I have arthritis in my thigh.'

The second and third steps of Burge's thought experiment highlight the relationship between the proper evaluation of an individual's beliefs and thoughts and the linguistic community of which he is a member. In both the actual and the counterfactual situation we take for granted that the contents of a person's beliefs and thoughts are properly expressed by the ordinary mentalistic attributions made by the members of his linguistic community. What is different in the counterfactual case is the proper use and definition of 'arthritis', and hence also the notion expressed by that word. So the second and third steps of Burge's thought experiment help us see that the proper evaluation of Alfred's beliefs is not settled solely by his linguistic dispositions and his physical properties.

106. Norms for Understanding, Conventional Linguistic Meaning, and Cognitive Value

Alfred knows enough about arthritis to entertain beliefs and thoughts involving the notion of arthritis, but he does not know that one cannot have arthritis in one's thigh, and so he has an "incomplete understanding" of the notion of arthritis. Alfred's "incomplete understanding" of the notion of arthritis is "the key to the thought experiment."[17] We can construct a similar thought experiment "in any case where it is intuitively possible to attribute a mental state or event whose content involves a notion the subject incompletely understands."[18] Burge recommends that we view Alfred's "incomplete understanding" of the notion of arthritis as an illustration of fundamental *normative* aspects of our mentalistic discourse. In this section I will reconstruct Burge's framework for elucidating what he calls "norms for conventional understanding." In the next section I will use my reconstruction of Burge's framework to clarify the phenomenon of incomplete understanding, and describe how the arthritis thought experiment may be seen to depend on it.

Burge elucidates our mentalistic discourse from our perspective as *participants* in our linguistic community, viewed as "a vast, ragged network of interdependence, established by patterns of deference which lead back to people who would elicit the assent of others."[19] A speaker's linguistic competence is exhibited in her linguistic activity: "the language does not present a standard of competence independent of individuals' activity. Minimal competence consists in conformity to the practice of others. 'Greatest competence' consists in abilities to draw distinctions, to produce precisifications, to use numerous linguistic resources, to offer counterexamples to proposed equivalences—that elicit the reflective agreement of other competent speakers."[20] In Burge's view, linguistic competence is inextricably linked to "reflective agreement" among competent speakers. The most competent speakers are those who have the most convincing *reasons* for their assertions and beliefs.

For many terms used in a given linguistic community there are widely accepted beliefs expressed by *using* the term. Thus we use the term 'arthritis' to express our belief that *arthritis is a disease that can occur in the joints and muscles,* and we use our term 'contract' to express our belief that *a contract is a legally binding agreement.* Some beliefs expressed by using a term X reflect a community's best judgment about what Xs are, and so they "set a norm for conventional linguistic understanding" in the community;[21] these beliefs constitute the "conventional linguistic meaning" of X. Burge's account of "conventional linguistic meaning" is rooted in his view of how the members of the community arrive at, support, and test their beliefs about what Xs are. He describes a "dialectic of meaning-giving characterizations" the dynamics of which reveal the normative force of the conventional linguistic meaning of a term.

Imagine that we are together trying to come up with a dictionary entry for the term 'chair'. Before we begin our dialectic, we already regularly use the term 'chair', and all of us know a chair when we see one. Thus we agree on what Burge calls "archetypical applications"—"perceptually backed, indexically mediated applications (or imagined projections from these) to 'normal' or 'good' examples."[22] The dialectic of meaning-giving characterizations "consists of an attempt to find a fit between such examples and the characterizations that are dominant in selecting them."[23]

Suppose we start by thinking that *a chair is a movable seat with a back and legs*. Our question is whether this characterization fits with our archetypical applications of the word 'chair'. One of us may recall that some deck chairs—the kind that are attached to the side of a ship's cabin—are not movable and have no legs. If we agree that deck chairs are chairs,[24] we must revise our preliminary characterization. We may propose, for example, that *a chair is a seat with a back*. We then ask whether this new characterization fits with our archetypical applications of the word 'chair'. One of us may recall that a bench is a seat with a back. We all agree that a bench is not a chair. So we refine our characterization again: *a chair is a seat for one with a back*. The dialectic continues in this way until we are convinced that our characterization fits with all archetypical applications of our word 'chair'.

The resulting characterization provides the "conventional linguistic meaning" of the term 'chair'. The conventional linguistic meaning of a term is the characterization that "sets a norm for conventional understanding of the term." Burge explains that "to provide a meaning, a proposed normative characterization must accord with archetypical applications and must treat the characterizations that competent users actually give, as at least approximations to the norm. The conventional linguistic meaning of a term has been correctly specified when, under these restrictions, the most competent speakers have reached equilibrium on a characterization."[25] When the most competent speakers of a language have reached equilibrium on a characterization, all competent members of the linguistic community either know the characterization or ought to defer to those know it; and the most competent members of the community also know the reasons why the community reached equilibrium on the characterization. In this sense the characterization "sets a norm for conventional understanding."

When we defer to the meaning-giving characterization of a more competent speaker in our community, we are not simply caving in to her personal whims, but accepting her *reasons* for rejecting our previous characterization. Burge emphasizes that

> in the course of the dialectic we stand corrected: we recognize ourselves as convicted of *mistakes*, not merely infelicitous strategies for communication. We come to know something that

characterizes empirical entities and sets standards for characterizations to which we regard *ourselves* as antecedently committed ... the most competent speakers are pre-eminent not merely because they impress the impressionable. Their influence is based on persuasion that is subject to dispute and cognitive checks.[26]

Thus to arrive at and sustain a particular meaning-giving characterization, the members of a linguistic community must be able to defend it against challenges, and to allay doubts that it is correct. In principle *any* meaning-giving characterization—even those we take to be obvious—can be challenged or doubted.

We must therefore distinguish between the *normative* force of conventional linguistic meaning and the *truth* of particular normative characterizations. The normative force of a particular characterization rests on agreement among the most persuasive members of the linguistic community. But the truth of a characterization is not guaranteed by this kind of agreement. Agreement on a characterization always involves presuppositions or explicit citations of "extralinguistic fact"—substantive beliefs that may be false. But "there is no transcendental guarantee that people cannot agree on making mistakes."[27]

This leads Burge to distinguish between the *conventional linguistic meaning* of a term and its *cognitive value*. The cognitive value of a term is the *notion* expressed by it. The conventional linguistic meaning may be revised without changing the notion expressed by the term. In our successive characterizations of a term, we take for granted that we are characterizing the same notion. And when our beliefs involving a notion undergo a fundamental revision we develop a new meaning-giving characterization of the old notion.

Putnam's kinetic energy example can be adapted to illustrate Burge's distinction between conventional linguistic meaning and cognitive value. Recall that 'kinetic energy' has the same reference in both pre-relativistic and relativistic physics. At one time all competent physicists treated the pre-relativistic equation as a definition, and so by Burge's criterion the pre-relativistic equation was the "meaning-giving characterization" of 'kinetic energy'. Later physicists revised the equation to accommodate Einstein's relativity theory. Thus the meaning-giving characterization of 'kinetic energy' changed, but the *notion* expressed by 'kinetic energy'—its cognitive value—remained the same.

Burge's account of conventional linguistic meaning can be seen as a development of Putnam's observations about the relationship between "meaning" and what Putnam calls our "linguistic obligations." We saw earlier (§101) how Putnam's talk of "linguistic stereotypes" highlights our requirements for "minimal competence" in the use of a term. Burge's dialectical account of conventional linguistic meaning is an account of a linguistic community's requirements for "maximal competence" in the use of a term. Just as a speaker must have some beliefs if her use of language is to pass muster in her linguistic community, so a speaker must have a reflective understanding of how to use a term, and the ability to persuade others that her understanding is correct, if she is to be counted among the most competent members of her linguistic community.

107. Complete and Incomplete Understanding and the Structure of Burge's Thought Experiments

Burge's description of the dialectic of meaning-giving characterizations shows how our understanding of a notion is linked to the conventional meaning-giving characterization of the notion. This suggests that, in Burge's special use of the phrase:

CU   A subject S *completely understands* notion N when S knows the conventional meaning-giving characterization of N.

To say that S "completely understands" N in this sense is to say that S knows what the most competent speakers in S's linguistic community *believe to be* the correct meaning-giving characterization of N.[28] But we have seen that the conventional meaning-giving characterization of N may be wrong even if everyone accepts it. So S may "completely understand" notion N in the sense defined by CU even if S and everyone else in S's linguistic community is wrong about what Ns are.[29]

S has an incomplete understanding of N when S does not completely understand N. There are two ways in which S may incompletely understand N:

IU   A subject S *incompletely understands* notion N if and only if either (a) some of S's beliefs involving N are false ac-

cording to the conventional meaning-giving characterization of N, or (b) S is agnostic about some statements whose
truth values are settled according to the conventional
meaning-giving characterization of N.

Burge's arthritis example illustrates (a): Alfred is minimally competent in the use of the term 'arthritis', but he believes that he has
arthritis in his thigh, and this belief is false according to the conventional meaning-giving characterization of arthritis.[30] To illustrate (b) we may suppose that Charles, who is also minimally
competent in the use of the term 'arthritis', is *unsure* whether one
can have arthritis in one's thigh.

Like CU, IU defines a subject's "incomplete understanding" in
terms of what the most competent speakers in the subject's linguistic community *believe to be* a correct characterization of N. But
there is no *guarantee* that the most competent speakers will reach
equilibrium on a correct meaning-giving characterization.

This means that the suppositions (first) that Alfred has an
"incomplete understanding" (as defined by IU) of arthritis, and
(second) that Twin Alfred has a "complete understanding" (as
defined by CU) of what they call 'arthritis' on Twin Earth, are not
sufficient to support Burge's conclusion that when Alfred and Twin
Alfred sincerely utter the words 'I have arthritis in my thigh,' they
express beliefs with different truth values. This conclusion presupposes that the notions expressed by 'arthritis' in the actual and
counterfactual situations are different. In the context of Burge's
thought experiment, we can confidently conclude that the notions
expressed by 'arthritis' in the actual and counterfactual situations
are different only if we suppose that the meaning-giving characterizations in both the actual and counterfactual steps are correct.

To see why, let us consider a similar thought experiment in which
the meaning-giving characterizations of the two communities are
not both correct. Every detail of this new thought experiment is the
same as Burge's original arthritis thought experiment except that
the competent speakers in the counterfactual community agree on
an incorrect characterization of what they call 'arthritis'. This leaves
open the possibility that their term 'arthritis' expresses the notion
arthritis.[31] Under these circumstances, both Alfred and Twin Alfred
believe that they have *arthritis* in their thigh, even though according

to IU Alfred incompletely understands the notion arthritis and Twin Alfred does not.

In Burge's version of the arthritis thought experiment the competent speakers in the counterfactual community agree on the *correct* characterization of what they call 'arthritis'. Burge relies on this assumption when he concludes that Alfred and Twin Alfred express beliefs involving different notions when they sincerely utter 'I have arthritis in my thigh'. Thus Burge presupposes that the meaning-giving characterizations are correct in both the actual and the counterfactual communities.

Now we can describe Burge's arthritis thought experiment schematically as follows. (Read N as a blank space in which you imagine some word like 'arthritis', and 'N' as a name of the word you imagine in place of N.) In the first step we imagine a community whose conventional meaning-giving characterization of N is correct, and a competent speaker S in that linguistic community who incompletely understands N in the sense defined by (a) of IU: some of S's beliefs involving N are false according to the conventional meaning-giving characterization of N. In the second step we imagine that Twin S, whose physical structure and linguistic dispositions are the same as S's, lives in a community in which 'N' is correctly characterized differently, so that none of the beliefs Twin S expresses using 'N' are false according to the conventional meaning-giving characterization of the notion expressed by 'N' in his linguistic community. Since we assume that both communities *correctly* characterize the notions they express with 'N', we can conclude that 'N' expresses different notions in the two communities, and that S and Twin S express beliefs with different contents when they sincerely assent to sentences containing 'N'. Thought experiments of this form show that when a subject S has an incomplete understanding of N, the contents of S's beliefs and thoughts involving N are not settled solely by S's physical structure and linguistic dispositions.

Thought experiments of this form can be run in reverse, so that in the first step none of S's beliefs involving N are false according to the conventional meaning-giving characterization of N, and in the second step Twin S has an incomplete understanding of the notion expressed by 'N' in Twin S's linguistic community. For example, we can imagine that Alfred correctly believes that one cannot have arthritis in one's thigh. Twin Alfred also assents to the sentence 'One can't have arthritis in one's thigh', but in his linguistic community the word 'arthritis' is correctly defined to apply to rheumatoid ailments in one's joints and muscles, including the thigh. So Twin Alfred is surprised to learn from his doctor that he has what they call 'arthritis' in his thigh. A minimally competent speaker, Twin Alfred defers to his doctor. When Twin Alfred utters the sentence 'I don't have arthritis in my thigh', he thereby expresses a false belief whose content does not involve the notion *arthritis*. This reverse version of Burge's arthritis thought experiment shows that even when none of S's beliefs and thoughts involving notion N are false according to the conventional meaning-giving characterization of N, the contents of S's beliefs and thoughts involving N are not settled solely by S's physical structure and linguistic dispositions.[32]

We can also construct thought experiments that begin with a subject who incompletely understands a notion N in the sense defined by (b) of IU. Thus suppose that in the first step Charles is unsure whether one can have arthritis in one's thigh. Charles asks his doctor whether he can have arthritis in his thigh, and his doctor tells him that he cannot. Suppose that in the counterfactual community, 'arthritis' is correctly applied to rheumatoid ailments in the muscles as well the joints. So when Twin Charles asks his doctor, "Can one have arthritis in one's thigh?" the doctor says, "Yes". Charles and Twin Charles have an incomplete understanding of the notion expressed by the word 'arthritis' in their respective linguistic communities, and they express beliefs with different contents when they use their term 'arthritis'. Thus when Charles sincerely utters the sentence 'Arthritis is a disease one can have in the joints', he expresses the belief that arthritis is a disease one can have in the joints, but when Twin Charles utters that sentence, he expresses a different belief.

This thought experiment has the following form. In the first step we imagine a community whose conventional meaning-giving characterization of a notion N is correct, and a competent speaker S in that linguistic community who incompletely understands N in the sense defined by (b) of IU—S is agnostic about some statements whose truth values are settled according to the conventional meaning-giving characterization of N. In the second step we imagine that Twin S, whose physical structure and linguistic dispositions are the same as S's, lives in a community in which the word 'N' is correctly defined slightly differently. Since we assume that both communities *correctly* characterize the notions they express with the word 'N', we conclude that 'N' expresses different notions in the two communities, and that S and Twin S express beliefs with different contents when they sincerely assent to sentences containing 'N'. Like Burge's original arthritis thought experiment, thought experiments of the form just described show that when a subject S has an incomplete understanding of a notion N, the contents of S's beliefs and thoughts involving N are not settled solely by S's physical structure and linguistic dispositions.

108. Essentialism and Rationalism about Notions

We have seen that Burge's thought experiments rest on the supposition that the meaning-giving characterizations in both the actual and counterfactual steps are *correct*. But what *makes* a meaning-giving characterization correct or incorrect?

This question seems pressing and difficult because of the links between our ideas of meaning, essence, and necessity. Quine once disparagingly remarked that "meaning is what essence becomes when it is divorced from the object of reference and wedded to the word."[33] Burge apparently endorses this remark (though not its disparaging tone) when he says that a correct meaning-giving characterization of a word 'N' gives "essential" information about Ns, and thus states a "necessary truth" about Ns.[34] Thus any satisfactory account of what makes a meaning-giving characterization of N *correct* must at the same time be an explanation of how it gives "essential" information about Ns, and of why it is "necessarily true." Since talk of "essential" information and "necessary truth" is notoriously obscure, we understandably feel a special urgency about the question of what makes a meaning-giving characterization correct or incorrect.

We are apparently faced with two alternatives: either (a) a meaning-giving characterization of N is correct or incorrect *in virtue of linguistic convention,* or (b) a meaning-giving characterization of N is correct or incorrect *in virtue of its "correspondence" or lack of "correspondence" with N itself.* According to (a), the "necessity" attaching to the correct meaning-giving characterizations is somehow rooted in linguistic convention; according to (b), the "necessity" attaching to the correct meaning-giving characterizations is somehow based in the notions themselves. Alternative (a) suggests that notions are in some sense constituted or constructed by our decisions about how to use our words, whereas alternative (b) suggests that notions are independently existing "objects" whose essential properties we aim to represent accurately with our meaning-giving characterizations.

Since Burge defines the meaning of a term as a characterization of the way it is used by competent speakers, it may seem that the most competent speakers simply *decide* what is to count as the correct meaning-giving characterization of many of our words. This apparently favors alternative (a). But in Burge's view *there is no term whose correct meaning-giving characterization is decided by linguistic convention.*

To see this, recall that the aim of the dialectic of meaning-giving characterizations is to find a fit between the archetypical applications of a given term and the characterizations that are dominant in selecting these applications. When the most competent speakers reach an equilibrium on a characterization, it sets a norm for linguistic understanding, and in this sense it gives what Burge calls the "conventional linguistic meaning" of the term. It is central to Burge's account of the dialectic of meaning-giving characterizations that the "conventional linguistic meaning" of a term can be challenged and revised. The crucial consideration is that

> there is no separating truths of meaning or truths of logic (or criterial truths, or truths of reason, or necessary truths) from truths of fact. . . . In stating a truth of meaning (however one construes the notion), one is not stating a degenerate truth. To put this crudely: in explicating one's "meanings," one is equally stating non-degenerate truths—"facts." So *giving a true explication is not separable from getting the facts right.*[35]

This undermines the suggestion that a meaning-giving characterization might be true *in virtue of* linguistic convention, independent of empirical "facts."

But if the truth of a conventional meaning-giving characterization of a notion N is not decided by convention, it seems that it must somehow be determined by *the notion itself*. This leads to (b), according to which a meaning-giving characterization of N is correct or incorrect *in virtue of its "correspondence" or lack of "correspondence" with N*. Alternative (b) is strongly suggested by Burge's distinction between the conventional meaning-giving characterization of a term and its "cognitive value"—the notion it expresses. Burge seems to picture the cognitive value or notion expressed by a term as ontologically independent of our conventional meaning-giving characterizations of it. According to this metaphysical picture, a conventional meaning-giving characterization of a given notion N is correct only if N has the essential property attributed to it by the characterization. Thus for example, if *arthritis is a rheumatoid ailment that afflicts the joints only* is the correct meaning-giving characterization for the notion *arthritis*, then *arthritis* has the essential property of being a disease one can have only in the joints. This is what I call *essentialism about notions*.

Burge sometimes endorses a corresponding rationalist picture of the epistemology of understanding. He writes, for example, that "our cases develop a theme from the Socratic dialogues: Thought can correct meaning."[36] The metaphysical and rationalistic overtones of this allusion to Socrates are sounded again in another remarkable passage:

> we distinguished different levels of understanding, culminating in ideal, articulable mastery of a conventional normative characterization. Is there a further sort of ideal understanding associated with cognitive value? There is no simple answer.... Usually the best understanding one can achieve of a cognitive value is that offered by accepted normative characterizations and whatever background information accompanies them. Thus full understanding of cognitive value is normally not distinct from ideal understanding of ordinary usage and meaning. (In such cases, the cognitive value expressed by a term is, however, still individuated differently from its linguistic meaning.) When thought does correct meaning, one may achieve a revised understanding of cognitive value based on theoretical realization that goes beyond ordinary usage and meaning. *Understanding of this sort bears comparison with the sort of ultimate insight, championed by the*

> rationalist tradition, that was regarded as concomitant with deep foundational knowledge.[37]

Here Burge suggests that above and beyond the ordinary dialectic of meaning-giving characterizations, which results in a conventional linguistic meaning for a term, there is a deeper kind of rational insight given to only a few extraordinary members of a linguistic community.[38] This may lead us to embrace what I call *rationalism about notions,* according to which we have a special intellectual faculty for "grasping" or "seeing" the essential properties of the notions that lie behind our actual linguistic practices.

So it seems we must embrace essentialism about notions to explain what it is for a meaning-giving characterization to *be* correct; and we need to accept rationalism about notions to explain how we can *discover* the correct characterization.

109. A Strategy for Deflating Burge's Anti-Individualism

In the last two chapters I tried to show that if we start from our perspective as participants in ordinary and scientific inquiries, and we remind ourselves of familiar and unproblematic ways in which ordinary features of our use of language fit together in a natural and coherent system, we arrive at a deflationary anti-individualism that does not presuppose any substantive metaphysical theses. I announced (in §102) that my goal in this chapter is to add detail to my deflationary picture of anti-individualism by highlighting central aspects of our practices of evaluating our beliefs and thoughts, and I stressed (in §103) that Burge's anti-individualistic descriptions of our use of language are rooted in our perspective as participants in ordinary and scientific inquiries. But now it seems that Burge's anti-individualistic descriptions of our participant perspective on mentalistic discourse require that we accept essentialism and rationalism about notions—two substantive and obscure metaphysical theses. Instead of adding detail to the deflationary picture of anti-individualism sketched in Chapter Seven, Burge's anti-individualism apparently undermines it.

This threatens my central goal, which is to articulate and defend a compelling alternative to metaphysical realism and scientific naturalism. Essentialism about notions amounts to a version of metaphysical realism (§95). It is clear that if my anti-individualistic descriptions of our linguistic practices lead inevitably to essentialism about notions, I have not sketched an alternative to metaphysical realism. It is less clear but equally important that if my anti-individualistic descriptions of our linguistic practices commit me to essentialism about notions, then I have not sketched a compelling alternative to Quine's scientific naturalism. In Chapter Six I tried to convince you that Quine's behavioristic descriptions of our use of language prevent us from understanding our linguistic practices, whereas a careful description of our use of language from the participant perspective shows how familiar aspects of our use of language fit together in a natural and coherent system. As I see it, the plausibility and appeal of my alternative to Quine's scientific naturalism rest primarily on the effectiveness of my attempts to show that the participant perspective is free of any problematic metaphysical or epistemological assumptions. So if my participant perspective inevitably presupposes essentialism about notions, I have not sketched a compelling alternative to Quine's naturalism.

Properly viewed, however, Burge's descriptions of our mentalistic discourse do not presuppose essentialism and rationalism about notions. In the next three sections I will try to show that Burge's thought experiments and his dialectic of meaning-giving characterizations, suitably reconstructed, add illuminating details to my deflationary picture of anti-individualism by highlighting central aspects of our practices of evaluating our beliefs and thoughts.

The key to my reconstruction is to reject the assumption that *if a meaning-giving characterization is correct, there must be something in virtue of which it is correct.* This assumption was implicit in the reasoning that led us to conclude in the previous section (§108) that Burge's descriptions of our mentalistic discourse foster essentialism and rationalism about notions. Once we reject this implausible assumption, we can see that even though (a) is unacceptable, we are not thereby driven to (b), since we don't need a theory of what "makes" a meaning-giving characterization correct.[39] We are then free to develop a deflationary reconstruction of Burge's talk of "the dialectic of meaning-giving characterizations." With this deflationary reconstruction we can tame Burge's talk of "essential" information and "necessary truth."

I sketch my reconstruction in the next three sections. First (in §110) I draw on "Philosophical Discoveries" by R. M. Hare to clarify and deflate our idea of the participant perspective, and to contrast it with Quine's behavioristic descriptions of linguistic behavior. Then (in §111) I show how to understand Burge's dialectic of meaning-giving characterizations from this deflated participant perspective, and (in §112) I explain what truth, notions, and contents amount to on this deflationary reconstruction of Burge's anti-individualism. I try to show that if we systematically deflate Burge's descriptions of our mentalistic discourse, we can reject Quine's behavioristic descriptions of language use without indulging in obscure metaphysical or epistemological theories of meaning and understanding.

110. Hare on Dancing the Eightsome Reel

In "Philosophical Discoveries," R. M. Hare's aim is "to elucidate the nature of the discovery called 'discovering the use of words' "[40] by describing how a group of dancers would resolve their dispute about how to dance a certain dance. For our purposes the central interest of Hare's discussion of the dancers' dispute is that it illuminates familiar and unproblematic aspects of our ordinary use of language, aspects that can only be described from our perspective as participants in ordinary and scientific inquiries. Hare begins with the following description of the dancers' dispute:

> Suppose that we are sitting at dinner and discussing how a certain dance is danced. Let us suppose that the dance in question is one requiring the participation of a number of people—say one of the Scottish reels. And let us suppose that we have a dispute about what happens at a particular point in the dance; and that, in order to settle it, we decide to dance the dance after dinner and find out. We have to imagine that there is among us a sufficiency of people who know, or say they know, how to dance the dance—in the sense of 'know' in which one may know how to do something without being able to say *how* it is done.[41]

Several additional suppositions set the context for Hare's imagined dispute about how to dance the dance:

Let us suppose that the dance is a traditional one which those of the company who can dance it have all learnt in their early years; let us suppose that they cannot remember the circumstances in which they learnt the dance; nothing of their early dancing-lessons remains in their memory except: how to dance the dance. And let us further suppose that there are no books that we can consult to see if they have correctly danced the dance—or, if there are books, that they are not authoritative.[42]

Against this background we suppose that the dancers know how to dance the eightsome reel. Their dinner dispute arises when they try to give a detailed description of how the eightsome reel is to be danced. It is a dispute about what one *ought* to do if one wishes to dance the eightsome reel *correctly*.

To resolve the dispute, the dancers dance the eightsome reel after dinner. Suppose that when they dance the eightsome reel, they agree on how the dance is to be danced and immediately resolve their dispute. This could happen if the dispute was due to a momentary confusion of the eightsome reel with a different dance. A more interesting possibility is that some of the dancers get out of step with the others at the disputed point and the dance comes to a halt with some dancers claiming that the others have made a mistake. Suppose that under these circumstances one of the dancers claims that her fellow dancers are wrong. She might try to show, for example, that her fellow dancers have oversimplified a complex part of the dance, or that they fail to see a certain pattern exemplified by several recurring parts of the dance. In both cases—and in countless similar ones—she would remind the dancers of what they already know about how to dance the dance, and show how the steps with which they are so familiar fit together in a coherent pattern which they have overlooked or forgotten. If she convinces her fellow dancers, the dispute is resolved.

The dispute concerns the *proper* way to dance the eightsome reel. When the dancers resolve their dispute, they agree on a *normative characterization* of the eightsome reel—an account of how the eightsome reel is to be danced. Thus when they write out their account of how to dance the eightsome reel, "what has been put down is not: how a particular set of dancers *did* dance on a particular occasion, but: how *the* eightsome reel *is* danced. It is implied that if *any* dancers dance like *this* they are dancing an eightsome reel correctly."[43] The dancers' dispute is resolved when they all *agree* on a single account of how the dance is danced.

We can make sense of disputes or disagreements about how to dance a particular dance only if we have some way of identifying the dance independently of an explicit description of how it is to be danced. That there is a single dance about whose description the dancers disagree is shown by their shared ability to dance and to recognize performances of the eightsome reel. They learned to perform the eightsome reel when they were young. In a practical sense they both know and remember how to dance the eightsome reel, even though they do not know or remember an explicit description of how to dance the eightsome reel. Both their understanding of the dispute and their method for resolving it presuppose their ability to dance the eightsome reel.

This brings us to the central point of the story of the dancers' dispute: *if we are to understand the dispute and its resolution, we cannot restrict ourselves to descriptions available to someone who is unable to recognize or participate in performances of the eightsome reel.*

To highlight this crucial point, consider the perspective of anthropologists who do not know how to dance the eightsome reel, and cannot by themselves distinguish between performances of the eightsome reel and performances of many other dances. The anthropologists view the dancers and their dance from the "outside." They cannot by themselves identify the eightsome reel. At best they can indirectly identify the eightsome reel by observing the behavior of people who *say* they are dancing "the eightsome reel." Hare observes that

> if a party of anthropologists sat down to dinner before starting their study of a particular dance, they could not fall into the sort of argument that I have imagined. Nor could they fall into it *after* starting the study of the dance. This sort of argument can arise only between people who, first of all, know how to dance the dance in question or to recognize a performance of it, but secondly are unable to say how it is danced. In the case of the anthropologists the first condition is not fulfilled.[44]

Hare notes that the anthropologists have no independent grasp of how to dance the dance, relative to which various proposed characterizations of how it is danced could be evaluated:

The anthropologists ... have not learnt to dance the dance
which they are going to see danced after dinner; and therefore,
even if they have decided to *call* the dance that they are to see
danced 'dance no. 23', this name is for them as yet unattached
to any disposition of theirs to recognize the dance when it is
danced. The anthropologists will not be able to say, when a
particular point in the dance is reached, 'Yes, *that's* how it
goes'. They will just put down what happens, and add it to
their records.[45]

In contrast, since the dancers know how to dance the eightsome
reel, they are in a position to make discoveries about how the
eightsome reel is danced. In this sense they are in a position to
make discoveries about what the name 'eightsome reel' means:
"the people in my example, when they say 'eightsome reel', are not
using an arbitrary symbol for *whatever* they are going to observe;
the name 'eightsome reel' has for them already a determinate
meaning, though they cannot as yet say what this meaning is."[46]
The name 'eightsome reel' has the meaning given by the proper
characterization of how the dance is to be danced. Since the dancers
have a practical ability to dance the dance, they in a sense already
know the meaning, before they "discover" it via comparisons of
particular characterizations with actual performances of the dance.

111. Burge's Dialectic Deflated

I will now try to convince you that we can describe our use of
language from the participant point of view and accept a deflated
version of Burge's dialectic of meaning-giving characterizations
without falling into obscure metaphysical and epistemological
assumptions, such as essentialism and rationalism about notions. I
will argue that the dialectic of meaning-giving characterizations is
as lucid and unproblematic as the method used by the dancers to
resolve their dispute about how to dance the eightsome reel. My
strategy is to note parallels between the method used by the dancers
to resolve their dispute about how to dance the eightsome reel and
the method used in the dialectic of meaning-giving characterizations of the term 'chair' (§106).

There are two preliminary points of comparison. First, the

dancers' ability to dance the eightsome reel is analogous to our competent use of the term 'chair'. Just as the dancers' practical knowledge of how to dance the eightsome reel is exhibited in their actual performances of that dance, our competence in the use of the term 'chair' is exhibited in our "archetypical applications" of that term. Second, the dancers' method of reaching agreement on a description of the eightsome reel is analogous to our method of reaching equilibrium on a dictionary entry for the term 'chair'. Just as the dancers search for a description of the eightsome reel that fits with their actual performances of the eightsome reel, so we search for a characterization of chairs that fits with our "archetypical applications" of 'chair'.

We saw in the previous section that if we are to understand the dancers' dispute and its resolution we cannot restrict ourselves to descriptions available to Hare's anthropologists, who are unable to dance the eightsome reel, or to distinguish between the eightsome reel and other dances. We also saw that there is nothing mysterious about the dancers' perspective as participants in the dispute about how to dance the eightsome reel.

We are now in a position to see that the anthropologists' perspective on the dancers' dispute and its resolution is analogous to Quine's naturalistic perspective on our use of the term 'chair'. If we are to understand the dialectic of meaning-giving characterizations for the term 'chair', we cannot restrict ourselves to Quine's behavioristic descriptions of our use of the term 'chair'.

To see this, consider again why the anthropologists' perspective bars us from understanding the dancers' dispute. In the previous section we saw that we can make sense of disputes or disagreements about how to dance a particular dance only if we have some way of identifying the dance without an accurate or explicit description of how it is to be danced. The dancers' shared ability to dance and to recognize performances of the eightsome reel shows that there is a single dance about whose description they disagree. Since the anthropologists cannot dance the dance or recognize performances of it, they are blind to an aspect of the dancers' situation without which which their dispute could not arise.

Similarly, we can make sense of a dialectic of meaning-giving characterizations of the term 'chair' only if we have some way of identifying chairs without an accurate or explicit characterization of what chairs are. That there is a common subject of our dialectic is shown by our competence in the use of the term 'chair', expressed in our confident "archetypical applications" of the term 'chair' and our willingness to defer to more persuasive members of our linguistic community. Different speakers participating in the same dialectic take for granted that their fellow speakers are minimally competent in the use of the word 'chair', and so they take each other's archetypical applications of the word at face value.[47] This aspect of our language use can only be described from our perspective as participants in a common language that includes the term 'chair'.

Our perspective as participants in a common language looks mysterious if we confine ourselves to Quine's descriptions of our linguistic behavior. But our recent comparisons suggest that there is no more mystery to our participation in a common linguistic practice than there is to the dancers' participation in performances of the eightsome reel.

112. A Deflationary View of Truth, Notions, and Contents

I suggest that nothing more than our participation in the use of a common language is required to make sense of Burge's anti-individualistic descriptions of our mentalistic discourse. In particular, we need not presuppose essentialism or rationalism about notions. The key to my deflationary interpretation is to reject the assumption that there must be something *in virtue of which* our meaning-giving characterizations are correct.

Consider truth first. Through our participation in our shared linguistic practices of criticizing and correcting our assertions, we see that truth does not follow from consensus. With a disquotational truth predicate we can easily express this aspect of our linguistic practices. We can say, for example, that 'Chairs are portable seats with a back and legs' is true if and only if chairs are portable seats with a back and legs. This does not tell us whether chairs are portable seats with a back and legs, whether anyone believes that chairs are portable seats with a back and legs, or how we should go about trying to evaluate this statement. Hence to make the point that truth does not follow from consensus, a disquotational truth predicate is enough; we do not need a substantive theory of what "makes" our statements true.

Nor do we need a theory of the cognitive values, or notions, expressed by our terms. Properly viewed, the term "notion" is just a way of speaking that helps us see aspects of our use of language that we might otherwise miss.[48] Talk of "notions" and "characterizations" helps us see, for example, that a competent speaker can believe that he has arthritis in his thigh, even though one cannot have arthritis in one's thigh. Talk of the distinction between the "notion" *arthritis* and the "characterization" *arthritis is a rheumatoid ailment that afflicts only the joints* serves to highlight the use of the term 'arthritis' in expressions of beliefs and thoughts that conflict with the characterization, as for example when we assert that *arthritis is not a disease that afflicts only the joints.*

The apparently problematic idea that a meaning-giving characterization can be *correct* should be deflated with a disquotational truth predicate. To say that a meaning-giving characterization is correct is just to say that it is disquotationally true. On this deflationary view, our understanding of what is it is for a meaning-giving characterization to be "correct" is exhausted by our understanding of actual and possible ways in which we arrive at, challenge, and revise our meaning-giving characterizations.

Since a community's meaning-giving characterizations of a term reflect more or less entrenched beliefs and interests of members of the community, what counts for them as the proper use of a term is inextricable from their substantive beliefs. This means that there is no sharp distinction between what Burge calls "the dialectic of meaning-giving characterizations" and other aspects of our everyday and scientific inquiries. When we are constructing a dictionary, we may be engaged in this kind of dialectic with no other conscious aim. But in the midst of everyday and scientific inquiries, competent speakers may correct each other's "characterizations" of a term, just as they may correct each other's "empirically" false beliefs. So, strictly speaking, there is no such thing as the dialectic of meaning-giving characterizations. Talk of "the dialectic of meaning-giving characterizations" is just a way of highlighting one inextricable aspect of our everyday and scientific inquiries.

In the same deflationary spirit, we should accept Burge's suggestion that to say that a meaning-giving characterization of N gives "essential" information is just to say that if an object x does not satisfy the characterization, "we would correctly and almost automatically refuse to count x an instance of the type."[49] So, for example, to say that "arthritis is a rheumatoid ailment of the joints only" gives "essential" information about arthritis is just to say that one cannot have arthritis in one's thigh—that we would correctly and automatically refuse to count a disease in a person's thigh as a case of *arthritis*. And to say that a meaning-giving characterization of N states a "necessary truth" about N is to say that it gives "essential" information about N in the deflationary sense just described.

I also recommend that talk of the "contents" of a speaker's beliefs and thoughts be replaced by deflated descriptions of how we should evaluate her beliefs and thoughts. To say that the "contents" of two of her beliefs are different is then just to say that the beliefs should be evaluated differently. In Burge's arthritis thought experiment, the belief that Alfred expresses with his sincere assertions of 'I have arthritis in my thigh' is false, whereas the belief that Twin Alfred expresses with his sincere assertions of 'I have arthritis in my thigh' is true. Burge's claim that these beliefs have different "contents" can be replaced by the observation that the beliefs should be evaluated differently.

Thus I propose that all of the details of Burge's thought experiments—his talk of "contents" and "notions," of "the dialectic of meaning-giving characterizations," and of "complete" and "incomplete" understanding—be replaced by deflated descriptions of our practices of attributing and evaluating particular beliefs and thoughts. Reconstructed in this way, Burge's anti-individualistic descriptions of how we evaluate our beliefs and thoughts add detail to my deflationary picture of anti-individualism.

NINE

Realism, Self-Knowledge, and Skepticism

113. A Challenge from within the Participant Perspective

In this chapter I will confront a fundamental challenge to the coherence of the deflationary picture of anti-individualism sketched in Chapters Six to Eight. For reasons I will explore in detail, our anti-individualistic descriptions of our commonsense and scientific inquiries tempt us to think we can raise skeptical possibilities that undermine self-knowledge—the familiar fact that we know our own beliefs and thoughts without empirical investigation.

In discussing these issues there is a danger of getting swamped by unusually heavy seas of language. For instance, I take for granted that to say we have self-knowledge is to say we "know the contents" of our own thoughts without special "empirical" investigation. Unfortunately, these words are commonly associated with ideas that prevent us from properly understanding self-knowledge. The word "empirical" typically brings to mind the idea of a sharp distinction between "conceptual" and "empirical" consequences of our beliefs and thoughts—an idea that anti-individualism undermines, for reasons I will explain below. We will see that talk of "contents" and of "knowing the contents" of one's own thoughts is also misleading. If we don't keep our eye on such problematic expressions, entrenched ways of understanding them are sure to distort our picture of the phenomena to which they are supposed to apply. To signal my doubts about standard ways of thinking about self-knowledge and related issues, I put quotation marks around words and phrases I find especially problematic.

In the rest of this opening section, I will sketch a skeptical problem for self-knowledge, and describe my strategy for dis-solving it.

Recall that in my view the anti-individualist starts by taking at face value our ordinary judgments about what speakers believe, what they are talking about, and when they agree or disagree with each other. For example, we ordinarily take for granted that if a competent English speaker who has at least a minimal mastery of the term 'water' sincerely utters the sentence 'There is water in the basement' in appropriate circumstances, he thereby expresses his belief that there's water in the basement, even if he doesn't know that water is H_2O. The anti-individualist's thought experiments clarify our understanding of such ordinary belief attributions. As we saw in Chapter Eight, these thought experiments show that the proper evaluation of a speaker's beliefs may be settled in part by social and physical factors. I recommended (§112) that talk of the "contents" of a speaker's beliefs be replaced by descriptions of how to evaluate them. In this deflationary sense, the anti-individualist's thought experiments show that the "contents" of a speaker's beliefs may be partly settled by social and physical factors he knows very little about.

At first it seems obvious that if the "contents" of our beliefs are settled in part by social and physical factors, then we don't "know the contents" of our beliefs unless we know those social and phys-ical factors. It seems obvious, for example, that if the proper eval-uation of a person's belief that there is water in the basement is settled in part by the fact that water is H_2O, then if that person does not know that water is H_2O, he does not know all that is involved in properly evaluating his belief that there is water in the basement, and so he does not "know the content" of that belief.[1]

But we should not be so quick to conclude that anti-individualism is incompatible with self-knowledge. Anti-individualists question the assumption that if the "contents" of our thoughts are settled in part by social and physical factors, we don't "know the contents" of our thoughts unless we know those social and physical factors.[2] More important, in my view, anti-individualists should say that just as there is an ordinary sense in which a competent speaker who does not know that water is H_2O may believe there is water in the basement, so there is an ordinary sense in which a competent speaker who believes there is water in the basement "knows the content" of that belief, even if he does not know that water is H_2O. On the picture of self-knowledge that I will propose, to "know the contents" of our own beliefs is just to be able to use our sentences in discourse—to make and evaluate assertions, to ask questions, to describe possibilities, and so forth. To evaluate this proposal, we must move beyond the facile first impression that anti-individualism is incompatible with self-knowledge.

Deeper doubts about the compatibility of anti-individualism and self-knowledge arise when we formulate skeptical "hypotheses" that seem to call into question even our most basic presuppositions about the meanings of our words and the "contents" of our thoughts. Ordinarily I take for granted that when I sincerely utter the sentence 'There's water in the basement,' I thereby express the thought that there is water in the basement. After a little reflection I realize that in a world in which my word 'water' doesn't refer to water, my sincere utterances of the sentence 'There's water in the basement' don't express the thought that there is water in the basement. But if I accept anti-individualism it seems I can raise the skeptical "possibility" that I am actually *in* a world in which my word 'water' does not refer to water. If I *am* in such a world, then when I utter the sentence 'There's water in the basement' I don't thereby express the thought that there is water in the basement. Moreover, I can describe any number of possible situations in which my word 'water' does not refer to water. How then can I "know the contents" of the thoughts I express with my sincere utterances of sentences containing the word 'water'?

If I know that my word 'water' refers to water, then of course I know that I am not in a world in which my word 'water' does not refer to water. But it seems that to know what I mean by 'water' and what thoughts I express when I sincerely utter sentences containing the word 'water', I must *first* discover which of many different "possible" worlds I am in. It also seems that I can't discover this without "empirical" investigation. So it appears that if we accept anti-individualism we can make sense of skeptical "possibilities" that are incompatible with our most basic "assumptions" about the meanings of our words and the "contents" of our thoughts. Such

skeptical "possibilities" apparently undermine our ordinary conviction that we needn't engage in a special "empirical" inquiry to
"know the contents" of our thoughts.[3]

This skeptical reasoning is more challenging than our first facile
impression that anti-individualism is incompatible with self-
knowledge. Nevertheless, as I will try to show, the reasoning
sketched in the last two paragraphs also rests on a mistake. The
skeptic invites us to suppose that *we may actually be in a world in
which our word 'water' does not refer to water*. I will argue that this
supposition is incoherent, since if it were true we would not be able
to express or understand it. The skeptic may reply that the incoherence of his supposition amounts to a *reductio ad absurdum* of
anti-individualism. But I will argue that the fault lies with the skeptic's supposition, which reflects a fundamental misunderstanding
of anti-individualism.

The misunderstanding is to think that it makes sense to attribute
a wide range of ordinary beliefs and thoughts to an individual who
doesn't "know the content" of those beliefs and thoughts. In my
view, to understand the relationship between belief and self-
knowledge we must investigate our actual practices of attributing
beliefs to a person, and of judging whether or not he knows what
he is talking about. As I have already suggested, careful descriptions of ordinary situations in which philosophers are inclined to
say that a speaker "knows the contents" of his own beliefs and
thoughts show that to "know the contents" of the thoughts we
express with our sentences is just to be able to use our sentences in
discourse—to make and evaluate assertions, to ask questions, to
describe possibilities, and so forth. The same linguistic activities
that lead us to attribute beliefs and thoughts to an individual also
show that he "knows the contents" of those beliefs and thoughts.[4]
It is therefore a misunderstanding to suppose that someone could
express a wide range of beliefs and thoughts in the usual way, yet
not "know the contents" of those beliefs and thoughts.[5]

A related misunderstanding is to think that an individual can
"know the contents" of his thoughts even if he suspends all his
"empirical" beliefs. As I see it, our understanding of belief and
self-knowledge is inextricably linked to our assessments of whether
or not an individual is competent in the use of language. A speaker
is not competent in the use of language, nor does he "know the

contents" of his beliefs, unless he takes for granted some background (or other) of "empirical" beliefs. To say that we "know the contents" of our beliefs without "empirical" investigation is to say that at any given time, relative to a background of revisable "empirical" beliefs, we need not engage in any special "empirical" investigation to be able to use our words to make assertions and evaluate assertions, ask questions, and so on. Self-knowledge is neither purely "formal" nor in need of special "empirical justification."

Despite appearances, I will argue, this view of self-knowledge does not beg the question against skepticism, since to characterize a possibility as "skeptical" we must have some idea of what that possibility is. Since we must take many of our beliefs for granted just to *understand* and *describe* possibilities that are in conflict with some of our beliefs, there are many supposedly "skeptical" possibilities whose descriptions show that they are not actual. Properly viewed, the deflationary picture of anti-individualism deepens our understanding of belief and self-knowledge, and undermines certain entrenched "intuitions" about what is possible.

114. Realism and Self-Knowledge in Context

Before we consider the skeptical possibilities that are supposed to raise difficulties for self-knowledge, let us briefly note familiar aspects of our ordinary use of language that ground our commonsense ideas about realism and self-knowledge. For these preliminary observations I will presuppose that skepticism is not in question.

As we saw in Chapter Six, Putnam's kinetic energy example shows that some of our theoretical beliefs about energy have radically changed. This and similar examples highlight the diachronic aspect of our ordinary and scientific inquiries—no matter how well entrenched our beliefs about a given topic may be, there is always the potential for revision. The deflationary picture of anti-individualism sketched in Chapters Seven and Eight includes descriptions of radical diachronic and synchronic differences in belief, and thereby highlights diachronic and synchronic aspects of the division of linguistic labor. These anti-individualistic descriptions of our linguistic practices clarify two core ideas of commonsense realism—that our beliefs are not guaranteed to be true, and that our physical and social environments exist independently of us.

Surprisingly, the same descriptions undermine the metaphysical realist's idea that our conception of the things in our social and physical environments is independent of *all* of our "empirical" beliefs. Linguistic competence always presupposes some background or other of "empirical" beliefs. A speaker is minimally competent in the use of a particular word only if his use of the word "passes muster" in his linguistic community (§100), and he can participate in what Burge calls "the dialectic of meaning-giving characterizations" (§106). So from our perspective as participants in ordinary and scientific inquiries, we see that the objects in our physical and social environments *exist* independently of us, but our *conception* of the things in our physical and social environments is not independent of all our "empirical" beliefs (§99).

Now consider self-knowledge—the familiar fact that we "know the contents" of our own beliefs and thoughts without special "empirical" investigation. Unfortunately, ideas we typically associate with the words "know" and "content" prevent us from properly describing this phenomenon. One obstacle is our tendency to take certain ordinary uses of the word "know" as our paradigm for understanding what it means to say a speaker "knows the contents" of his own thoughts without "empirical" inquiry. Ordinarily someone says, "I know that the basement is flooded," for example, only if (first) there is some question about whether the basement is flooded, (second) the person is able to give a reason for his claim, and (third) there is an investigation that, if carried out, would settle the question.[6] If we take this ordinary use of "know" as our paradigm, we will be puzzled as to how a person could be said to "know the contents" of his own beliefs and thoughts without "empirical" investigation. For the question of whether someone "knows the contents" of his own beliefs and thoughts does not ordinarily arise, and there is no established practice of making, challenging, and defending claims to have self-knowledge.

Another obstacle to our understanding of self-knowledge is the word "content." For some philosophers, to say that a speaker "knows the contents" of his own beliefs brings to mind the idea of a relation between the speaker and something x that is the "content" of his belief. Sparked by this idea, some philosophers try to construct metaphysical theories of the special "cognitive" relationship a speaker bears to the "contents" of his own thoughts. In contrast, I assume that our understanding of "content" is exhausted by our actual practices of attributing and evaluating beliefs and thoughts (§112). We may use the sentence 'Oscar believes that there is water in the basement' to express the "content" of one of Oscar's beliefs, and to say how this belief is to be evaluated. We need not suppose that contents are *objects* to attribute and evaluate beliefs in this way. Hence to say that Oscar can tell without "empirical" inquiry that he believes there is water in the basement is not to presuppose that there is a mysterious "cognitive" relationship between Oscar and something x that is the "content" of his belief.[7]

To avoid such misunderstandings, I propose that we clarify the phenomenon of self-knowledge by looking at those aspects of our linguistic practices that lead us to say (misleadingly) that we "know the contents" of our own beliefs and thoughts without special "empirical" investigation. As I see it, self-knowledge is an ordinary aspect of competence in the use of language. The key point is that to "know the contents" of the thoughts we express with our sentences is just to be able to use our sentences in discourse: to make and evaluate assertions, ask questions, describe possibilities, clear up confusions, and so on. Thus the same linguistic activities that lead us to attribute beliefs and thoughts to an individual also show that he "knows the contents" of those beliefs and thoughts. Oscar's use of the word 'water' to make and evaluate assertions shows that when he sincerely utters the sentence 'There's water in the basement', he "knows the content" of his belief that there is water in the basement without special "empirical" inquiry.[8]

In this sense a speaker can "know the contents" of his beliefs without "empirical" investigation, even if such investigation would be required to determine whether one of his beliefs "has the same content" as another. Kevin Falvey and Joseph Owens highlight this aspect of our ordinary practice with the following story:

Suppose that Rudolf is acquainted with cilantro. He knows it to be an herb that figures prominently in Mexican cuisine, and he is familiar with its distinctive aroma. He says ... "cilantro should be used sparingly," thereby expressing the thought that cilantro should be used sparingly. In addition, Rudolf frequently employs dried coriander in his cooking; indeed he is as familiar with coriander as he is with cilantro. Coriander, too, he thinks, should be used sparingly, and he says so . . . "coriander should be used sparingly."[9]

Falvey and Owens assume that Rudolf is competent in the use of the terms 'cilantro' and 'coriander', and so he "knows without empirical investigation" what beliefs he expresses when he says "cilantro should be used sparingly" and "coriander should be used sparingly." Falvey and Owens suggest that since coriander is cilantro, Rudolf's belief that cilantro should be used sparingly and his belief that coriander should be used sparingly "have the same content."[10] Rudolf does not know that cilantro is coriander, and so he does not know whether these two beliefs "have the same content." But this does not undermine our ordinary judgment that Rudolf is competent in the use of the terms 'cilantro' and 'coriander', and that without special "empirical" inquiry he "knows the contents" of his beliefs that cilantro should be used sparingly and that coriander should be used sparingly.

This and similar examples have led some philosophers to think that self-knowledge is independent of all "empirical" beliefs.[11] But in making and evaluating assertions, raising questions, clearing up confusions, and so on, we always take for granted some background or other of "empirical" beliefs.[12] So when we say that we "know the contents" of our own thoughts without "empirical" investigation, we do not mean that our "self-knowledge" is independent of all our "empirical" beliefs. We mean that we are in a position to use our words in discourse without first engaging in a special "empirical" investigation of the "contents" of our thoughts.

115. Self-Knowledge and Metalinguistic Beliefs

Our ordinary attributions of self-knowledge do not presuppose that the attributee has any metalinguistic beliefs. Yet we are each in a position to talk about our own words, even if we have never previously done so. I can say, for example, that *when I sincerely assert the sentence 'There's water in the basement' I thereby express the thought that there is water in the basement,* and that *my word 'water' refers to water.* And once I have made these statements I may wonder whether they are true.

I can see that if these statements were not true, my sincere utterances of the sentence 'There's water in the basement' would not express the thought that there is water in the basement. I realize that if my sincere utterances of the sentence 'There's water in the basement' don't express the thought that there is water in the basement, then I don't "know the content" of my thought that there is water in the basement.[13] Since I take for granted, without special "empirical" inquiry, that I "know the content" of my thought that there is water in the basement, I naturally conclude, without special "empirical" inquiry, that my sincere utterances of the sentence 'There's water in the basement' express the thought that there is water in the basement, and that my word 'water' refers to water.

We are each in a position to see that if we have self-knowledge, then our disquotational metalinguistic statements of the forms "my sincere utterances of the sentence '___' express my thought that ___" and "my word '___' refers to ___" are true. Once we express such metalinguistic statements about our own words, we can see that if those statements aren't true, then we don't "know the contents" of our beliefs and thoughts. We take for granted that we "know the contents" of our beliefs and thoughts without special "empirical" inquiry, and so we naturally conclude that the disquotational metalinguistic statements of the forms "my sincere utterances of the sentence '___' express my thought that ___" and "my word '___' refers to ___" are true.[14]

116. Problematic Possibilities

The skeptic about self-knowledge claims that our confidence in this natural conclusion should be undermined by skeptical possibilities that follow directly from the anti-individualist's thought experiments. In these thought experiments we hold constant a person's physical structure and behavior, described nonintentionally and without reference to his environment, while we stipulate that his environment is different in certain respects. When we generalize the anti-individualist's method of constructing thought experiments, we see that for each of us, one could describe countless *subjectively equivalent worlds* in which our sensory surfaces are affected in the same way, but our environments are radically different. In each of these worlds, we express our beliefs and thoughts using sentence-tokens with the same syntactic shapes. Moreover, it *appears* that in each of these worlds our "first-person experiences" would be the same.[15] It is therefore tempting to conclude that from the first-person point of view, although we know which sentences we are using, this does not tell us which of our subjectively equivalent worlds we are actually in.

But if we can't tell solely on the basis of our first-person experiences which of our subjectively equivalent worlds we are actually in, then we can't tell solely on the basis of our first-person experiences that, for example, our sincere utterances of the sentence 'There's water in the basement' express the thought that there is water in the basement. And if we can't tell solely on the basis of our first-person experiences that our sincere utterances of the sentence 'There's water in the basement' express the thought that there is water in the basement, then it seems that without special "empirical" inquiry we can't "know the contents" of the beliefs and thoughts we express with that sentence. More generally, if we can't tell solely on the basis of our first-person experiences which of our subjectively equivalent worlds we are actually in, then it seems we can't "know the contents" of our own beliefs and thoughts without special "empirical" inquiry.

The skeptic's reasoning is most gripping when it is illustrated by descriptions of particular subjectively equivalent worlds in which the "contents" of our beliefs and thoughts are different from what we actually take them to be. For example, consider the subjectively equivalent world in which I am born, raised, and now live on Twin Earth, where the word 'water' refers to twin water, not water. In that world my sincere utterances of 'There's water in the basement' express the thought that there is twin water in the basement. This is a different thought from the one I actually take myself to express with my sincere utterances of 'There's water in the basement'. Using this subjectively equivalent world to illustrate his point, the skeptic about self-knowledge reasons as follows. "If I focus on my subjective experience of using my sentence 'There's water in the basement', I am unable to tell whether or not I was born, raised, and now live on Twin Earth, and so it seems that I can't know without empirical investigation whether I am expressing the thought that there is water in the basement, or the thought that there is twin water in the basement."

We can describe another troubling possibility that is slightly closer to home. Among my subjectively equivalent worlds is one in which I am transported without my knowledge from Earth to Twin Earth. It seems that by our ordinary standards of belief attribution, we would say that after a time (say five years),[16] I count as a competent member of the twin-English-speaking community. Then my sincere utterances of 'There's water in the basement' express the thought that there is twin water in the basement. Before the move, my sincere utterances of this sentence expressed the thought that there is water in the basement. Yet in that subjectively equivalent world I am unaware of the move. Using this subjectively equivalent world to illustrate his point, the skeptic about self-knowledge reasons as follows. "If I focus on my 'subjective experience' of using my sentence 'There's water in the basement', I am unable to tell whether or not I was transported five years ago to Twin Earth, and so it seems that I can't know without empirical investigation whether I am expressing the thought that there is water in the basement, or the thought that there is twin water in the basement."

To understand this skeptical reasoning, it is crucial to see that skepticism about self-knowledge does not follow just from the observation that in some of our subjectively equivalent worlds the "contents" of our beliefs and thoughts are different from what we take the "contents" of our beliefs and thoughts to be in the actual world. It is a mistake to move directly from (a) there are subjectively equivalent worlds in which our beliefs and thoughts are different from what we take them to be in the actual world, to (b) without special "empirical" investigation we can't tell whether or not we are in one of these strange subjectively equivalent worlds. To move from (a) directly to (b) is in effect to slide from "my beliefs and thoughts *might have been* different from what I actually take them to be" to "my beliefs and thoughts *may be* different from what I actually take them to be." Taken by itself, this move is unjustified. And anyone who thinks that anti-individualism is compatible with self-knowledge accepts (a) but not (b). To challenge this position the skeptic needs to justify his move from (a) to (b).[17]

To get from (a) to (b), one might think it is enough to assert that all knowledge of "contingent truths" requires special "empirical" investigation. We saw in §115 that if we "know the contents" of our beliefs and thoughts without special "empirical" investigation, then we may also conclude without special "empirical" investigation that, for example, our sincere utterances of the sentence 'There's water in the basement' express the thought that there is water in the basement, and our word 'water' refers to water. One might accept this "conditional," but insist that our acceptance of such "contingent truths" requires "empirical" justification of a kind we can't provide, and infer by *modus tollens* that we *don't* "know the contents" of our beliefs and thoughts without special "empirical" investigation.[18]

This argument may *appear* promising, but in fact it just begs the question against a principled anti-individualist, who has good reason to resist the widely accepted view that our acceptance of "contingent truths" requires special "empirical" justification. The key point is that from the anti-individualist's perspective, our ordinary understanding of self-knowledge is inextricable from our actual practices of attributing beliefs and thoughts, and hence also from our ordinary discriminations between competent and incompetent uses of language. In §114 I noted that our attributions of belief and self-knowledge to an individual always presuppose that he takes for granted some background (or other) of "empirical" beliefs. To say that an individual "knows the contents" of his own thoughts without special "empirical" inquiry is to say he is in a position to use his words in discourse without first engaging in a special "empirical" investigation of the "contents" of his thoughts. And in §115 I argued that if an individual "knows the contents" of his beliefs and thoughts without special "empirical" investigation, then if he can construct disquotational metalinguistic sentences of the forms "my sincere utterances of the sentence '___' express my thought that ___" and "my word '___' refers to ___," he can accept without special "empirical" investigation that those metalinguistic sentences are true.[19] Thus, for instance, without special "empirical" investigation he can accept that his sincere utterances of the sentence "There's water in the basement' express the thought that there is water in the basement, and that his word 'water' refers to water. In this sense he accepts some "contingent truths" without special "empirical" investigation.[20] To raise a serious skeptical challenge to this view of self-knowledge, the skeptic must show us how to move from (a) to (b) without just taking for granted that to accept a "contingent truth" we must have special "empirical" justification.

How then does the skeptic justify the move from (a) to (b)? As I understand it, the skeptic's road from (a) to (b) is paved by the natural and tempting assumptions that (i) in all of our subjectively equivalent worlds our "first-person experiences" would be the same, and (ii) our self-knowledge must be justified by our "first-person experiences." Neither (i) nor (ii) directly begs the question against the anti-individualistic view of self-knowledge sketched in the previous paragraph. Yet (i) and (ii), together with (a), lead the skeptic to conclude that our "evidence" for our self-knowledge claims does not discriminate between any of our subjectively equivalent worlds.

Given (i) and (ii), the *realism* implicit in anti-individualism—the recognition that our beliefs are not guaranteed to be true, and that our physical and social environments exist independently of us—supports the skeptic's claim that *for all we know on the basis of our "first-person experiences" we may actually be in any one of our subjectively equivalent worlds.* If we accept this claim, we are apparently forced to accept (b)—that without special "empirical" investigation we don't know whether or not we are in one of these strange subjectively equivalent worlds. But if we can't tell without "empirical" investigation which of our subjectively equivalent worlds we are in, then we can't tell without "empirical" investigation what beliefs and thoughts we express with sincere utterances of our sentences. In this way we feel driven to conclude that anti-individualism is incompatible with self-knowledge.

117. Why Skepticism about Self-Knowledge Is Incoherent

In our attempt to answer the skeptic's challenge, we are seduced into thinking that if we can *picture* ourselves existing in any one of our subjectively equivalent worlds, then we may *actually be* in any one of our subjectively equivalent worlds. And to say that we may *actually be* in any one of our subjectively equivalent worlds is to concede that we don't know the meanings of our words or the "contents" of our thoughts. Yet I will argue that if we accept anti-individualism, then to show that we may actually be in any one of our subjectively equivalent worlds, it is not enough to *picture* ourselves existing in any of our subjectively equivalent worlds. The gripping idea that we may actually be in any one of our subjectively equivalent worlds is illusory.

There are two central components to the illusion. On the one hand, there is the first-person "subjective" view of our use of sentences, and on the other, a radically "external" third-person "objective" view of the physical and social factors that "determine" the meanings of our sentences and thereby also "determine" the "contents" of our beliefs and thoughts. The "subjective" view of our use of sentences is based in the idea that we can somehow "subtract" any "empirical" assumptions we make about our social and physical environment from our first-person experience of using our sentences. This subtraction seems natural if we take for granted that our first-person experiences are the same in all of our subjectively equivalent worlds.[21] We assume that we can describe, from a fully "objective" point of view, an array of possible situations we may be in, and note that our "subjective" experience would be the same in each of them. This seems to lead inevitably to the conclusion that our knowledge of our "beliefs" and "thoughts" is limited to what little we can glean from our "subjective" experiences of using sentences of various syntactic types.

But this "subjective" view of our own sentence use makes sense only if it is contrasted with a corresponding "objective" view of the "external" factors that "determine" the meanings of our sentences and the "contents" of the beliefs and thoughts. Those who accept the skeptical reasoning sketched in the previous section think that we *can* make sense of this contrast between the "subjective" and the "objective" view of our sentences. Why do they accept this?

The idea of an "objective" view of our "subjective" situation stems from a natural but fundamental misunderstanding of the anti-individualist's thought experiments. The anti-individualist's thought experiments are usually presented from the third-person point of view, with the subjects of the thought experiments viewed from the "outside." From this third-person point of view, we assume that *we* know what features of the subjects' social and physical environments partly determine the "contents" of their beliefs and thoughts. We think *we* know the "contents" of the subjects' beliefs and thoughts, even if *the subjects themselves* can't tell without special "empirical" inquiry which subjectively equivalent world they are in. This sets up the contrast between the two perspectives: the "subjective" point of view of the subject of the thought experiment, and the "objective" point of view of the person conducting the thought experiment. To apply the conclusion of the thought experiments to ourselves, *we simply imagine ourselves in the position of the subject.* We assume that the contrast between the "subjective" first-person point of view and the "objective" third-person point of view can be easily applied to our own case. So we think of our own sentence use from the "subjective" point of view, and imagine that from the "objective" third-person point of view our sincere utterances express thoughts whose "contents" we can't know without "empirical" investigation.

The trouble is that this radical contrast between the "subjective" and the "objective" points of view does not make sense. The incoherence of the contrast is brought home when we try to reason about our own thoughts from both perspectives. Consider the following elaboration on our earlier attempt to reach a skeptical conclusion:

> Among my subjectively equivalent worlds is one in which five years ago I was transported without my knowledge from Earth to Twin Earth, and I am now a competent member of the twin-English-speaking community. In that situation my sincere utterances of 'There's water in the basement' do not express the thought that there is *water* in the basement, they express the thought that there is *twin water* in the basement. I can't tell without empirical investigation whether or not I am in this subjectively equivalent world. So I can't tell without empirical investigation whether my sincere utterances of 'There's water in the basement' express the thought that there is *water* in the basement or the thought that there is *twin water* in the basement.

This reasoning slips back and forth between taking a "subjective" view of my use of sentences and using them to describe "objective" possibilities. On the one hand, I am saying that I do not know what "objective" situation I am in, and so I don't know whether my sincere utterances of 'There's water in the basement' express the thought that there is *water* in the basement or the thought that there is *twin water* in the basement. On the other hand, if I am to *use* my sentence 'There's water in the basement' to *describe* the possible world in which my sincere utterances of 'There's water in the basement' express the thought that there is water in the basement, I must take for granted that, viewed "objectively," my sincere utterances of 'There's water in the basement' express the thought that there is water in the basement. But the attempt to shift back and forth between the "subjective" and "objective" points of view on my use of sentences is deeply confused. For if I can use my sentences to describe possibilities at all, then in effect I undermine the general conclusion that all I know of the "contents" of my thoughts must be based in my "subjective" experience of using my sentences.

The skeptic apparently fails to see that to "know the contents" of the thoughts we express with our sentences is just to be able to use our sentences to make and evaluate assertions, to ask questions, and to describe possibilities. We can agree with the skeptic that doubts about disquotational metalinguistic statements should undermine our confidence that we know what we are talking about. But if such doubts undermine our confidence that we know what we are talking about, the same doubts also undermine our confidence that we can use our sentences to make and evaluate assertions, to ask questions, and to describe "objective" possibilities. When we use our words to express the skeptic's reasoning, we in effect undermine the general conclusion that we don't "know the contents" of our thoughts unless we first find out which of our subjectively equivalent worlds we are in. To use our words to express the various "objective" possibilities that the skeptic raises is to *show* that we "know the contents" of our thoughts without special "empirical" investigation. Hence the skeptic's attempt to shift back and forth between the "subjective" and "objective" points of view on our use of language is incoherent.

One might think that this incoherence is the result of our being trapped within our "subjective" first-person point of view. Someone who accepts this account of the problem will still find the "objective" perspective intelligible, even if he can't express it from his first-person "subjective" point of view. Such a person may imagine a completely "objective" perspective on his own situation, expressed in some idealized philosophical metalanguage the meanings of whose sentences are independent of the environment he is in. When he is reasoning about his own situation from the "objective" point of view, he will then imagine that he is using the sentences of this idealized metalanguage, and this will shield his reasoning from the consequences of anti-individualism.

The trouble with this response is that if we accept anti-individualism we have no idea how we *could* express the "thoughts" we imagine ourselves to express using the idealized metalanguage. We can't express these "thoughts" in language, for the whole point of the idealized metalanguage is to take up a detached "objective" point of view on *all* of our linguistic behavior. But since we can't actually *express* the "thoughts" we imagine ourselves to express using the idealized metalanguage, our *imagining* these "thoughts" can't save the skeptical reasoning from incoherence.

Philosophers who feel they understand the skeptical reasoning may not find this reply immediately convincing. Such philosophers may insist that our theorizing about language and content must start with a metaphysical picture of the objective "external" world. Within this more encompassing metaphysical framework, we can then ask whether our words refer to the independently conceived entities that we suppose exist in the "external" world, and if so, how this is possible.

If we think of anti-individualism in this way, the problem summarized four paragraphs ago looks merely pragmatic: every time we *try* to express our skeptical concern that we are in some strange world in which our words do not mean what we think they mean, we end up expressing a different thought from the one (we imagined that) we were trying to express. Confident that we can make sense of this puzzling situation, we reason as follows:

> When I think that maybe I was transported to Twin Earth, and so my utterances of 'There's water in the basement' express the thought that there is twin water in the basement, I find that I have not properly expressed my skeptical insight. I was trying to view my use of language from a perspective independent of both situations, and to observe that if I am in the world in which I was transported to Twin Earth, my sentences would not mean what I think they mean. The trouble is that if I accept anti-individualism, I must accept that the contents of my descriptions of these possibilities are themselves settled by the world I am actually in. So every time I try to express my metaphysical doubts from a perspective independent of my actual situation, my actual physical and social environments

determine which thoughts I am expressing with my sentences, and my aim is frustrated. *I know what I am trying to say, but I can't express my meaning in language.*

Our initial confidence should falter when we realize that we can't express the "objective" skeptical possibilities that we imagine. Once we see that can't express the "objective" skeptical possibilities that we imagine, we can see that the imagined metaphysical perspective is illusory, and thus the skeptical "problem" of the previous section dissolves.

The incoherence of the skeptic's reasoning is like the incoherence of an Escher drawing whose seemingly sensible parts don't fit together into a sensible whole. To raise a skeptical problem about self-knowledge, it is not enough to *picture* ourselves in place of one of our twins in a subjectively equivalent world, since a picture is not a thought, and the "possibility" our skeptic has "pictured" does not amount to a coherent possibility at all.

118. The Misunderstanding behind Skepticism about Self-Knowledge

Someone in the grip of the skeptical reasoning might regard the argument I just presented as a *reductio ad absurdum* of anti-individualism. This attitude presupposes that the skeptical reasoning is an inevitable consequence of anti-individualism. But the skeptic's illusion that we may actually be in any one of our subjectively equivalent worlds reflects a fundamental misunderstanding of anti-individualism. Anti-individualism starts by taking at face value our ordinary judgments about what individuals believe, what they are talking about, and when they agree or disagree with each other. From this perspective we see that when a competent speaker of English sincerely utters the sentence 'There's water in the basement', she thereby expresses her belief that there is water in the basement, and when a competent speaker of Twin English sincerely utters the sentence 'There's water in the basement', she thereby expresses her belief that there is twin water in the basement. I have already pointed out that there is an unproblematic sense in which competent speakers in both communities "know the contents" of their beliefs and thoughts without special "empirical" inquiry: they are able to use their words in discourse. The mistake behind the skeptical reasoning is to think that we can accept the anti-individualistic belief attributions, even if we conclude that the attributees can't use their words in discourse, and hence don't "know the contents" of their beliefs and thoughts without special "empirical" inquiry.

I have already stressed that "knowing the contents" of one's beliefs without special "empirical" inquiry is an ordinary aspect of competence in the use of language. Since Oscar typically applies the word 'water' to samples of *water*, and he is disposed to submit the judgments he makes using his word 'water' to criticism and correction by more knowledgeable members of his linguistic community, we see that he is competent in the use of the English word 'water', and that without special "empirical" inquiry he "knows the contents" of the beliefs his sincere utterances of sentences that contain the English word 'water' express. Similarly, without special "empirical" inquiry Twin Oscar "knows the contents" of the beliefs his sincere utterances of sentences that contain the Twin English word 'water' express. This is not to speculate about psychological processes that occur "inside" Oscar's and Twin Oscar's heads, but to describe our actual practices of attributing beliefs and self-knowledge.

The skeptic about self-knowledge may reply that to attribute the belief that there is water in the basement to a competent English speaker who sincerely utters the sentence 'There's water in the basement', we need suppose not that she "knows the content" of this belief without special "empirical" investigation, but only that she *believes* that she "knows the content" of her belief without special "empirical" investigation.

This reply presupposes that a competent English speaker can *believe* that she "knows the contents" of her beliefs without special "empirical" investigation, even if in fact she does not "know the contents" of her beliefs without special "empirical" investigation. But this presupposition does not make sense either. We saw in the previous section that I "know the contents" of my thoughts without special "empirical" inquiry if I can describe the "objective" possibility that my sincere utterances of the sentence 'There's water in the basement' express the thought that *there is water in the basement*, and not the thought that *there is twin water in the basement*. We saw

that I cannot *simultaneously* accept that I am considering these possibilities, and that I may not be considering them after all. The same
kind of reasoning shows that no one *else* can consider the possibility
that her sincere utterances of 'There's water in the basement'
express the thought that there is water in the basement unless *she*
"knows the contents" of the thought expressed by her sentence
'There's water in the basement'.

At this point the skeptic about self-knowledge may simply insist
that the anti-individualist's attributions do *not* express the "contents" of a competent speaker's beliefs and thoughts. But this is not
to *discover* a problematic consequence of accepting anti-
individualism. Instead it amounts to a rejection of anti-
individualism. In most ordinary cases we can't make sense of the
anti-individualist's attributions of a belief to an individual unless
we see that she "knows the content" of that belief without special
"empirical" inquiry. And if we can't make sense of anti-
individualism, we can't accept it either.[22]

I conclude that if we are convinced that the anti-individualist's
attributions make sense, we can't *also* insist that the attributees
don't "know the contents" of their beliefs and thoughts without
special "empirical" inquiry. This insistence would lead us back to
the incoherent contrast, sketched in §117, between our "subjective" use of sentences and the "objective" factors that determine
the contents of our beliefs and thoughts. The illusion of such
a contrast is fostered by a misunderstanding of the anti-
individualist's thought experiments. We can make sense of the
anti-individualist's attributions of particular beliefs and thoughts
to a person only if we see that she "knows the contents" of those
beliefs and thoughts without special "empirical" inquiry. Thus
we cannot both accept the anti-individualist's attributions of
beliefs and thoughts to a subject, and deny that she "knows the
contents" of those beliefs and thoughts without special "empirical" inquiry.

119. Problematic Possibilities Disarmed

We are now in a position to see that the problematic possibilities
described in §116 are not actual. We can see this by reflecting on our
description of those possibilities. Consider the following argument:

(A1) I am now using this sentence to express the thought that there is water in the basement.

(A2) If I were in the world in which I was born, raised, and now live on Twin Earth, I could not use sentence (A1) to express the thought that there is water in the basement.

(A3) Therefore, I am not in the world in which I was born, raised, and now live on Twin Earth.

As a competent speaker, without special "empirical" investigation I "know the content" of the thought I express with sincere utterances of (A1). (A2) is a consequence of our observation that when a competent speaker on Twin Earth sincerely utters the sentence 'There's water in the basement' he thereby expresses the thought that *there is twin water in the basement.* This is not the thought that there is water in the basement, since *water is not twin water.* Thus I can see that I am not in a world in which I was born, raised, and now live on Twin Earth.

The same kind of reasoning shows that I am not in the world in which I was transported to Twin Earth five years ago:

(B1) I am now using this sentence to express the thought that there is water in the basement.

(B2) If I were in the world in which I was transported to Twin Earth five years ago, I could not use sentence (B1) to express the thought that there is water in the basement.

(B3) Therefore, I am not in the world in which I was transported to Twin Earth five years ago.

As a competent speaker, without special "empirical" investigation I "know the content" of the thought I express with sincere utterances of (B1). (B2) is a consequence of our observation that when a competent speaker on Twin Earth sincerely utters the sentence 'There's water in the basement' he thereby expresses the thought that *there is twin water in the basement.* This is different from the thought that there is water in the basement, since *water is not twin water.* Thus I can see that I am not in a world in which I was transported to Twin Earth five years ago.

From (A1)–(A3) and (B1)–(B3) we see that there are subjectively equivalent worlds whose descriptions show they are not actual.[23] This undermines the skeptic's conclusion that for all we know without special "empirical" inquiry we may actually be in any one of our subjectively equivalent worlds.

120. Empirical Presuppositions and Skeptical Possibilities

Viewed out of context, arguments (A1)–(A3) and (B1)–(B3) can look like tawdry attempts to pull a rabbit—knowledge of "empirical" facts—out of an empty hat—self-knowledge. To clarify the context and dispel the air of hocus-pocus surrounding arguments (A1)–(A3) and (B1)–(B3), in this section I will sketch and criticize a position that combines a minimal disquotational picture of self-knowledge with a rejection of arguments like (A1)–(A3) and (B1)–(B3).

One might think that self-knowledge is restricted to knowledge of disquotational metalinguistic truths, and so it does not tell us, for example, whether or not water is twin water. Since premises (A2) and (B2) both depend on the "assumption" that water is not twin water, these premises depend on substantive "empirical" presuppositions that go beyond self-knowledge.[24] If we accept this restricted disquotational picture of self-knowledge, then it will seem that, contrary to my claim at the end of the previous section, there are no subjectively equivalent worlds whose descriptions alone show us that they are not actual. To establish that a particular subjectively equivalent world is not actual, "empirical" investigation is always required.[25]

In my view, this objection to arguments (A1)–(A3) and (B1)–(B3) reflects a confusion about the relationship between self-knowledge and background "empirical" beliefs. If we accept anti-individualism, it is a confusion to think that we can suspend all our "empirical" beliefs and still know what we are talking about well enough to understand why the "problematic possibilities" sketched in §116, and disarmed by arguments (A1)–(A3) and (B1)–(B3), are supposed to be "skeptical." It should go without saying that *to characterize a possibility as "skeptical," we must have some idea of what that possibility is.* Nevertheless, I will argue, the restricted disquotational picture of self-knowledge reflects a failure to see the consequences of this truism.

According to the restricted disquotational picture of self-knowledge, (i) I know without special "empirical" inquiry that such disquotational sentences as "My sincere utterances of the sentence 'There's water in the basement' express the thought that there is water in the basement" and "My word 'water' refers to water" are true, but (ii) my knowledge that these disquotational metalinguistic sentences are true can't *by itself* yield knowledge of any "empirical" or "contingent" facts. Someone in the grip of this picture of self-knowledge will reason as follows:

> Since I know without empirical inquiry that these metalinguistic sentences are true, by the simple disquotational property of the predicate 'is true', I can infer that I know without empirical inquiry that *my sincere utterances of the sentence 'There's water in the basement' express the thought that there is water in the basement*, and that *my word 'water' refers to water*. Since this knowledge is available *without* any empirical inquiry, it can't amount to knowledge of empirical or contingent facts.

We can sum up this reasoning as follows: *self-knowledge is restricted to knowledge of disquotational metalinguistic truths, and so by itself it can't yield knowledge of "empirical" facts.*

Someone who accepts this restricted disquotational picture of self-knowledge can grant that in ordinary contexts where skeptical hypotheses are not in question, it is harmless to rely on commonsense "empirical" beliefs. He can even agree that relative to our commonsense background of "empirical" beliefs, our knowledge of disquotational metalinguistic truths *seems* to yield knowledge of substantive "empirical" facts. But he will insist that this is an illusion created by a failure to distinguish self-knowledge, which is "empirically empty," from our commonsense "empirical" beliefs.

If we accept this picture of the relationship between self-knowledge and knowledge of "empirical" facts, we will think that (A1)–(A3) and (B1)–(B3) beg the question against the skeptical possibilities that they allegedly undermine. We will think that at best our self-knowledge yields "empirically empty" versions of (A1) and (B1), and so we will see no reason to accept premises (A2) and (B2), which both depend on the assumption that water is not twin water. We will reason as follows:

> Whether or not we are actually in either of the situations described, we have the purely disquotational, empirically

empty knowledge that our word 'water' refers to water. But this does not tell us what water is. In particular, it does not tell us whether or not water is twin water. If we take for granted that water is not twin water, then we in effect simply beg the question of whether our word 'water' refers to twin water. In the context of the skeptical hypotheses raised in §116, we are not entitled to assume that water is not twin water.

We can sum up this skeptical reasoning as follows. *Self-knowledge is knowledge of purely disquotational metalinguistic truths, and so it does not tell us whether or not water is twin water. This shows that premises (A2) and (B2) depend on substantive "empirical" presuppositions that go beyond self-knowledge.*

The basic problem with this conclusion is that it presupposes that self-knowledge is independent of all our background "empirical" beliefs. Those in the grip of the disquotational picture of self-knowledge do not realize that to suspend all our "empirical" beliefs is to undercut any skeptical force to the "possibility" that we are actually on Twin Earth, and that our word 'water' refers to twin water. For if we suspend all "empirical" beliefs about Twin Earth and twin water, we literally have no idea what we are talking about, and so we have no reasons for thinking that the "possibility" that we are on Twin Earth raises a *skeptical* threat to our ordinary beliefs. To put it paradoxically, the restricted disquotational picture of self-knowledge leads to the self-defeating conclusion that *to raise and evaluate skeptical hypotheses, we must assume that we do not know what we are talking about.*

To see this, suppose that we are confronted by a skeptic who accepts the restricted disquotational picture of self-knowledge, and challenges us to justify our belief that we are not in a subjectively equivalent world in which our word 'Earth' refers to Twin Earth and our word 'water' refers to twin water. Such a person might try to create the impression that this is a *skeptical* possibility by arguing as follows: "Without any question-begging empirical assumptions, you can't rule out the possibility that you are now on Twin Earth, and you have been there long enough to count as a competent speaker of Twin English. So without empirical investigation you can't know whether or not your word 'water' refers to twin water." This rhetoric directs our attention *away* from the question of why the "possibility" is supposed to be *skeptical*. When listening to this challenge, we take for granted our ordinary "empirical" beliefs that Earth is not Twin Earth and water is not twin water, so we feel we understand the skeptic's possibility, and feel obliged to say why it is not actual. But when we try to say why the possibility is not actual, we are told we can't assume that Earth is not Twin Earth and water is not twin water, for that would be "question-begging." Thus at first we feel we understand the skeptic's possibility but have no resources to rule it out. To succumb to this feeling is to be bamboozled by the skeptic's rhetoric.

A closer look reveals that the skeptic's "possibility" is not *skeptical* at all. The reason is that *to characterize a possibility as "skeptical" we must have some idea of what that possibility is.* Unless we have some idea of what Twin Earth and twin water are, we have no idea what possibility the skeptic is trying to raise, and so we have no reason for thinking that it is a *skeptical* possibility. If we do as the skeptic requires, and suspend all our background "empirical" beliefs, we simply have no idea what he is talking about. But if we understand what "possibility" he is raising well enough to see that it conflicts with our ordinary "empirical" beliefs, then, using arguments like (A1)–(A3) and (B1)–(B3), we can see that it is not actual.[26] So here is how we should answer the skeptic:

> What are you suggesting?[27] What do you mean by 'Twin Earth' and 'twin water'? If Twin Earth is Earth and twin water is water, then what you are suggesting is not skeptical at all. But if Twin Earth is not Earth and twin water is not water, then I see from your description that the supposedly skeptical possibility is not actual, since to understand it, I must take for granted that my word 'Earth' refers to Earth and my word 'water' refers to water. Either way the possibility you are raising is not a genuine threat to my ordinary beliefs.

At first we felt we *understood* the skeptic's possibility, but had no resources to rule it out. Now we can see that this feeling was confused. Either we understand the skeptic's "possibility" well enough to see that it conflicts with our ordinary beliefs, in which case we can use arguments like (A1)–(A3) and (B1)–(B3) to show that it is not actual, or we don't know what the skeptic is talking about, and so we have no reason to think that his "possibility" conflicts with our "empirical" beliefs.

In this case, the confused feeling that we *understood* the skeptic's "possibility" but had no resources to rule it out can be traced to the restricted disquotational picture of self-knowledge. If we accept this picture, we will assume that we can "know the contents" of our beliefs and thoughts even if we suspend all our "empirical" beliefs. This assumption fosters the illusion that we can understand the skeptic's possibility even if we suspend all our "empirical" beliefs.

But self-knowledge is not independent of "empirical" beliefs. I noted in §114 and §118 that self-knowledge is an aspect of competence in the use of language. If a speaker has no idea what he is talking about, and suspends all judgments expressed by using a term, then he is incompetent in the use of language. He may doubt some (perhaps even most) of his "empirical" beliefs, but he must rely on other "empirical" beliefs to give sense to his doubts. To be competent in the use of the word 'water', for example, a speaker must have some background (or other) of "empirical" beliefs about water, even if he is always revising these beliefs, and even if most of them are false. If the speaker suspends all his "empirical" beliefs, in the interests of not "begging the question" against skepticism, then he has no idea *what* he is talking about, and so we can no longer credit him with any beliefs expressed by using the term 'water'.

Once we see that self-knowledge always presupposes some background or other[28] of "empirical" beliefs, we can see that arguments (A1)–(A3) and (B1)–(B3) do not beg the question against the "possibilities" that we were born and raised on Twin Earth, or that we were transported there five years ago. For we must take some beliefs for granted if we are to have *any idea* of what these "possibilities" are. These background beliefs may be revised and criticized almost without limit. But given the way we ordinarily understand the skeptical "possibilities" that we were born and raised on Twin Earth or that we were transported there five years ago, we can see that they are not actual. This conclusion rests on "empirical" assumptions without which those "possibilities" would not even *appear* to conflict with our ordinary beliefs.

121. Two More Problematic Possibilities

Let's apply what we have learned about the inextricability of self-knowledge and "empirical" beliefs to two more problematic possibilities.

Consider a world in which an exact duplicate of my brain spends its entire "life" in a vat, but receives the same pattern of nerve impacts that my embodied brain actually receives.[29] Suppose this brain "utters" sentences with the same syntactic shapes as mine. Some would say that just as the "contents" of my utterances are dependent on the nature of the things to which I apply my words, so the "contents" of the brain's "utterances" are determined by the states of the machine that produces impacts at its nerve endings.[30] I doubt that a brain in such a situation could express any thoughts at all. But even if it could, its thoughts wouldn't have the same "contents" as ours. When I sincerely utter the sentence 'I am not a brain in a vat', for example, I express the thought that I am not a brain in a vat. But the brain in the vat doesn't causally interact with brains and vats, or with anything else that would enable it to form descriptions of brains and vats, and so it can't express any thoughts about brains or vats. If its "utterances" express any thoughts at all, they are not the thoughts I express with sentences of the same syntactic shapes.

Now consider a world in which five years ago a group of doctors removed my brain from my body, placed it in a vat of nutrients, and connected it to a machine that produces the same pattern of nerve impacts that my embodied brain actually receives. If we suppose again that a disembodied brain can "utter" sentences and express "thoughts," then it seems that after a while the meanings of my "utterances" and the "contents" of my "thoughts" would change. Let's say that after five years in the vat, my "utterances" of 'I am not a brain in a vat' no longer express my belief that I am not a brain in a vat. If my "utterances" of 'I am not a brain in a vat' express any thought at all, that thought does not have the same "content" as the thought that I am not a brain in a vat.

In light of our recent reflections on the inextricability of self-knowledge and "empirical" beliefs, we can see that we are not in either of these strange situations. The following reasoning shows that this "possibility" is not actual:

(C1) I am now using this sentence to express the thought that I am not a brain in a vat.

(C2) If I were always a brain in a vat, I could not use sentence (C1) to express the thought that I am not a brain in a vat.

(C3) Therefore, I am not always a brain in a vat.

As a competent speaker, without special "empirical" inquiry I "know the contents" of the thought I express with sentence (C1). (C2) follows from our description of the world in which a duplicate of my brain is always in a vat. On reflection we can see that if the duplicate brain's "utterances" of (C1) express any thought at all, it is not the thought I express with (C1).

Now consider the case in which my brain was transferred to a vat five years ago. The following reasoning shows that this "possibility" is not actual:

(D1) I am now using this sentence to express the thought that I am not a brain in a vat.

(D2) If my brain had been transferred into a vat five years ago, I could not now use sentence (D1) to express the thought that I am not a brain in a vat.

(D3) Therefore, my brain was not transferred into a vat five years ago.

Once again, without special "empirical" inquiry I "know the contents" of the thought I express with sentence (D1), and (D2) follows from our understanding of our description of the world in which my brain was transferred into a vat five years ago. On reflection we can see that if the transferred brain's "utterances" of (D1) express any thought at all, it is not the thought I actually express with (D1). This shows that my brain was not transferred into a vat five years ago.[31]

122. Empirical Presuppositions and Skeptical Possibilities Again

To support premises (C2) and (D2) we reasoned that if our brains were in vats for long enough, we would not be able to use (C1) or (D1) to express our belief that we are not brains in a vat. We took for granted the standard meaning-giving characterizations of our words 'brain', 'vat', 'machine', and 'stimulations'. We assumed, for example, that a brain is a mass of substance contained in the skull of humans and other vertebrates, and that a vat is a tub, tank, cask, or other large vessel used to hold a liquid.[32] These characterizations presuppose that we causally interact with brains and vats, that there are humans and other vertebrates in our physical environment, that there are tubs, tanks, and casks, and so on. It may seem question-begging to rely on these assumptions when we are trying to show that we aren't always brains in vats, and that our brains weren't transferred into vats five years ago.

Falvey and Owens have recently raised this kind of objection to arguments like (C1)–(C3) and (D1)–(D3). They hold a version of the restricted disquotational picture of self-knowledge described in §120. They assume that in their restricted disquotational sense we "know" without special "empirical" inquiry what beliefs we express with (C1) and (D1). They would argue that my reasons for accepting premises (C2) beg the question of whether I am always a brain in a vat (BIV) by *presupposing* the standard meaning-giving characterizations ("explications") of my words 'brain' and 'vat':

> in order to establish that the BIV's utterances of the words 'brain' and 'vat' differ in reference from our utterances of these words, we must appeal to the premise that our words 'brain' and 'vat' refer to certain definite physical objects in our environment. But these are all empirical propositions, which in fact are true only if we are not brains in vat. As such, the appeal to this premise is illegitimate in the present context. It begs precisely the question at issue ... our explications of our own words involve empirical propositions that are false if we are BIVs. Consequently, we cannot appeal to our knowledge of these explications in the course of an argument to the effect that we are not BIVs.[33]

If we are persuaded by this objection, we must conclude that (C1)–(C3) begs the question against the "skeptical" possibility that we are always brains in vats. For similar reasons, Falvey and Owens would say that (D1)–(D3) begs the question against the "skeptical" possibility that our brains were transferred into vats five years ago.

But Falvey and Owens don't realize that to suspend all our "empirical" beliefs is to undercut any skeptical force to the "possibility" that we are always brains in vats, or that our brains were transferred to vats five years ago. If we suspend all our "empirical" beliefs, then we have no reason for thinking that "our explications of our own words involve empirical propositions that are false if we are BIVs." *Either* we take the disquotational picture of self-knowledge seriously, and conclude that without special "empirical" investigation we have no idea what "possibilities" are allegedly "described" by such sentences as 'Perhaps we are always brains in vats' and 'Perhaps our brains were transferred into vats five years ago', *or* we take for granted our ordinary background of "empirical" beliefs, and so we are in a position to see that we aren't always brains in vats, and that our brains weren't transferred to vats five years ago.

So Falvey and Owens's imagined middle position—that without special "empirical" investigation we know what beliefs we express with (C1) and (D1), but we don't know whether we are always brains in vats, or whether our brains were transferred into vats five years ago—is incoherent. If we accept anti-individualism, we can't make sense of suspending all our "empirical" beliefs. Anti-individualism depends on our ordinary practices of attributing beliefs and thoughts to speakers, and these practices always presuppose a background of "empirical" beliefs. Our background beliefs are always open to challenge and revision, but we can't coherently doubt them all at once. Given the way we ordinarily understand the skeptical "possibilities" that we are always brains in vats, and that our brains were transferred into vats five years ago, we can see that these "possibilities" aren't actual. This conclusion rests on "empirical" assumptions without which the "possibilities" would not even *appear* to conflict with our ordinary beliefs.

123. Does Anti-Individualism Beg the Question against Skepticism?

One might think that anti-individualism *by itself* begs the question against skepticism, by assuming that we can't know what we think unless we presuppose a background of "empirical" beliefs. For this feature of anti-individualism undercuts the general skeptical "possibility" that we may actually be in any one of our subjectively equivalent worlds. In particular, as we have seen, it undercuts the idea that for all we know without special "empirical" investigation, we may actually be on Twin Earth, and our word 'water' may actually refer to twin water. If we presuppose that we know enough to see that if we were in that situation our beliefs would be different from what they actually are, we can also see that we are not in that situation. In the face of these "anti-skeptical" consequences, the traditional skeptic will charge that *from the start* anti-individualism begs the question against the skeptical "possibility" that we were born, raised, and now live on Twin Earth, and, more generally, against the skeptical "intuition" that for all we know without special "empirical" investigation, we may actually be in any one of our subjectively equivalent worlds.[34]

Before we face this objection directly, it is important to see that even if we accept anti-individualism and presuppose a background of "empirical" beliefs sufficient for competence and self-knowledge, there remain some far-fetched skeptical hypotheses that we can express and understand even if they are actually true. For example, I may have been transported without my knowledge to Twin Earth, where there is no water. Before I am there long enough to count as a competent speaker of Twin English, I will naturally think that the liquid I see in the lakes, streams, and oceans is *water,* and so many of my beliefs will be false. It is easy to cook up other far-fetched possibilities of the same kind. For example, perhaps last night my brain was removed and placed in a vat so that it now receives the same stimulations that it would have received had it not been put into the vat. If so, I have not yet been in the vat long enough to change the "contents" of my beliefs—I am not yet a "competent" speaker of "Vat English." Even when we take into account all we have said about anti-individualism, it is not incoherent to suppose that I am now a brain in vat. Even though I am confident that I am not actually a brain in a vat, I don't have to suspend *all* my "empirical" beliefs to think coherently that I may actually be a brain in vat.[35]

But of course this won't convince the traditional skeptic that anti-individualism does not beg the question against him. For the possibility that I was born, raised, and now live on Twin Earth looks just as coherent to a traditional skeptic as the possibility that last night I was transported without my knowledge to Twin Earth. And I have argued that if we accept anti-individualism, our very *description* of the "possibility" that we are now and always were on Twin Earth *shows* that this "possibility" is not actual. This seems to beg the question against the traditional skeptic, who assumes that it makes sense to suppose that we are in that situation.

The traditional skeptic assumes from the start that it is coherent to suppose that we may actually be in any one of our subjectively equivalent worlds. Even if we find this supposition compelling, we should be willing grant that the skeptic's "intuitions" about what is possible *may* be confused. The skeptic himself will probably refuse to grant that his "intuitions" may be confused. But if we are to take his challenges seriously, we must be convinced that his "intuitions" make sense.

The question then arises of how we are to *evaluate* the skeptic's claim that for all we know without special "empirical" investigation, we may actually be in any one of our subjectively equivalent worlds. In this chapter I have evaluated the skeptic's claim by highlighting aspects of our ordinary practices of attributing and evaluating beliefs and thoughts. Anti-individualists take for granted that our best understanding of belief and thought is expressed in our actual practices of attributing beliefs and thoughts to individuals. They start by taking at face value our actual practices of attributing beliefs and thoughts, and use thought experiments to elucidate aspects of these ordinary practices. The thought experiments show that the proper evaluation of our beliefs and thoughts is settled in part by features of our social and physical environments. I have argued that the same basic approach should be applied to our understanding of self-knowledge. Just as our understanding of belief and thought is expressed in our actual practices of attributing beliefs and thoughts to individuals, so our understanding of self-knowledge is expressed in our actual assessments of whether an individual is competent in the use of language. Self-knowledge is an aspect of competence in the use of language: to "know the contents" of the thoughts we express with our sentences is just to be able to use our sentences to make and evaluate assertions, to ask questions, to describe possibilities, and so on. When we say that a speaker "knows the contents" of his beliefs without special "empirical" investigation, we mean that we are in a position to use our words in discourse without first engaging in a special "empirical" investigation of the "contents" of our thoughts. If a speaker suspends all his background "empirical" beliefs, then he is incompetent in the use of language. To doubt some of his "empirical" beliefs, he must presuppose others. This shows that unless we presuppose a background of "empirical" beliefs we can't even *raise* a skeptical challenge to our ordinary beliefs. The inextricability of background "empirical" beliefs and self-knowledge undermines the traditional skeptic's assumption that for all we know without special "empirical" investigation, we may actually be in any of our subjectively equivalent worlds.

Faced with this criticism, the skeptic will be inclined to reassert his "intuition" that for all we know without special "empirical" investigation, we may actually be in any one of our subjectively equivalent worlds. He will be inclined to repeat his argument that our first-person experiences would be the same in all these worlds, and that our claims to have self-knowledge must be based solely on these experiences. His reasoning is gripping because we can *picture* ourselves existing in any of our subjectively equivalent worlds. But I have tried to show that such flights of fancy do not impart sense to the skeptic's claim that for all we know without special "empirical" investigation, we may actually be in any one of our subjectively equivalent worlds. I have argued that anti-individualistic elucidations of belief and self-knowledge undermine the skeptic's "intuition" that for all we know without special "empirical" investigation, we may actually be in any one of our subjectively equivalent worlds. In this context it is idle to assert that anti-individualism "begs the question" against the skeptic's "intuitions" about what is possible.

124. Truth and the Absolute Conception of Reality

We have seen why skepticism about self-knowledge is incoherent, that there are no coherent possibilities that conflict with the ordinary fact that we "know the contents" of our beliefs without special "empirical" inquiry, and so we can accept arguments (A1)–(A3), (B1)–(B3), (C1)–(C3), and (D1)–(D3). Thus the realism implicit in the deflationary conception of anti-individualism does not undermine self-knowledge.

There remains another serious challenge to the coherence of the deflationary conception of anti-individualism. It is fundamental to the deflationary conception that our best understanding of truth is given to us in our actual evolving commonsense and scientific inquiries. But we saw earlier (§99) that according to Thomas Nagel and Bernard Williams our participation in actual commonsense and scientific inquiries commits us to an "absolute conception" of truth that radically outstrips any imaginable corrections or refinements of our standards and procedures for evaluating assertions. If we are convinced that we grasp this "absolute conception" of truth and objectivity, we will feel forced to conclude that the deflationary picture of anti-individualism distorts our understanding of truth by tying it too closely to actual or imaginable standards and procedures for evaluating assertions.

Nagel and Williams believe that we grasp the "absolute conception" of truth and objectivity through a dialectic that begins with the commonsense idea that our "empirical" beliefs and thoughts result from causal interactions with an independently existing world. In the first step of the dialectic we note that our beliefs and thoughts are often false or misleading. For example, after a quick look at a particular tree, we may at first believe it is not perpendicular to level ground. Later, after more careful observations of the tree from a number of different positions, we may discover that it is perpendicular to level ground. Early in our lives we learn that appearances can be misleading in this way. Nagel and Williams suggest that such simple cases of perceptual relativity contain the seeds of an "absolute conception" of reality, a conception of how things are independently of all our beliefs or thoughts. To see some of our previous beliefs as false or limited, they argue, we need to adopt (what we take to be) a more "objective" perspective on the same situation, a perspective from which (we suppose that) we can explain and understand the error in those beliefs. And once we see that some of our *previous* beliefs were limited, we can imagine discovering that some of our *currently entrenched* beliefs are false or misleading. This involves imagining a more "objective" perspective that explains why some of our currently entrenched beliefs are false or misleading.

These observations apparently provide us with the ingredients of an infinitely extendable dialectic of perspectives. At any point in the dialectic we can ask whether there are "subjective" elements that distort our perspective. To ask this is to imagine a more encompassing circle of beliefs. This circle of beliefs can itself be questioned by imagining a still wider circle of beliefs. Nagel and Williams think that by reflecting on our commonsense and scientific beliefs in this way, we grasp the idea of an "absolute" perspective from which all other perspectives can be explained and understood.

Nagel and Williams think that for any actual or imaginable procedure for evaluating assertions, we can imagine a more "objective" perspective from which that procedure appears limited or unjustified. Their "absolute conception" of truth and objectivity is supposed to be in principle independent of the actual procedures and standards we use to evaluate our assertions, and of any imaginable extension of those procedures and standards.

So if we feel we understand the "absolute conception" of truth and objectivity, the deflationary picture of anti-individualism will seem to tie our understanding of truth too closely to our actual and possible procedures for evaluating assertions. We will inevitably conclude that the deflationary picture of anti-individualism is verificationism in disguise—an unacceptable distortion of our commonsense and scientific picture of truth and objectivity.

125. Nagel's Abstract Skepticism

Let us look at an example of how the absolute conception might be thought to undercut the deflationary conception of anti-individualism. Recall our argument (C1)–(C3) for the conclusion that we are not always brains in vats:

(C1) I am now using this sentence to express the thought that I am not a brain in a vat.

(C2) If I were always a brain in a vat, I could not use sentence (C1) to express the thought that I am not a brain in a vat.

(C3) Therefore, I am not always a brain in a vat.

We saw that without special "empirical" inquiry I "know the contents" of the thought I express with sentence (C1), that (C2) follows from our description of the world in which a duplicate of my brain is always in a vat, and that there is no coherent skeptical question for this argument to beg.

If we think we understand the absolute conception of reality, however, we may still find a way to doubt that the conclusion (C3) can be fully trusted. We may find a way to express a coherent skepticism akin to the kinds of doubts (discussed in §§115–118) that the skeptic about self-knowledge tries unsuccessfully to express. Let us see how this skepticism might be articulated.

The kernel of the idea is expressed in Thomas Nagel's objection to Putnam's argument that we are not always brains in vats. Although I cannot justify this claim here, (C1)–(C3) amounts to a streamlined reconstruction of the core of Putnam's reasoning,[36] so I will assume that Nagel's objection is also aimed at (C1)–(C3):

> If I accept the argument, I must conclude that a brain in a vat can't think truly that it is a brain in a vat, even though others can think this about it. What follows? Only that I can't express my skepticism by saying "Perhaps I am a brain in a vat." Instead I must say, "Perhaps I can't even think the truth about what I am, because I lack the necessary concepts and my circumstances make it impossible for me to acquire them!" If this doesn't qualify as skepticism, I don't know what does.[37]

Nagel is willing to grant that (C1)–(C3) is sound, but he is bothered by the idea that a brain that is always in a vat could "utter" sentences with the same syntactic shapes as (C1)–(C3). Let's pretend we can translate the brain's utterances into English by appending the phrase "in the image" to the sentences it "utters." "Uttering" sentences with the same syntactic shapes as (C1)–(C3), the brain "convinces" itself that *it is not always a brain in a vat in the image.* Despite this reassuring "antiskeptical" argument, however, the brain's cognitive perspective is *in fact* seriously limited. The brain doesn't have and can't acquire the concepts necessary to express the awful truth about its situation. What concerns Nagel is that *our* cognitive perspective may be analogously limited: perhaps we don't have and can't acquire the concepts necessary to express some similarly awful truth about our cognitive limitations.

Note that Nagel's skepticism about the "objectivity" of our concepts and beliefs is not merely the result of thinking that there may be true thoughts about our situation that we are not now able to express. We all accept this everyday fact without lapsing into skepticism about the "objectivity" of our current repertoire of concepts and thoughts. In learning new disciplines and languages we acquire the ability to express concepts and thoughts that previously we couldn't express. Some of these new thoughts may be true, some may be surprising or disappointing, but none completely undermines the "objectivity" of all our previous thoughts.

Nagel thinks if we accept (C1)–(C3), we must also accept that our cognitive situation is *analogous* to the cognitive situation of the brain that is always in a vat. Such a brain can't think that it is a brain in a vat, and can't acquire the concepts necessary to think this, and so it remains ignorant of this horrible fact about its situation. Let's say that a subject's representation of the world consists in all her beliefs and thoughts. Nagel thinks that the possibility of a brain that is always in a vat, and yet unable to express this thought, shows that a subject's representation of the world may be seriously limited, even if most of what it believes and thinks is true. Nagel's skepticism results from his worry that perhaps our representation of the world is analogously limited. He grants that if (C1)–(C3) is sound, we may not be able to grasp the way our situation is actually limited, but he apparently thinks that we can argue by analogy, as follows: our representation is more encompassing than the brain's, since it encompasses features of the brain's situation that the brain can't represent. To imagine that, for all we know, our representation of the world is limited, despite its internal coherence and truth, is to imagine that there is some representation (or other) that stands to our representation as ours stands to the brain's representation. So Nagel apparently accepts the following assumption:

(R) For all we know, there is some representation (or other) that is related to our representation as ours is related to the brain's representation.

Nagel's skepticism is based in his assumption (R). Relative to the supposed representation, our representation would look as limited as the brain's. It is almost as if Nagel is trying to make sense of the illusory possibility that we *are* in fact always brains in vat, and that when we accept (C1)–(C3), we are concluding that we are not always brains in a vat in the image. But Nagel apparently accepts, at least for the sake of argument, that this supposed "possibility" is illusory. So he changes tack: he tries to *indicate* his skeptical doubt without supposing that he can express in detail any of the possibilities he is concerned about. He grants that we are not always brains in vats, but argues that the "absolute conception" of reality casts doubt on the supposed "objectivity" of this conclusion. In Nagel's view, (C1)–(C3) actually *supports* the skeptical conclusion that just as the brain's cognitive situation is seriously limited in ways the brain can't express, so *our* cognitive situation may be seriously limited in ways that we can't express.[38]

Nagel's skepticism depends on the idea that we can conceive of a representation that is radically independent of all our substantive beliefs. To understand Nagel's argument by analogy we must be able to conceive of a representation that portrays the world using concepts we don't possess and can't acquire. We must be able to conceive of a representation that is radically independent of all our substantive beliefs. Nagel believes that we can understand such a representation as the limit of the dialectic described several paragraphs ago. We generalize from our local discoveries of distortions and limitations in our beliefs to attain the idea of the absolute conception of reality, from which all other representations are encompassed and explained. The absolute conception contains no subjective elements, no human limitations or distortions whatever. Surely if we can understand the absolute conception, we can understand how there could be a representation that stands to ours as ours stands to that of the brain which is always in a vat. This is why Nagel finds (C1)–(C3) skeptical. Given Nagel's *prior* and *independent* commitment to the metaphysical realism expressed by his absolute conception, he cannot take any of our present assessments of our cognitive situation at face value. Since Nagel takes for granted that we might always be brains in vats, he learns from (C1)–(C3) that this can't be so, but only because of Putnam's "theory of meaning," which Nagel does not in any case accept. So Nagel for the sake of argument is willing provisionally to accept anti-individualism, but does not relinquish his absolute conception of objectivity and truth. The result is that he remains just as skeptical as before; only now he expresses his skepticism by saying, "Perhaps I can't even think the truth about what I am, because I lack the necessary concepts and my circumstances make it impossible for me to acquire them!"[39]

126. The Dissolution of the Absolute Conception of Reality

So Nagel thinks that our ordinary and scientific inquiries commit us to a conception of objectivity and truth that is independent of all our substantive beliefs, and of all the standards or procedures we actually use or might use to evaluate our assertions and beliefs. Nagel's absolute conception apparently poses a serious internal challenge to the coherence of the deflationary conception of anti-individualism, according to which our best understanding of truth and objectivity is revealed in our actual and evolving procedures for evaluating our assertions. This challenge is more sophisticated than the skeptical reasoning sketched in §115, but it rests on a similar fantasy about the relationship between our linguistic practices and the "external" world. Nagel's challenge presupposes that we can make sense of there being a representation that is completely independent of any of our substantive beliefs. But if we accept the deflationary picture of anti-individualism I have sketched in the last several chapters, we can't make sense of the idea of a representation that is completely independent of any of our substantive beliefs.

The reason is that our understanding of a representation is essentially tied to our understanding of the "content" of a possible belief or thought. To see this, recall that a subject's representation of the world consists in all her beliefs and thoughts. More important, however, in Chapters Six, Seven, and Eight, we discovered that if we begin with our perspective as participants in ongoing linguistic practices, we see that the proper evaluations of our beliefs and thoughts are partly settled by our social and physical environments. We have no idea what the "contents" of our beliefs and thoughts are apart from our best judgments as to how they are to be evaluated, and these judgments are inextricable from our substantive beliefs. This is the discovery that led us to abandon the analytic-synthetic distinction. Essentially the same reasoning shows that the absolute conception of reality is empty. To give it content, we would have to be able to separate the idea of a representation from *any* of our substantive beliefs, and this is exactly what we discovered that we can't do.

Thus Nagel's idea of a representation that is completely independent of any of our substantive beliefs is an illegitimate generalization from our actual concept of a representation, which is essentially tied to actual or possible beliefs and thoughts that we can (in principle) express. This is not to say that we can't conceive of representations that we can't now express. As I noted above, we have all had the experience of learning new languages and disciplines, and in the process we have acquired the ability to express thoughts that we could not express before. My point is that our understanding of the possibility of thoughts we can't now express is inextricable from our substantive beliefs. To make sense of such thoughts, we must suppose that they could be encompassed in an extension of our present beliefs and thoughts. This shows that the dialectic that Nagel describes can't give content to his absolute conception.

Nagel tries to view the consequences of anti-individualism from his imagined "absolute" perspective on truth and objectivity. What he doesn't realize is that anti-individualism undermines the analytic-synthetic distinction, and hence also the distinction between representations and our substantive beliefs. Nagel's mistake is to think that we can extend our idea of the "contents" of possible beliefs and thoughts beyond our capacity to speculate about *how* our beliefs might be mistaken. Our understanding of objectivity is not limited by our present substantive beliefs, since we can make sense of discovering that we are wrong. But our understanding of how we might be wrong is inextricable from our substantive beliefs. We lose all grip on truth or falsity when we try to imagine a representation completely independent of all our substantive beliefs.

I conclude that anti-individualism undermines the idea of an absolute perspective from which all others can be encompassed and understood. Despite appearances, Nagel's dialectic of perspectives does not raise a serious internal challenge to the deflationary picture of anti-individualism.

TEN

Anti-Individualism and Rule-Following

127. Rule-Following Reconsidered

Let's return to the topic of rule-following. In Chapter One I argued that Kripke's skepticism about meaning and assertion depends on his interpretation of the idea that it is because we grasp and follow rules that our words are meaningful, that we can make assertions, and that we can agree or disagree at all. I explained in Chapter Two why Quine's skepticism about meaning is an inevitable consequence of his scientific naturalism. My point in Chapter Three was that it is fruitless to try to resist Kripke's or Quine's views of meaning and assertion until we can articulate an alternative.

At the end of Chapter Three I proposed a two-stage strategy for investigating the relation between meaning and assertion. In the first stage (Chapters Four to Six) I uncovered the roots of our perspective as participants in our linguistic practices. From these roots, in the second stage (Chapters Seven through Nine) I developed a deflationary anti-individualistic description of meaning and assertion.

In this concluding chapter I'll use my deflationary picture of anti-individualism to criticize and reject Kripke's and Quine's views of the relationship between meaning and assertion.

128. Kripke's Dialectical Skepticism

Kripke's skepticism about rule-following is dialectical. As I explained in Chapter One, Kripke begins with our feeling that it is because we grasp and follow rules that our words are meaningful, that we can make assertions, and that we can agree or disagree at all. He takes for granted that the meaning of an expression is its contribution to the truth conditions of (our assertions of) sentences in which the expression occurs, and that to grasp the meaning of an expression we must grasp its contribution to the truth conditions of our assertions. To grasp the truth condition expressed by the sentence 'Sixty eight plus fifty seven is one hundred twenty-five', for example, we must grasp the meaning of 'plus'. We ordinarily suppose that our word 'plus' means *plus.* Kripke presents an interpretation of what is required for this supposition to be true. It turns out that his requirements can't be satisfied, and so he concludes that nothing determines that our word 'plus' means plus. His reasoning is easy to generalize, and leads to the skeptical conclusion that our words are not objectively meaningful, even though they seem to be.

According to my reconstruction, in Kripke's view there are four related presuppositions about rules implicit in our commonsense assumption that our word 'plus' means plus. First, we find it natural to think that when we grasp the rule for addition, the answers to an indefinite number of addition problems are predetermined independently of any calculation we make. When we calculate the answer to an addition problem like 'sixty-eight plus fifty-seven is one hundred twenty-five', we feel that our grasp of the plus function had "in its own way already traversed" all the steps and determined the truth or falsity of our answer.

Second, Kripke claims that "when we consider a mathematical rule like addition, we think of ourselves as being *guided* in our application of it to each new instance."[1] This idea presupposes Kripke's first observation that in some sense the answers to addition problems are predetermined by the rules we grasp.

Third, Kripke stresses that meaning is a "normative" notion. When I use 'plus' to mean plus, I in effect "instruct myself what I *ought* to do to conform to the meaning."[2] The normative aspect of meaning is displayed in our ordinary practices of making and evaluating assertions. Our participation in these practices expresses our commitment to making an assertion only if we have some reason to believe it's true, and to withdrawing an assertion if we have good reason to think it is false.

Fourth, Kripke claims that our "*past* intentions regarding addition determine a unique answer for indefinitely many new cases in the *future*."[3] We can't raise skeptical doubts about what our words now mean—about whether our word 'plus' denotes plus, for example—without falling into a kind of pragmatic incoherence. Kripke's skeptical strategy is to suppose that our words are now meaningful, but to challenge our commonsense assumptions about what we meant in the *past*. If nothing determines what we meant in the past, Kripke reasons, then nothing determines what our words mean now, despite the pragmatic incoherence of using our own words to express the conclusion that they are meaningless.

Kripke challenges us to say what "facts" about our past mental or behavioral states determined that we meant plus by 'plus', and not one of the countless mathematical functions that agree on all the "answers" we had given at that time, but yield different answers to "addition problems" we had not yet encountered. If we accept Kripke's picture of meaning as instructions in the mind, we feel we understand the skeptic's "hypothesis" that we meant quus by 'plus', where x quus $y = x + y$, if both x and y are less than 57, and 5 otherwise. We don't realize at first that the skeptical "hypothesis" severs all links between the meanings of our words and our ordinary linguistic practices. As we try to answer Kripke's skeptical challenge, however, we find we have no idea how a mental state or behavioral state of ours could determine what we meant. But if nothing determines what our words meant in the past, then nothing determines what they mean in the present either. We feel driven to conclude that our words are meaningless, and so we can't make judgments or entertain thoughts at all.

129. Rule-Following from the Participant Perspective

In this and the next two sections I will draw on points made in earlier chapters to question Kripke's interpretation of the common-sense idea that it is *because* we grasp and follow rules that our words are meaningful, that we can make assertions, and that we can agree or disagree. The key idea behind my criticism is that we have no idea what it is to grasp or follow rules apart from what we call "obeying a rule" and "going against it" in actual cases.[4] If we properly describe our linguistic practices from the participant perspective, we see that Kripke's emphasis on the first-person experience of following a rule directs our attention to the wrong place, and leads to a distorted picture of what is required for following a rule. In particular, Kripke's skeptical "hypothesis" that by 'plus' we meant quus severs all links between our understanding of what is required for meaning and our ordinary practices of ascribing meanings, evaluating assertions, and resolving disputes. To reject the skeptical "hypothesis" is to reject Kripke's interpretation of what is required for meaning, and thereby to undermine his skeptical dialectic.

The proper perspective from which to describe and understand rule-following is not the first-person phenomenological one that Kripke stresses so much in his skeptical argument, but the perspective of participants in a shared linguistic practice. In Chapters Six through Nine I sketched a systematic deflationary picture of the participant perspective. Let me now briefly remind you of some of the central points of these chapters, and explain how they highlight aspects of our rule-following practices.

We saw in Chapter Six that Putnam's reasons for rejecting Carnap's analytic-synthetic distinction rest on descriptions of actual and possible cases in which our language and the references of our terms remain the same but our beliefs change. Putnam's method is to remind us of familiar ways in which ordinary features of our use of language fit together in a natural and coherent system. To undermine Carnap's analytic-synthetic distinction Putnam reminds us of statements we hold immune from disconfirmation even though they are not true in virtue of rules. The kinetic energy example shows that our beliefs about *energy* have radically changed. To make sense of this it helps to think of "energy" as a "law-cluster term" whose reference remains the same despite radical changes in our beliefs.

In Chapter Seven we saw that anti-individualism is a natural development of Putnam's rejection of the analytic-synthetic distinction. The heart of Putnam's anti-individualism is the division of linguistic labor, both at a given time and across time. He observes that the division of linguistic labor is dependent on entrenched beliefs and shared interests associated with a term. When we clarify our inquiries from within the participant perspective, we find that our idea that the things we refer to are independent of our beliefs is rooted in our understanding of ways we could find out that we are wrong—what Putnam calls "the contribution of the environment" is a reflection of the division of linguistic labor across time.

In Chapter Eight I described Burge's dialectical account of the conventional linguistic meaning of a term as a development of Putnam's idea that individual linguistic competence is a normative notion, to be understood relative to the beliefs, standards, and interests of a particular linguistic community. The key idea behind Burge's description of the meaning-giving dialectic is that some members of a linguistic community are more *persuasive* than others. Persuasion should not be confused with coercion or manipulation. A conventional meaning-giving characterization of a term can be challenged, questioned, reevaluated. Even the most authoritative and persuasive speakers may be criticized and in some cases corrected.

When we are persuaded that one of our beliefs could not have been true, as in Burge's arthritis case, we show our commitment to the standards of the community by deferring to the speaker who persuaded us. This does not mean that the most persuasive speakers in the community are right. They may reach equilibrium on a false characterization, and there is always the possibility, however remote, that under new pressure to justify their meaning-giving characterizations, they will revise their views, and persuade others to do so as well.[5]

The crucial point is that it is *only* from the perspective of our participation in shared linguistic practices that rule-following and meaning can be properly understood. Just as a group of dancers can have a dispute about how to dance a dance only if they share a practical ability to dance the dance and to recognize performances of it, so a community of speakers can dispute about how to apply their words in particular cases only if they share a practical ability to make and to recognize archetypical applications of their words. The deflationary picture of anti-individualism helps us to see that it is only from our perspective as participants in such disputes and discussions that we can understand what it is to obey a rule or go against it in actual cases.

The importance of the participant perspective is put to the test and further illuminated by the attempt to raise skeptical possibilities that undermine the familiar fact that we "know the contents" of our beliefs and thought without special "empirical" inquiry. In

Chapter Nine I observed that there is an unproblematic sense in which competent speakers "know the contents" of their own beliefs and thought without special "empirical" inquiry: they are able to use their words in discourse—to make assertions, raise questions, express possibilities, and so on. I argued that the attempt to raise possibilities that undermine self-knowledge is self-defeating, since if we can raise the possibilities that are supposed to undermine self-knowledge, on reflection we can see they are not actual. These conclusions about skepticism and self-knowledge reinforce my point that it is only from our participant perspective that we can understand our linguistic practices.

130. How to Resist Kripke's Picture of Meaning and Assertion

We are now in a position to see that Kripke's fundamental mistake is to think that we understand rules independently of our practices of obeying rules and going against them in actual cases. The mistake reflects Kripke's preoccupation with our first-person experiences of following rules:

> I feel confident that there is something in my mind—the meaning I attach to the 'plus' sign—that *instructs* me what I ought to do in all future cases. I do not predict what I will do ... but instruct myself what I ought to do to conform to the meaning. . . . But when I concentrate on what is now in my mind, what instructions can be found there? . . . The infinitely many cases of the table are not in my mind for my future self to consult. . . . What can there be in my mind that I make use of when I act in the future? It seems that the entire idea of meaning vanishes into thin air.[6]

Kripke's preoccupation with the idea that when I apply my words I "consult" something "in my mind" leads him to think that our words are meaningful only if some fact about us determines what rules we follow.

The presupposition is a natural consequence of a tempting misunderstanding of familiar but puzzling features of our ordinary use of language. It can be harmless to say that the truth conditions of our addition assertions are "determined in advance," since this phrase can be understood to express the difference between correctly calculating a sum and making a mistake. But if we forget or ignore the contexts that give content to this phrase, we will be misled into thinking that our grasp of a rule like *plus* is independent of our use of language. Thus Kripke's emphasis on our *experience* of "grasping a rule in a flash" leads him to think that we understand rules independently of our practices of obeying rules and going against them in actual cases. He then wonders how we follow one rule rather than another one, if they both fit with all the steps we have taken so far. He thinks there must be some "fact" about us, conceived independently of our actual ascriptions of meaning, that determines that we are intending to follow one of the pictured rules, not the other. This leads inevitably to his skeptical conclusion.

We are tempted to think that our experience of suddenly grasping a rule can be explained or understood only if we suppose that quite apart from our participation in actual practices of ascribing meanings, evaluating assertions, and resolving disputes, there is something in our minds that tells us what we ought to do if we are to conform to the rule. But if we begin with what I call the participant perspective on our use of language, and accept my deflationary sketch of anti-individualism, we will no longer be as tempted to make this mistake.[7]

If we have no understanding of rules apart from our practices of obeying rules and going against them in actual cases, then we can't make sense of Kripke's skeptical "hypothesis" that in the past our word 'plus' meant quus not plus. Kripke tries to persuade us that we can make sense of this "hypothesis" by focusing on our first-person experience of trying to follow a rule. This directs our attention to mental states that accompany our attempts to follow rules, and thereby leads us unwittingly to accept Kripke's view that a speaker's intention to follow a rule is just a matter of his being in a certain mental state, conceived independently of our actual practices of ascribing meanings, evaluating assertions, and resolving disputes. Taking our deflationary anti-individualism for granted, we can now see that our understanding of rules is not independent of our practices of obeying rules and going against them in actual cases. Without Kripke's view of meaning to sustain it, our feeling that we understand Kripke's skeptical "hypothesis" fades. And without Kripke's skeptical "hypothesis" to motivate it, his skepticism about meaning dissolves. Since the skeptic has not raised a genuine possibility, there is no need to try to rule it out. Our ordinary procedures for raising and resolving doubts about our meaning ascriptions are untouched by Kripke's skeptical argument.[8]

131. A Skeptical Reply

One might be tempted to reply to my diagnosis of Kripke's mistake by challenging the thought that a *community* of language users is able to follow rules. Such a challenge might be raised as follows

> Kripke's skepticism about meaning applies to linguistic communities, not only to individuals considered in isolation from their linguistic communities. For the totality of all uses of words by all past and present members of a linguistic community is finite, and therefore can be interpreted in many different ways. To answer Kripke's skeptical challenge, we must find a fact that determines what rules are followed in our linguistic community. We can't answer this challenge by appealing to the totality of all uses of words by all past and present members of a linguistic community, for this is just what is in need of interpretation. And if we insist that this skeptical challenge does not make sense, on the grounds that a community's evolving use of language is *definitive* of what it is to follow a rule correctly, then we abandon the idea of objective rules, and collapse into a radical kind of idealism. Thus an appeal to the participant perspective on our rule-following practices will not solve or dissolve Kripke's skeptical problem about rule-following.

This objection stems from a fundamental misunderstanding of the reasons I gave for rejecting Kripke's skeptical argument. It is instructive to see why.

I argued that Kripke's skeptical reasoning presupposes that our understanding of rules is independent of our practices of obeying and going against rules in actual cases. This is what led him to look for a fact that determines which rules we are trying to follow. I urged that if we accept my deflationary picture of anti-individualism, we will see that our picture of the rules we follow does not have any application apart from our rule-following practices. Taking the deflationary picture for granted, we can see that Kripke is wrong about what is required for rule-following.

The skeptical objection voiced near the beginning of this section does not address this method of dissolving Kripke's skeptical reasoning. When the skeptic claims that Kripke's skepticism about meaning applies to the entire community, whether or not we can adopt a participant perspective on our use of rules from within that community, he is simply *reasserting* his view that our understanding of rules is independent of our practices of obeying and going against rules in actual cases—a view of rules that the deflationary picture of anti-individualism calls into question.

The skeptic's claim that the deflationary picture of anti-individualism is a form of linguistic idealism reflects a similar misunderstanding of my attempt to dissolve Kripke's skeptical challenge. I take the participant perspective for granted when I attempt to show that we have no conception of rules that are radically independent of anything we can do to evaluate our assertions. It makes sense to think the deflationary picture of anti-individualism is a form of idealism only if our grasp of rules is independent of our actual practices of agreeing, disagreeing, evaluating assertions, and resolving disputes. Simply to *claim* that the deflationary picture of anti-individualism is a kind of idealism is to avoid my diagnosis of what is wrong with Kripke's metaphysical picture of rules.

Although the labels "realism" and "idealism" have been used in many different ways, my deflationary anti-individualism is best viewed as a form of realism, not idealism. In Chapters Six through Nine I emphasized that no matter how well entrenched our beliefs about a given topic may be, there is always the potential for criticism and correction. To make sense of familiar aspects of our commonsense and scientific inquiries, I proposed that we view *diachronic* agreements, disagreements, and belief revisions as the result of a division of linguistic labor *across time,* and *synchronic* agreements and disagreements as a result of a division of linguistic labor *at a given time.* The resulting descriptions of our linguistic practices clarify the two core ideas of commonsense realism: that our beliefs are not guaranteed to be true, and that our environment exists independently of us.

132. Quine's Scientific Skepticism

In Chapter Two I explained that Quine does not try to derive skeptical consequences about meaning solely by reflecting on our commonsense judgments about meaning. His skepticism about the determinacy of meaning and translation is of a piece with his doctrinal naturalism, the view that "it is within science itself, and not in some prior philosophy, that reality is to be identified and described."[9] Since there is no legitimate perspective higher or firmer than science, what counts as science cannot be defined. Science for Quine is displayed in the doctrines of the mature disciplines like physics, chemistry, and biology.

Both Quine's naturalized epistemology and his indeterminacy thesis are consequences of his doctrinal naturalism. Since for Quine there is no perspective higher or firmer than science, neither naturalized epistemology nor the indeterminacy thesis can undermine our ability to use sentences of our mature physical theories to make "transparent" identifications and descriptions of reality.

Quine's naturalized epistemology is the inevitable result of his doctrinal naturalism, and his commitment to empiricism. From Quine's naturalistic point of view, the "motivating insight" behind empiricism is that "we can know external things only through impacts at our nerve endings."[10] His naturalized epistemology aims to analyze and describe the associations between impacts at our nerve endings and the sentences of our scientific theories. Viewed naturalistically, a scientific theory is a fabric of sentences variously associated with one another and linked to impacts at our nerve endings by the mechanism of conditioned response.[11] The aim of naturalized epistemology is to describe the relationship between "meager input"—the impacts at our nerve endings—and "torrential output"—our assent to and dissent from sentences under various prompting stimulations.

The "minimal verifiable aggregate" of a scientific theory is what Quine calls an "observation sentence." The *stimulus meaning* of a sentence S for speaker A is the ordered pair comprising all irradiation patterns of the eye (and other sense modalities) that prompt A's assent to S, together with all those irradiation patterns that would prompt A's dissent from S. An *observation sentence* is one whose stimulus meaning is the same for all members of the linguistic community. With this definition Quine captures in purely naturalistic terms the intersubjectivity of our observation reports, which are the checkpoints for our theories of nature.[12]

Most of the sentences of a theory are not directly keyed to sensory stimulation; the intersubjective empirical content of these sentences cannot be identified with their stimulus meanings. When a speaker assents to a nonobservational sentence, his assent depends not only on current prompting stimulation, but also on associations of that sentence with other sentences. Only the speaker's theory taken as a whole can be said to have a net intersubjective sensory import. "The unit of empirical significance is the whole of science."[13]

The ontological commitments of our theories are "mere nodes of the structure" that constitutes our total theory of nature, according to Quine. Viewed naturalistically, predicates like 'electron', 'dog', and 'table' are "devices for working a manageable structure into the flux of experience."[14] This seems to undercut our ordinary assumption that when we use sentences of our scientific theories, we are in some sense "really" talking about or referring to such things as electrons, dogs, and tables. But Quine's answer to this worry is that when we use our theories of nature, there is no perspective from which we can wonder whether we are "really" referring to independently existing things. Our "identifications and descriptions of reality" can be made only from within our scientific theories. We should not "look down on the standpoint of theory as make-believe" since "we can never do better than occupy the standpoint of some theory or other, the best we can muster at the time."[15]

This attitude toward theories is reflected in Quine's acceptance of disquotational paradigms for truth and reference. We can say that 'electrons' refers to electrons, and that 'Electrons exist' is true if and only if electrons exist. In Quine's view, we have no understanding of reference or truth apart from these paradigms. We are all in a position to apply these disquotational paradigms to expressions and sentences of our own theories; we can say clearly and directly what our words refer to, and when our sentences are true. The disquotational paradigms are not threatened by naturalized epistemology, and so there is no conflict for Quine between these two perspectives on our scientific theories.

Quine's indeterminacy thesis is also an inevitable consequence of his doctrinal naturalism. From Quine's naturalistic point of view, the objective content of every sentence is completely exhausted by its associations with sensory stimulation, but *observation sentences* are the only ones whose objective contents are exhausted by their *stimulus meanings*. Although translators do not in practice appeal to stimulus meaning, in fact the translation of an observation sentence S is a matter of finding a sentence of the translator's language that has (approximately) the same stimulus meaning as S. Thus the translation of observation sentences is objective and determinate, according to Quine's view of translation in chapter 2 of *Word and Object*. But the translation of other sentences is not uniquely determined. By Quine's naturalistic standards there are many different manuals for translating one language into another. Each manual preserves the "net empirical contents" of the two languages by means of translations that by ordinary standards may appear radically inequivalent. There are no scientific grounds for choosing one of these manuals over another. Since there are no standards higher or firmer than science for judging truth, we must conclude that there is no fact of the matter about translation beyond the constraint to preserve the "net empirical content" of a speaker's "theory."

This conclusion is not restricted to what are ordinarily called "foreign languages." From Quine's naturalistic point of view, "radical translation begins at home." For any two speakers of the same natural language the homophonic manual is just one of many "translations" that preserve the "net empirical content" of their idiolects. For the same reason, each speaker's idiolect can be mapped onto *itself* in many different but empirically equivalent ways. Thus even the "translation" of my own language into itself is objectively indeterminate.

We can nevertheless use the sentences of our own idiolects to make assertions. Our use of sentences of our own idiolects is not undercut by the indeterminacy thesis. For Quine, we must use the sentences of our idiolects to express our "theories of nature." And it is only "within [our theories themselves], and not in some prior philosophy, that reality is to be identified and described."[16] There is no legitimate perspective from which we can view the standpoint of our best theories as "make-believe" or "subjective."

To resolve the apparent conflict between the indeterminacy thesis and our use of sentences to make statements, Quine draws on the distinction between *using* the sentences of our languages and *mentioning* them in naturalistic descriptions of the associations between sentences and sensory stimulation. In Quine's view, we are each in a position to use disquotational paradigms for truth and reference, despite the indeterminacy of translation.

Finally, from Quine's naturalistic point of view, to say that two speakers agree or disagree is just to say that their linguistic dispositions to assent to (or dissent from) sentences "mesh" (or "clash"). Even though we each use our own words without "translating" them, all of our ordinary evaluations of when we "agree" or "disagree" with other speakers rest on entrenched but ultimately unfounded "choices" as to how to "translate" their words into ours.

133. How to Resist Quine's Picture of Meaning and Assertion

My strategy for resisting Quine's picture of the relationship between meaning and assertion has been to try to show that if we start from our perspective as participants in actual linguistic practices, we will see that two speakers of the same public language can express their agreements and disagreements directly, without implicitly "choosing" a translation manual. In Chapters Six through Nine, drawing on Kripke's, Putnam's, and Burge's suggestive examples and remarks, I have developed a deflationary anti-individualistic picture of how familiar aspects of our linguistic practices fit together in a natural and coherent system. Working from within this alternative picture of the relationship between meaning and assertion, we can resist Quine's indeterminacy thesis *without* asserting that there are facts independent of our translation practices that determine how our words should be translated.

In Chapter Six we saw that Putnam's criticism of the analytic-synthetic distinction begins with the idea that the languages that we should take as methodologically basic are the languages that we actually use in our inquiries. Putnam's radical move was to give up on replacing the languages we actually use in science and everyday life, and to clarify them from within. To undermine Carnap's analytic-synthetic distinction, Putnam sketches new ways of looking at familiar aspects of actual linguistic practices.

We saw in Chapter Seven how this method led to his anti-individualism, the core of which is the observation that there is a division of linguistic labor among speakers of the same natural language. On my reconstruction, talking of a "division of linguistic labor" is Putnam's way of highlighting that in most ordinary situations it is unproblematic to say that two uses of the same word within a single public language have the same reference.

The roots of the division of linguistic labor have been explored and further articulated by Burge, as we saw in Chapter Eight. Burge sees the division of linguistic labor as a reflection of our participation in a dialectic of meaning-giving characterizations of our terms. As participants in the dialectic, we defer to other members of our community who disagree with us, or try to persuade them that we are right and they are wrong. The crucial point is it is only from our perspective as participants in these linguistic activities that we can properly describe what it is to agree, disagree, evaluate assertions, and resolve disputes.

To illustrate this point I developed Hare's analogy between agreements and disagreements among speakers of a single language about how to use words, and disputes among dancers about how to dance the eightsome reel. Hare supposed that a group of dancers, each of whom has a practical ability to dance the eightsome reel, get into a dispute over how to dance the eightsome reel. The dispute is over a particular part of the dance. To resolve the dispute, the dancers together dance the dance.

I stressed that to understand the dancers' dispute about how to dance the eightsome reel we must keep in mind that they know how to dance the eightsome reel, and they can recognize performances of it, even if they don't yet agree on an *explicit* account of how it is to be danced. I proposed that their dispute and its resolution be described from their perspective as *participants* in performances of the dance. Such descriptions are available only to those who share a practical ability to dance the dance.

If a group of anthropologists who do not know how to dance the eightsome reel try to say how the eightsome reel is danced, they must rely solely on their observations of the movements of dancers whom they believe to be dancing the eightsome reel. They will not be in a position to say how the dance *ought* to be danced, and so they will miss an important aspect of the practices they observe.

There may be some uses for the anthropologists' detached description of behaviors displayed when people dance, but such descriptions can't give us any insight into how the eightsome reel is properly danced. The anthropologists' descriptions are not more "objective" than the descriptions the dancers themselves can give after discussion and practical investigation, so there is no reason to insist that an "objective" account of what it is to dance the eightsome reel can be given only from the anthropologists' perspective.

The dancers' dispute about how to dance the eightsome reel and their procedure for resolving this dispute are rooted in a shared practical ability and a commitment to resolving disputes by appealing to aspects of that shared practical ability. Analogously, the agreements and disagreements that we express in our everyday and scientific inquiries are rooted in our shared practical ability to make archetypical applications of our words, and in our commitment to resolve disputes about the conditions for properly applying our words by appealing in part to that shared practical ability.

From this perspective we can see that Quine's indeterminacy thesis is not established by his behavioristic descriptions of language use. There is no real conflict between Quine's behavioristic descriptions of language use and the descriptions that we can give from the participant perspective. Properly viewed, Quine's behavioristic descriptions of our linguistic practices are no more troubling than an anthropologist's behavioristic descriptions of performances of a particular dance.

Quine's reasons for the indeterminacy thesis can persuade only those who do not see the possibility of a deflationary alternative to his scientific naturalism. Now that we have articulated a natural and coherent alternative to Quine's austere behavioristic picture of language, we can see that there is no reason to accept his indeterminacy thesis.

134. A Quinean Reply

No one who has ever been in the grip of Quine's picture of meaning and assertion will be immediately convinced by the foregoing reasons for resisting it. Our philosophical commitments and temptations, especially if they are deeply rooted and systematic, have a momentum of their own. Ideally, each person must continue to think through the consequences of Quine's philosophical starting point, and of various alternative starting points, before eventually arriving at a stable conclusion about where we ought to begin if we are to achieve a clear view of the relationship between meaning and assertion. But it is time to conclude my discussion of Quine's view.

To highlight and consolidate my strategy for resisting Quine's view, let us look briefly at Quine's claim that "in general the underlying methodology of the idioms of propositional attitude contrasts strikingly with the spirit of objective science at its most representative."[17] Quine's unfavorable comparison of the "the underlying methodology of the idioms of propositional attitude" with "objective science" rests on his naturalistic reconstruction of "the underlying methodology of the idioms of propositional attitude." In Quine's view, to use sentences of the forms 'S says that P', 'S believes that P', 'S thinks that P', and so on, is in effect to engage in "indirect quotation"—to report what S says, believes, or thinks by using a sentence of one's own idiolect in place of sentences of S's idiolect. The trouble with "indirect quotation," and hence with propositional attitudes generally, is that there are no strict standards for evaluating such reports:

> In indirect quotation we project ourselves into what, from his remarks and other indications, we imagine the speaker's state of mind to have been, and then say what, in our language, is natural and relevant for us in the state thus feigned. An indirect quotation we can usually expect to rate only as better or worse, more or less faithful, and we cannot even hope for a strict standard of more or less; what is involved is evaluation, relative to special purposes, of an essentially dramatic act. Correspondingly for the other propositional attitudes, for all of them can be thought of as involving something like quotation of one's own imagined verbal response to an imagined situation.[18]

Quine concludes that "in the strictest scientific spirit . . . the essentially dramatic idiom of propositional attitudes will find no place."[19] In the context of Quine's scientific naturalism, this conclusion distances us from our perspective as participants in our ordinary practices of attributing and evaluating beliefs and thoughts. In the glare created by Quine's naturalistic descriptions of language use, our participant perspective looks subjective and unimportant.

This view of the participant perspective is of a piece with Quine's idiolectical picture of language use, and his thesis that there are countless naturalistically acceptable yet inequivalent ways to "translate" our fellow speakers' words. For Quine, a speaker's dispositions to assent to and dissent from sentences are all we have to go on in determining what he means or believes, and so any attribution that preserves all speech dispositions preserves all there is to meaning and belief. Thus Quine's skepticism about the participant perspective is the natural consequence of his assumption that all our attributions of beliefs and thoughts must ultimately be based on independently specified "evidence" or "facts" that support our "hypotheses" about what a person means and believes.

Properly viewed, however, our actual attributions of beliefs and thoughts to individuals do not depend on "evidence" or "facts" in the way Quine assumes. From the participant perspective we see, for example, that in the circumstances described in Chapter Eight Alfred believes he has arthritis in his thigh. This is not just one among many different options we have for saying what belief Alfred expressed when he sincerely uttered the English sentence 'I have arthritis in my thigh'. From our participant perspective we see that Alfred was wrong. Alfred himself defers to his doctor upon learning that he can't have arthritis in his thigh. Relying on such observations about our linguistic practices, in Chapters Six through Eight we saw that there is no reason to accept Quine's idiolectical picture of language, or his thesis that our actual linguistic interactions embody just one of many acceptable but inequivalent "translations" of our fellow speakers' words.

NOTES

Introduction

1. W. V. Quine, "Things and Their Place in Theories," in W. V. Quine, *Theories and Things* (Cambridge, Mass.: Harvard University Press, 1981), 1–23; quotation from 21.

2. John McDowell, "Wittgenstein on Following a Rule," *Synthese 58* (1984): 325–363.

3. Ludwig Wittgenstein, *Philosophical Investigations*, 3rd ed., trans. G. E. M. Anscombe (New York: Macmillan, 1968), §201.

One. Kripke's Skepticism about Meaning

1. Throughout this book I use ordinary quotation marks to quote speech and text, and as "scare quotes"—to indicate that I am willing to use the quoted expression for the sake of discussion, but that I do not recommend it. I use single quotation marks to refer to linguistic expressions themselves.

2. Saul Kripke, *Wittgenstein on Rules and Private Language* (Cambridge, Mass.: Harvard University Press, 1982).

3. Kripke describes Ludwig Wittgenstein's *Philosophical Investigations*, 3rd ed., trans. G. E. M. Anscombe (New York: Macmillan, 1968), the source of Kripke's reflections on meaning and rules, as a "perpetual dialectic, where persisting worries, expressed by the voice of the imaginary interlocutor, are never definitively silenced." (Kripke, *Wittgenstein on Rules*, 3). Kripke highlights one aspect of Wittgenstein's dialectic and reads it as a skeptical attack on the idea that it is because we grasp and follow rules that our words are meaningful, we can make assertions, and agree or disagree at all.

4. A dialectical skeptic about knowledge, for example, begins with an analysis of our judgments about what is required for knowledge and aims to show that it is impossible for us to meet those requirements. In chap. 1 of *The Significance of Philosophical Skepticism* (Oxford: Clarendon Press, 1984), Barry Stroud plays the role of a dialectical skeptic about knowledge.

In contrast, a *scientific* skeptic presents a scientific analysis or reconstruction of some phenomenon, and uses it to criticize our commonsense judgements about that phenomenon. To succeed it is not important that the scientific skeptic convince us that prior to encountering his arguments we were already implicitly committed to the scientific analysis that leads to his skeptical conclusion. A classic example of scientific skepticism is David Hume's critique of our commonsense idea that causes necessitate their effects. A more recent example is W. V. Quine's critique of our common-sense ideas about meaning and translation. I discuss Quine's scientific skepticism in Chapters Two, Three, Five, Six, Eight, and Ten.

5. See for example Simon Blackburn, "The Individual Strikes Back," *Synthese 58* (1984): 281–301; Paul A. Boghossian, "The Rule-Following Considerations," *Mind 98* (1989): 507–549; Warren Goldfarb, "Kripke on Wittgenstein on Rules," *Journal of Philosophy 82* (1985): 471–488; John McDowell, "Wittgenstein on Following a Rule," *Synthese 58* (1984): 325–363; Colin McGinn, *Wittgenstein on Meaning* (Oxford: Basil Blackwell, 1984); and Crispin Wright, "Wittgenstein's Rule-Following Considerations and the Central Project of Theoretical Linguistics," in Alexander George, ed., *Reflections on Chomsky* (Oxford: Basil Blackwell, 1989), 233–264.

6. Kripke, *Wittgenstein on Rules*, 7.

7. Ibid., 8.

8. Ibid., 10.

9. Ibid., 17–18.

10. Ibid., 21–22.

11. This formulation is modeled on Michael Dummett's interpretation of Frege's view of the sense of a word: "for Frege ... the sense of [a] word consists in a rule which, taken together with the rules constitutive of the senses of the other words, determines the condition for the truth of a sentence in which the word occurs" (Michael Dummett, *Frege: Philosophy of Language,* 2nd ed., Cambridge, Mass.: Harvard University Press, 1981, 194). I intend my use of the phrase "truth conditions" to be neutral between various competing conceptions of truth. Disquotational truth is all one needs to make sense of the "intuitions" about the relationship between truth and meaning that I will feature in this section.

12. In *The Origins of Analytical Philosophy* (Cambridge, Mass.: Harvard University Press, 1994), Michael Dummett writes of Frege's view of "the mirroring of thoughts by sentences" (6) and quotes Frege: "The sentence can be regarded as an image of the thought in that to the relation between the part and the whole within the thought there by and large corresponds the same relation between the part of the sentence and the sentence" (G. Frege, *Posthumous Writings,* trans. P. Long and R. White,

Oxford: Basil Blackwell, 1979, 255; quoted by Dummett, *The Origins of Analytical Philosophy*, 6).

13. Wittgenstein, *Philosophical Investigations*, §185.

14. Ibid., §188.

15. Kripke, *Wittgenstein on Rules*, 52.

16. Kripke dismisses Wittgenstein's alternative understanding of our commonsense talk of meaning: " 'We are,' he says in §194 . . . 'like savages, primitive people, who hear the expressions of civilized men, put a false interpretation on them, and draw the queerest conclusions from it.' Maybe so. Personally I can only report that, in spite of Wittgenstein's assurances, the 'primitive' interpretation often sounds rather good to me" (Kripke, *Wittgenstein on Rules*, 66). Using this confessional style, Kripke suggests that his understanding of grasping a rule is more honest than Wittgenstein's. To come to terms with Kripke's skeptical argument, we must see through such rhetorical tricks, yet remain open to the attractions of his picture of meaning.

17. Throughout §§138–242 of *Philosophical Investigations* Wittgenstein acknowledges and attempts to demystify this striking aspect of understanding. See §§151–155, 179–184, 188, 191, 197, 218–219, 238.

18. Kripke, *Wittgenstein on Rules*, 21–22.

19. Ibid., 65.

20. To paraphrase Dummett (*Frege*, 299), we feel it is mandatory to strive to make what we assert or judge agree with what is the case.

21. Kripke, *Wittgenstein on Rules*, 37.

22. Boghossian makes a similar point on p. 513 of "The Rule-Following Considerations."

23. Kripke in effect acknowledges this in the following passage: "it ought to be agreed that if I meant plus, then *unless I wish to change my usage*, I am justified in answering (indeed compelled to answer) '125' " (Kripke, *Wittgenstein on Rules*, 11, my emphasis).

24. Ibid., 12.

25. Ibid., 13.

26. Ibid., 13.

27. Ibid., 9.

28. Goldfarb, "Kripke on Wittgenstein on Rules," 473–474.

29. Kripke, *Wittgenstein on Rules*, 10.

30. In the first chapter of *Philosophical Scepticism*, Stroud argues that to know that p, for any "empirical" proposition p, we must rule out the skeptical possibility that we are dreaming that p, even though this possibility is never taken seriously in ordinary life. Similarly, Kripke argues that to justify our commonsense presupposition that by 'plus' we meant plus, we must cite some fact that rules out the skeptical possibility that

by 'plus' we meant quus, even though this possibility is never taken seriously in ordinary life. Stroud and Kripke believe that their skeptical challenges are based in our commonsense judgments about what is required for knowledge and meaning, and so they are *dialectical skeptics* (in the sense explained in §5).

31. Goldfarb, "Kripke on Wittgenstein on Rules," 474.

32. Kripke, *Wittgenstein on Rules*, 14.

33. Ibid.

34. Ibid., 15.

35. Ibid., 11.

36. Crispin Wright argues that if the skeptic is not questioning my memory, but he is challenging my assumption that I remember that I meant plus by 'plus', then he must be imposing limits on the nature of the "facts" themselves: "there is an explicit and unacceptable reductionism involved at the stage at which the Skeptic challenges his interlocutor to recall some aspect of his former mental life which might constitute his, for example, having meant addition by 'plus'. It is not acceptable, apparently, if the interlocutor claims to recall precisely that. Rather the challenge is to recall some *independently characterized* fact, in a way which does not simply beg the question of the existence of facts of the disputed species, of which it is then to *emerge*—rather than simply be claimed—that it has the requisite properties (principally, normative content across a potential infinity of situations). The search is thus restricted to phenomena of consciousness which are not—for the purpose of the dialectic—permissibly assumed 'up front' to have a recollectable *content*. . . . If the Skeptic is allowed to put the challenge in this way, then it is no doubt unanswerable. But so put, it is merely an implicit prejudice against the ordinary notions of meaning and intention, according to which we may and usually do non-inferentially know of our present meanings and intentions, and may later non-inferentially recall them" (Crispin Wright, "Wittgenstein's Rule-Following Considerations and the Central Project of Theoretical Linguistics," in Alexander George, ed., *Reflections on Chomsky*, Oxford: Basil Blackwell, 1989, 236.) Like Goldfarb's, this objection to Kripke's skeptic stems from a failure to appreciate Kripke's dialectical strategy.

37. Kripke, *Wittgenstein on Rules*, 51.

38. Ibid.

39. Ibid, 52, my emphasis.

40. Wittgenstein, *Philosophical Investigations*, §197.

41. Boghossian, "The Rule-Following Considerations," 542.

42. Wittgenstein, *Philosophical Investigations*, §197.

43. Boghossian, "The Rule-Following Considerations," 542.

44. My central point in this section is that since most readers don't understand Kripke's dialectical strategy, they naturally see no force in Kripke's reasons for rejecting primitive meaning facts. I am *not* claiming that the reasoning I attribute to Kripke can *force* a determined interlocutor to relinquish the view that there are primitive meaning facts that predetermine the truth conditions of our assertions. In this restricted sense I agree with Ed Minar that Kripke's reasons for rejecting such primitive meaning facts are "unlikely to convince a determined interlocutor who holds to intrinsically meaningful (and private) items." See Edward Minar, "Paradox and Privacy: On §§201–202 of Wittgenstein's *Philosophical Investigations*," in *Philosophy and Phenomenological Research* 65 (1994): 43–75, quotation from n. 28, p. 78.

45. Recall that an *addition problem* is any expression of the forms '___ plus . . .' and '___ + . . .', where the blanks are filled by English number-words and Arabic numerals respectively. 'Sixty-eight plus fifty-seven' and '68 + 57' are both addition problems in this sense, regardless of how they are interpreted. See §7.

46. We continue to assume that 'sixty-eight' denotes sixty-eight, '68' denotes 68, and so on.

47. Kripke, *Wittgenstein on Rules*, 15.

48. In the midst of his rejection of dispositional accounts of rule-following, Kripke raises the problem of accounting for ordinary mistakes: "Most of us have dispositions to make mistakes. For example, when asked to add certain numbers some people forget to 'carry'. They are thus disposed, for these numbers, to give an answer different from the usual addition table. Normally, we say that such people have made a *mistake*. That means, that for them as for us, '+' means addition, but for certain numbers they are not disposed to give the answer they *should* give, if they are to accord with the table of the function they actually *meant*. But the dispositionalist cannot say this. According to him, the function someone means is to be *read off* from his dispositions; it cannot be presupposed in advance which function is meant." (Kripke, *Wittgenstein on Rules*, 28–30). A simpler version of the same problem confronts the proposal that the meaning of our word 'plus' is determined by the answers we have already given to addition problems. Most of us have made *mistakes* when attempting to answer addition problems, and so the meaning of our word 'plus' can't be *read off* from the answers we have already given to addition problems, even if we ignore the problem of how our past answers to addition problems determine what answers we should give to addition problems we have not yet encountered.

49. Kripke, *Wittgenstein on Rules*, 15–16.

50. Ibid., 15.

51. Ibid., 16.

52. Ibid., 41.

53. Ibid., 43.

54. Ibid., 38–40.

55. Ibid., 22–23.

56. Ibid., 24.

57. Ibid., 23.

58. Ibid., 21.

59. Ibid., 56.

60. Goldfarb, "Kripke on Wittgenstein on Rules," 475–476.

61. See Wittgenstein, *Philosophical Investigations* §§193–194; and Kripke, *Wittgenstein on Rules,* 33–37 and n. 24.

62. Kripke, *Wittgenstein on Rules,* 22.

63. Ibid., 65.

Two. Quine's Scientific Skepticism about Meaning

1. W. V. Quine, *Word and Object* (Cambridge, Mass.: MIT Press, 1960), 27.

2. W. V. Quine, "Things and Their Place in Theories," in *Theories and Things* (Cambridge, Mass.: Harvard University Press, 1981), 1–23; quotation from 21.

3. On the fundamental role of science in Quine's philosophy, see Thomas Ricketts, "Rationality, Translation, and Epistemology Naturalized," *Journal of Philosophy 79* (1982): 117–136.

4. W. V. Quine, "Notes on the Theory of Reference," in W. V. Quine, *From a Logical Point of View,* rev. 2nd ed. (Cambridge, Mass.: Harvard University Press, 1961), 130–138; quotation from 138.

5. Quine emphasizes that "where it makes sense to apply 'true' is to a sentence couched in the terms of a given theory and seen from within the theory . . . To say that the statement 'Brutus killed Caesar' is true, or that 'The atomic weight of sodium is 23' is true, is in effect simply to say that Brutus killed Caesar, or that the atomic weight of sodium is 23" (*Word and Object,* 24).

6. Quine, "Things and Their Place in Theories," 23.

7. In *Pursuit of Truth,* rev. ed. (Cambridge, Mass.: Harvard University Press, 1992), Quine explicitly links his view of our talk of facts with his use of a disquotational truth predicate: "Instead of saying that 'Snow is white' is true if and only if it is a fact that snow is white we can simply delete 'it is a fact that' as vacuous, and therewith facts themselves: 'Snow is white' is true if and only if snow is white. To ascribe

truth to the sentence is just to ascribe whiteness to snow; such is the correspondence, in this example. Ascription of truth just cancels the quotation marks. Truth is disquotation" (80).

8. Quine, *Word and Object*, 161.

9. Ibid., 3–4.

10. Ibid., 221.

11. Ibid., 2.

12. W. V. Quine, "Epistemology Naturalized," in W. V. Quine *Ontological Relativity and Other Essays* (New York: Columbia University press, 1969), 69–90, quotation from 82–83.

13. My paraphrase; see Quine, *Word and Object*, 11.

14. Ibid., §46.

15. To make sense of this *Word and Object* definition of an observation sentence, we must understand how a sentence can have the same stimulus meaning for two or more speakers. In *Pursuit of Truth* Quine abandons the assumption that stimulus meanings can be compared across speakers, and settles for a looser definition, according to which a sentence is observational for a group if "each member would agree in assenting to it, or dissenting, on witnessing the occasion of utterance" (43). By either definition, an observation sentence is one whose association with sensory stimulation is firm and direct. For a brief discussion of the ramifications of Quine's new definition, see my review of *Pursuit of Truth*, in *Philosophical Review* 103 (1994): 535–541.

16. Quine, *Word and Object*, 10–11.

17. Ibid., 11.

18. W. V. Quine, "Two Dogmas of Empiricism," in W. V. Quine, *From a Logical Point of View*, rev. 2nd ed. (Cambridge, Mass.: Harvard University Press, 1961), 20–46; quotation from 42.

19. Quine, "Two Dogmas," 44.

20. Quine, "Epistemology Naturalized," 83.

21. Quine, *Word and Object*, 22.

22. Quine, "Epistemology Naturalized," 81.

23. Ibid., 89.

24. Ibid.

25. Quine, *Word and Object*, 27.

26. Quine, "Epistemology Naturalized," 81.

27. Ibid., 82.

28. The quoted words and phrases are taken from the following sentence: "Any translations of English sentences into Arunta sentences will be as correct as any other, so long as the net empirical implications of the theory as a whole are preserved in translation" (ibid., 80).

29. In "On Quine's Indeterminacy Doctrine," *Philosophical Review 98*

(1989): 35–63, Andrzej Zabludowski argues that by Quine's own account of "empirical content," there can be no truth values that aren't settled by speech dispositions, and so if two translations preserve all speech dispositions, they will agree in truth values, contrary to Quine's indeterminacy thesis. But Quine's account of "empirical content" is not a "theory" or "analysis" of truth conditions, as Zabludowski supposes, and so there is no incompatibility between Quine's account of "empirical content" and the indeterminacy thesis.

30. Quine, *Word and Object*, 37.

31. Even though the linguist does not translate by explicit appeal to stimulus meanings, Quine believes that "stimulus meaning . . . may be properly looked upon . . . as the objective reality that the linguist has to probe when he undertakes radical translation" (ibid., 39).

32. Ibid., 38.

33. Quine, "Epistemology Naturalized," 80.

34. Even for observation sentences, however, we can't filter out information that all members of a linguistic community share.

35. W. V. Quine, "Ontological Relativity," in *Ontological Relativity and Other Essays*, 26–68; quotation from 30–31.

36. Quine, *Word and Object*, 53.

37. Quine, "Ontological Relativity," 33.

38. Quine, *Word and Object*, 72.

39. Ibid., 72.

40. Ibid., 73–74.

41. Quine, *Pursuit of Truth*, 50.

42. Noam Chomsky, "Quine's Empirical Assumptions," in D. Davidson and J. Hintikka, ed., *Words and Objections: Essays on the Work of W. V. Quine* (Dordrecht: D. Reidel, 1969), 53–68; quotation from 61.

43. W. V. Quine, "Reply to Chomsky," in ibid., 302–303.

44. Quine makes this point vividly in the following passage from his "Reply to Chomsky": "Though linguistics is of course a part of the theory of nature, the indeterminacy of translation is not just inherited as a special case of the under-determination of our theory of nature. It is parallel but additional. Thus, adopt for now my fully realistic attitude toward electrons and muons and curved space-time, thus falling in with the current theory of the world despite knowing that it is in principle methodologically under-determined. Consider, from this realistic point of view, the totality of truths of nature, known and unknown, observable and unobservable, past and future. The point about indeterminacy of translation is that it withstands even all this truth, the whole truth about nature. This is what I mean by saying that, where indeterminacy of translation applies, there is no real question of right choice; there is

no fact of the matter even to *within* the acknowledged under-determination of a theory of nature" (303). The connection between Quine's talk of "facts of the matter" and naturalism is made explicit in a passage from "Things and Their Place in Theories": "I have argued that two conflicting manuals of translation can both do justice to all dispositions to behavior, and that, in such a case, there is no fact of the matter of which manual is right. The intended notion of fact of the matter is not transcendental or yet epistemological, not even a question of evidence; it is ontological, a question of reality, and to be taken naturalistically within our scientific theory of the world" (23).

45. For an elaboration of this kind of objection see Paul Boghossian, "The Status of Content," *Philosophical Review 99* (1990): 157–184.

46. In §43 of *Word and Object,* Quine considers what he calls "the fallacy of subtraction"—the argument that "if we can speak of a sentence as meaningful, or as having meaning, then there must be a meaning that it has, and this meaning will be identical with or distinct from the meaning another sentence has." Quine dismisses this argument with the retort "Whistling in the dark is not the method of true philosophy" (206–207).

47. Ibid., 27. This is Quine's first formulation of the indeterminacy thesis; in the next paragraph he says that the thesis of the indeterminacy of translation is "the same point . . . put less abstractly."

48. Quine, "Ontological Relativity," 46.

49. Quine, *Word and Object,* 27.

50. Ibid., 27. In Quine's vivid simile, "Different persons growing up in the same language are like different bushes trimmed and trained to take the shape of . . . elephants" (*Word and Object,* 8).

51. Ibid., 27.

52. Quine, "Notes on the Theory of Reference," 134.

53. Quine, "Ontological Relativity," 47.

54. Quine, *Word and Object,* 78.

55. Quine, "Ontological Relativity," 48.

56. Ibid., 49.

57. For example, John Searle, "Indeterminacy, Empiricism, and the First Person," *Journal of Philosophy 84* (1987): 123–146.

58. Quine, *Philosophy of Logic,* 11.

59. Ibid., 3.

60. Ibid., 98, 102.

61. To see that logic has "universal applicability" we need not actually be able to apply it to sentences of every language that may be used to make assertions about the subjects treated within our total theory of nature. To generalize over sentences we must be in a position to use them, and there are many languages we have not and may never learn.

62. Quine, "Things and Their Place in Theories," 21.

63. Quine, *Word and Object*, 2.

64. Quine, "Epistemology Naturalized," 81.

65. Quine, "Ontological Relativity," 29.

66. See Boghossian, "The Status of Content."

Three. The Very Idea of a Participant Perspective

1. John McDowell, "Wittgenstein on Following a Rule," *Synthese 58* (1984): 325–363.

2. Ludwig Wittgenstein, *Philosophical Investigations*, 3rd ed., trans. G. E. M. Anscombe (New York: Macmillan, 1968), §201.

3. W. V. Quine, *Word and Object* (Cambridge, Mass.: MIT Press), 206.

4. In *Naming and Necessity* (Cambridge, Mass.: Harvard University Press, 1980), Kripke writes: "some philosophers think that something's having intuitive content is very inconclusive evidence in favor of it. I think it is very heavy evidence in favor of anything, myself. I really don't know, in a way, what more conclusive evidence one can have about anything, ultimately speaking" (42).

5. Wittgenstein, *Philosophical Investigations*, §201.

6. McDowell, "Wittgenstein on Following a Rule," 341–342.

7. Ibid., 325, my emphasis.

8. Ibid.

9. Ibid.

10. Ibid., 330.

11. Ibid., 331. The passage in single quotes is from Wittgenstein, *Philosophical Investigations*, §198.

12. Wittgenstein, *Philosophical Investigations*, §201.

13. McDowell, "Wittgenstein on Following a Rule," 332.

14. Wittgenstein, *Philosophical Investigations*, §201.

15. McDowell writes: "The paradox that Wittgenstein formulates at §201 is . . . the genuine and devastating paradox that meaning is an illusion ("Wittgenstein on Following a Rule," 343).

16. Ibid., 336.

17. Ibid.

18. Crispin Wright, *Wittgenstein on the Foundations of Mathematics* (Cambridge, Mass.: Harvard University Press, 1980), 355. Quoted by McDowell, "Wittgenstein on Following a Rule," 327.

19. Wright, *Wittgenstein on the Foundations of Mathematics*, 220.

20. McDowell, "Wittgenstein on Following a Rule," 335.

21. Ibid., 335–336.

22. For instance, Wright emphasizes that: "if 'correctness' means

ratification-independent conformity with an antecedent pattern, there is apparently absolutely nothing which we can do to make the contrast active between the consensus description and the correct description. Of course, it may happen that the community changes its mind; and when it does so, it does not revise the judgment that the former view enjoyed consensus. But that is a fact about our procedure; to call attention to . . . the circumstance that *we make use of the notion that we can all be wrong* . . . is not to call attention to anything which gives sense to the idea that the wrongness consists in departure from a ratification-independent pattern" (*Wittgenstein on the Foundations of Mathematics*, 219–220, my emphasis). Similarly, in *Wittgenstein on Rules and Private Language* (Cambridge, Mass.: Harvard University Press, 1982), Saul Kripke interprets Wittgenstein as saying that the notions of correctness or incorrectness of language use can be understood only in the context of a linguistic community. But like Wright, Kripke denies that in Wittgenstein's view the reactions of the community *define* truth: "One must bear firmly in mind that Wittgenstein has no theory of truth conditions—necessary and sufficient conditions—for the correctness of one response rather than another to a new addition problem. Rather he simply points out that each of us *automatically* calculates new addition problems (without feeling the need to check with the community whether our procedure is proper); that the community feels entitled to correct a deviant calculation; that in practice such deviation is rare, and so on. Wittgenstein thinks that these observations about sufficient conditions for justified assertion are enough to illuminate the role and utility in our lives of assertion about meaning and determination of new answers. *What follows from these assertability conditions is not that the answer everyone gives to an addition problem is, by definition, the correct one, but rather the platitude that, if everyone agrees upon a certain answer, then no one will feel justified in calling the answer wrong*" (*Wittgenstein on Rules*, 111–112, my emphasis).

23. McDowell, "Wittgenstein on Following a Rule," 336.

24. Ludwig Wittgenstein, *Remarks on the Foundations of Mathematics*, 3rd ed. ed. R. Rhess and G. E. M. Anscombe, trans. G. E. M. Anscombe (Oxford: Basil Blackwell, 1978), VI, §35; quoted by McDowell, "Wittgenstein on Following a Rule," 340.

25. Ludwig Wittgenstein, *On Certainty*, ed. G. E. M. Anscombe and G. H. von Wright, tran. Denis Paul and G. E. M. Anscombe (Oxford: Basil Blackwell, 1969), §204; quoted by McDowell, "Wittgenstein on Following a Rule," 341.

26. McDowell, "Wittgenstein on Following a Rule," 341.

27. Ibid., 336.

28. Ibid., my emphasis.

29. Ibid., 347.

30. Ibid., 346.

31. Ibid.

32. Ibid., 346–347.

33. Ibid., 347.

34. Ibid., 353.

35. Ibid., 342.

36. Ibid., 339.

37. Ibid., 351. Here McDowell quotes from Wright, *Wittgenstein on the Foundations of Mathematics*, 354.

38. McDowell, "Wittgenstein on Following a Rule," 350, my emphasis.

39. Ibid., 350–351, my emphasis.

40. Ibid., 352.

41. Ibid.

42. Ibid., 351.

43. Ibid., 352.

44. Ibid., 352–353.

45. Ibid., 347, my emphasis.

46. Ibid., 336.

47. Ibid., 350.

48. Ibid., 336, my emphasis.

49. Ibid., 353.

Four. Carnap's Analytic-Synthetic Distinction

1. Rudolf Carnap, "Intellectual Autobiography," in Paul A. Schilpp, ed., *The Philosophy of Rudolf Carnap* (La Salle, Ill.: Open Court, 1963), 3–84; quotation from 44–45.

2. In §2 of *The Logical Syntax of Language*, trans. Amethe Smeaton (London: Kegan Paul, Trench, Trubner & Co., 1937), Carnap writes: "Of the so-called philosophical problems, the only questions which have any meaning are those of the logic of science. To share this view is to *substitute logical syntax for philosophy*" (8).

3. In §2 of *Logical Syntax*, Carnap writes: "The inquiries which follow are of a purely formal nature and do not depend in any way upon what is usually known as philosophical doctrine" (8).

4. For a detailed justification of this claim, see Thomas Ricketts, "Carnap: From Logical Syntax to Semantics," in R. Giere and A. Richardson, ed., *Origins of Logical Empiricism* (Minneapolis: University of Minnesota Press, 1995). My exposition of Carnap's view owes a great

deal to "Carnap: From Logical Syntax to Semantics" and to Ricketts's paper "Rationality, Translation, and Epistemology Naturalized," *Journal of Philosophy* 79 (1982): 117–136. In §72 of Chapter Five I present my central criticisms of Ricketts's reading of Carnap.

5. In *Logical Syntax*, for example, Carnap showed that by means of the arithmetization of syntax a language sufficient to express the theorems of elementary number theory can specify its own syntactical transformation rules. The full logical consequence relation for such a language cannot be defined within the language, however, as Gödel's incompleteness theorems show. The consequence relation is nevertheless syntactical in an extended sense that allows what Carnap called "indefinite" inference rules. (See *Logical Syntax*, §43, §45, §§47–48.)

6. Carnap draws the distinction between pure and descriptive syntax and semantics in the same way from *Logical Syntax* on. See, for example, §2 and §§24–25 of *Logical Syntax*, and §5 of *Introduction to Semantics* (Cambridge, Mass.: Harvard University Press, 1942).

7. In *Logical Syntax* Carnap proposed that we specify the consequence relation for language in purely syntactical terms; he used axioms and proof-theoretic syntactical rules of inference, including what he called "indefinite" rules (see note 5). Later, after he learned of the significance of Tarski's method for defining truth for formalized languages, Carnap proposed that we explicate the logical consequence relation for a language L in semantical terms. First he laid down rules of designation and gave a truth definition for L. He then used his definition of truth to define what he called 'L-true' for the language L, his explication of 'analytic in L'. A definition of 'L-true' for a language L defines the logical consequence relation for L, since S_2 is a logical consequence of S_1 in L if and only if the conditional with S_1 as antecedent and S_2 as consequent is L-true in L.

8. Carnap, "Intellectual Autobiography," 54–55.

9. Carnap, *Logical Syntax*, §17, p. 52.

10. In his "Intellectual Autobiography", Carnap emphasizes his openness to alternative metatheoretical resources: "A few years after the publication of the book [*Logical Syntax*], I recognized that one of its main theses was formulated too narrowly. I had said that the problems of philosophy ... are merely syntactical problems; I should have said in a more general way that these problems are metatheoretical problems. The narrower formulation is historically explained by the fact that the syntactical aspect of language had been the first to be investigated by exact means by Frege, Hilbert, the Polish logicians, and in my book. Later we saw that the metatheory must also include semantics and pragmatics; therefore the realm of philosophy must likewise be conceived as comprising these fields" (56).

11. In his "Intellectual Autobiography" Carnap writes: "The chief motivation for my development of the syntactical method ... was [that] ... it seemed to me that the development of a suitable metalanguage would essentially contribute toward greater clarity in the formulation of philosophical problems and greater fruitfulness in their discussions" (55).

12. In a letter to Charles W. Morris, written in 1936, Quine explained that "Carnap would regard the contribution of the *Syntax* as methodological rather than systematic; and its methodological power has worked not only to cope satisfactorily with some philosophical problems, but also to clear the way for further ones, which remain to be attacked by the same methods." (The letter is printed in Richard Creath, ed., *Dear Carnap, Dear Van,* Berkeley and Los Angeles: University of California Press, 1990, 204–206; the quotation is from 205.) I take Quine to be reporting Carnap's pragmatic attitude toward his own proposals in *Logical Syntax.*

13. Carnap, "Intellectual Autobiography," 47.

14. Ibid., 64.

15. In "Logical Truth and Analyticity in Carnap," in W. Aspray and P. Kitcher, ed., *History and Philosophy of Modern Mathematics,* Minnesota Studies in Philosophy of Science, vol. 11 (Minneapolis: University of Minnesota Press, 1988), Michael Friedman claims that Carnap "is concerned above all with the Kantian question 'How is mathematics ... possible' ... Carnap never gives up his belief in the importance and centrality of this question—nor does he ever waver in his conviction that he has the answer: the possibility of mathematics and logic is to be explained by a sharp distinction between formal and factual, analytic and synthetic truth" (82). I disagree, for packed into Friedman's claim that Carnap is interested in this "Kantian question" is the mistaken assumption that Carnap had explanatory ambitions that could only be realized by a substantive "theory" of allegedly "universal" methods for specifying the rules for a language system.

16. W. V. Quine "Truth by Convention," first published in 1936, reprinted in W. V. Quine, *The Ways of Paradox and Other Essays,* rev. and enl. ed., (Cambridge, Mass.: Harvard University Press, 1976), 77–106.

17. W. V. Quine, "Carnap and Logical Truth," in Paul A. Schilpp, ed., *The Philosophy of Rudolf Carnap* (La Salle, Ill.: Open Court, 1963), 385–406.

18. For Carnap the "transcription" thesis is trivialized by his method of constructing language systems: virtually any "axiom" can be included as a primitive truth of a language system.

19. See "Truth by Convention," 87–88.

20. Axiomatizations of truth-functional logic are covered in many introductory logic texts, including Quine's *Methods of Logic*, 4th ed., (Cambridge, Mass.: Harvard University Press, 1982), §13.

21. Quine, "Carnap and Logical Truth," 391–392.

22. Lewis Carroll, "What the Tortoise Said to Achilles," *Mind* 4 (1895): 278–280.

23. Quine, "Truth by Convention," 105.

24. Ibid., 106.

25. Hilary Putnam has summarized Quine's objection (which Putnam also claims to find in Wittgenstein) as follows: "The 'exciting' thesis that logic is true by convention reduces to the unexciting claim that *logic is true by conventions plus logic*. No real advance has been made." From "Analyticity and Apriority: Beyond Wittgenstein and Quine," reprinted in Hilary Putnam, *Realism and Reason* (Cambridge: Cambridge University Press, 1983), 115–138; quotation from 116.

26. Rudolf Carnap, "W. V. Quine on Logical Truth," in Paul A. Schilpp, ed., *The Philosophy of Rudolf Carnap* (La Salle, Ill: Open Court, 1963), 915–922.

27. Ibid., 916.

28. In Quine's lectures on Carnap's philosophy, delivered at Harvard in 1934, Quine seems to have a clear grasp of Carnap's deflationary view of analytic truth: "Kant's recognition of *a priori* synthetic propositions, and the modern denial of such, are thus to be construed as statements of conventions as to linguistic procedure. The modern convention has the advantage of great theoretical economy; but the doctrine that the *a priori* is analytic remains only a syntactic decision. It is however no less important for *that* reason: *as a syntactic decision it has the importance of enabling us to pursue foundations of mathematics and the logic of science without encountering extra-logical questions as to the source of the validity of our a priori judgments* ... it shows that all metaphysical problems as to an *a priori* synthetic are gratuitous, and let in only by ill-advised syntactic procedures" (*Dear Carnap, Dear Van*, 65–66, my emphasis). In this passage Quine does not attribute any explanatory ambitions to Carnap. By 1935, when Quine wrote "Truth by Convention," he had apparently changed his mind about Carnap's view.

29. Thus Carnap would reject the kind of radical conventionalism that Dummett attributes to Wittgenstein, where for each new statement of logic or mathematics it is somehow "up to us" whether it should count as a theorem. See Dummett's papers "Wittgenstein's Philosophy of Mathematics," reprinted in Michael Dummett, *Truth and Other Enigmas* (Cambridge, Mass.: Harvard University Press, 1978), 166–185, and "Wittgenstein on Necessity: Some Reflections," reprinted in

Michael Dummett, *The Seas of Language* (Oxford: Clarendon Press, 1993), 446–461.

30. In "Quine on Logical Truth," Carnap writes: "The main point of [Quine's] criticism seems to be that [my account of logical truth] is 'empty' and 'without experimental meaning.' With this remark I would certainly agree, and I am surprised that Quine deems it necessary to support this view by detailed arguments. In line with Wittgenstein's basic conception, we agreed in Vienna that one of the main tasks of philosophy is clarification and explication. Usually, a philosophical insight does not say anything about the world, but is merely a clearer recognition of meanings or of meaning relations" (917).

31. Carnap, "Intellectual Autobiography," 63–64.

32. Rudolf Carnap, *Meaning and Necessity* (Chicago: University of Chicago Press, 1947), 4. L_1 is different from Carnap's language system S_1 (see pp. 3–5 of *Meaning and Necessity*); I simply transpose his constraint on the interpretation of 'human being' and 'rational animal' to L_1.

33. For a concise exposition of Tarski's method of defining truth for formalized languages, see chap. 3 of W. V. Quine, *Philosophy of Logic*, 2nd ed. (Cambridge, Mass.: Harvard University Press, 1986).

34. This is a paraphrase of Carnap, *Meaning and Necessity*, §2–1, p. 10.

35. Carnap apparently sees this as analogous to Tarski's Convention T, which states a material condition of adequacy on a definition of a truth predicate for formalized languages.

36. Each of L_1's state descriptions, together with the interpretations of the names of L_1, corresponds with an assignment of extensions to the predicates of L_1 (in a universe U that contains all and only those objects denoted by names of L_1). To say that a sentence S of L_1 is *L-true* in Carnap's sense is (in effect) to say that S is true under every assignment of extensions to the predicates of L_1 (in U). Equivalently, S is *L-true* in L_1 if and only if the truth of S can be deduced from the Tarski-style truth definition for L_1, regardless of which state description holds, and hence regardless of the extensions of the predicates of L_1. Both of these explications of logical truth for L_1 depend on a prior distinction between logical and descriptive signs of L_1. For a time Carnap searched for a general definition of this distinction (note his attitude in §§13–16 of *Introduction to Semantics*), but in later years (as seen, for example, in "Quine on Logical Truth") he gave up the search, without abandoning his semantical conception of logical truth. I discuss this aspect of Carnap's explications of analyticity in §56 and §§69–70.

37. See Carnap, *Meaning and Necessity*, 15.

38. In "Two Dogmas of Empiricism," reprinted in W. V. Quine, *From a Logical Point of View*, rev. ed. (Cambridge, Mass.: Harvard University

Press, 1961), 20–46, Quine makes essentially the same observation about Carnap's explication of analyticity in terms of state descriptions: "the criterion of analyticity in terms of state-descriptions serves only for languages devoid of extra-logical synonym-pairs, such as 'bachelor' and 'unmarried man' . . . the criterion in terms of state-descriptions is a reconstruction at best of logical truth, not of analyticity" (23–24).

39. Here I give only one of Carnap's several equivalent explications of 'analytic in L_2'. See the options he offers in "Meaning Postulates" (reprinted in *Meaning and Necessity*, 222–229); I am using definitions (9) and (10) from p. 226. Carnap's definition (8) shows how meaning postulates can be added to a Tarski-style truth theory to yield an equivalent explication of 'analytic in L_2'. The basic idea is that S is *L-true* in L_2 if and only if S can be deduced from the Tarski-style truth definition for L_2, together with the meaning postulates of L_2, regardless of which state description holds, and hence regardless of the extensions of the predicates of L_2 (except insofar as those state descriptions and extensions are constrained by the meaning postulates).

40. In "Meaning Postulates," Carnap emphasizes that: rules of designation "are not necessary for the explication of analyticity, but only for that of factual (synthetic) truth." (224)

41. Carnap, "Meaning Postulates," 224–225.

42. "Meaning Postulates," 225.

43. Rudolf Carnap, "Quine on Analyticity," in Richard Creath, ed., *Dear Carnap, Dear Van* (Berkeley: University of California Press, 1990), 427–432; the quotation is from 432. Carnap is also explicit about this in "Quine on Logical Truth": "My proposals for the explication of analyticity have always been given for a formalized (codified, constructed) language L, i.e., a language for which explicit semantical rules are specified that lead to the concept of truth . . . The explication is given by additional rules, essentially by a list of meaning postulates" (918).

44. This account of pure and descriptive semantics is taken from Carnap's *Introduction to Semantics*, §5. His view of the distinction changed little throughout his career.

45. My paraphrase of Carnap's hypothesis (5), on p. 920 of "Quine on Logical Truth."

46. Rudolf Carnap, *Introduction to Semantics*, §5, my emphasis. In §25 of *Logical Syntax* Carnap writes: "we can distinguish two different theories: the axiomatic syntax which we have just been discussing (with or without axioms) and physical syntax. The latter is to the former as physical geometry is to axiomatic geometry. Physical geometry results from axiomatic geometry by means of the establishment of the so-called *correlative definitions* (cf. Reichenbach . . . [*Philosophie*]) . . . It is only by

means of these definitions that the axiomatic system is applicable to empirical sentences" (*Logical Syntax*, 78). "Reichenbach [*Philosophie*]" is Carnap's reference to Hans Reichenbach, *Philosophie der Raum-Zeit-Lehre*, originally published in Berlin in 1928, and known in English translation as Hans Reichenbach, *The Philosophy of Space and Time*, trans. Maria Reichenbach and John Freund (New York: Dover, 1958). In "Wilfred Sellars on Abstract Entities in Semantics," Schilpp, ed., *Carnap*, 923–927, Carnap notes parenthetically that to understand the analogy we must not think of pure geometry as purely syntactic or axiomatic: "in pure semantics we cannot give an analysis of the concept of designation in its ordinary sense because for this purpose psychological concepts are required. The situation is analogous to the relation between pure geometry and physical geometry (where pure geometry is understood as represented, not by an uninterpreted axiom system, but rather by a purely logical theory concerning a certain structure). . . pure geometry can mirror the logical connections holding between physico-geometrical concepts or propositions" (927).

47. Reichenbach, *The Philosophy of Space and Time*, 16.

48. Ibid., 19.

49. In his book *Philosophical Foundations of Physics: An Introduction to the Philosophy of Science* (New York: Basic Books, 1966), Carnap endorses Reichenbach's view of the epistemology of geometry, but objects to Reichenbach's talk of "coordinative *definitions*," on the grounds that in many cases we cannot explicitly define the relationship between theoretical terms and observations. Despite this terminological dispute, Carnap accepts that "we might give an explicit definition, by empirical procedures, to a concept such as length, because it is so easily and directly measured, and is unlikely to be modified by new observations" (239).

Most philosophers of physics now reject Reichenbach's view of the epistemology of geometry. See Michael Friedman's exemplary criticism of Reichenbach's view, in §3, chap. 7 of Friedman's book *Foundations of Space-Time Theories: Relativistic Physics and Philosophy of Science* (Princeton: Princeton University Press, 1983).

50. Carnap, "Quine on Logical Truth," 920.

51. Ibid.

52. In "Meaning and Synonymy in Natural Languages" (reprinted in Carnap, *Meaning and Necessity*, 233–247), Carnap's most extended discussion of the epistemology of descriptive semantics, he is no more explicit about the kinds of coordinative definitions needed for descriptive semantics.

53. In "Foundations of Logic and Mathematics," *International Encyclo-*

pedia of Unified Science, vol. 1, no. 3 (Chicago: University of Chicago Press, 1939), Carnap emphasizes that the semantical rules of a natural language are underdetermined by the facts about how its expressions are used: "We now proceed to restrict our attention to a special aspect of the facts concerning the language B which we have found by observations of the speaking activities within the group who speak that language. We study the relations between the expressions of B and their designata. On the basis of those facts we are going to lay down a system of rules establishing those relations. We call them *semantical rules.* These rules are not unambiguously determined by the facts. Suppose we have found that the word 'mond' of B was used in 98 per cent of the cases for the moon and 2 per cent for a certain lantern. Now *it is a matter of our decision whether we construct the rules in such a way that both the moon and the lantern are designata of 'mond' or only the moon.* If we choose the first, the use of 'mond' in those 2 per cent of cases was right—with respect to our rules; if we choose the second, it was wrong. *The facts do not determine whether the use of a certain expression is right or wrong, but only how often it occurs and how often it leads to the effect intended, and the like. A question of right or wrong must always refer to a system of rules.* Strictly speaking, the rules which we shall lay down are not rules of the factually given language B; they rather constitute a language system corresponding to B which we will call *the semantical system B-S"* (148–149, my emphases). As I see it, this passage reflects Carnap's view that descriptive semantics, like physical geometry, depends on our choice of coordinative definitions. The semantical description of the "factually given" language B consists of the semantical system B-S, together with coordinative definitions that link B-S to the "speaking activities" of those who use language B.

54. This is just like Quine's reply to Chomsky. See §27 above.

55. In "Quine on Logical Truth," Carnap writes: "Quine's arguments to the effect that the lexicographers actually have no criterion for their determinations did not seem at all convincing to me" (920). This was written before *Word and Object,* but it seems to me that there is nothing in chap. 2 of *Word and Object* that should change Carnap's evaluation of Quine's arguments. To accept Quine's indeterminacy thesis, Carnap would have to abandon his lifelong conception of the starting point and task of philosophy. In Chapter Five I will argue that Quine's objections do not undermine Carnap's framework from within.

56. Carnap, "Meaning and Synonymy in Natural Languages," 234, my emphasis.

57. In "Rationality, Translation, and Epistemology Naturalized," Ricketts formulates Quine's challenge to Carnap in this way. In §72 I

evaluate Ricketts's reconstruction of Quine's arguments against Carnap's analytic-synthetic distinction.

58. Presented in §§5–6 of E. W. Beth's paper "Carnap's Views on the Advantages of Constructed Systems over Natural Languages in the Philosophy of Science," in Schilpp, ed., *Carnap*, 469–502.

59. Rudolf Carnap, "E. W. Beth on Constructed Language Systems," in Schilpp, ed., *Carnap*, 927–933; quotation from 929, my emphases. Carnap makes the same point in earlier works. For example, in "Testability and Meaning," part 4, *Philosophy of Science 4*, no. 1 (1937): 1–40, Carnap writes: "In order to formulate the rules of an intended language L, it is necessary to use a language L' which is already available. L' must be given at least practically and need not be stated explicitly as a language system, i.e. by formation rules. We may take as L' the English language" (4).

60. Carnap, "E. W. Beth on Constructed Language Systems," 930.

61. Ibid., 931, my emphasis.

62. My reconstructions of Beth's objection and Carnap's reply to it are inspired by "Carnap and the Philosophy of Mathematics," by Warren Goldfarb and Thomas Ricketts, in D. Bell and W. Vossenkuhl, ed., *Science and Subjectivity: The Vienna Circle and Twentieth Century Philosophy* (Berlin: Akademie Verlag, 1992), 61–78.

Five. Quine's Reasons for Rejecting Carnap's Analytic-Synthetic Distinction

1. In the opening paragraph of "Carnap and Logical Truth," however, Quine adopts a rare conciliatory tone: "My dissent from Carnap's philosophy of logical truth is hard to state and argue in Carnap's terms. This circumstance perhaps counts in favor of Carnap's position.... It was only by providing ... a background of my own choosing that I was able to manage the more focussed criticisms in the later pages" (W. V. Quine, "Carnap and Logical Truth," in Paul A. Schilpp, ed., *The Philosophy of Rudolf Carnap*, La Salle, Ill.: Open Court, 1963, 385–406; quotation from 385.)

2. See, for example, Peter Hylton, "Analyticity and the Indeterminacy of Translation," *Synthese 52* (1982): 167–184, and Christopher Hookway, *Quine: Language, Experience, and Reality* (Stanford: Stanford University Press, 1988). Hookway writes "I do not think that Quine believes that abandoning the analytic/synthetic distinction commits us to the indeterminacy of translation. However, if there is such indeterminacy, it can provide further arguments against Carnap's position" (129).

3. From a letter from Carnap to Quine, July 15, 1954, in Richard

Creath, ed., *Dear Carnap, Dear Van* (Berkeley and Los Angeles: University of California Press, 1990), 435–436; quotation from 435.

4. From a letter from Quine to Carnap Aug. 9, 1954, in ibid., 437–439; quotation from 438.

5. Rudolf Carnap, *Introduction to Symbolic Logic and Its Applications*, trans. W. H. Meyer and J. Wilkinson (New York: Dover, 1958), 1.

6. Ibid.

7. W. V. Quine, *Word and Object* (Cambridge, Mass.: MIT Press, 1960), 161.

8. W. V. Quine, "Things and Their Place in Theories," in *Theories and Things* (Cambridge, Mass.: Harvard University Press, 1981), 1–23; quotation from 21.

9. In an unpublished passage cited by Burton Dreben in "Putnam, Quine, and the Facts," *Philosophical Topics 20*, no. 1 (1992): 293–315, Quine writes: "Folk wisdom has it that we communicate successfully because our sentences *mean* alike for us. Reflecting on how one learns language, foreign or domestic, we now see rather that meaning alike for us merely means, if anything, that we are communicating successfully. And we communicate successfully because we learned the language or languages from one another in shared observable circumstances. We shaped and adjusted our verbal behavior to mesh with that of our fellows, whatever the circumstances, with a minimum clashing of gears" (305).

10. Carnap, *Introduction to Symbolic Logic*, 7, my emphasis.

11. Quine, *Word and Object*, 160.

12. Ibid.

13. Despite countless exchanges with Carnap in the intervening years, in "Carnap and Logical Truth," written in 1954, Quine *repeats* the main objection he raised eighteen years earlier in "Truth by Convention" (first published in 1936, reprinted in W. V. Quine, *The Ways of Paradox and Other Essays*, rev. and enl. ed., Cambridge, Mass.: Harvard University Press, 1976, 77–106).

14. Sometimes the simplicity of a scientific theory is our sole criterion for judging that it offers a better explanation than a more complex one. In Quine's view simplicity is a central consideration when we are evaluating the merits of rival logical theories. For Quine this is enough to show that the task of logic is continuous with the explanatory tasks of, for example, physics and biology. One might object that the choice of a suitable canonical notation does not issue in new predictions or observations, whereas the choice of a physical or biological theory does. But for Quine this is a difference of degree, not of kind: "such is the nature of physical reality that one physical theory will get us around better

than another; but similarly for canonical notations" (Quine, *Word and Object*, 161).

15. Quine is explicit about this in "Carnap and Logical Truth," where he writes: "What has made it so difficult for us to make satisfactory sense of the linguistic doctrine of logical truth is the obscurity of 'true by language'. Now 'synonymous' lies within that same central obscurity; for, about the best we can say of synonymous predicates is that they are somehow 'coextensive by language.' The obscurity extends, of course, to 'analytic' " (403).

16. W. V. Quine, "Two Dogmas of Empiricism," reprinted in W. V. Quine, *From a Logical Point of View*, rev. ed. (Cambridge, Mass.: Harvard University Press, 1961), 20–46; quotation from 22–23.

17. Ibid., 23.

18. Ibid.

19. There are well-known ways of specifying in syntactic terms what is to count as an admissible reinterpretation of the nonlogical components of sentences in the standard notation of first-order logic. For example, see Quine's *Methods of Logic*, 4th ed. (Cambridge, Mass.: Harvard University Press, 1982), §§26–28.

20. For Carnap pure semantics is part of pure logic, as are all the techniques discussed in Part I of his *Introduction to Symbolic Logic*. Thus Quine is challenging Carnap's boundary between pure logic and empirical science.

21. Quine, "Two Dogmas," 24.

22. Ibid., 25.

23. Ibid., 26.

24. From Quine's naturalistic point of view, mere definitional abbreviation of terms already in use amounts to "legislative postulation." In "Carnap and Logical Truth," Quine concedes that legislative postulation "affords truth by convention unalloyed," but insists that "so conceived, conventionality is a passing trait, significant at the moving front of science, but useless in classifying the sentences behind the lines. It is a trait of events and not of sentences" (395).

25. In §1 of "Two Dogmas" Quine writes: "the criterion of analyticity in terms of state-descriptions serves only for languages devoid of extralogical synonym-pairs, such as 'bachelor' and 'unmarried man'— synonym-pairs of the type which give rise to the 'second class' of analytic statements. The criterion in terms of state-descriptions is a reconstruction at best of logical truth, not of analyticity" (23–24). Quine defers discussion of Carnap's restrictions on what counts as a state description until §4, since these restrictions depend on Carnap's notion of a semantical rule.

26. Quine, "Two Dogmas," 34.

27. Carnap begins his paper "Quine on Analyticity," in which he replies to "Two Dogmas," with the following sentence: "It must be emphasized that the concept of analyticity has an exact definition only in the case of a language-system, namely a system of semantical rules, not in the case of an ordinary language, because in the latter the words have no clearly defined meaning" (*Dear Carnap, Dear Van*, 427).

28. Quine, "Two Dogmas," 32.

29. Since Quine feels he has already shown that the idea of a language system is not helpful, he dismisses it in one brief paragraph toward the end of §4 of "Two Dogmas": "It might conceivably be protested that an artificial language L (unlike a natural one) is a language in the ordinary sense plus a set of explicit semantical rules—the whole constituting, let us say, an ordered pair; and that the semantical rules of L then are specifiable simply as the second component of the pair L. But, by the same token and more simply, we might construe an artificial language L outright as an ordered pair whose second component is the class of its analytic statements; and then the analytic statements of L become specifiable simply as the statements in the second component of L. Or better still, we might just stop tugging at our bootstraps altogether" (35–36).

30. Quine, "Two Dogmas," 33, my emphasis.

31. In "Quine on Analyticity," Carnap writes: "In case Quine's remarks are meant as a demand to be given one definition applicable to all systems, then such a demand is manifestly unreasonable; it is certainly neither fulfilled nor fulfillable for semantic and syntactic concepts, as Quine knows" (430). Carnap expands on this point in "W. V. Quine on Logical Truth": Quine "said in ['Two Dogmas'] that the semantical rules are recognizable only by the heading 'Semantical Rules' which itself is meaningless. I was puzzled by this remark because neither Quine nor anybody else has previously criticized the obvious fact that, e.g., the admitted forms of sentences of a formalized language L are only recognizable by a label like 'Sentence Forms in L' preceding a list of forms of expressions, or the fact that the axioms of a logical calculus are only recognizable by the label 'Axioms.' Why should the same fact be objectionable in the case of meaning postulates?" (Carnap, "Quine on Logical Truth," in Schilpp, ed., *Carnap*, 918). There is no answer to this, for Quine, except that the notion of a semantical rule is obscure, but the notion of a sentence is clear. As we shall see in later sections of the text, Quine's indeterminacy thesis spells out his reasons for thinking that the notion of a semantical rule is obscure.

32. Thus Carnap's comparison with the definition of "sentence" for

formalized languages (see the previous note) does not answer Quine's challenge. Carnap and Quine have different conceptions of the starting point and task of logic, but Carnap does not see this, and so he is mystified by Quine's rejection of the notion of a semantical rule.

33. Quine, "Two Dogmas," 35.

34. Ibid.

35. An indirect answer to this question comes in "Carnap and Logical Truth," where Quine distinguishes between legislative and discursive postulates, the former instituting "truth by convention" of a sort. Quine observes that these classifications merely reflect our current linguistic dispositions, not lasting traits of the sentences themselves. This answer to Carnap presupposes the more general answer to Carnap I sketch in the next paragraph of the text.

36. This is exactly what Carnap says at the end of "Quine on Logical Truth": "I believe that the distinction between analytic and synthetic statements, expressed in whatever terms, is practically indispensable for methodological and philosophical discussions. . . . As an example, let me refer to a philosopher whose work I esteem very highly, although I cannot agree in all points with his views. This philosopher once undertook to destroy a certain doctrine, propounded by some other philosophers. He did not mean to assert that the doctrine was false; presumably he regarded it as true. But his criticism concerned its particular kind of truth, namely that the truth of the doctrine was of the analytic kind. To be sure, he did not use the word 'analytic', which he did not seem to like very much . . . What he showed was that various attempts to assign an experimental, empirical meaning to this doctrine remained without success. Finally he came to the conclusion that the doctrine, even though not false, is 'empty' and 'without experimental significance' " (922).

37. Philosophers influenced by Wittgenstein may see the seeds of a more subtle criticism of Carnap in Quine's claim that the notion of a semantical rule is meaningful only relative to "one or another particular enterprise of schooling unconversant persons in sufficient conditions for truth of statements of some natural or artificial language L" (Quine, "Two Dogmas," 35). But Quine's own attempts to develop his criticisms of the idea of a semantical rule depend on his naturalistic empiricism and behaviorism, with which Wittgenstein would have little sympathy. To my knowledge, no one has yet developed a Wittgensteinian critique of Carnap's notion of a semantical rule. A proper Wittgensteinian critique would have to undermine the *very idea* of a semantical rule as it is used within pure semantics.

38. Quine, "Things and Their Place in Theories," 21.

39. Quine, *Word and Object*, 2.

40. This is a paraphrase of a sentence in *Word and Object*, 11.

41. In "Epistemology Naturalized," in W. V. Quine, *Ontological Relativity and Other Essays* (New York: Columbia University Press, 1969), 69–90, Quine writes: "But why all this creative reconstruction, all this make-believe? The stimulation of his sensory receptors is all the evidence anybody has to go on, ultimately, in arriving at his picture of the world. Why not just see how this construction really proceeds? Why not settle for psychology?" (75).

42. Thomas Ricketts, "Rationality, Translation, and Epistemology Naturalized," *Journal of Philosophy* 79 (1982): 117–136. Ricketts claims that Quine's criticisms do not "pass Carnap's conception of rational reconstruction by" (133), since Carnap must have a criterion of analyticity if he is to avoid an "epistemic solipsism destructive of the very ideal of rationality Carnap wants to articulate and vindicate" (124).

43. Ibid., 123–124, emphasis on the second and third sentences is mine.

44. Ibid., 125.

45. Here is a passage that supports this interpretation of Ricketts's requirement: "Quine's criticisms of Carnap's criterion of analyticity reveal a further condition that must be met if investigators are to share a common bench before which to litigate their differences. They must share a framework for empirical psychology which yields a criterion of analyticity" (ibid., 134).

46. Ricketts writes that "Carnap does recognize Quine to be asking after the grounds for attributing linguistic frameworks. Carnap attempts to meet this challenge by presenting a 'behavioristic, operational procedure' for identifying the analytic sentences of a person's language by reference to the person's speech dispositions. . . . Description of these dispositions is . . . couched in concrete, more or less behavioral terms. . . . But . . . the mere acknowledgement of this demand vitiates Carnap's conception of rational inquiry" (ibid., 125).

47. Ibid., 124.

48. Quine, "Two Dogmas," 41.

49. Hookway, *Quine*, 27.

50. Ibid., 30.

51. Pierre Duhem, *The Aim and Structure of Physical Theory* (first published in French in 1906), trans. Philip P. Wiener (New York: Atheneum, 1962).

52. Carnap, "Quine on Logical Truth," 921.

53. Hookway, *Quine*, 35.

54. Ibid., 37.

55. Ibid., 38.

56. These considerations also tell against Peter Hylton's view in "Analyticity and Indeterminacy of Translation," *Synthese* 52 (1982): 167–184. Like Hookway, who includes this paper among the references for his book on Quine, Hylton sees Quine's rejection of Carnap's analytic-synthetic distinction as a consequence of the holism of theory testing. In Hylton's view, Quine's observations about the holism of theory testing show that Carnap's notion of a semantical rule, which Carnap needs to articulate his ideal of rational adjudicability, has no basis in our actual scientific practices: "If [Carnap's] ideal of rational adjudicability were reasonable as an abstract account of actual epistemic practice, this would be because we did in fact, in our justificatory procedures, act differently towards rules of language, on the one hand, and statements within a language, on the other hand. [But] ... our justificatory practices show no such distinction. If this is correct, then no method of analysing those practices can create such a distinction" (175). Yet Hylton concedes that this argument would not persuade Carnap: "Quine's attack on the analytic-synthetic distinction involves a *reconceiving* of what it means to give an account of science. The normative aspect falls away" (176, my emphasis). What Hylton fails to see is that since Quine's attack on the analytic-synthetic distinction depends on Quine's naturalistic account of science, the attack is inextricable from Quine's indeterminacy thesis. In Hylton's view, Quine's indeterminacy thesis "appears as a part of [Quine's] debate with Carnap over analyticity, but ... is not essential to the most fundamental issues at stake in that debate" (176). In §§48–73 I have explained in detail why I reject this view of Quine's arguments against Carnap's analytic-synthetic distinction.

57. For Quine a speaker's idiolect is not an essentially "private" language that no one else can understand.

Six. Putnam's Reasons for Rejecting Carnap's Analytic-Synthetic Distinction

1. Hilary Putnam, "The Analytic and the Synthetic," reprinted in Hilary Putnam, *Mind, Language, and Reality* (Cambridge: Cambridge University Press, 1975), 33–69.

2. For example, Putnam sounds like Carnap when he describes how the analytic-synthetic distinction can be drawn for formalized languages: "We draw an analytic-synthetic distinction formally only in connection with formalized languages whose inventors list some statements and rules as meaning postulates. That is, it is stipulated that to

qualify as correctly using the language one must accept *those* statements and rules. *There is nothing mysterious about this"* (ibid., 54–55, my emphasis).

3. Early in "The Analytic and the Synthetic" Putnam writes: "I think that appreciating the diverse natures of logical truths, of physically necessary truths in the natural sciences, and of what I have for the moment lumped together under the title of framework principles—that clarifying the nature of these diverse kinds of statements is the most important work that a philosopher can do. Not because philosophy is necessarily about language, but because we must become clear about the roles played in our conceptual systems by these diverse kinds of truths before we can get an adequate view of the world, of thought, of language, or of anything" (41). For reasons that will become clearer later in the text, I see this passage as an expression of Putnam's view that the most important task for philosophy is to remove obstacles to the proper description of our practices of agreeing, disagreeing, evaluating assertions, and resolving disputes.

4. Putnam's conception of the starting point and task of philosophy is similar to that of Hans Reichenbach, Putnam's teacher. In *Experience and Prediction* (Chicago: University of Chicago Press, 1938), Reichenbach criticizes the logical positivists for failing to describe the criteria of the languages we actually use in science and ordinary life. These criticisms reflect Reichenbach's view that the aim of an adequate epistemology must be to describe the criteria that govern our actual inquiries. There are several crucial differences between Reichenbach and Putnam, however, the most important of which are that Reichenbach was committed to empiricism and that he thought that the analytic-synthetic distinction is essential to a proper reconstruction of scientific assertions.

5. Putnam, "The Analytic and the Synthetic," 42–43.

6. Ibid., 44.

7. Ibid., 45, emphasis mine.

8. Ibid., 51.

9. Ibid., 52–53.

10. Ibid., 52.

11. As Putnam says, "One should always be suspicious of the claim that a principle whose subject term is a law-cluster concept is analytic. The reason that it is difficult to have an analytic relationship between the law-cluster concepts is that such a relationship would be one more law. But, in general, any one law can be abandoned without destroying the identity of the law-cluster concept involved." (ibid.).

12. Ibid., 45–46.

13. Ibid., 48–49.

14. Hilary Putnam, "It Ain't Necessarily So," reprinted in Hilary Putnam, *Mathematics, Matter, and Method* (Cambridge: Cambridge University Press, 1975), 237–249; quotation from 240.

15. I discuss the role of rational persuasion in our understanding of agreement and disagreement in Chapter Eight.

16. In Putnam's view, the standard examples, not some a priori philosophical theory of meaning, give us the best reason for thinking there are analytic statements. This attitude is clear in the following passage: "the analytic-synthetic distinction rests on a certain number of classical examples. We would not have been tempted to draw it or to keep drawing it for so long if we did not have a stock of familiar examples on which to fall back. . . . I am inclined to sympathize with those who cite the examples and who stress the implausibility, the tremendous implausibility, of . . . the thesis that the distinction which certainly seems to exist does not in fact exist at all" ("The Analytic and the Synthetic," 34).

17. See Putnam's story in "The Analytic and the Synthetic," 58.

18. Thus Putnam writes: "It is logically possible that all bachelors should have a certain neurosis and that nobody else should have it; it is even possible that we should be able to detect this neurosis at sight. But, of course, there is no such neurosis. This I know in the way that I know most negative propositions. It is not that I have a criterion for as yet undiscovered neurosis, but simply that I have no good reason to suppose that there might be such a neurosis. And in many cases of this kind, lack of any good reason for supposing existence is itself the very best reason for supposing nonexistence" (ibid., 58–59).

19. Ibid., 46.

20. W. V. Quine, "Carnap and Logical Truth," as it appears in Paul A. Schilpp, ed., *The Philosophy of Rudolf Carnap* (La Salle, Ill.: Open Court, 1963), 385–406).

21. In §5 of "Carnap and Logical Truth," Quine explains that a *legislative definition* "introduces a notation hitherto unused, or used only at variance with the practice proposed, or used also at variance, so that a convention is wanted to settle the ambiguity," and that a *legislative postulate* "institutes truth by convention, and seems plausibly illustrated by set theory" (394). Neither legislative definition nor postulation is defined in terms of Carnap's notion of a semantical rule.

22. Ibid., 405.

23. Quine, *Word and Object*, 57.

24. Ibid., 56.

25. Ibid., 57, n. 8.

26. Quine, "Ontological Relativity," 29.

27. In "Analyticity, Linguistic Practice, and Philosophical Method," in Klaus Puhl, ed., *Meaning Scepticism* (Berlin: de Gruyter, 1991), 218–250, Elizabeth Fricker suggests that Quine's willingness to appeal to "intuitions of analyticity," and his sympathy with Putnam's talk of one-criterion words and law-cluster concepts, are in conflict with Quine's scientific naturalism about meaning. She writes: "In admitting this new source of data . . . Quine is departing radically from his official program of allowing only semantic notions which can be constructed from stimulus meanings. We may distinguish between two perspectives on a language: the spectator's stance, and the participant's. Construction from stimulus-meanings utilises only what can be known from the spectator stance—which comprises all the data which are "objective" in a certain sense which Quine approves. In admitting speakers' intuitions, Quine allows data only available, at least in the first instance, from the participant stance: facts which only those already inside the language have access to" (230–231). In my own way I have drawn a similar contrast between descriptions of language use from our participant perspective, and Quine's view of a speaker's language as a complex of present dispositions to verbal behavior. But here Fricker suggests that there is a tension *within Quine's own views* about how to describe our use of language. As I see it, however, Quine notes our "intuitions" about analyticity and sameness of reference despite radical changes in belief only to explain them away. He views all "intuitions" we have from our participant perspective as reflections of our scientifically arbitrary choices about how to "translate" our fellow speakers' words. Such choices may become entrenched within a given population of speakers, but in Quine's view that just makes it more difficult to see that they are scientifically arbitrary.

28. This phrase is from Quine, "Carnap and Logical Truth," 405.

29. Quine, *Word and Object*, 57.

30. Ibid., 24.

31. See, for example, Thomas Ricketts, "Rationality, Translation, and Epistemology Naturalized," *Journal of Philosophy* 79 (1982): 117–136.

32. An example is Michael Friedman; see his "Physicalism and the Indeterminacy of Translation," *Nous* 9 (1975): 357–374.

33. In "Putnam, Quine—and the Facts," *Philosophical Topics* 20 (1992): 293–315, Burton Dreben writes: "Quine is saying that there is no need to postulate an 'ether', an underlying medium that successful communication reflects" (305). This suggests that anyone who questions Quine's indeterminacy thesis believes that there is "an underlying medium that successful communication reflects." But Dreben knows that Quine's indeterminacy thesis is not merely the denial of an underlying medium

of communication. The indeterminacy thesis states that there are count-less radically different manuals of "translation" that capture all that is objective to meaning. This raises a crucial question: Why does Quine think that all of these manuals capture all that is objective to meaning? The answer is Quine's naturalistic empiricism—the view that the totality of speech dispositions linking sentences to one another and to sensory stimulation exhausts the "facts" relevant to both epistemology and semantics. Quine's indeterminacy thesis depends on this naturalistic empiricism, and there is no plausible way to view Quine's naturalistic empiricism as the mere denial of the idea that there is "an underlying medium that successful communication reflects."

34. In "Reply to Gary Ebbs," *Philosophical Topics* 20 (1992): 347–358, Putnam reports that "The Analytic and the Synthetic" was written in 1957. Quine's first published his argument for indeterminacy in 1960, as chap. 2 of *Word and Object*.

35. Quine once criticized Carnap for his "make-believe" epistemology of science: "why all this creative reconstruction, all this make-believe? The stimulation of his sensory receptors is all the evidence anybody has to go on, ultimately, in arriving at his picture of the world. Why not just see how this construction really proceeds? Why not settle for psychology?" (W. V. Quine, "Epistemology Naturalized," in W. V. Quine, *Ontological Relativity and Other Essays*, New York: Columbia University press, 1969, 69–90; quotation from 75). Quine designed his behavioristic epistemology and seman-tics to fit his own "motivating insight" that "stimulation of his sensory receptors is all the evidence anybody has to go on, ultimately, in arriving at his picture of the world." From our perspective as participants in actual linguistic practices, however, Quine's behavioristic epistemology is just more make-believe, even if it is expressed in seemingly scientific terms.

36. Nor is there is any good reason to suppose that our ordinary translation practices guarantee that translation is an equivalence rela-tion, or that there are propositions. Note that if we knew that transla-tion were an equivalence relation, then we could define the proposition expressed by a sentence S as the class of sentences that translate S, including S itself.

37. Recall that in *Word and Object* Quine rejects the idioms of proposi-tional attitude as unscientific: "the underlying methodology of the idioms of propositional attitude contrasts strikingly with the spirit of objective science at its most representative.... An indirect quotation we can usually expect to rate only as better or worse, more or less faithful, and we cannot even hope for a strict standard of more or less; what is involved is evaluation, relative to a special purpose, of an essentially dramatic act" (218–219).

Seven. From the Rejection of the Analytic-Synthetic Distinction to Anti-Individualism

1. Hilary Putnam, "Dreaming and 'Depth Grammar'," reprinted in Hilary Putnam, *Mind, Language, and Reality* (Cambridge: Cambridge University Press, 1975), 304–324; quotation from 310.

2. Putnam notes that for Malcolm "saying that this virus was *the* cause of multiple sclerosis was changing the concept" (ibid., 310).

3. See, for example, Michael Friedman in "Physicalism and the Indeterminacy of Translation," *Nous 9* (1975): 357–374.

4. In saying that these ordinary judgments are "philosophically unproblematic," I do not mean to suggest that they are not open to criticism and correction. The crucial point is that to evaluate such judgments we need no special philosophical theory of the epistemology or metaphysics underlying ordinary criticisms and corrections of such judgments.

5. For Quine, even this apparently innocent judgment reflects my "choice" of the homophonic "translation" from my past idiolect into my present idiolect. We are already straying from Quinean doctrine when we treat our ordinary judgments of sameness or difference of reference between temporal stages of our own idiolects as philosophically unproblematic. An extreme idiolectical view similar to Quine's is embraced by Donald Davidson in "A Nice Derangement of Epitaphs," in E. LePore, ed., *Truth and Interpretation* (Oxford: Basil Blackwell, 1986), 433–466.

6. Saul Kripke, *Naming and Necessity* (Cambridge, Mass., Harvard University Press, 1980), 27.

7. Ibid., 83–84.

8. Ibid., 84.

9. Ibid., 93.

10. Ibid., 96.

11. See, for example, Gareth Evans,"The Causal Theory of Names," *Aristotelian Society Supplementary Volume 97* (1973): 187–208.

12. Hilary Putnam, "Explanation and Reference," reprinted in Putnam, *Mind, Language, and Reality*, 196–214; quotation from 198.

13. Ibid., 203.

14. Ibid., 199–200.

15. Putnam's observation that "law-cluster" terms are "transtheoretical" also highlights the fundamental incompatibility of his view with Quine's. See §84.

16. Putnam makes this correction in "Language and Reality," reprinted in Putnam, *Mind, Language, and Reality*, 272–290. He writes

that "knowledge of laws cannot be attributed to individual speakers who happen to have acquired 'energy' or 'voltage' or 'electron'; thus, even if the 'law cluster' theory were right as an account of the *social determination of reference,* it could not be right as an account of what every speaker implicitly 'means' " (281–282).

17. Kripke does, however, note that a name may be introduced by a description that uniquely fixes its reference. See *Naming and Necessity,* 96.

18. Putnam, "Explanation and Reference," 200.

19. Ibid.

20. Ibid., 201.

21. Hilary Putnam, "The Meaning of 'Meaning'," reprinted in Putnam, *Mind, Language, and Reality,* 215–271; quotation from 225.

22. As Putnam points out, "whether or not something is ... the same liquid as *this* may take an indeterminate amount of scientific investigation to determine" (ibid., 225). Given our ordinary beliefs about human beings, it would be wrong to say that whether or not something is the same human being as *this* (a particular baby) may take an indeterminate amount of scientific investigation to determine. There may be some difficult cases, but scientific investigation is not what is needed to settle them.

23. In Quine's view, "we must speak from within a theory, albeit any of various [theories]. . . . What evaporates is the transcendental question of the reality of the external world—the question of whether or in how far our science measures up to the *Ding an sich*" (W. V. Quine,"Things and Their Place in Theories," in *Theories and Things,* Cambridge, Mass.: Harvard University Press, 1981, 1–23; quotation from 22).

24. Keith Donnellan, "Kripke and Putnam on Natural Kind Terms," in C. Ginet and S. Shoemaker, ed., *Knowledge and Mind* (Oxford: Oxford University Press, 1983), 84–104; quotation from 98, my emphasis.

25. Ibid., 99.

26. Ibid., 98.

27. Ibid., 100.

28. Ibid., 101.

29. Ibid., 102.

30. Ibid., 102–103.

31. Ibid., 103.

32. Ibid.

33. Ibid., 104.

34. Putnam, "The Meaning of 'Meaning'," 238–239.

35. Ibid., 240–241.

36. Ibid., 241.

37. Ibid.

38. Ibid., 242.

39. See Hilary Putnam, "It Ain't Necessarily So," reprinted in *Mathematics, Matter, and Method* (Cambridge: Cambridge University Press, 1975), 237–249. Putnam was a bit unclear at that time (1962) about whether it would be a change in the "meaning" of 'cat' to say that all cats are robots controlled from Mars, but the trouble here has more to do with the word "meaning" than our understanding of the reference of the word 'cat' under the circumstances Putnam describes. Here is where his uncertainty comes out: "Once we find out that cats were created from the beginning by Martians, that they are not self-directed, that they are automata, and so on, then it is clear that we have a problem of how to speak... My own feeling is that to say that cats turned out not to be animals is to keep the meaning of both words unchanged" (239). Note, however, that Putnam uses the word 'cats' in his description of this bizarre possibility, and thus shows, just as in the pencil case and the multiple sclerosis thought experiment, that 'cat' is not a one-criterion term.

40. Donnellan apparently assumes that a speaker's beliefs and linguistic activity (perhaps together with the beliefs and linguistic activities of his contemporaries) settle what his words refer to, and so the discoveries and beliefs of future generations cannot have anything to do with what our words refer to *now*. A similar assumption may be what motivates Mark Wilson to place the following constraint on his anti-individualistic view of meaning: "The evidence for an assignment of an extension to a predicate should be limited to such linguistic behavior as can be reasonably extrapolated from the community's contemporaneous practice and should not reflect accidental features of the society's later history" (Mark Wilson, "Predicate Meets Property," *Philosophical Review* 91 [1982]: 549–589; quotation from 553). If by "an assignment of an extension to a predicate" we take Wilson to mean (in part) "a judgment as to the how the predicate is correctly applied," then there is some initial plausibility to this constraint. For we may want to determine whether or not a given term has been properly used during some period, *relative to the entrenched beliefs and interests of the community during that period.* In such cases it is natural to disregard "accidental features of the society's later history." But Donnellan goes further. He maintains that if the use of 'gold' evolves in a way that we could not have "extrapolated" from present use, then the extension of 'gold' (its correct application) has *changed.* (Wilson also takes this idea seriously; see p. 580 of "Predicate Meets Property.") But this overlooks the division of linguistic labor across time.

41. If Donnellan does not assume that there is any difference in the distribution of the isotopes on the two planets, and if the two linguistic communities really are identical before the development of chemistry, then there would be no reason at all for a divergence in the extension of 'gold'. But suppose such a divergence developed nonetheless. Would that show that it is based in "psychological quirks"? No, not by itself. It could still turn out that one or the other group has *misunderstood* its own use of the term 'gold'. This kind of possibility is briefly explored in the next paragraph of the text, and more fully in Chapter Eight.

42. Donnellan, "Kripke and Putnam on Natural Kind Terms," 101.

43. Putnam notes parenthetically that the example he uses to illustrate the contribution of the environment "can be construed as involving the division of labor across time" ("The Meaning of 'Meaning'," 229). As I see it, however, this is not a parenthetical point.

44. Putnam, "The Meaning of 'Meaning'," 229.

45. Ibid.

46. See Bernard Williams, *Descartes: The Project of Pure Inquiry* (Harmondsworth: Penguin, 1978), 64–65, and Thomas Nagel, *The View from Nowhere* (Oxford: Oxford University Press, 1986), chaps. 2 and 5.

47. Thus Putnam writes: "speakers are *required* to know something about (stereotypical) tigers in order to count as having acquired the word 'tiger'; something about elm trees (or anyway, about the stereotype thereof) to count as having acquired the word 'elm'; etc." ("The Meaning of 'Meaning'," 248).

48. Moreover, these minimal requirements may change within the same community; and at one time in any given linguistic community there may be more than one group of practical applications of a term, including beliefs expressed *using* the term, that is minimally sufficient for passing muster in the use of the term.

49. Putnam, "The Meaning of 'Meaning'," 249.

50. Ibid.

51. Within the same community, entrenched background interests and beliefs may change without changing the reference of terms. This creates some subtleties in our present judgments about whether someone in the distant past is minimally competent in the use of a term. For example, we must not judge whether or not a speaker who lived in 1750 is competent in the use of a term by the standards of today. Instead we must imagine ourselves in the position of competent members of the English-speaking community in 1750, and from that perspective judge whether or not the speaker was competent in the use of the term. If he was competent, then by the division of labor across time, which links his use of

the term to ours, we should take him to be a member of our (temporally extended) linguistic community.

52. Putnam, "The Meaning of 'Meaning'," 252.

53. Kripke, *Naming and Necessity*, 93. On pp. 68–70 Kripke explains why a successful theory of reference must not be circular.

54. In "The Elusiveness of Reference," in Peter A. French, Theodore E. Uehling, and Howard K. Wettstein, ed., *Midwest Studies in Philosophy*, vol. 12 (Minneapolis: University of Minnesota Press, 1988), 179–194, Thomas Blackburn argues that there is no way to develop a theory of reference from the sketches Putnam and others have given us. His conclusion is more general than mine, and he does not sketch a systematic account of the starting point and method that lead to Putnam's causal picture of reference. Unlike Blackburn, I think Putnam's causal picture of reference is interesting *because* it can't be developed into a theory; my reconstruction of Putnam's starting point and method shows why.

Eight. Participation, Deference, and Dialectic

1. My reconstruction draws primarily on two of Burge's papers: "Individualism and the Mental," in Peter A. French, Theodore E. Uehling, and Howard K. Wettstein, ed., *Midwest Studies in Philosophy*, vol. 4 (Minneapolis: University of Minnesota Press, 1979), 73–121, and "Intellectual Norms and Foundations of Mind," *Journal of Philosophy 83* (1986): 697–720.

2. Burge, "Individualism and the Mental," 87.

3. Ibid., 74.

4. Ibid.

5. Ibid.

6. Ibid., 76.

7. Ibid., 75.

8. Ibid., 77.

9. This is not to say that Alfred's competence *consists in* his disposition to defer to more competent speakers. For reasons discussed in §§100–101, we cannot give a (noncircular) theory of necessary and sufficient conditions for linguistic competence.

10. Burge, "Individualism and the Mental," 101.

11. For reasons I will discuss later in the text, we must also assume that those dictionary entries are themselves correct, although this further condition makes no *practical* difference.

12. Burge, "Individualism and the Mental," 100, my emphasis.

13. Ibid., 93.

14. Ibid., 77–78.

15. Ibid., 78.

16. Burge supposes that in the counterfactual community there are recognized standards for applying 'arthritis'. We can't tell what those standards are from Burge's sketch, and so we can't say what notion, if any, is expressed by the term 'arthritis' as it is used on Twin Earth. But Burge's conclusion does not depend on our being able to specify the beliefs Twin Alfred expresses by using the term 'arthritis'.

17. Burge, "Individualism and the Mental," 79.

18. Ibid., 79.

19. Burge, "Intellectual Norms and Foundations of Mind," 702.

20. Ibid.

21. Ibid., 703.

22. Ibid.

23. Ibid.

24. This raises the question of whether our applications of 'chair' to deck chairs is "archetypical." A complicating factor in the dialectic is that our assessment of whether an application is "archetypical" may itself change in the face of a new characterization. There is an interdependence between our characterizations of a term and our view of what counts as an "archetypical" application of that term.

25. Burge, "Intellectual Norms and Foundations of Mind," 703–704.

26. Ibid., 704.

27. Ibid., 706.

28. To know the conventional meaning-giving characterization for N, S must have some understanding of why competent speakers accept it.

29. One might think that we should revise CU to include the condition that the conventional meaning-giving characterization of N is correct. But any adequate account of what Burge means by "complete understanding" must preserve the *normative* link between understanding and conventional linguistic meaning. One might think that the "correct" meaning-giving characterization is the one that survives at "the end of inquiry." But we have no clear idea what would or could "end inquiry," and so this definition of "correctness" is empty. If we try to add a primitive notion of correctness to CU, we sever the connection between complete understanding and the normative force of a conventional meaning-giving characterization. For the normative force depends on the *persuasiveness* of competent speakers, and persuasiveness guarantees only reasonable belief, not truth.

30. Here are two more examples: (1) Suppose that Bertrand has mostly true beliefs about sofas, but believes in addition that some very large stuffed armchairs are sofas. According to the conventional meaning-giving characterization of a sofa, stuffed armchairs are not

sofas. Hence Bertrand has a belief about sofas which could not be true according to the conventional meaning-giving characterization of a sofa. (2) Suppose that Carl believes that a contract is a legally binding agreement, and he correctly believes that he has willingly entered into many contracts, but in addition he believes that an explicit verbal agreement is not a contract, because it is not written. According to the conventional meaning-giving characterization of a contract, some explicit verbal agreements are contracts. Hence Carl has a false belief about what contracts are.

31. Even though we do not have a theory of sameness or difference for notions, our ordinary practices of translation show that terms from different languages can express the same notion. For example, the French word 'eau' is translated by the English word 'water', and this shows that 'eau' expresses the notion *water.*

32. Burge writes that "the reversal of the thought experiment brings home the important point that *even those propositional attitudes not infected by incomplete understanding* depend for their content on social factors that are independent of the individual, asocially and nonintentionally described" ("Individualism and the Mental," 84–85). A different version of the reversal of the thought experiment can be developed to show that even if a speaker completely understands a notion N, her thoughts and beliefs involving N are not settled solely by her physical structure and linguistic dispositions. We can see in our actual linguistic practices that speakers can know a correct dictionary entry for a word if they are told what it is, and perhaps given some reasons for it, by knowledgeable members of their linguistic community. This allows for the possibility that a speaker knows the conventional linguistic meaning for her term 'arthritis', but her twin, who has received misleading information from apparently knowledgeable members of her linguistic community, does not. The rest of the thought experiment is just like the one sketched in the text.

33. W. V. Quine, "Two Dogmas of Empiricism," reprinted in W. V. Quine, *From a Logical Point of View,* rev. ed. (Cambridge, Mass.: Harvard University Press, 1961), 20–46; quotation from 22. In Quine's view, of course, meaning is guilty by association with essentialism.

34. Burge writes that "the dialectic attempts to arrive at what might be called *normative characterizations.* These are statements about *what Xs are* that purport to give basic, 'essential,' and necessarily true information about Xs" ("Intellectual Norms and Foundations of Mind," 703). In n. 2 (p. 698) Burge qualifies his talk of "necessary truth": "the argument need not rest on an assumption about necessity. What we need are general thoughts or statements so central to the correct identification of a

type of thing, property, or event, that, under ordinary conditions, if the thought failed to apply to some given entity *x*, we would correctly and almost automatically refuse to count *x* an instance of the type." Despite this qualification, I will argue in this section that Burge's talk of necessity and essential information raises puzzling questions.

35. "Intellectual Norms and Foundations of Mind," 714., my emphasis. Burge presents his account of the relationship between "purely linguistic truths" and "extra-linguistic facts" as a development of what he calls Quine's "first point against positivism." In my view, however, Burge's position is better viewed as a development of Putnam's central criticism of the analytic-synthetic distinction.

36. Ibid.

37. Ibid., 718, my emphasis. Burge goes on to say that "perhaps foundations and ultimacy are not to be expected. But our cognitive commitments and potential go beyond the boundaries set by conventional (or idiolectic) linguistic meaning."

38. Burge's sympathy with rationalism is clear from the start of "Intellectual Norms and Foundations of Mind," where he states his intention to explicate that notion of *intellectual responsibility* that "undergirds the proprietary concepts of dialectic, rationality, understanding, spirit, and rule-following that Plato, Aristotle, Kant, Hegel, and Wittgenstein, respectively, tried to explicate" (698).

39. Some philosophers with strong empiricist sympathies find (a) more promising than (b). Alan Sidelle argues that essentialism is unacceptable, and so we must try to explain the truth of statements that are alleged to be necessary a posteriori (like some of Burge's "truths of meaning") by appealing to linguistic conventions. Like many others, Sidelle takes for granted that *there must be something in virtue of which a necessary a posteriori statement is true.* He is primarily interested in Kripke's and Putnam's claims that some statements are necessary a posteriori, but similar reasoning would presumably lead him to reject (b) and reconsider (a). See his book *Necessity, Essence, and Individuation* (Ithaca: Cornell University Press, 1989). In my view, we should reject both alternatives, and stop trying to say what makes these statements true.

40. R. M. Hare, "Philosophical Discoveries," reprinted in Richard Rorty, ed., *The Linguistic Turn: Recent Essays in Philosophical Method* (Chicago: University of Chicago Press, 1967), 206–217; quotation from 209.

41. Ibid., 208.

42. Ibid., 209.

43. Ibid., 211.

44. Ibid., 210.

45. Ibid.

46. Ibid.

47. Burge in effect acknowledges this point when he writes that "a notable feature of the dialectic is that, as the participants work toward an expression of communal meaning, *they typically do not discuss the matter as outsiders*" ("Intellectual Norms and Foundations of Mind," 705, my emphasis).

48. Akeel Bilgrami has criticized Burge for offering a merely "disquotational" specification of what "concepts" (which I am here calling "notions") are. Bilgrami's central criticism is that if "concepts" cannot be given any further specification, then they are "mysterious" and "ineffable." He rejects talk of "notions" on what he takes to be broadly Wittgensteinian grounds: "Following Wittgenstein, I find mystery in these matters if something is altogether, and by its nature, inexpressible. Whereof one cannot speak, thereof one is mystery-mongering." ("Can Externalism Be Reconciled with Self-Knowledge?" *Philosophical Topics* 20 [1992]: 223–267; quotation from 249). I agree that Burge's talk of notions is mysterious if it is interpreted as committing us to an ontology of notions that somehow lie behind our use of language. But I think that there is no reason why we have to interpret Burge's talk of notions in this way. In the end, if we take my deflationary view of anti-individualism, there are no notions for us to theorize about.

49. Burge, "Intellectual Norms and Foundations of Mind," 698, n. 2.

Nine. Realism, Self-Knowledge, and Skepticism

1. In "Can Externalism Be Reconciled with Self-Knowledge?" *Philosophical Topics* 20 (1992): 223–267, Akeel Bilgrami expresses this first impression that there is a conflict between self-knowledge and anti-individualism (which he calls "externalism") as follows: "if the contents of our thoughts are not constituted only by things internal to us in some suitably Cartesian sense, then it may seem at least *prima facie* natural to think that we will often not know what our thoughts are, since we may often not know crucial things about items external to us" (235).

2. For example, in "Individualism and Self-Knowledge," *Journal of Philosophy* 79 (1988): 649–663, Tyler Burge compares self-knowledge to perceptual knowledge, and argues that when skepticism is not at issue, "knowing one's own thoughts no more requires separate investigation of the conditions that make the judgment possible than knowing what one perceives" (657).

3. Anthony Brueckner goes further, and argues that if anti-individualism is true, we can't know the "contents" of our beliefs *whether or not we appeal to empirical evidence*. In his paper "Skepticism

about Knowledge of Content," *Mind* 99 (1990): 447–451, he argues for this radical skeptical conclusion as follows: "I claim to know that I am thinking that some water is dripping. If I know that I am thinking that some water is dripping, then I know that I am not thinking, instead, that some twater is dripping. But I do not know that I am not thinking that some twater is dripping, since, according to externalism [anti-individualism], if I were on twin earth thinking that some twater is dripping, things would seem exactly as they now seem (and have seemed). So I do not know that I am thinking that some water is dripping" (448). Brueckner's reasoning is in essentials just like the reasoning I presented in the text, although his conclusion is stronger (and correspondingly less plausible).

4. This view of self-knowledge conflicts with some standard philosophical models of what might be called the "logical form" of self-knowledge. For example, in "Individualism and Self-Knowledge," Burge writes that "knowledge of one's own mental events . . . consists in a reflexive judgment which involves thinking a first-order thought that the judgment itself is about. The reflexive judgment simply inherits the content of the first-order thought" (656). In this sense Burge thinks that self-knowledge is "second-order." In contrast, I think that our ordinary attributions of self-knowledge are *inextricable* from our ordinary attributions of "first-order" thoughts and beliefs. To assign different logical forms to them is to suggest that self-knowledge of "first-order" thoughts and beliefs must be somehow *constituted* by mental states *over and above* the "first-order" thoughts and beliefs themselves. This picture of self-knowledge is partly responsible, I think, for the widespread failure to see that it makes no sense to attribute "first-order" thoughts and beliefs to an individual who does not "know the contents" of his beliefs and thoughts without special "empirical" inquiry.

5. Of course, I don't deny that the phrase 'know the contents' could be interpreted in such a way that to "know the contents" of one's own beliefs and thoughts is *not* enough to be able to use one's words in discourse.

6. These three features common to many ordinary uses of the word "know" are identified by Normal Malcolm in his paper "Defending Common Sense," *Philosophical Review* 58 (1949): 201–220; see p. 203 for Malcolm's list of the three features.

7. In "Knowing One's Own Mind," *Proceedings and Addresses of the American Philosophical Association* 60 (1987): 441–458, Donald Davidson notes that the sense of mystery that surrounds the topic of self-knowledge stems in part from our tendency to picture the "contents" of our beliefs and thoughts as "objects before the mind."

8. This sense of self-knowledge is of a piece with a familiar sense in which speakers know the meaning of their words, described by Putnam as follows: "To know the meaning of a word may mean (a) to know how to translate it, or (b) to know what it refers to, in the sense of having the ability to state explicitly what the denotation is (other than by using the word itself), or (c) to have tacit knowledge of its meaning, in the sense of being able to use the word in discourse. The only sense in which the average speaker of the language 'knows the meaning' of most words is (c)" (Hilary Putnam, *Representation and Reality*, Cambridge, Mass., MIT Press, 1988, 32).

9. Kevin Falvey and Joseph Owens, "Externalism, Self-Knowledge, and Skepticism," *Philosophical Review* 103 (1994): 110.

10. Falvey and Owens talk about one thought (or belief) being the "same" as or "different" from another, as in this passage: "Is Rudolf's thought that cilantro should be used sparingly the same as or different from his thought that coriander should be used sparingly? . . . Whether Rudolf's thoughts are the same or different is determined in part by relevant features of his environment, among which is the fact that cilantro is coriander" (ibid., 110). In n. 3 they suggest that two thoughts are the "same" if they have the "same content." They summarize the point of their cilantro example as follows: "facts about the world and the language he employs are relevant in determining sameness and difference in the contents of Rudolf's propositional attitudes, facts that he can come to know only by investigation of his environment" (ibid., 111, n. 3). I accept this way of speaking only if it is qualified by a strong dose of skepticism about the clarity of the word "content." The question of whether a belief expressed by using a sentence S and a belief expressed by using a different sentence S' "have the same content" is not well posed until we settle on some account of what content is. In my view, for reasons sketched in Chapters Seven and Eight, a deflationary anti-individualist has almost nothing general and informative to say about what content is. One might say that S and S' "have the same content" if they are properly evaluated in the same way, but this of course depends on what is meant by "proper evaluation." To elucidate this phrase, I recommend that we describe how we evaluate *particular* assertions and beliefs (§112).

11. Falvey and Owens claim that we "know the contents" of our own thoughts even if we doubt all our "empirical beliefs." Against this I will argue (in §120 and §122) that if we suspend all our "empirical beliefs," we have no idea what we are talking about.

12. In "The Meaning of 'Meaning'," reprinted in Hilary Putnam, *Mind, Language, and Reality* (Cambridge: Cambridge University Press,

1975), 215–271, Putnam emphasized the importance of empirical beliefs to a speaker's minimal competence in the use of a term. Recall the following passage from Putnam's discussion of linguistic stereotypes: "Suppose our hypothetical speaker points to a snowball and asks, 'is that a tiger?'. Clearly there isn't much point in talking tigers with him. *Significant communication requires that people know something of what they are talking about*" (248, my emphasis). Given the anti-individualist's starting point, this observation is not limited to communication, but has immediate consequences for our understanding of the content of a speaker's beliefs, and his own knowledge of what he is talking about. As we saw in Chapter Seven, what a speaker must believe in order for him to count as competent in the use of a term depends on the beliefs and interests entrenched in his linguistic community. There is no simple rule for determining whether or not a speaker is competent in the use of a language, no informative set of necessary and sufficient conditions for competence. The best we can do is investigate and elucidate various actual and counterfactual situations in which we judge that speakers are competent.

13. I am deliberately playing into the hands of the skeptical challenge developed in §116 by treating the "supposition" that *my sincere utterances of the sentence 'There's water in the basement' don't express the thought that there is water in the basement* as the antecedent of a conditional. This *suggests* (but doesn't require) that the "supposition" *may actually be true.* In §§117–118 I will argue that we can't really make sense of the skeptic's "supposition" that for all I know on the basis of my first-person experiences, I may actually be in a world in which *my sincere utterances of the sentence 'There's water in the basement' don't express the thought that there is water in the basement.*

14. I assume that each individual is in a position to use a disquotational truth predicate to generalize for himself the reasoning of the previous paragraph of the text, and that he can *use* and *affirm* his own sentences of the forms "my sincere utterances of the sentence '___' express the thought that ___" and "my word '___' refers to ___." Those who find it distracting to use a disquotational truth predicate here should just replace the schemata with particular metalinguistic statements, such as *my sincere utterances of the sentence 'Water boils at 212 degrees Fahrenheit' express the thought that water boils at 212 degrees Fahrenheit; my word 'water' refers to water; my sincere utterances of the sentence 'Gold is a metal' express the thought that gold is a metal; my word 'gold' refers to gold;* and so on.

15. In my view, this appearance is illusory. But to present the skeptic's reasoning in the most gripping way, I shall not directly question

the illusion that our "first-person experiences" are the same in all our subjectively equivalent worlds. My use of the phrase "subjectively equivalent world" does not commit me either way.

16. In "Content and Self-Knowledge," *Philosophical Topics* 17 (1989): 5–26, Paul Boghossian takes for granted that the meanings of our terms and the "contents" of our thoughts could change in one day. This leads to the strange consequence that we may not know what thought our sincere utterances of 'There's water in the basement' expressed *yesterday*. Boghossian rightly questions whether the possibility of such a rapid change is compatible with the assumption that we had self-knowledge yesterday, or, for that matter, that we have self-knowledge today. In my view, however, our practices of attributing meanings and thoughts show that changes in the meaning of a sentence cannot occur in just one day. It is not clear exactly how *much* time is required for such changes to occur, but we need not settle this question to evaluate the skeptical reasoning I present in this section.

17. The slide from "my beliefs and thoughts *might have been* different from what I actually take them to be" to "my beliefs and thoughts *may be* different from what I actually take them to be" is an example of the kind of modal fallacy that G. E. Moore identified in his classic papers "Four Forms of Skepticism" and "Certainty," in G. E. Moore, *Philosophical Papers* (London: Allen and Unwin, 1959), 196–225 and 226–251. Moore observed that anyone who claims to know that p, for some "contingent" proposition p, will accept that p might have been false; but to say "p may actually be false" is in effect to say "I do not know that p." Hence a skeptic who argues from "p might have been false" to "p may actually be false" begs the question of whether I know that p. Even if we accept that p might have been false, that by itself gives us no reason to conclude that p may actually be false.

18. I will argue in §§117–118 that it is a confusion to think we may *not* actually have self-knowledge—that we are merely *supposing* that we do have it. At this stage in the dialectic, however, I am presenting the skeptic's reasoning *as though* it makes sense to treat the presupposition that we have self-knowledge as the antecedent of a conditional that could be used, by *modus tollens*, to support the conclusion that we do *not* have self-knowledge.

19. I take for granted that each individual is in a position to use a disquotational truth predicate to generalize for himself the reasoning of the second paragraph of §115, and that he can *use* and *affirm* his own sentences of the forms "my sincere utterances of the sentence '___' express the thought that ___" and "my word '___' refers to ___." See note 14.

20. One might wonder how these sentences *could* express "contingent truths" if it is reasonable to accept them without special "empirical" justification. In §120 and §122 I address a sophisticated version of this concern.

21. Note again that I don't myself accept this assumption.

22. If we were convinced by the skeptic's reasoning, we would try to find "beliefs" and "thoughts" that capture what is common to the subject's first-person point of view in all of her subjectively equivalent worlds. We may try to characterize these "beliefs" and "thoughts" in terms of what Brian Loar calls their "realization conditions." See Loar's paper "Social Content and Psychological Content," in R. Grimm and D. Merrill, ed., *Contents of Thought* (Tucson: University of Arizona Press, 1988). For an interesting critical discussion of Loar's notion of "realization conditions," see Stalnaker, "Narrow Content," in C. Anthony Anderson and Joseph Owens, ed., *Propositional Attitudes* (Chicago: CSLI Lecture Notes, 1990), 131–145.

But one needn't think anti-individualism is incompatible with self-knowledge to be interested in a distinction between "wide" and "narrow" content. One might find a use for "narrow" content in cognitive psychological explanations, for example, even if one thinks that anti-individualism is compatible with self-knowledge.

23. There is no argument analogous to (B1)–(B3) that shows that I am not in the subjectively equivalent world in which I lived on Twin Earth from birth until five years ago, when I was transported without my knowledge to Earth, where I now count as a competent speaker of English. It is instructive to see that this strange possibility does not undermine self-knowledge, and that it is consistent with anti-individualism. Let us consider a few of the details. After the change, what I used to call 'Twin Earth' is Earth, and what I used to call 'Earth' is Twin Earth. By supposition, before the change I was a competent speaker of Twin English, the language spoken on Twin Earth, and so my utterances five years ago of 'There's water in the basement' expressed the thought that there is twin water in the basement. Now that I have settled on Earth, however, my sincere utterances of 'There's water in the basement' express the thought that there is water in the basement. Without special "empirical" inquiry I accept that my sincere utterances of 'There's water in the basement' express the thought that there is water in the basement even though I don't know without special "empirical" inquiry whether or not five years ago my utterances of 'There's water in the basement' expressed the same thought. As we saw in §114, a speaker can "know the contents" of his beliefs without special "empirical" inquiry, even if special investigation *would* be required

him to find out whether one of his beliefs "has the same content as" another. The supposition that five years ago I lived on Twin Earth does not lead to incoherence, yet I am confident that it isn't true, since I am confident that there is no Twin Earth, and that even if there were, I could not have been transported from there to Earth without my knowledge.

24. One might be tempted to think that we can simply *stipulate* that water is not twin water. If it is *true by stipulation alone* that water is not twin water, then it is also true by stipulation that if we were in either of the two situations described in §116, our word 'water' would not refer to water. Such a stipulation would *seem* to be independent of our ordinary background of "empirical" beliefs.

The trouble is that if we accept anti-individualism, we can't make sense of the idea that it is true by stipulation, completely independent of any "empirical" facts, that water is not twin water. For even if we now take for granted that water is not twin water, this belief is not independent of our ordinary background of "empirical" beliefs.

To see this, it is enough to tell a far-fetched story about how we might someday "discover" that water is twin water. To tell this story we must suspend some of our deeply entrenched "empirical" beliefs. We take for granted, for example, that Twin Earth is a fictional planet, a figment of Putnam's imagination. But suppose that (here we lapse into fiction):

Long ago, before Putnam wrote "The Meaning of 'Meaning'," he discovered a planet that looks exactly like Earth. He dubbed this planet 'Twin Earth', and conjectured that wherever there is water on Earth, there is a different liquid, which he called 'twin water', on Twin Earth. His discovery got him thinking about the relationship between linguistic meaning and our social and physical environments, and this led him to develop the Twin Earth thought experiments he presents in "The Meaning of 'Meaning'." He never told anyone (except some of his closest friends, who have kept it secret) that Twin Earth exists, since he was not sure that there is no water on Twin Earth, and this supposition is important to his thought experiments. He decided to keep his discovery of Twin Earth secret, and to ask readers to *suppose* that Twin Earth exists, and that on Twin Earth there is no water, only twin water.

To "understand" this story we must suspend some of our ordinary "empirical" beliefs. What makes the story unbelievable is precisely that it conflicts with some of our most deeply entrenched background "empirical" beliefs. Yet if we are willing to suspend many of these "empirical" beliefs, we can "understand" the remote possibility that someday we will "discover" that water is twin water. Thus suppose for example that (here we again lapse into fiction):

Sometime early in the next century Putnam makes his discovery of Twin Earth public. Astronomers study planet Twin Earth, and tentatively confirm Putnam's initial conjecture that the lakes, streams, and oceans of Twin Earth are filled with twin water, and there is no water at all on Twin Earth. Philosophers are surprised to find that the planet they called Twin Earth really exists, but they soon adjust to this situation, and continue their exploration of our ordinary practices of belief ascription using variations on Putnam's original Twin Earth thought experiments. They accept that their word 'twin water' refers to a real liquid, the stuff that fills the lakes, streams, and oceans of Twin Earth. Finally, after several centuries astronauts from Earth make a trip to Twin Earth and discover that twin water is really water after all, undermining our initial "stipulation," made several centuries earlier, that water is *not* twin water.

This story shows that it is not true *by stipulation alone* that water is not twin water. When we assume that water is not twin water, we are tacitly supposing that Twin Earth is a figment of Putnam's imagination, and so the story I just told is pure fiction. The story is so far-fetched that in ordinary contexts our stipulation that water is not twin water seems independent of any "empirical" assumptions. Nevertheless, the story shows that we do not know *by stipulation alone,* independent of all "empirical" assumptions, that twin water is not water. A similar story can be constructed to show that we do not know by stipulation alone, independent of all "empirical" assumptions, that Twin Earth is not Earth. These stories should be taken in the same spirit as Putnam's fantasy (in "The Analytic and the Synthetic," reprinted in Putnam, *Mind, Language, and Reality,* 33–69) of "discovering" that our term 'bachelor' is a "law-cluster" term, even though we are confident that it's a "one-criterion" term.

25. The position I will sketch is similar to the position defended by Falvey and Owens in "Externalism, Self-Knowledge, and Skepticism." They present what amounts to a version of what I call the restricted disquotational picture of self-knowledge, claim that this picture of self-knowledge is compatible with anti-individualism, and argue that when we are evaluating skeptical arguments, we can't take any of our "empirical" beliefs for granted. Here is a characteristic passage: "I know the propositions expressed by all the T-sentences of a homophonic truth theory for English. It is partly in virtue of the fact that I possess this knowledge that it is correct to characterize me as a speaker of English. But what I may not know, and what I may for the purposes of the [skeptical] argument under discussion assume that I do not know, are the propositions expressed by the T-sentences of any *non*homophonic truth theory for English" (127).

26. I do not mean to suggest that we can disarm all skeptical chal-

lenges in this way. I am concerned here with the kinds of possibilities raised in §116 and disarmed by (A1)–(A3) and (B1)–(B3). Not all problematic possibilities can be dissolved in this way.

27. I am alluding here to J. L. Austin's use of this sentence to make a different (but related) point in his paper "Other Minds," in J. O. Urmson and G. J. Warnock, ed., *J. L. Austin, Philosophical Papers*, 3rd ed. (Oxford: Oxford University Press, 1979). After describing our ordinary procedures for making and evaluating a person's claim to know that there is a goldfinch in the garden, Austin notes that a traditional skeptic will not be convinced that we have ruled out all doubts about this claim. Austin argues that the apparently meaningful skeptical question "Is it a real goldfinch?" does not in fact raise any genuine doubt at all: "The doubt or question 'But is it a *real* one?' has always (must have) a special basis, there must be some 'reason for suggesting' that it isn't real, in the sense of some specific way, or limited number of specific ways, in which it is suggested that this experience or item may be phoney. Sometimes (usually) the context makes it clear what the suggestion is: the goldfinch might be stuffed but there's no suggestion that it's a mirage, the oasis might be a mirage but there's no suggestion that it might be stuffed. If the context doesn't make it clear, then I am entitled to ask 'How do you mean? Do you mean it may be stuffed or what? *What are you suggesting?*' The wile of the metaphysician consists in asking 'Is it a real table?' (a kind of object which has no obvious way of being phoney) and not specifying or limiting what may be wrong with it, so that I feel at a loss 'how to prove' it is a real one" (87). The question *What are you suggesting?* is especially pressing within the context of an anti-individualistic approach to belief and thought. We must have some idea of what we are talking about just to see whether or not a given possibility is in conflict with some of our "empirical" beliefs. But once we take for granted "empirical" beliefs that give content to such possibilities, in many (though not all) cases it is obvious that they are not actual.

28. In "Knowledge of Content and Knowledge of the World," *Philosophical Review* 103 (1994):327–343, Anthony Brueckner considers (what in effect amounts to) the superficially similar claim that *there is some background of empirical beliefs (some "pieces of knowledge") which every competent speaker has*. He rightly rejects this claim on the grounds that we can't "isolate those pieces of knowledge which are required in order to understand [our words]" (343, n. 19). What Brueckner apparently overlooks is that our actual evaluations of competence show that *every competent speaker has some background (or other) of empirical beliefs*. This observation undermines the purely formal conception of self-knowledge

without presupposing that we can "isolate those pieces of knowledge which are required in order to understand [our words]," and so it is not vulnerable to Brueckner's objection. Brueckner seems to have missed the importance of the quantifier shift, from *there is some background of empirical beliefs (some "pieces of knowledge") which every competent speaker has* to *every competent speaker has some background (or other) of empirical beliefs.*

29. To avoid distracting complications, I will also suppose that both the brain and the machine came into existence by accident, and that there are no individuals that exist outside the vat. This is a modified version of the case Putnam considers in chap. 1 of *Reason, Truth, and History* (Cambridge: Cambridge University Press, 1981). In my paper "Skepticism, Objectivity, and Brains in Vats," *Pacific Philosophical Quarterly* 73 (1992): 239–266, I reconstruct and defend Putnam's argument that we are not in this situation.

30. This is one of the alternatives Putnam considers (see p. 14 of *Reason, Truth, and History*), though he pretends to state the meanings of the brain's "utterances" by appending "in the image" to ordinary English sentences. This misleadingly suggests that the brain's "utterances" of 'I am a brain in a vat' are true if and only if it is having sense experiences as of being a brain in a vat. In "Skepticism, Objectivity, and Brains in Vats," 249–250, I explain why this is unacceptable.

31. There is no argument analogous to (D1)–(D3) which shows that I am not in the world in which I was a brain in a vat until five years ago, when my brain was transferred into my body, so that now after five years of embodied existence I count as a competent speaker of English. It is another question whether we can really make sense of that strange "possibility."

32. Both of these characterizations are from *The New Shorter Oxford English Dictionary.*

33. Falvey and Owens, "Externalism, Self-Knowledge, and Skepticism," 107–108.

34. Michael Williams argues in this way in his paper "Skepticism and Charity," *Ratio* 12 (1988): 176–194. First he sketches the skeptic's problematic: "The skeptic insists on assessing all our knowledge, or all our knowledge of the world, all at once. This means that the skeptical problem is necessarily addressed from a first-person perspective, since *nothing to do with the world or whatever other people there may be in it can be taken for granted*" (187). Williams argues that anti-individualism begs the question against skepticism, because anti-individualism depends on assumptions about how things are independent of our subjective first-person perspective: Anti-individualism "turns out to involve the idea of unproblematic access to certain causal relations between speakers and

objects in the world. If, in the context of the skeptic's question, we grant ourselves this access, the game is over before it begins" (188). In this passage, Williams is criticizing Donald Davidson's anti-individualistic position in particular, but if his criticism is legitimate, it also applies to Putnam's and Burge's anti-individualism. Thus Williams concludes that anti-individualism begs the question against the skeptic's assumption that for all we know without "empirical" investigation we are in any one of our subjectively equivalent worlds. In a sense I agree with Williams that if we accept anti-individualism the skeptical game is over before it begins. But this is so because anti-individualism undermines the skeptic's "intuitions" about what may actually be true, and *not* because anti-individualism begs a coherent skeptical question.

35. Even if it is not *immediately* incoherent, however, the supposition that I am actually a brain in a vat would corrode my confidence in my background of "empirical" beliefs, and ultimately undermine my confidence that I can use my words to make statements and evaluate assertions at all. So what appears to be a coherent possibility, given all we have said about anti-individualism, may not be coherent after all. The line between coherent and incoherent "possibilities" is not clear.

36. (C1)–(C3) is similar to the reconstruction I present and defend in my paper "Skepticism, Objectivity, and Brains in Vats." The central points of the rest of this chapter are adapted from this paper. To investigate the deepest consequences of Putnam's reasoning, in "Skepticism, Objectivity, and Brains in Vats" I began with the following formulation of Putnam's argument:

(i) I can raise the question: *Am I always a brain in a vat?*
(ii) If I were always a brain in a vat, I could not raise this question.
(iii) Hence I am not always a brain in a vat.

This reconstruction goes beyond Putnam's own presentation in chap. 1 of *Reason, Truth, and History*, but captures the spirit of it. Version (i)–(iii) is due in essentials to Thomas Tymoszco, "In Defense of Putnam's Brains," *Philosophical Studies* 57 (1989): 281–297. I now think that version (C1)–(C3) is better because it builds into premise (C1) a reference to the sentence I use to express my thought that I am not a brain in a vat. This avoids an awkward loophole that I tried to fill in the appendix of "Skepticism, Objectivity, and Brains in Vats." I now think that both the loophole and the appendix can be avoided by using version (C1)–(C3).

37. Thomas Nagel, *The View from Nowhere* (Oxford: Oxford University Press, 1986), 68.

38. Graeme Forbes has also has recently concluded that "a metaphys-

ical possibility exists, the specifics of which are beyond the envatted brain's grasp. So why should there not be such a possibility the specifics of which are beyond *our* grasp?" ("Realism and Skepticism: Brains in a Vat Revisited," *Journal of Philosophy* 92 [1995]: 205–222; quotation from 220) Forbes notes that Crispin Wright draws a similar conclusion in "On Putnam's Proof That We Are Not Brains-in-a-Vat," *Proceedings of the Aristotelian Society* 92 (1992): 76–94.

39. One might object to this argument for skepticism on the grounds that, even if it is possible that there be a representation that is related to our representation as ours is related to the brain's representation, we have no reason to believe that there is. But this reply is weak. For, assuming that we accept (R), we have no reason for believing that such a representation does not exist. And without such a reason, Nagel would insist, we aren't justified in believing that our representation of the world is not seriously limited. One might press further here, and urge that we give up the assumption that unless we can provide concrete evidence that rules out a skeptical possibility, we have no justification for believing that it does not obtain. But this is not the most interesting place at which to challenge the argument.

Ten. Anti-Individualism and Rule-Following

1. Saul Kripke, *Wittgenstein on Rules and Private Language* (Cambridge, Mass.: Harvard University Press, 1982), 17–18.

2. Ibid., 21–22.

3. Ibid., 7.

4. Here once again I am echoing Ludwig Wittgenstein's famous remark, in §201 of *Philosophical Investigations,* 3rd ed., trans. G. E. M. Anscombe (New York: Macmillan, 1968), that "there is a way of grasping a rule which is not an interpretation, but which is exhibited in what we call 'obeying a rule' and 'going against it' in actual cases."

5. Burge describes the dialectic of meaning-giving characterizations in abstraction from other practices of evaluating our assertions and judgments. But we saw in Chapter Eight that there is no way to separate our "empirical" beliefs from the meaning-giving characterizations which set conventional norms for the proper use of our terms. There is no sharp line between a dialectic of meaning-giving characterizations and rational inquiry in general.

6. Kripke, *Wittgenstein on Rules,* 22.

7. In *Philosophical Investigations* Wittgenstein emphasizes that to understand puzzling features of our use of language, such as the philosophically perplexing but familiar phenomenon of grasping a rule "in a

flash," we must learn to see those features in their proper context. In my own way, I have tried to make a similar point.

8. So in the end I agree with Warren Goldfarb that Kripke's skeptical "hypotheses" should be resisted (see the Goldfarb passage quoted in §13 of Chapter One). Unlike Goldfarb, however, I think that it is instructive to see how Kripke's interpretation of our commonsense views about meaning, coupled with our natural temptation to take the skeptical "hypothesis" seriously, leads to his skeptical conclusion. In my view, to resist Kripke's skeptical dialectic, we must see why our understanding of rules is inextricable from our actual practices of agreeing, disagreeing, evaluating assertions, and resolving disputes.

9. W. V. Quine, "Things and Their Place in Theories," in W. V. Quine, *Theories and Things* (Cambridge, Mass.: Harvard University Press, 1981), 1–23; quotation from 21.

10. W. V. Quine, *Word and Object* (Cambridge, Mass.: MIT Press, 1960), 2.

11. This is a paraphrase of a sentence from *Word and Object,* 11.

12. In *Pursuit of Truth* (Cambridge, Mass.: Harvard University Press, 1990), Quine explicitly disavows his earlier view that we can mirror the intersubjectivity of observation reports in purely naturalistic terms. In this concluding chapter I will direct my criticisms at the classic Quinean position on observation sentences and translation presented in chap. 2 of *Word and Object.*

13. W. V. Quine, "Two Dogmas of Empiricism," in W. V. Quine, *From a Logical Point of View,* rev. 2nd ed. (Cambridge, Mass.: Harvard University Press, 1961), 20–46; quotation from 42.

14. Ibid., 44.

15. Quine, *Word and Object,* 22.

16. This is my adaptation of a sentence I have quoted several times before. See Quine, "Things and Their Place in Theories," 21.

17. Quine, *Word and Object,* 218.

18. Ibid., 219.

19. Ibid.

INDEX